"The Kensingtons"
PRINCESS LOUISE'S KENSINGTON REGIMENT
Second World War

THE KENSINGTONS
SECOND WORLD WAR

REGIMENTAL
OLD COMRADES
ASSOCIATION

Portrait by Dorothy Wilding, London.

H.R.H. THE PRINCESS ROYAL WHO UNVEILED THE 1939–1945 WAR MEMORIAL AT HEADQUARTERS ON MAY 8TH, 1949.

[*Frontispiece*

"The Kensingtons"

PRINCESS LOUISE'S KENSINGTON REGIMENT

Second World War

The Naval & Military Press Ltd
for The Regiment

Published by

The Naval & Military Press Ltd
Unit 5 Riverside, Brambleside
Bellbrook Industrial Estate
Uckfield, East Sussex
TN22 1QQ England

Tel: +44 (0)1825 749494

www.naval-military-press.com
www.nmarchive.com

In reprinting in facsimile from the original, any imperfections are inevitably reproduced and the quality may fall short of modern type and cartographic standards.

PRINCESS LOUISE'S KENSINGTON REGIMENT

The arms of the Royal Borough of Kensington
Quid nobis ardui.

"South Africa, 1900–02."

The Great War—3 Battalions.—"Neuve Chapelle," **"Aubers," "Somme, 1916, '18,"** "Albert, 1916, '18," "Guillemont," "Ginchy," "Flers-Courcelette," "Morval," "Le Transloy," **"Arras, 1917, '18,"** "Scarpe, 1917, '18," **"Ypres, 1917,"** "Langemarck, 1917," **"Cambrai, 1917, '18,"** "Hindenburg Line," "Canal du Nord," "Valenciennes," "Sambre," "France and Flanders, 1914–18. **"Doiran, 1917,"** "Macedonia, 1916–17," **"Gaza,"** "El Mughar," "Nebi Samwil," **"Jerusalem,"** "Jericho," "Jordan," "Megiddo," **"Sharon,"** "Palestine, 1917–18."

Battle Honours for 1939–45 not awarded at time of going to press.

N.B.—Those in heavy type are borne on the Regimental Colour.

DEDICATION

This book is dedicated to the memory of those who died whilst serving with the Kensingtons and forms part of the Regimental War Memorial. Its publication was substantially assisted by funds raised for that purpose.

PREFACE

By Colonel Hugh Campbell, D.S.O., O.B.E., T.D.

It has been my privilege to be associated with the "Kensingtons" in one way or another for fifty years, for eighteen years of which I was indeed proud to be the Honorary Colonel of this famous Territorial Regiment. Anything therefore that I may write in its praise may justly be regarded as coming from one who is favourably biased.

Let, then, the following pages, which tell the story of the two Kensington Battalions in the Second World War, speak for themselves.

They will show that the "imperishable glory" which the Kensingtons won in the First War, and which is so vividly chronicled in the earlier volume, *The Kensingtons*, has not been dulled by time or exorcised by events. Rather has it been burnished anew until it shines as a glorious example to the fine lads who form the Kensingtons of today.

My heart is filled with thankfulness and pride that the generation of Kensingtons which followed mine has so amply fulfilled the pledge and honoured the sacrifices made by its predecessors, and having seen something of the Regiment as it is constituted today, I am certain that the men in it will carry the torch of courage and comradeship still higher, if ever called upon to do so.

The story which follows will help them to emulate the wonderful heroism and fortitude which has earned for the Princess Louise's Kensington Regiment a worthy place in the undying annals of British military history.

HUGH CAMPBELL, Colonel.

BLYTHEWOOD,
    ASCOT.

AUTHORS' ACKNOWLEDGMENTS

THE Authors wish to express their gratitude to those who lent diaries, notes, etc., those who read the completed manuscript making valuable suggestions, and those who rendered assistance in many other ways. They also acknowledge their indebtedness to His Majesty's Stationery Office for permission to publish extracts from *The Highland Division* by Eric Linklater and the map of the Maginot Line. They are also indebted to the Imperial War Museum and *The Kensington News* for permission to publish various photographs, and to Dorothy Wilding, London, for the portrait of H.R.H. The Princess Royal.

B. V. C. HARPUR
B. R. WOOD
J. J. EVANS
S. JACOBSON
R. J. CANNON

INTRODUCTION

When Her Royal Highness, Princess Louise, Duchess of Argyle, wrote the preface in 1935 for *The Kensingtons*, few could have thought that the occasion for another war-history of two battalions of the Kensingtons would so soon arise; still less that it would chronicle battles fought over some of the same war-scarred countryside, and even more remote was the possibility that some of the same men who carried the Kensington badge into Flanders in 1914–18 would wear that badge in France again in 1939–45.

But these were the few. In the main it was another generation of Kensingtons which wore the arms of the Royal Borough and carried them to the Maginot Line in 1940, through the fighting withdrawal across France, back to St. Valéry, and the hell of an evacuation under fierce enemy pressure; and later into Belgium and Holland; into North Africa, through the long length of Italy, and into Austria. It is their story which is now to be told, the story of the 1st and 2nd Battalions, Princess Louise's Kensington Regiment. And while that story was being woven, in the mud of Flanders and Holland, the dust and heat of Africa, the rains and snow of Italy and Austria, the Royal lady who was Titular Chief of the Regiment for so many years, passed quietly away to her last long rest and so was not in her accustomed place to welcome home again "her Kensington Regiment", of which she was so proud, and which returned triumphantly bearing fresh laurels to lay around her exalted name.

But nót all who went returned; in a war so wide-spread, so devastating and ruthless, that could not be. It is indeed a miracle that so many came back, and it remains a wonder that in this Second World War, so infinitely greater and more destructive than the First, military casualties were so much less. It is to the memory of those who died that this volume is dedicated; it forms part of the Regimental War Memorial, which is completed by the handsome addition to

INTRODUCTION

the existing Memorial in the Drill Hall at Regimental Headquarters. To the relatives who mourn the fallen this will be a lasting reminder of the heroic part they played in the fight to preserve freedom in a darkening world.

To the Kensingtons of today and tomorrow this book, together with its companion volume, *The Kensingtons,* will reveal more fully the great traditions which they inherit and thus foster that esprit de corps the existence of which is so vital a necessity to a happy and successful regiment. They will find in it a mine of information and recognise many of the problems and difficulties as their own; but much of it they will find as strange and obsolete as the horse transport lines and infantryman's puttees of 1914 seemed to the men of 1939.

For the rôle of the Regiment has changed more than once in the past fifteen years, and may change again. It is a far cry from the brass band and the red and grey uniforms of 1914 to the highly technical, wireless-equipped vehicles of 1951; the glamour that surrounded the close-dressed ranks of 1000 men led by officers mounted on chargers does not extend to the grim-looking, efficient small motorised units of today. Yet the spirit is the same and, thank God, the men are the same.

The book has not been produced without considerable difficulty, for in spite of the great help the Old Comrades' Association was able to give by storing war diaries and other papers of inestimable value during hostilities, the records were by no means complete, and the accounts given in the following pages do not pretend to be exact in every particular. One of the disadvantages of a Territorial unit is that upon embodiment it marches out of headquarters and leaves nothing behind but bare walls. In the daily stress of life in the field, and the interminable moves which are inherent in the Services, it is not easy to compile and keep intact an accurate record of the life of a regiment, and few people have an eye to a subsequent history.

But we did learn something from previous experience, when after the First War it took us fifteen years to piece together and publish a full history, and without the great help from Commanding Officers on this occasion, and the foresight of the Honorary Secretary of the O.C.A. this record could not now be available.

Great credit is due to the men who have actually written the various parts of this history, all of them very much preoccupied with their own personal problems in an uneasy post-war world. What we wanted were authors *who had actually taken part* in the events they described, and for a long time this seemed to be impossible. Suggestions to enlist professional assistance were resisted stoutly and at last patience was rewarded; men were found who, at considerable sacrifice of time and leisure, collated the immense mass of material available and wrote the story. We think the inevitable delay has been well worth while. The story may not be complete but it is as full and as accurate as we can make it; there may be errors and there must be omissions, but we trust they are few, and for what there are we apologise.

All in all, it is a great record of duty magnificently done by men who wore the arms of the Royal Borough of Kensington and carried out its motto, *'Quid Nobis Ardui'*, to the full. May we always remember the many who did not come back, remember with humility and with thankfulness, for

'Greater love hath no man than this,
That a man lay down his life for his friends'.

HAROLD M. HOLLIER,
Chairman,
History Sub-committee.

Foreword to the 2025 Commemorative Edition
by Major General John Kendall VR
Deputy Commander Field Army

President
Princess Louise's Kensington Regimental Association

The first edition of 'THE KENSINGTONS' Second World War History was originally published by the Regimental Old Comrades Association in 1951. Over the passing years a copy of this history has become a rare and much sort after World War Two Regimental History.

Now, in 2025 The Princess Louise's Kensington Regimental Association (formally the Regimental Old Comrades Association) has decided that in this 80th anniversary year of the ending of the Second World War it would be fitting to reprint the Regimental World War Two history as a commemoration and tribute to the service and sacrifice of those Kensingtons who served in that conflict.

It is hoped that by reprinting this edition and making it more widely available it will make a significant contribution to the history of the Second World War alongside the many regimental histories already published on the subject.

QUID NOBIS ARDUI

Major General John Kendall VR

CONTENTS

THE 1ST BATTALION

CHAPTER		PAGE
I	1936 to the Outbreak of World War II	3
II	Mobilisation	11
III	France: The First Phase (April–May 1940)	18
IV	France: The Second Phase (June 1940)	29
V	Return to Home Forces	42
VI	Another Year with Home Forces	47
VII	Marking Time, 1942	53
VIII	Prepare for Action, 1943	59
IX	North African Prelude	65
X	The Sicilian Campaign	72
XI	Taranto to the Apennines	85
XII	Winter Fighting and Cassino	108
XIII	Summer Offensive: Italy (May–July 1944)	137
XIV	Egyptian Interlude (July 22nd–September 16th, 1944)	161
XV	Into Battle Again (September–December 1944)	165
XVI	Static Warfare and the Final Offensive (January 1st–May 2nd, 1945)	198
XVII	A Glimpse of the Austrian Aftermath (May 1945–April 1946)	221
XVIII	Grecian Twilight (April 1946–September 1946)	232
XIX	"Quid Nobis Ardui" The Captive Kensingtons	238

THE 2ND BATTALION

CHAPTER		PAGE
	Foreword	251
	Part I: Defence and Preparation	252
XX	Home Service (September 1st, 1939–October 14th, 1941)	255
XXI	Iceland (October 14th, 1941–September 8th, 1942)	263
XXII	Training for Invasion (September 8th, 1942–June 6th, 1944)	275
	Part II: Invasion and Victory	284
XXIII	Battalion H.Q. and H.Q. Coy. (June–December 1944)	285
XXIV	A Coy. (June 8th–December 31st, 1944)	298
XXV	B Coy. (June 5th–December 31st, 1944)	309
XXVI	C Coy. (June–December 31st, 1944)	324
XXVII	D Coy. (June–December 31st, 1944)	335
XXVIII	Victory and Occupation	348

POST-WAR (1947–51)

XXIX	Post-war (1947–51)	367
	Roll of Honour	376
	1st Battalion Honours and Awards	378
	2nd Battalion Honours and Awards	380
	Index	381

LIST OF MAPS

1st Battalion

Maginot Line, France, 1940	*page* 20
Somme–St. Valéry, France, 1940	38
Sicilian Campaign, July–September 1943	*facing* 80
Termoli and Trigno, October–November 1943	81
Operations in the Advance to the Sangro, October–November 1943	96
Sangro Operations, November 1943	97
Central Apennines, December 1943–February 1944	*page* 110
Cassino Panorama, February–May 1944	*facing* 208
Trasimeno Operations, June 1944	209
Operations, October 1944–February 1945	224
Po Valley Operations, March–April 1945	225

2nd Battalion

Iceland, 1941–42	*page* 264
Final Dispositions in the Normandy Bridgehead	294
Initial Locations on the "Island"	349

LIST OF ILLUSTRATIONS

H.R.H. The Princess Royal, C.I., G.C.V.O., G.B.E. — *Frontispiece*

1st Battalion

	FACING PAGE
Sgt. Thompson instructing on the Vickers machine-gun at Beaulieu Camp, 1939	48
Typical Machine-gun Post, France, 1940	49
Carriers enter Centuripe after its epic capture	64
The Sangro River with fifteen spans of the Main Bridge demolished	65
Convoys grind tortuously into the Apennines	112
Activity on the Mortar Lines of "B" Group near Ronchi	113
A Mule Train plods forward through the snow near Rionero	128
Cassino shrouded by smoke from enemy shellfire and our own screens	129
Transport awaits road repairs near Sassaleone	192
Medium machine-guns of a "D" Group Platoon firing from a house during the Senio attack	193

2nd Battalion

M.M.G. Carriers halt in the village of Rauray, Normandy	288
Sgt. Durbin indicates a target during the operations in Normandy.	289
4·2-inch mortars in action on the Belgium–Holland Frontier	304
The Island between Arnhem and Nijmegen	305
H.R.H. Princess Juliana inspecting the Battalion at Nijmegen	368

Post-war

The Army Phantom Signal Regt. (Princess Louise's Kensington Regiment) marches past the Mayor of Kensington on "Adoption Day," 15th April, 1951	369

THE 1st BATTALION

By

MAJOR B. V. C. HARPUR, M.C.

AND

MAJOR B. R. WOOD, T.D.

(1936—12th June, 1940) (and P. O. W. Chapter)

MAJOR J. J. EVANS, T.D.

(13th June, 1940—May, 1943)

CHAPTER I

1936 TO THE OUTBREAK OF WORLD WAR II

THE year of 1936 opened on a note of sadness. His Majesty King George V was gravely ill, and on the night of January 20th many millions of subjects heard the poignant message which came over the radio: "The life of His Majesty the King is passing peacefully to its close". The death of His Majesty occurred about an hour after the officers of the Regiment, dining at headquarters in Mess, had drunk the loyal toast, and it was perhaps the last occasion on which the health of King George V was drunk in Mess. The funeral took place on January 28th, and the Regiment had the rôle of lining the route in Piccadilly near Hyde Park Corner; the pressure of the enormous crowds, who had gathered to pay their last respects to a much-beloved monarch, was so great that the troops had to combine police duties with their military duties.

Training in the early months of the year and at occasional week-ends was directed towards the annual camp, which was being held at West Lavant, near Goodwood, and amongst noteworthy events during this period was the Annual Prize-giving held in May, when the prizes were presented by General Sir Walter Kirke, Director-General of the Territorial Army. Later in the month the regimental drums were selected to play before one of the evening performances at the Royal Tournament.

Camp was held from July 11th to 25th, and the Kensingtons went as part of the newly-formed brigade under Col. G. M. Giles, together with the H.A.C. infantry battalion, the L.R.B., and the London Scottish; in addition to learning a great deal all ranks thoroughly enjoyed themselves.

On its return from camp the battalion marched from Victoria Station to Kensington Palace, where it was inspected by the Titular Chief of the Regiment, H.R.H. the Princess Louise, Duchess of Argyll, C.B.E., C.I.

After a brief interval, training was resumed at H.Q. and in September the Commanding Officer, Col. W. A. Stone, M.C., T.D., inspected the Latymer Upper School Cadet Corps, which was affiliated to the Regiment and wore the regimental badges. Soon afterwards the Kensington Defence Company was formed, under the command of Capt. J. Cary, a former company commander and Quartermaster of the Kensingtons; he enrolled many members of the Old Comrades' Association, which was, as usual, giving much valuable support to the Regiment. The purpose of the Defence Companies was to have available, in the event of war, a force which could take over guard duties, etc., thereby relieving troops for more active rôles.

In November the Annual Armistice Day Parade was held, and the Princess Louise attended the service in the Drill Hall. H.R.H. placed a wreath on the Regimental War Memorial and took the salute when the Regiment, with the O.C.A., marched to the Kensington War Memorial and thence to the Cenotaph.

The close of the year was marked by the abdication of King Edward VIII, who was succeeded by his brother as King George VI.

For many years now the sport at which the Kensingtons had always excelled was boxing, and in 1937 the regimental team won the Brigade Boxing Championship for the twelfth year in succession and were second in the Divisional Championship. There is little doubt that this side of the Regiment's activities helped to procure many recruits.

In April, Major G. C. Pim, late Scots Guards, was appointed Second-in-Command to succeed Major E. L. Stacey, who had resigned in July 1936, and at the end of the month General Sir Harry H. S. Knox, the Adjutant-General, presented the prizes at the Annual Prize-giving.

On Coronation Day, May 12th, 1937, Territorial regiments were not permitted to parade in full strength for the Coronation procession, but the Regiment was represented in the procession by an officer, a warrant-officer, a sergeant, and a lance-corporal. In addition, a detachment of two officers and twenty-five other ranks took part in lining the route. Seven days later, however, the Regiment paraded at full strength with colours, band, and drums when it lined the route in the Strand on the occasion of Their Majesties' State Drive to the Guildhall, and all ranks were pleased to learn that H.R.H. the Princess Louise, had been appointed a Dame Grand Cross of the Royal Victorian Order.

To celebrate the Coronation, the O.C.A. held a successful ball at Thames House Restaurant, Millbank, on May 21st, and members of the Regiment were present in force. On Sunday, June 27th, H.M. King George VI held a review of ex-servicemen in Hyde Park, and amongst the eighty thousand men who marched past was a large contingent from the O.C.A. headed by the regimental drums.

Camp was held at Lympne, and the Regiment was fortunate in having excellent weather, so that the maximum benefit was obtained from the fortnight's training. On the return it was learnt that the title was being changed to PRINCESS LOUISE'S KENSINGTON REGIMENT, THE MIDDLESEX REGIMENT (DUKE OF CAMBRIDGE'S OWN), and that the Regiment would in future form part of the Middlesex Regiment instead of being affiliated to the K.R.R.C.

In October, Col. Stone was re-transferred to the H.A.C. infantry reserve of officers, and all ranks said good-bye with deep regret. Lt.-Col. F. G. Hancocks, M.C., T.D., of the L.R.B. was appointed Commanding Officer, and Capt. N. E. Hoare, The Buffs, became Adjutant in place of Capt. Boyle, who had rejoined his regiment on promotion to Major. Col. Hancocks had first joined the T.A. in 1913, and coming to London the following year joined the L.R.B. in which he was commissioned in 1915. After demobilisation and when the T.A. was reconstituted he rejoined the ranks of the L.R.B. and was recommissioned in 1926.

On October 18th a Guard of Honour attended on H.M. Queen Mary when she opened the new Jubilee extension of the West London Hospital, and in addition to taking part in the Annual Armistice Day Parade the Regiment attended a Civic Sunday Service at St. Mary Abbots Church.

Early in 1938 an extremely enjoyable ball was held at H.Q., and thereafter the Regiment embarked upon serious training for camp with the determination to obtain as many recruits as possible. In April and May respectively the Prize-giving and Regimental Rifle Meeting were held; at the former Major-General P. C. R. Commings, C.B., C.M.G., D.S.O., commanding the London Division, presented the prizes. At the London District Rifle Meeting at Pirbright the Regiment won, for the first time, The Dewar (M.G.) Trophy.

During the period prior to camp several week-end exercises were held, and the experience so gained undoubtedly helped to earn the praise which the Regiment received from the Brigade Commander at the camp at Burley in the New Forest. Although probably more hard work and training were done at this camp than at any other, everyone voted it the most enjoyable yet. Whilst at camp it was learnt with much pleasure that the rôle of the battalion was being changed from an infantry battalion to a fully mechanised machine-gun battalion, equipped with Vickers ·303-m. machine-guns.

No sooner had the Regiment returned than the "September Crisis" arose. The Q.M., much to his surprise and delight, suddenly received stores and equipment for which he had been asking in vain for years, and when the key personnel were called up a mobilisation scheme was laid on to enable the embodiment, if and when it was ordered, to be carried out smoothly. However, after long-drawn-out days of anxiety and the completion of much essential work at H.Q. by all ranks, the Prime Minister returned from his final meeting with Hitler saying that he had secured "Peace in our time". It would be difficult to place anything to Hitler's credit, but at least at this time he earned the thanks of the T.A. for gaining it a very large number of recruits.

With the crisis out of the way, temporarily rather than permanently, so thought most members, the Regiment prepared to move from its H.Q. at Iverna Gardens, Kensington, where it had been since 1885, to the imposing building which had been erected at 190 Hammersmith Road, Hammersmith. Although many were sorry to leave the old familiar H.Q., it was realised that the Regiment had long ago outgrown it, and the new H.Q. was certainly the most modern and best-equipped in London, from both a military and a social angle. The one real regret was the fact that it was not possible for the new building to be erected in the Royal Borough of Kensington, from which the Regiment took its name and in which its roots were so firmly established.

Recruiting continued slowly but surely during January 1939, and by the middle of February the strength of the battalion was 20 officers and 377 other ranks. In March, the C.O., Lt.-Colonel F. G. Hancocks, accompanied by several newly-commissioned officers, attended a levee at Buckingham Palace: normally such functions were held at St. James's Palace, but this was required for one of the many conferences which were a feature of pre-war London. For the first time the C.O. wore the full-dress uniform of the Regiment, including the famous spiked helmet, which he succeeded in putting through the roof of the taxi when departing from the Palace, much to the chagrin of the driver and to the enjoyment of the junior officers.

During this month two very successful dances were held at the new H.Q. One was arranged by the A.T.S. who were now attached to the Regiment, and the other was run jointly by the O.C.A. and the Regiment. Easter fell soon afterwards, and all companies carried out machine-gun firing at Pirbright. Whilst there, news was heard of Mussolini's second act of aggression, namely, the invasion of Albania, and many minds were set wondering as to the ultimate consequences. It had, however, one immediate and gratifying result, namely a greatly increased flow of recruits.

In the middle of April 1939, the 21st Annual Dinner of the Old Comrades' Association was held at the Clarendon Restaurant, with the Honorary Colonel, Colonel Hugh Campbell, D.S.O., O.B.E., T.D., in the chair. The dinner marked the silver jubilee of the O.C.A., which had gone from strength to strength since its foundation in 1914 by Captain A. Ridley, M.B.E.

It was at this time that the Prime Minister made the momentous announcement in the House of Commons that, for the first time in the history of our island, conscription was to be introduced in peace-time. This was a result of the Continental situation caused by the entry of German forces into Czechoslovakia in defiance of the Munich Agreement of September 1938. The period of service was to be six months and was to apply to all youths aged between eighteen and twenty, but anyone who joined the Territorial Army before a certain date would be exempt. It was further proposed to double all existing T.A. units.

For the next few days H.Q. was besieged by hundreds of would-be volunteers, and the 1st Battalion was soon up to war establishment and recruiting began for the 2nd Battalion. Major Cecil Pim, 2/i/C. of the 1st Battalion, was appointed C.O. of the 2nd Battalion, and with the leasing of premises opposite the H.Q. the 2nd Battalion not only had a home of its own but was soon up to strength.

An additional fillip had been given to recruiting for the "Kensingtons" by *Picture Post*, which published an article on the Territorial Army amply illustrated with photos of H.Q. and showing a night in the life of a recruit.

As usual in May, the Royal Tournament was held at Olympia and the Regiment supplied two officers and a machine-gun platoon to take part each night in the final scene. Later on in the month, the Whitsun week-end was utilised for M.G. firing and practising range-taking at Pirbright. On the first Sunday in July, H.M. the King took the salute in Hyde Park at a march-past of contingents representing all units of the T.A., and the 1st Battalion furnished a number of officers and other ranks. The following week-end a very successful T.E.W.T. was held for the officers by the C.O. in the New Forest.

Since the appointment of Major Pim to command the 2nd Battalion, the 1st Battalion had been without a 2/i/C. This was remedied just prior to the annual camp by the arrival of Major C. N. C. Howard, an "old Kensington"; he joined the battalion on Sunday, July 30th, when it assembled at H.Q. ready to move to camp by M.T. in company groups. Despite, or because of, the present size of the T.A., equipment of all kinds was extremely slow in reaching units and the journey to camp had to be made by motor-coaches, with the company commanders using cars which had been specially hired. Nevertheless, the journey provided good experience of a move by road. Each company had a halt on the Hog's Back, where the Honorary Colonel was waiting to welcome the arrivals, and eventually without any untoward incident the battalion arrived at Bagshot Moor Camp, Beaulieu.

The camp was provided with excellent facilities unknown in a T.A. camp previously, such as shower-baths and drying-sheds, but it was noted with concern that on some of the older Ordnance maps the site was marked as a swamp. Over 80 per cent. of the battalion were recruits, and all ranks were anticipating with pleasure a fortnight of good, solid training. The first three days were in fact so spent, but late on Wednesday night the rain came down in torrents and very soon the entire camp was under water. After breakfast all kit was placed high, and for the moment dry, on tables in the messing tents, and under the able guidance of the pioneers and many other would-be experts, drainage schemes were started. In the meantime, billeting arrangements were being made in case of need, and when another deluge came the order was given to evacuate the camp and to occupy the billets in the neighbouring villages. These were occupied for the remainder of the camp with the exception of a night in the second week when, the rain having ceased and the ground become reasonably dry, it was decided that the camp should be reoccupied. One need not say that no sooner had this been done when the rain again came down in torrents.

All this seriously interrupted training and led to the cancellation of the night exercises. However, many things were learnt, and the battalion returned on Sunday, August 13th, 1939, well cemented together. As the 1st Battalion moved out of the camp, the 2nd moved in and were to enjoy a fortnight of almost perfect weather. When the battalion was dismissed at H.Q. on that Sunday afternoon in August there were many signs that ere long all would be in khaki again to carry on where the others left off in 1918.

During the rest of August the Drill Hall was to be closed, but it soon appeared that Hitler was planning another act of aggression, and this time a halt would have to be called. On August 24th, 1939, key personnel were called up to prepare for embodiment under a scheme previously prepared, and at the same time many old warriors were recalled who comprised the Kensington's National Defence Company. The latter shared the Drill Hall with the battalions' key personnel until they (the N.D.C.) took over the 2nd Battalion H.Q. when the 2nd moved to Hammersmith Old Town Hall.

CHAPTER II

MOBILISATION

FOLLOWING the invasion of Poland by the Germans on September 1st, the T.A. was embodied at 3 p.m. and from thence on the men streamed in to report, receive their embodiment grant, be medically examined, and be taken under company arrangements to the respective quarters.

The rôle allotted to the battalion was support of the Civil Power, i.e. to assist the police in the event of air-raids, prevent looting from bombed houses, etc., to allay panic, and to deal with any parachutists or saboteurs that the enemy might drop. Areas allocated were as follows: A Coy., Kensington; B Coy., Chiswick; C Coy., Hammersmith; D Coy., Notting Hill. All companies were billeted in empty houses, schools, etc., and were to be ready for any immediate action required. One officer and a D.R. were to be on duty at the police-station in the respective areas of their companies. Advance Bn. H.Q. was at Hammersmith police-station, and Rear Bn. H.Q. and H.Q. Coy. at 190 Hammersmith Road. The battalion was attached temporarily to 6 Infantry Brigade, 2 London Division, Brigadier Wreford, Irish Guards, commanding.

The day following embodiment was spent by all companies in putting their quarters in order and trying to find the answers to many questions. Pending the receipt of R.A.S.C. rations the messing was in the hands of a private firm of caterers, and there were many other difficulties to be smoothed over. In the evening a terrific thunderstorm broke over London and many thought the capital was being bombed. The House of Commons, for the first time for many years, was in session on a Saturday and the Prime Minister had announced that Mussolini was endeavouring to mediate between ourselves and Germany.

Sunday, September 3rd, 1939, was not to prove a day of rest as there were still many things to be done. At 11 a.m.

it was learnt that no reply had been received to our ultimatum that all German forces should withdraw from Poland, and in view of the failure of Mussolini's attempt at mediation, the Prime Minister broadcast to the nation that a state of war existed between England and Germany. Mr. Chamberlain said that the things we were fighting against were "the evil things, brute force, bad faith, injustice, oppression, and persecution".

Hardly had he finished speaking when the air-raid sirens sounded their dread warning and the British public were given their first sample of what was to be a familiar sound in later years. Fortunately, it transpired that the warning was given in error and the battalion was not, therefore, called upon to take any action.

During the next few days various officers and men were posted to training centres as instructors or went on courses, and meanwhile companies endeavoured to carry out machine-gun training in addition to their duties in aid of the Civil Power. Towards the end of the month, in view of the "phoney war" the battalion was partially released from its duties, thereby enabling companies to carry out the maximum M.G. training possible. To facilitate training there was a re-allocation of areas and A, B, and C Companies were to take over a slightly wider area to enable D Coy. to be withdrawn from the Civil Power assistance duties altogether. This company was to act as a training cadre and to it were sent a number of junior N.C.O.s to be trained as instructors.

A very impressive ceremony took place on October 15th, when the Regimental colours were laid up at St. Mary Abbots Church, Kensington. The colours were carried by Lieut. P. Beevor and 2/Lieut. B. R. Wood, with Sgts. Clarke, Rees, and Hibberd forming the escort, and the service was conducted by the Vicar of Kensington, the Rev. Prebendary Smith. The church was filled with contingents from all companies and by a large gathering of members of the O.C.A.

A few days later the battalion was relieved altogether of its duties in aid of the Civil Power and was to provide three companies to guard "V.P.s" (Vulnerable Points, not

Very Important Persons) on the outskirts of London—A Coy. at Balloon Barrage H.Q. at Stanmore; B and C Coys. around Mill Hill and Hendon; D Coy remaining at Chiswick as a cadre training unit. Although the guard duties were onerous there were many compensations. The R.A.F. billets were excellent, likewise the food, and good relations were soon established between the Kensingtons and R.A.F. and the W.A.A.F.—particularly the latter; football, boxing matches, and excellent ENSA shows helped to brighten the off-duty hours.

Armistice Day fell on a Saturday and a service was attended at St. Mary Abbots, Kensington, on Sunday, November 12th, by serving members of the Regiment and a strong contingent of the O.C.A. After the service the entire congregation, led by the Mayor, attended a brief ceremony at the War Memorial, where wreaths were laid by Brig.-Gen. Lewis, C.B., C.M.G., T.D., on behalf of H.R.H. Princess Louise, by Major Howard for the Regiment, and by Captain Tosland for the O.C.A.

On November 16th it was learned that the battalion was leaving for Somerset on the 19th to join and train with 44 (Home Counties) Division, commanded by Major-General Osborne, popularly, if irreverently, known as "Snow-White". The pleasure of all ranks at learning the news was dampened when they heard that Col. Hancocks was relinquishing the command. He was extremely popular with all ranks, had a vast experience of machine-guns, and it says much for his enthusiasm and ability if one merely studies the growth of the battalion and its record since he took over command. Major Howard was appointed to the command, Major Hoare became 2/i/C. and Captain Bryar Adjutant in place of Major Hoare.

A, B, and C Companies left their respective stations early on Sunday, November 19th, 1939, to join up with Bn. H.Q., H.Q. Coy and D Coy. at Addison Road, Kensington, where on the platform were assembled Col. Hugh Campbell, Hon. Col. of the Regiment, Col. (now Major-General) Sir Donald Banks, D.S.O., Lt.-Col. F. G. Hancocks, and many members of the O.C.A. The train drew out for Ilminster, where Bn. H.Q., H.Q. Coy., C and D Coys. were to be billeted, A and B Companies being billeted at South Petherton, a village about seven miles away.

On arrival at Ilminster at 16.00 hrs. the Bn. detrained; the advance party had a hot meal ready in what was to be the mess hall of the battalion, a disused shirt factory. Afterwards, the companies were taken to their respective quarters, which were mainly old factories, schools, and skittle alleys, and in most cases the accommodation was primitive. A and B Companies' billets at South Petherton were no better and it was some days before the respective company officers were satisfied that the troops were even fairly comfortable. Recreational facilities were not impressive either at Ilminster or at South Petherton, but all ranks soon became very popular with the local residents and had open invitations for Sunday dinner and baths.

Serious training was now embarked upon, lectures on fire control for all N.C.O.s, M.G. handling for the men, and lectures on fire control and T.E.W.T.s for the officers. In addition, long route-marches enabled the battalion to get fit, and in fact, except for Sundays, there was little time for leisure. Towards the end of November drafts arrived from the K.R.R.C. and Middlesex Regiment and also ex-machine-gunner reservists from the Yorks and Lancs, East Yorks and East Lancs Regiments, and it says much for their qualities that they soon became 100 per cent. Kensingtons. These drafts were necessary to replace the large number of Kensingtons under the age of twenty (then the minimum age for service abroad) to whom the battalion had had to say "*au revoir*" with great regret, prior to the departure for Somerset. In the main these went to the 2nd Bn., but a few were sent to O.C.T.U.

With very deep regret the battalion learned, on December 4th, 1939, that H.R.H. Princess Louise had passed away the previous night. Throughout the years H.R.H. was associated with the Regiment, she maintained a never-failing interest in its welfare and never, except through illness, missed an Armistice Day Parade. The 1st Bn. was represented at the funeral by the Commanding Officer and the Adjutant.

After three weeks' intensive M.G. training, including

night exercises, the battalion was included in a divisional "digging-in" exercise on Batcombe Down, and during the six days and nights that the exercises took place it was bitterly cold, with thick snow on the ground. No surprise was occasioned, therefore, when the local council stated afterwards that the entire area had been denuded of signposts, traffic signs, and anything which could be burnt.

Before Christmas, the battalion was pleased to welcome an "Old Kensington", Major Prismall, who came from the depot to take command of B Coy., and he was followed a little later by Major J. B. Dodge, who took over command of D Coy.

December 20th, 1939, saw the start of Christmas leave; three parties, each of seven days, and as a present all ranks were vaccinated and were promised T.A.B. inoculations in the New Year. The battalion also received at this time its full complement of trucks, much to the delight of Lieut. "Tiny" Milton, the M.T.O., who with his very able assistant the O.M.E., Lt. Rae, gave the transport such great care that the battalion never had a major breakdown throughout training in England and the campaign in France. For those left with the battalion on Christmas Day, a magnificent dinner was laid on by the Q.M., Lt. "Rocky" Knight.

When Christmas leave was over, A, B, C, and D Companies proceeded to Tidworth for a week of field-firing, leaving Bn. H.Q. and H.Q. Coy. to look after the billets. For the first time since the outbreak of war the troops were billeted in proper quarters and the officers were able to establish a Mess together, the only bleak spot during a very enjoyable and instructive week being the weather. Thick snow fell on the second day and stayed for the whole week and a long time thereafter. It was with much trepidation that the companies left for Somerset again on Sunday, January 21st, 1940, as the roads, due to intense cold and snow, were like skating rinks and speed consequently restricted to 8 M.I.H. However, with the exception of two crashes the companies reached their destination intact, though very late. In one of the accidents, involving the car of the column commander, which was being towed, Capt. Tregoning was injured and was in hospital for a long time.

Despite the continuation of snow and many other difficulties due to the appalling cold, training continued apace. At the end of the month it was learnt that a reconnaissance and billeting party was to leave for France on February 5th, and the battalion was to follow shortly. On the 7th the Division was inspected by H.M. the King at Crewkerne, and in the absence of the C.O. through illness Major Hoare commanded the battalion. The day after the inspection the battalion was informed that the move to France was off and the reconnaissance and the billeting parties returning. A rumour went around that the Kensingtons were to form part of a force ear-marked for Finland which was to assist, unofficially, that gallant little nation in its defence against the Russians, but it remained a rumour.

The crossing to France having been indefinitely postponed, training was resumed, and Major Hoare assumed command temporarily of the battalion as Lt.-Col. Howard had been struck off the strength of the unit, having been absent through illness for more than twenty-one days. To assist with training, the depot sent Major Walden, a regular officer of the Middlesex Regiment who had been on leave from Hong-Kong when war broke out, and with him came Capt. Salmon.

Capt. Holding now assumed command of B Coy., and intensive company and battalion training was augmented by field-firing at Swyre. Whilst this was taking place, Lt.-Col. F. G. Parker of the Middlesex Regiment was posted to command the battalion, Major N. E. Hoare returned to his own regiment, The Buffs, and Major Walden was appointed 2/i/C. and Capt. Padfield from the depot became O.C. C Coy.

As the battalion was warned for service overseas early in April, training became even more vigorous, broken only by four days' embarkation leave starting on March 19th. On April 5th the advance party once again proceeded to France, and this was to be followed on April 6th by a party consisting of the drivers and transport, with the remainder of the battalion leaving on April 13th. Hasty preparations were now made to get all kit packed in the trucks, and on April 5th, 1940, everything was in readiness for the transport to move off on the following day.

MOBILISATION

It may be of interest to show here in outline the approximate lay-out of the battalion on joining the B.E.F.

Bn. H.Q.
C.O., Lt.-Col. F. G. Parker
2/i/C., Major F. Walden
Adjt., Capt. B. L. Bryar*
I.O., 2/Lt. E. P. Shanks
Q.M., Capt. E. D. Knight, M.M.*
M.O., Capt. J. Smith, R.A.M.C.
Padre, Capt. F. Bennett, C.F.
R.S.M. Hill†
R.Q.M.S. Edgecombe*

H.Q. Coy.
O.C., Major A. A. de C. Chimay*
M.T.O., Lieut. R. D. Milton*
Signal Officer, 2/Lt. I. H. Battye
O.M.E. (attached), Lieut. D. Rae, R.A.O.C.
C.S.M. Butler*
C.Q.M.S. Humphreys*
P.S.M. Chilton*

A Company
O.C., Capt. G. D. Paterson*
2/i/C., Capt. H. R. Mountford*

Platoon Comdrs.:
    2/Lt. B. R. Wood*
    2/Lt. A. R. Meikle*

P.S.M. Thompson*

C.S.M. Darling*
C.Q.M.S. Minski*

B Company
O.C., Capt. E. W. Holding*
2/i/C., Capt. R. Wasey*

Platoon Cmdrs.:
    2/Lt. P. F. Smythe*
    2/Lt. S. F. Caulfield-Kerney

P.S.M. Frost*

C.S.M. Hibberd*
C.Q.M.S. King*

C Company
O.C., Capt. C. Padfield
2/i/C., Capt. P. Beevor*

Platoon Cmdrs.:
    2/Lt. W. E. Walker*
    2/Lt. H. A. C. Page
P.S.M. Gordon*

C.S.M. Skinner*
C.Q.M.S. Morris*

D Company
O.C., Major J. B. Dodge, D.S.O., D.S.C.
2/i/C., Capt. A. H. Salmon

Platoon Cmdrs.:
    2/Lt. R. Hammond*
    2/Lt. H. J. Lavington*
P.S.M. Mullender*

C.S.M. Satchwell†
C.Q.M.S. Wasley*

First-Line Reinforcements (Officers):
Capt. C. K. Williamson*
2/Lt. A. L. Burton*
2/Lt. G. Kent*
2/Lt. J. J. Evans*

* Pre-War T.A. Members of the Regiment.   † Pre-War Permanent Staff.

CHAPTER III

FRANCE—THE FIRST PHASE (APRIL–MAY 1940)

At 06.30 hrs. on Monday, April 6th, 1940, the Battalion transport was drawn up along Strawberry Hill at Ilminster, and despite the fact that the battalion's A.A. platoon was dispersed along the length of the column one was grateful that the "phoney" war was still in force and, given good luck, no enemy planes should be about. Even at this early hour it seemed as if the entire population of Ilminster had turned out, and after the numerous D.R.s had left under command of Lt. Milton to police the route, the first company moved off at 07.30 hrs. On arrival at Southampton the column drove straight into the docks, where it was welcomed by an old Kensington, Major Bellamy, the E.S.O. The petrol was at once drained from all trucks and loading on board the transport ship commenced.

Whilst at Southampton all ranks were billeted at a rest camp which was previously a school, and during breakfast the next day it was announced on the wireless that Norway had been invaded by the Germans. Many now wondered whether the battalion would see France. By Wednesday morning all the trucks had been loaded and in the afternoon the troops embarked on the transport *Isle of Man*. Accommodation on board ship was very crowded, and it was a difficult matter to acquaint all ranks with action to be taken in event of air or submarine attack. Sharp at 19.00 hrs. the *Isle of Man* left the docks and steamed into the Solent, where it anchored whilst the rest of the ships joined the convoy. Anchors were weighed at midnight, and when dawn broke, after an uneventful night, Le Havre was in sight. The ship carrying the transport had also arrived, and as soon as the troops had been disembarked preparations were made to drive away the vehicles, as they were unloaded, to the billet. The billet for the advance party was in a large château at Valliquerville, a small village between Yvetot and

Bolbec, with the usual large avenue of trees leading up to it which provided good cover from the air for the transport. Accommodation was rather primitive, and all ranks soon realised that France had a long way to go as regards sanitation. During the evening the French liaison officer, Lt. Drouet, who was to be attached to the battalion, arrived, and it was not surprising that he spoke perfect English as he had lived nearly all his life in Birmingham. For the next two days, whilst the remainder of the transport was being unloaded, the officers in the advance party arranged billets for the battalion due to arrive on Sunday, April 14th. The only accommodation was barns, not very clean at that, and it was found that it needed a very large area to meet the requirements of a battalion.

In the meantime the battalion in England, deprived of its transport, guns, and equipment, spent the days route-marching and the evenings in giving fond farewells to the many friends who made life so much more pleasant during the stay in Somerset. On April 13th the battalion left Ilminster, and once again the population turned out in force. Two trains took the battalion to Southampton, and in the early afternoon all ranks were safely aboard the S.S. *Amsterdam*. At 08.00 hrs. the following morning Le Havre was reached, and the First-Line Reinforcements left for the base depot. After a meal the battalion entrained for Yvetot, where the battalion transport was drawn up waiting to convey the companies to their respective billets.

On the following day orders were received for the battalion to proceed to Armentières. This was to be our farewell to 44 Division, which was destined for a further period of training in France; what the future held in store was not divulged until after our arrival in Armentières, when we were placed under the command of 5 Division on the Belgian frontier. A billeting party left forthwith and companies began feverish preparations to move. At 08.30 hrs. the next day the battalion moved off, and after passing through Yvetot and St. Saens the beautiful countryside of the Forêt D'eu was sighted, which made a pleasant change from the flat fields whose monotony was broken only by the avenues of trees lining the roads. After a halt for half an

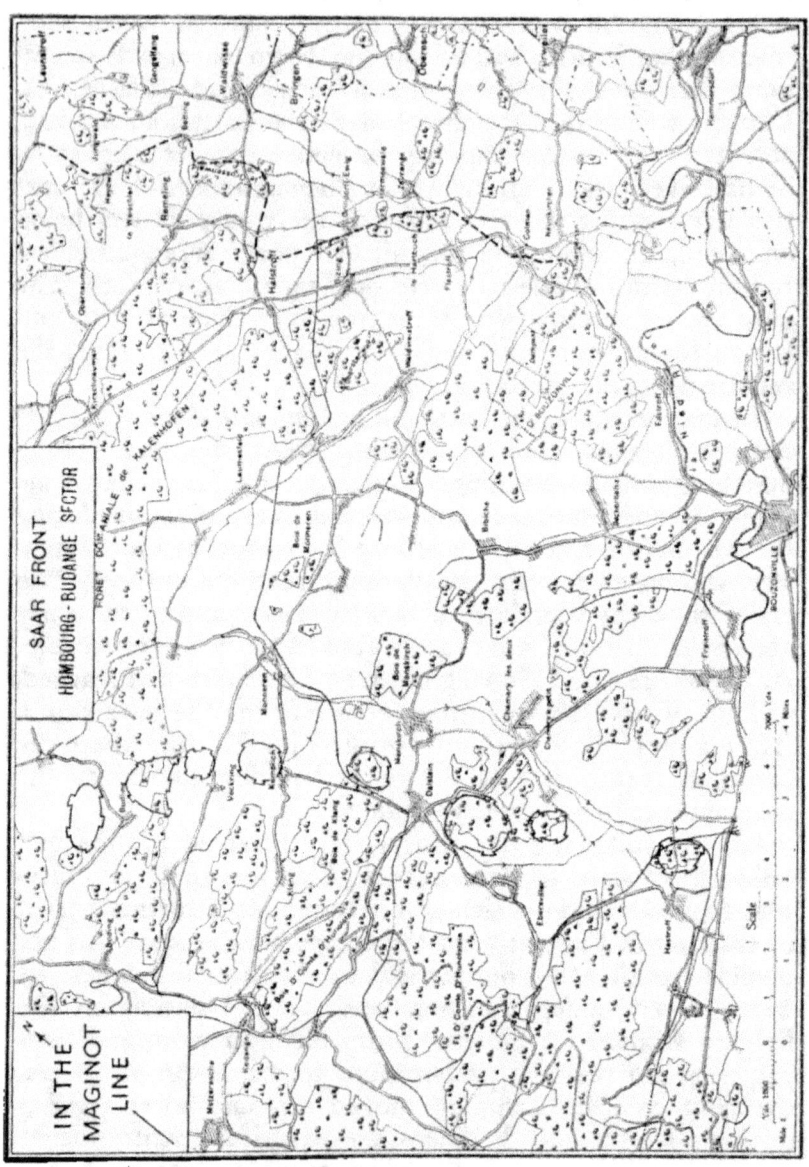

---- = Approximate Line of Outposts, 51 Division.

hour at Neufchatel, the Pas de Somme was reached, scene of so much bitter fighting in the last war. The night was spent near Blangy, and early the next morning the battalion was off again over the flat countryside of the Somme; the River Somme was crossed at Abbeville, and over cobbled streets the trucks sped past Crecy and St. Pol. The industrial area of France was now being reached, and town succeeded town with the endless cobblestones and the vast slag-heaps reaching high. After passing through Lillers (known to old soldiers as Loos), Merville was reached, where a halt was made for lunch washed down with "blond" beer from the *estaminets*.

The battalion entered Armentières at 14.30 hrs., and companies were soon directed to their various billets, consisting of empty shops, houses, and factories. Armentières was not a very large town, and one was left wondering how it obtained the notoriety it achieved from the popular song of the last war. Certainly, all ranks found it hard to discover a present-day mademoiselle equal to the lady of 1914-18 renown, and it was not for want of trying ! ! ! The following day large-scale maintenance of transport was carried out, and in the evening the battalion was informed that it would be joining the 51 (Highland) Division, which was destined for the Saar Front.

For some time, British units of a strength not larger than a brigade were being attached for service in front of the Maginot Line on the Lorraine-Saarbruecken border. The idea was to acclimatise the troops to battle conditions, in other words "to blood them." In April it was decided to send a British division to take over a French divisional sector, and 51 Division was selected for the rôle. Many problems had to be solved, not least of which was the difference in strength and fire-power between a French and a British division.

The C.O. and French liaison officer left on April 19th for Metz, which was the French IX Corps H.Q., in order to meet the divisional commander, Major-General Victor Fortune, C.B., D.S.O., and with his brigadiers and other unit commanders to make a "recce" of the divisional front. Meanwhile, the battalion undertook several long marches to keep fit, and in the evenings companies carried out several large moves by road. Many places familiar to last-war Kensingtons were seen, such as Estaires, and there were still many signs of that war, including pill-boxes and partly-filled-in trenches. Sunday was made the occasion for a drum-head service on the main square, and during the day many troops went for walks to the Belgian frontier.

Lt.-Col. Parker returned to Armentières to lead the battalion down on April 25th on the long journey of over 280 miles, an advance party having left already to arrange the billeting in the assembly area close to the front at the villages of Hagondange and Talange, near Metz. Famous towns were passed on the first day's route, such as Béthune, Arras, Cambrai, and St. Quentin. Rheims was passed through on the second day, and the night was spent at La Neuville du Pont. Early the following morning the battalion, in order to avoid detection from the air, moved to a hide in the beautiful Forest of Argonne and, when night fell, left on the last lap of the journey to Hagondange and Talange. On arrival at the two villages in the early hours of the morning the companies were quickly led to their respective billets, and all ranks settled down to a good rest.

A Coy. now had the great misfortune to lose their able and popular company commander, Capt. Paterson, who was sent to hospital at Metz with appendicitis. Major de Chimay was sent from H.Q. Coy. to command A Coy. in his place, and Capt. Wasey assumed command of H.Q. Coy.

Once again large-scale maintenance of transport was carried out whilst the company commanders were reconnoitring the positions their companies were to occupy in the outpost line some twelve miles in front of the Maginot Line. Although the majority of elderly people in the neighbourhood spoke only German, having been under the Huns' yoke from the Franco–Prussian War of 1871 to after the 1914–18 War, they were extremely kind to all ranks.

In the early evening of April 30th, 1940, C and D Companies prepared to move, as soon as darkness fell, to their positions in the "Ligne de Contacte" about twelve miles in front of the Maginot Line. The Maginot Line consisted of numerous forts both large and small, built of thick concrete and blended with the landscape: it ran on high ground connected by woods, and in front were "dragons' teeth", barbed wire, and wide anti-tank ditches. The countryside dominated by the Maginot Line had been entirely stripped of every shrub, bush, and tree for about two miles until the "Bois Militaires" were reached, in which was the "Ligne de Recueil", consisting mainly of trenches and outposts, then about two miles farther on was the "Ligne de Soutien", and six miles in front of this the actual "Ligne de Contacte" about six miles from the Siegfried Line, with the enemy advance-posts from 200 yards to 1,000 yards away.

The "Ligne de Contacte" consisted of scattered outposts, mere dug-outs made of logs and surmounted by barbed wire. In a wood of about 400 yards in length there would be generally four outposts about 100 yards apart, consisting of a machine-gun section at each end of the wood and two infantry sections in the centre. From dusk to dawn everyone remained in their respective fox-holes, and anyone or anything moving outside was considered to be an enemy, unless warning had been received that a British patrol would be out.

51 Division was taking over from the French the line Heydwald Wood–Welschler–Grossenwald–Grindorf–Hartbuch–Colmen–Neunkirchen. The Germans were actually in the villages of Grindorf and Neunkirchen, and the village of Betting was apt to change hands frequently. C Coy. were taking over the Heydwald–Grossenwald sector, with Coy. H.Q. at Remeling, and D Coy. Grindorf–Colmen, with Coy. H.Q. at Waldweisstroff. Bn. H.Q. also moved up in front of the Maginot Line and established themselves at Bibiche.

The French had reported that the area had been very quiet, but it was evident that the enemy realised a change-over was taking place, and although the days remained quiet, except for desultory shelling in the morning, the nights were full of incidents. Many enemy patrols endeavoured to penetrate the woods but they were repulsed by grenades, rifles, and tommy-guns. Machine-guns could be used only on fixed lines at night, and if the night-firing apparatus were used the woods resembled Piccadilly Circus in a normal peace-time. Thus the Kensingtons could use only small arms to protect themselves, which they did very effectively. During the day the wire was repaired, if necessary, and constant improvements made in the dug-outs, etc. The opportunity was also taken to obtain well-earned sleep, as everyone had to be on the alert all night.

Although the infantry units had sustained a few casualties, the first battalion casualty was on May 5th, when P.S.M. Frost, of B Coy., a first-class platoon commander, was killed in the act of throwing a grenade during an evening raid on his platoon, by a bullet from a tommy-gun fired at very close range.

On May 6th, A and B Companies took over from C and D Companies respectively, having moved up to Bibiche the day previous. The nights, as usual, were full of activity and several patrols were sent out by the division in order to meet the enemy on their own ground.

In the early hours of May 10th, large fleets of enemy bombers flew over, and returned some hours later with several gaps in the formations. Soon afterwards it was learned that the Low Countries had been invaded and every post was on the alert, as a large-scale enemy attack was expected. This was not long delayed, and at 16.00 hrs. heavy shell-fire was put down by the enemy on the Heydwald and Grossenwald, and heavy firing could be heard from the French section farther north. Eventually the enemy, armed with flame-throwers, attacked and captured the Welscher Wood but were prevented from crossing the gap to the Heydwald, where 6 Platoon of A Coy., commanded by Lt. Meikle, were awaiting them, by the cross-fire from 4 Platoon, commanded by Lt. Wood, in the Grossenwald. At the same time all sections in the Grossenwald were actively engaged with the enemy, whose strength was estimated as a Brigade. The Kensingtons and Gordons were assisted by Bren-gun carriers from the Lothian and Border Horse, who had two put out of action. During this battle 4 Platoon Kensingtons nearly ran out of ammunition, but were saved by supplies brought up by the company cooks in a Bren-gun carrier along a fire-swept road. In the meantime Betting village, occupied by a platoon of the Black Watch, was surrounded, and covering fire was put down by the machine-guns to enable the Jocks to withdraw. This they did successfully, and said afterwards that the sound of the bullets going over their heads was like music in their ears, which was more than could be said of their bagpipes, which they played at every conceivable opportunity!

In the other sector, B Coy. also had a spirited battle and were subjected to a terrific artillery barrage. The Jocks lost several outposts, but managed to recapture some before the battle ended, and suffered many casualties. However, there is no doubt that the devastating fire of B Coy.'s machine-guns played no small part in driving the enemy back.

The next day A and B Companies were relieved by C and D Companies and took up their positions in the "Ligne de Recueil". The enemy, by no means dispirited by their lack of success, fired many shells into a company front within a short space of time and made several attacks, which were all repulsed though not without many casualties to both sides. With repeated attacks on the outposts it was now apparent that the existing line was becoming untenable, and on May 15th the Germans launched a full-scale attack along the whole front and made several penetrations between the outposts. During this attack Sgt. Willmott, Platoon Sergeant of Lieut. Hammond, was shot through the head and died later of his wounds. General Condé, commanding the Third French Army, now decided, in conjunction with General Fortune, that the time had come to conform with the withdrawal of the French Armies on either flank. Consequently the necessary orders were issued for the troops holding the "Ligne de Contacte" to withdraw through the "Ligne de Recueil" (which would become the "Ligne de Contacte") behind the Maginot Line. Arrangements had been made some days previously to meet such an eventuality, and so far as the Kensingtons were concerned it meant that the machine-guns were to cover the withdrawal of the infantry units, and to enable this to be done alternative machine-gun-section positions were selected. As the machine-gunners would be the last to withdraw, all non-essential items of equipment were to be sent back to company H.Q. on receipt of the appropriate orders.

The withdrawal was to prove no easy operation, due to the proximity of the enemy, and all M.G. sections had their moments of anxiety. D Coy. had the farthest distance to march back to the Maginot Line and they "borrowed" the mules (belonging to the Indian R.A.S.C. attached)—on which Sgt. Greenhill had brought up the rations—the first for three days—to carry their guns, etc. Sgt. Pratt, of a C Coy. Platoon commanded by Lieut. Walker, was called upon to use his section in laying down covering fire to enable a company of the 5 Gordons to extricate themselves from the Welschler Wood, where they were pinned down by enemy fire : two of the enemy machine-guns were silenced and the company managed to withdraw with only one casualty, and finally Sgt. Pratt evacuated his section without loss. For this he subsequently was awarded a well-earned D.C.M., and thus became the first Kensington to win a decoration in the Second World War.

After C and D Companies, with the infantry battalions, had withdrawn through the line held by the rest of the division on the ridge of Kalenhofen in front of the Maginot Line, for some reason the enemy did not follow up, probably due to the mines and demolition, but the *Luftwaffe* was very active in reconnaissance and in bombing cross-roads, etc. After a couple of days or so, A and B Companies were relieved by companies of the 7 Royal Northumberland Fusiliers and withdrew behind the Maginot Line to a secondary position, thereby enabling the troops to have a well-earned rest.

There had always been an agreement whereby any British division or brigade on the Saar Front would be permitted to join the main B.E.F. in the event of an enemy offensive, and all ranks were cheered to hear on May 21st that 51 Division was to travel north. On the release of the division from service with the Third French Army, General Condé, in an Order of the Day, said: "The Highlanders of 1940 have renewed the tradition of Beaumont-Hamel," and the Kensingtons were vain enough to hope that they had helped in maintaining that tradition.

The move back from the Saar began at 21.00 hrs. on May 21st and no lights were, of course, allowed on the vehicles, which made travel very hazardous, as numerous French units, motorised and horsed, were going both ways! However, without undue incident, St. Marie-aux-Chenes was reached at 03.00 hrs., and in the morning overdue maintenance was carried out on the transport and machine-guns. Although, in view of the trying experience in the out-posts, a longer rest was hoped for, the battalion left again for Hautecourt the next night and here two days were spent in cleaning up. On the second day it was rumoured that the enemy had broken through at Sedan and the village was rapidly put into a state of defence. The rumour was not strictly correct, but the news was bad, the French were being heavily pressed near Sedan and the battalion was at one hour's notice to move; on the night of May 25th the 51 Division was ordered up as a reserve to the area Grandpre–Varennes, north-west of Verdun. On arrival there, whilst awaiting further orders, which as soon as received were countermanded, the battalion harboured in a large wood and spent the day watching "dog-fights" in the skies between French and German planes.

Meanwhile in the north the situation was worsening: through the capture of Boulogne and Calais by enemy armoured formations, France was split in two and the 51 Division cut off from the B.E.F.; moreover, the Belgian Army was withdrawing under heavy pressure. The G.Q.G. in Paris had decided that the capital must be defended at all costs, and selected the Division to help in the matter. An advance party left during the afternoon of May 26th and the motorised part of the division was to leave that night. The first halt of the Kensingtons was to have been St. Vitry le François, but on arrival there in the early morning it was found to be a smoking ruin and after a short rest the journey was resumed in daylight. Many planes were heard and seen in the sky and leading units in the column were bombed on the road ahead, so at Sezanne the battalion was diverted into the grounds of a large château. Here it was learnt that the defence of Paris by the division was cancelled, and instead it was to proceed to the Somme to join 1 Armoured Division recently landed and the other British Units attached to the French IX Corps.

On May 29th Foucarmont, an important road junction in the Forêt D'eu, was reached and the transport was parked under trees on the main roads leading to Dieppe and Neufchatel, as it seemed likely that the enemy might bomb the cross-roads. The town was only about twenty miles from the front line and so road blocks were erected and machine-gun positions sited in case of trouble. Refugees were flocking into the town from all directions, seriously interfering with military traffic, and as the battalion was not at that time actively engaged with the enemy the C.O. obtained permission to use all available vehicles to evacuate them. By this means the population was reduced by over five thousand men, women, and children, including the few belongings they had with them.

During the move from the Saar to the Somme 2/Lt. E. P. Shanks, the I.O., and the D.R.s did sterling work in policing and mapping the route. At Foucarmont Lt. Kent joined B Coy., replacing P.S.M. Frost, who was killed on May 5th.

Meanwhile the B.E.F. was being evacuated from Dunkirk and it was obvious that the full weight of the enemy forces would soon be directed against the Somme front. The Germans had in fact already crossed the river and established bridgeheads at Abbeville and St. Valéry-sur-Somme (not to be confused with St. Valéry-en-Caux, of which more will be heard later). The French IX Corps, commanded by General Altmayer, including a French armoured division commanded by a General De Gaulle and supported by a British Armoured Division, had already attempted to throw the enemy back across the river but had been repulsed, with particularly heavy losses to 1 Armoured Division. The 51 Division was placed under command of the French, and on May 31st had taken over the sector from approximately Erondelle to just short of the south bank of the mouth of the Somme, which was held by French marines. 152 Brigade was on the right, 153 in the centre, and 154 on the left, with the 7 R.N.F. as the M.G. battalion in support.

CHAPTER IV

FRANCE—THE SECOND PHASE (JUNE 1940)

On June 2nd it was learnt that preparations were being made for another attack on the Abbeville and St. Valéry-sur-Somme bridgeheads, and A Coy. Kensingtons was to support 1 Gordons of 153 Bde. in the attack. The troops had managed to catch up on heavy arrears of sleep and maintenance and were eager at the thought of an attack instead of the nerve-racking defensive rôle on the Saar. In the early evening of June 3rd, A Coy. left for 153 Bde. and, as it went over a ridge towards the village of Lambricourt, near Miannay, came under heavy shell-fire from the enemy guns on the other bank of the Somme, but there were fortunately no casualties. On arrival, A Coy. found the village unoccupied except for a company of the Gordons and the Black Watch and an old lady of seventy, who said she had not run away from the Boche in the last war and did not intend to in this.

At dawn the next day 1 Gordons were to clear the enemy out of the Bois de Cambron, and this attack would coincide with a general offensive along the whole front with the support of the R.A.F. and French tanks. After a reconnaissance of the area by the platoon commanders just before dusk, the platoons moved into position during the night about 1,000 yards from the enemy positions. It was a difficult task trying to dig machine-gun pits in the hard earth without making too much noise, but when dawn came this had been accomplished. In front were shot-up tanks of 1 Armoured Division and the remains of trucks belonging to the R.N.F. as a result of the previous attack.

Meanwhile, back at Foucarmont, the enemy had bombed the town at dusk, causing great damage and numerous casualties, but by a miracle the remainder of the battalion suffered only slight damage to vehicles and one or two minor casualties. One hesitates to ponder how many civilians would have been casualties had not the battalion in the last few days evacuated so many refugees.

Soon after the raid, orders were received for another M.G. Coy. to take part in the attack the next day, and Major Dodge, commanding D Coy., left forthwith to contact 152 Bde. which, with the French tanks, were to attack Caubert from all sides.

Half an hour before dawn on June 4th the divisional artillery fired salvo after salvo on to the enemy for nearly an hour. At times the woods in front were blotted out by smoke and flame and it seemed impossible that anyone could be left alive in the inferno. However, when the shelling ceased and the infantry went into action it was apparent that the enemy was still there in force. As the Gordons of 153 Bde. attacked through the Bois de Cambron, Verey lights were put up to show the position of the leading troops, and the machine-guns of A Coy. fired belt after belt just ahead of them, switching their fire from time to time to the Grand Bois de Cambron, from which enemy fire was being directed on to A Coy.'s position. As the Gordons neared the end of the wood heavy mortar fire fell on A Coy., causing several serious casualties, including Sgt. Bailey and Pte. Nesbitt, but the M.G.s continued firing and the divisional artillery was requested to deal with the mortars. The enemy was now retreating across the gap from the Bois de Cambron to the Grand Bois, and afforded a magnificent target for the M.G.s. As the Bois de Cambron had been cleared, one of A Coy.'s platoons was sent there to support the Gordons in case the enemy counter-attacked.

Lt.-Col. H. Wright, commanding 1 Gordons, personally congratulated A Coy. on the excellent support which his battalion had received during the attack.

On the right flank 152 Bde. had attacked at the same time as the enemy had decided to mount an offensive, and when a company of 4 Camerons, supported by a section of D Coy. Kensingtons, advanced through the cornfields they were met by withering fire from well-sited machine-guns and mortars. Due to bitter hand-to-hand fighting it was not easy for the Kensingtons to lay down effective counter-fire without hitting the Camerons, but whenever the opportunity occurred the Germans were given a great deal of their own medicine and this undoubtedly helped to lessen the severe casualties sustained. On the left, another Coy. of Camerons, supported by a further M.G. section and French tanks, proceeded to attack Caubert and succeeded after fierce engagements in reaching the first objective, only to be met, as they advanced, by intense machine-gun fire from a ridge dominating the countryside, which was supposed to have been captured by the French tanks. Unfortunately, many tanks were blown up by undetected mines or accurate anti-tank gun-fire, and those that did reach their objective ran out of fuel and so became casualties.

The 4 Seaforths, on the right of the Camerons, supported by another platoon of D Coy. Kensingtons and French tanks, met with similar misfortune. In the open country, the tanks were speedily eliminated but despite this the Seaforths, supported by the Kensingtons' fire, went on against a stream of enemy machine-gun fire and a hail of mortar bombs and shells. The casualties sustained were enormous, but without armour there was no hope of forcing the enemy from his positions, and eventually, many companies having been practically annihilated, the attack was called off. In the day's fighting 152 Bde. had lost nearly six hundred all ranks.

As a result of the failure of the attack of 152 Bde. and the French tanks, 153 Bde. were unable to follow up the advantage they had gained. In the early afternoon the division was warned to expect an enemy counter-attack, but as this had not materialised by dusk it was obvious it would come at dawn. To support this contention enemy planes were very active towards dusk on reconnaissance and Stukas dive-bombed Miannay, completely blocking the important road junction there.

Dawn broke on June 5th with a mist, and half an hour later it was reported that the enemy had counter-attacked on the divisional front of twenty miles and towards the coast had broken through 154 Bde. This attack left 153 Bde. in an untenable position and orders were issued for a withdrawal of the remainder of the front; as this was being effected the mist cleared, showing the enemy advancing.

Due to the bombing of Miannay the withdrawal of 153 Bde. was carried out with difficulty and under the close fire of the enemy, but A Coy. eventually reached its destination at Moyenneville. 153 Bde. were now along the line of Miannay–Hymmeville and A Coy. were soon called to their support, and during a short action sustained several casualties, including Pte. Tondeur, who was badly wounded in the back. Soon afterwards, Sgt. Milnes, Pte. West, and Pte. Paul were also wounded.

On the right 152 Bde. were falling back to roughly the line Oisemont–St. Maxent, covered by the Lothian and Border Horse and remnants of French 31 Division. Earlier on in this operation a section of Lt. Lavington's platoon of D Coy. Kensingtons was overrun by the enemy.

The entire front was now badly dented and showing a very odd shape, and throughout the day the enemy pressure was maintained, well supported by the *Luftwaffe*, which dive-bombed many units. At times, brigades were out of touch with each other, but somehow or other they always managed to regain contact. By now, B and C Companies of the Kensingtons were in action endeavouring to hold a front larger than ever thought possible, but nevertheless managing to prevent the enemy from completely splitting the division into small pieces. It was now decided to try to hold the line of the River Bresle and a gradual withdrawal thereto would take place.

When dawn arrived most of the division had moved back towards the Bresle, with the enemy closely following, so that many times M.G. platoons of the Kensingtons were rushed hither and thither to lay down rapid defensive fire. As the hours went by the enemy never seemed to the tired British troops to relax his pressure, and it soon became apparent that the withdrawal over the River Bresle would have to be speeded up. Eventually orders were issued for the river to be crossed in the early evening, if possible, and the new front would run from Blangy to the sea, again a distance of over twenty miles.

By midnight most of the division was across the river, and although all ranks would have longed for a good night's sleep it was essential to dig in along the outskirts of the

Bois Militaire running along the line of the river. During the withdrawal, B Coy., commanded by Capt. Holding, were left behind owing to non-receipt of orders and found themselves at dawn on the wrong side of the river, in the midst of the enemy. However, as soon as the position was realised the company speedily cleared out, crossed the river over a bridge not yet blown, and again took up their place with the division right in the front line.

Towards the coast the enemy was already across the river but was eventually forced to withdraw after intensive shelling and machine-gunning by the divisional artillery and Kensingtons. During the day many excellent targets were offered to the battalion by enemy trucks bringing up fresh troops. The enemy air force was, however, very active, and each brigade had its fair share of bombing and many cursed the absence of the R.A.F. The wonderful feats of the British airmen over Dunkirk were, of course, unknown, as everyone was far too tired by the constant fighting by day and withdrawal by night to worry about what was happening elsewhere. However, during the afternoon of June 7th, a few British planes were seen and everyone was cheered to see enemy planes being brought down.

Meanwhile, the news from the right of the division was very disquieting: enemy armoured forces were reported to be advancing on Rouen; if true it meant that the "little" B.E.F. would soon be cut off from its base. A probing attack was made by the enemy against 153 Bde. soon after dawn on the 8th, but was beaten off with only a few casualties, of which A Coy. was fortunate in having only one. B and C Coys. on the right were still holding an incredibly thin and long line and when it became known that enemy armour was breaking through in force towards Rouen it was obvious that, despite the French Army Commander's order that there would be no withdrawal from the River Bresle, something would have to be done if the French and British troops were not to be cut off.

In the afternoon orders were issued that the division, including the "mixed" force composed of base reinforcements from Rouen which had joined the division the day before, would withdraw during the night to the line River

Aisne–Béthune running from Dieppe in the west to Neufchatel in the east. By this time all ranks were dog-tired, having had no sleep for many nights, let alone a wash, and nerves and tempers were becoming frayed. In these circumstances, it was amazing how determined everyone was not to be down-hearted. That night's march was to prove the worst of any yet undertaken; the motorised units had to follow the infantry, which led to engines getting overheated; dust was everywhere, and drivers fell asleep at the wheel through sheer exhaustion. To make matters worse enemy planes were constantly overhead dropping parachute flares to spot targets, on which they dropped bombs.

Dawn of June 9th found the division across the river with the exception of the divisional cavalry, the Lothian and Border Horse, who were covering the withdrawal and were still in touch with the enemy. Divisional H.Q. and Bn. H.Q. of 1 Kensingtons were situated at La Chaussée, and A and B Coys. awaited orders in woods outside Dieppe, which was being heavily bombed and was ablaze in many parts. C Coy. was about to proceed to Forges when news was received that enemy armoured forces were already there. It was obvious that Rouen would soon fall to the enemy and that the Allied forces had no hope of crossing the Seine and withdrawing behind the line which General Weygand, the new French C.-in-C., was supposed to have established there.

It would, of course, have been easy for 51 Division to withdraw forthwith to Le Havre and evacuated France, but this would have left the French forces in the lurch as, being mostly horse-drawn, they could not possibly keep up with a motorised division. It was therefore decided to withdraw to Le Havre in easy stages, and General Fortune fixed June 12th as the earliest date for evacuation. 154 Bde. (which had suffered heavy casualties), with "A" Bde., the mixed force, was to leave forthwith with B and C Coys. under command of Brig. Stanley-Clarke, to establish a line through which the rest of the division and French IX Corps would eventually withdraw.

In the early hours of June 10th, 1940, General Fortune was informed that enemy tanks were only six miles away from his H.Q.s. Twenty-five-pounder guns firing over open sights and A/T gunners soon barred their progress, but even graver news came in—that the enemy was astride the roads of withdrawal near Fécamp.

After a conference it was decided, if it was impossible to reach Le Havre, to try to evacuate from the small fishing-port of St. Valéry-en-Caux, around which a perimeter would be drawn, and British and French troops would be taken on board Allied ships in equal numbers.

As definite news about the enemy was very vague a mixed "recce" force was hastily gathered together at Div. H.Q. consisting of the Lothian and Border Horse, commanded by Lt.-Col. Lord Ansell, an A/T battery of 51 A.T. Regiment commanded by Major Peacock, and a M.G. platoon of A Coy. Kensingtons under the command of Lt. Wood. This force was to proceed along three parallel roads towards Fécamp and Le Havre in three bounds and report each bound clear to Div. H.Q., and deal if possible with any opposition. The division was to follow up gradually, ready for instant battle, with French IX Corps on the flank.

The "recce" unit threaded its way towards Fécamp, and only on the left flank was serious opposition encountered and suitably dealt with. Nearing Fécamp it was obvious there were considerable forces between this town and Le Havre and there was no alternative but to prepare to defend St. Valéry and trust in the Navy. A "recce" was thereupon made of this area and local opposition speedily eliminated. What was left of French IX Corps was allotted the southern portion of the perimeter, 153 Bde. with A Coy. Kensingtons, the western, and 152 Bde. with D. Coy. the eastern. Div. H.Q. was to be in St. Valéry itself.

In the early morning the perimeter was fully manned and at 10.00 hrs. General Fortune issued the following directive: "The Navy will probably make an effort to take us off by boat, perhaps tonight, perhaps in two nights. I wish all ranks to realise that this can only be achieved by the full co-operation of everyone, men may have to walk five or six miles. The utmost discipline must prevail. Men will board the boats with equipment and carrying arms. Vehicles will be rendered useless without giving away what is being done.

Carriers should be retained as the final rearguard. Routes back to the nearest highway should be reconnoitred and officers detailed as guides. Finally, if the enemy should attack before the whole force is evacuated, all ranks must realise that it is up to them to defeat them. They may attack with tanks and we have quite a number of anti-tank guns behind. If the infantry can stop the enemy's infantry, that is all that is required, while anti-tank guns and rifles inflict casualties on armoured fighting vehicles."

After a few probing attacks in the late morning the battle began in earnest in the afternoon; the enemy, needless to say, was vastly superior in tanks, guns, and mortars and their dive-bombers held undisputed sway in the sky. Against this overwhelming superiority the Allied force stood firm but, owing to the short time available for the reconnaissance and for digging in, the perimeter was very thin in places and casualties, of which the Kensingtons had their share, were numerous. Eventually, after extremely bitter fighting in all sectors, the enemy broke through and captured, from the French, a hill overlooking the town, which was being steadily bombed and shelled. At one time German tanks nearly entered the town, but the gunners, firing over open sights, forced them temporarily to withdraw. Whilst the battle was at its height orders were issued for the evacuation to begin at 22.30 hrs. Everything, including vehicles, was to be destroyed, with the exception of personal arms and ammunition, and the troops manning the perimeter were to be withdrawn through a smaller perimeter round the town itself held by two infantry battalions and two platoons of the Kensingtons. Beaches were allotted to the respective French and British troops.

When dusk fell the enemy was still attacking and the fighting was so confused as to make description impossible. The troops on the outer perimeter, after withdrawal, had orders to report at the railway station in the town, where they would get further instructions. However, on arrival there, after a hazardous journey through the defile leading to the town, with the enemy not far away, they found no one there in authority. The streets, packed with soldiers of all units, were lit up by the blazing houses, and shells were landing from time to time amongst them, but still the soldiers retained wonderful discipline. The inner perimeter was still managing to prevent the enemy penetrating into the town, but there were no boats in the harbour to take off the troops. Naval ships had in fact arrived the previous night, but finding no one there had departed out to sea where they had been heavily bombed from the air and shelled from the cliffs.

After midnight a destroyer and two sloops were seen and a few troops managed to board the landing-boats before the enemy appeared along the beach and forced the landing-boats to withdraw. Hand-to-hand fighting now took place along the beach and in the caves, and as the first light of dawn appeared it was obvious that there was no hope of evacuation (at least until the following night), particularly as the three boats which had managed to come close to the shore had been sunk. During the last few hours of fighting, Ptes. Farlander, Haslam, Paley, and Summers had been killed.

Now, to make matters more uncomfortable, it began to rain, but at least this would prevent the enemy air force from being in at the kill, and the dog-tired, wet, and hungry soldiers, never for one moment despairing, prepared to bolster up the perimeter in the forlorn hope of holding off the enemy for yet another day: an enemy which already dominated the town with artillery, mortars, and tanks. Against them were troops worn out by almost constant fighting since May 1st, having had no sleep for countless nights, with only personal arms, a very, very small quantity of ammunition, and little or no food. It was realised that as soon as the enemy attacked with all the weapons at his disposal there would be only one result—massacre. General Fortune had the hardest decision any soldier is ever called upon to make: whether to continue a hopeless fight, with the consequent huge number of casualties, or to surrender. His decision, bitter as it was to him and to his division, was the only one possible, particularly as the French, disorganised and dispirited, had already surrendered some hours previously.

Thus at 10.00 hrs. on Wednesday, June 12th, 1940, the

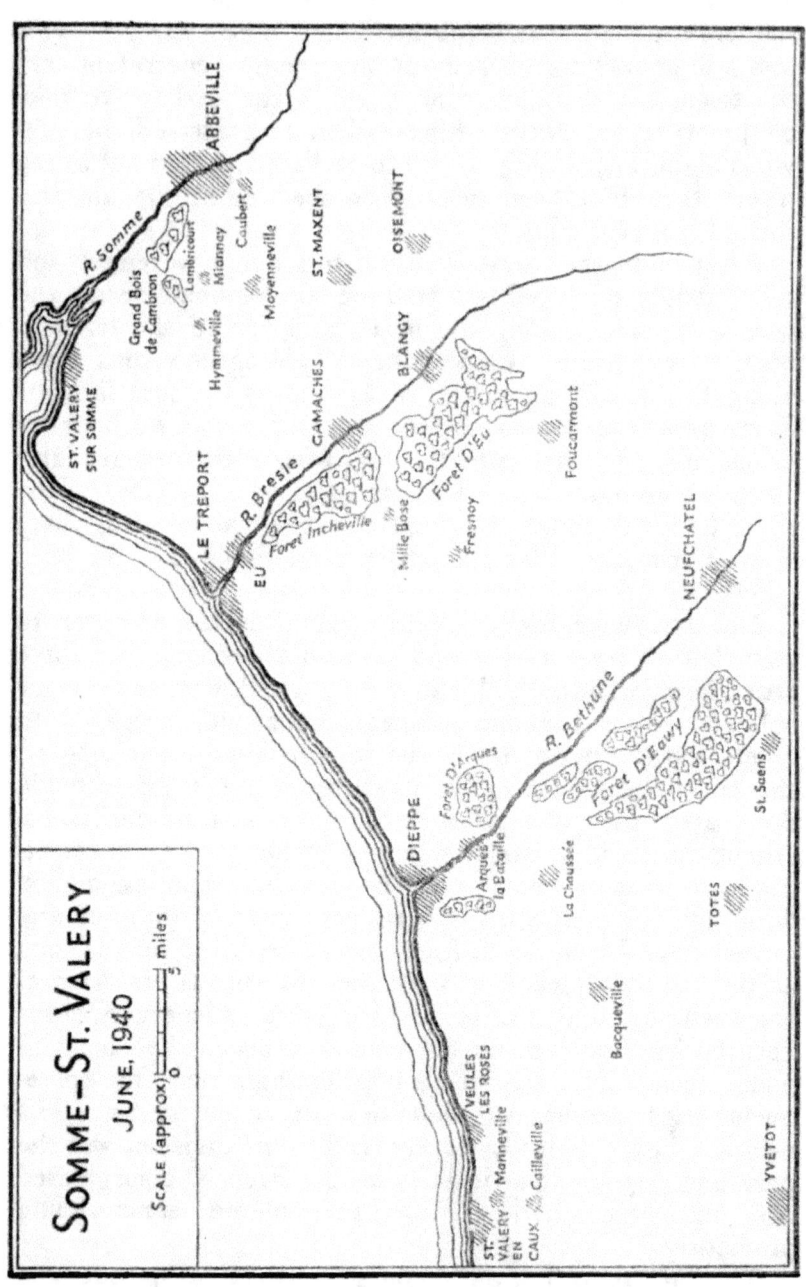

51 Division with A and D Coys. Kensingtons, game to the last, but with the dice loaded too heavily against them, laid down their arms, and a Major-General Rommel (whom the Allies were to hear of again later), commanding a German armoured division, drove into the town.

Meanwhile, a few miles to the east of St. Valéry, part of 152 Bde. and attached troops of the division had been in action during the night near a small port, Veules-les-Roses. To this port came some units of the Navy engaged in the embarkation and they succeeded, despite intense machine-gun and shell-fire, in taking off a number of troops, including Major de Chimay, commanding A Company, C.S.M. Satchwell and twelve other ranks of D Coy. Many of the Scots unable to get down the fire-swept paths leading to the shore made improvised ropes of rifle slings and, thus outwitting the enemy, reached the beaches.

Whilst the last act of the drama was being played at St. Valéry the rest of the battalion, namely Bn. H.Q., H.Q. Coy., B and C Coys., forming part of Brig. Stanley-Clarke's force, had reached, on the morning of June 10th, the coast road near Fécamp. The night had been pitch-black, and the drivers' task made no easier by the masses of refugees and French units on the road. The force was about to occupy a line Fécamp–Lillebonne when it was reported that the enemy had penetrated into Fécamp. In fact, the Germans had entered the town about twenty minutes after the tail of the Kensington column had left. Thus, with the division virtually split in two, it was decided to man a forward line between Goderville and Lillebonne with "A" Brigade, 17 Field Regt. R.A., and C Coy. Kensingtons. An inner line would be held between Octeville and Montvilliers by the remnants of 154 Bde., 75 Field Regt. R.A., and B Coy. Kensingtons.

Fighting took place during the late afternoon in the forward line and was particularly heavy near Fécamp, and on the following morning Brig. Stanley-Clarke learnt that 51 Division was completely cut off and the Navy were to attempt to evacuate it from St. Valéry. Attempts had already been made to make contact with General Fortune, but these had been unsuccessful. The Brigadier therefore ordered that his command and the garrison of Le Havre would begin evacuation from Le Havre that night, and thus the troops manning the forward line were accordingly withdrawn and embarked. Fortunately, whilst this was taking place the first rain for many weeks fell and only a few German aircraft appeared. During the day the town had been subjected to very heavy air-raids and several ships had been sunk in the port and a transit camp gutted.

The inner line was to commence withdrawal at noon on June 12th, but at the request of the French Command this was postponed for a further twelve hours in order to enable some of their scattered units of IX Corps to reach Le Havre. During the afternoon the Kensington Coy. Commanders, whilst an air-raid was in progress, "recced" the two-mile route to the docks from the place where the vehicles were to be left. Eventually the inner line withdrew, covered by B Coy. Kensingtons, and at the dispersal points two miles from the docks all vehicles, equipment, and stores were destroyed and flames and columns of smoke from this operation and as a result of the previous raids covered the town, thereby making air reconnaissance very difficult.

Despite this a further heavy raid occurred whilst the troops, carrying personal weapons and machine-guns, marched through the empty streets cluttered with debris. Buildings everywhere were blazing and collapsing, making an eerie and frightening spectacle. However, the docks were reached without loss so far as the Kensingtons were concerned, and just before the *Lady of Man* sailed, B Coy. less 1 Platoon arrived and were embarked.

The ship, however, sailed not for England but for Cherbourg, where the troops disembarked and it was expected that they would be put back into the line near Rouen. Owing to the decimated state of all units this was not a practical proposition and eventually re-embarkation was ordered and the ship sailed for Southampton, which was reached late on the afternoon of June 13th. Although disembarkation was ordered, all units were at two hours' notice to return to France.

A few days later 2/Lt. Kent and 68 other ranks of B Coy., who had been unable to rejoin their company near Le

FRANCE—THE SECOND PHASE (JUNE 1940)

Havre, arrived back in England with all their guns and equipment, having managed to cross the River Seine and board a ship near Cherbourg. For his initiative and meritorious conduct, 2/Lt. Kent was mentioned in dispatches, and 2/Lt. E. P. Shanks was similarly honoured.

Thus ended the first campaign of the Kensingtons in the 1939-45 War, and although tremendous experience was gained the cost was heavy. In addition to many casualties, 7 officers and 267 other ranks were reported missing, most of whom, however, were subsequently reported Prisoners of War. No finer words can be found to sum up the brief yet arduous campaign than Eric Linklater's "There is no sterner test of discipline than a long rearguard action, unless it be the sight of supporting troops who have been broken in the fight". The Fifty-First survived those tests and the division was a division to the end. It had shown, both on the Saar and on the Somme, a fine, aggressive spirit and great stubbornness in defence. In spite of its accumulated weariness, the frustration of all its hope, the failure on its flank, and its grievous losses, its spirit was unbroken. It suffered many casualties, but not the fatal one. Its hard core was fighting to the end and discipline "was last in the field".

CHAPTER V

RETURN TO HOME FORCES

WHILST a very tired party of approximately 350 all ranks, having disembarked from the steamer *Lady of Man*, rested at the Southampton transit camp, the Commanding Officer, Lt.-Col. F. G. Parker, conversed with the War Office concerning the next destination of 1st Bn. Kensingtons. Those evacuated from 51 Div. were collecting at Stirling, but there was room for the Bn. at the barracks of the parent unit, the Middlesex Regt., and finally the C.O.'s logic won the day. So, on June 15th, the party entrained for Mill Hill, where Col. M. Browne (commanding the Machine-gun Training Centre there) was extremely kind in welcoming the Bn. by arranging transport to barracks and finding billets for the officers for whom there was no accommodation in the Mess or in the very comfortable barrack rooms and wooden huts. On the 16th the Bn. Padre, Capt. Rev. F. L. M. Bennett, held a special service, and those present registered their own thankfulness and prayed for the large number of brother Kensingtons whose fate was still uncertain.

In the next few days, during which the Bn. was granted forty-eight hours' privilege leave, the C.O. was instructed that 1 Kensingtons would forthwith be re-equipped and trained as a Medium Machine-gun Bn. on the British Expeditionary Force establishment. On June 27th, against an establishment of about 30 officers and 700 other ranks, the Bn. strength was around 23 officers and 500 o/r, but over 140 reinforcements arrived on June 30th, and Lt. H. S. Jupp, who was later awarded the Military Cross for gallantry, was also posted to the Bn. with the 34 other ranks whom he had succeeded in bringing out of France in a fighting withdrawal.

Officers and personnel were re-allocated and the guns and equipment brought back from France distributed amongst the M.G. Coys. Lt.-Col. F. G. Parker appointed Capt. E. P. Shanks as Adjutant; the Coy. Commanders were Maj. de Chimay, A; Capt. E. W. Holding, B; Maj. C. J. C. Padfield, M.B.E., C; Capt. C. K. Williamson, D; Capt. B. L. Bryar, H.Q. No time was wasted, and training of the new teams commenced straight away.

Maj. F. Walden, Bn. 2/i/C., left Mill Hill on July 3rd with an advance party for Ashford, Kent, and A Coy. proceeded on a week's leave, for which the remaining Coys. were to wait until the Battle of Britain had been fought and won over their heads! On the 5th the Bn., less A Coy., left by rail for Ashford and marched three or four miles to Hothfield Place, a delightful three-storey building in extensive grounds with the Great Stour River flowing lazily through.

The Bn. was now attached to old friends, the 56 (1 London) Division, with a black cat as Div. sign; in addition to 1 and 2 London Infantry Brigades, 35, 135, and 198 Bdes. were also under command. The infantry included Queen's, London Rifle Brigade, London Scottish, and Queen's Westminsters. On the day after arrival the Bn. was ordered to take up a two-Coy. front in support of the infantry on the coast, with the remainder of the Bn. in Div. Mobile reserve; B and C Coys. commenced "recces" forthwith, and on July 8th B Coy. occupied section positions at Herne Bay, Sarr, Bishopstone, Reculver, and Minnis Bay, with H.Q. at Broadoak in support of 1 Lon. Inf. Bde. C Coy. occupied positions at Greatstone and Whitstable, supporting 135 Bde., with a Pl. on wheels at Horton Park with 2 Lon. Inf. Bde. Thirty-six new Vickers guns were received by the Quartermaster the same day; this seemed to mark a welcome resumption of the offensive.

There was plenty to do for those on the coast; during daylight, positions had to be either prepared or improved, and closer reconnaissance always found a better position just as the present one was nearing completion, so to the private soldier it appeared that every time one saw a strange officer, one could expect a move shortly; the Coy. H.Q. also improved their localities frequently. Daily there was thirty minutes of "stand-to" at dusk and dawn, and throughout darkness there were always sufficient men at the guns to bring them into action and to arouse the remainder of the section—asleep but dressed and close at hand. However, there was generally a preparable gap through the beach defences of barbed wire and mines to enable sea-bathing daily, which was a blessing many civilians missed that summer. Both B and C Coys. reported bombs close at hand on several occasions, but although buildings were damaged there were no serious personal casualties. Borrowed R.A.S.C. 3-ton vehicles were almost the only means of transport, but motor-cycles and trucks arrived in small numbers from time to time.

Bn. H.Q. and H.Q. Coy. were engaged in administering the Bn.; whilst A and D Coys. around Hothfield were doing elementary training and getting to know the country by occasional exercises. Mobile cinemas showing first-class films, concerts by the Ashford Players, and Coy. parties helped to pass the evenings. Unfortunately, at this time Pte. Cresswell of H.Q. Coy. was killed in an accident whilst on motor-cycle duties on the Ashford–Canterbury road, and was buried with full military honours.

In August news was first received officially that some members of A and D Coys. in France were Prisoners of War; finally, by March 1941, almost all personnel were accounted for. The Bn., and in particular the Old Comrades' Association, had already been busy in organising cigarettes and other parcels and these were now dispatched to many friends in captivity, and letters when received were very widely read. The O.C.A. was also very active in securing and forwarding welfare articles to the 1st Bn., and wireless sets, indoor games, outdoor sports equipment, books, and papers came in regularly to the P.R.I. and were very welcome in the Coys. when distributed. Later on, with the assistance of the Officers' Ladies' Committee, parcels of socks, mittens, and Balaclava helmets arrived, and these articles proved most valuable to all recipients; so much so, that they were collected, cleaned, and stored by the Q.M. from one winter until the next.

In August, B Coy. moved their H.Q. to Minster Abbey, taking over a wing from the Nuns, and 6 officers arrived at

Hothfield with 120 other ranks from M.G.T.C., and the Bn. was up to strength, including First-Line Reinforcements. Around the middle of the month A and D Coys. relieved C and B on the coast, the latter returning to Hothfield. Capt. John Smith, R.A.M.C., the Bn.'s popular doctor, died of injuries sustained in the greatly increasing aerial activity; Lt. R. W. Brown, R.A.M.C., was attached.

One night in August full "stand-to" was ordered on account of "unnatural fog in Channel"; this produced quite a "flap", but by the time the code-words had been de-coded and all preparations for receiving the enemy checked upon, no invaders appeared, so normal alert returned. Enemy bombing and machine-gunning raids were now frequent all over Kent, and the front-line fighter aerodromes, including Manston, Lympne, and Hawkinge, were attacked several times daily, and the Kensington Coys. forward were often upon or close to these objectives. As many as two hundred German planes were at times counted in formation in the air and they were being shot down in good numbers by British fighters and A.A. guns, and on August 31st the 1st Bn. added their own contribution; a Dornier 17 bomber, flying very low along the beach after raiding Manston aerodrome, was shot down by the Vickers guns of a section of 15 Pl., D Coy., mounted near Sandwich; the crew of four were taken prisoner.

At the beginning of September two Pls. from Reinforcements Coy. took up positions at Pegwell Bay and on Sheppey. The nearness of the enemy was realised when D Coy. reported cross-Channel shelling on Sandwich area. On the 30th, the 4 Cheshires took over from D and F.L.R. Coy., who returned to Hothfield, and privilege leave was generally resumed. Inter-Coy. reliefs continued and training proceeded whilst the Coys. were inland around Hothfield area.

In October 1940, Maj. F. Walden, the Bn.'s most efficient 2/i/C. and P.R.I., was appointed to command 2/8th Middlesex, another M.M.G. Bn. Maj. de Chimay became Bn. 2/i/C., whilst Maj. Padfield took over the duties of P.R.I.—a heavy task, as the Bn. and Coy. canteens were all doing a tremendous turnover, with beer, cakes, sweets, and cigarettes still available in large quantities. With Capt. Holding, Lt. M. Jupp, M.C., and 2/Lt. Kent posted to East Africa, and Capt. Williamson to Hong Kong (later killed whilst fighting Japanese there) the revised layout was: A Coy., Capt. S. F. Caulfield-Kerney; B, Capt. R. Wasey; C, Maj. C. J. Padfield; D, Maj. B. L. Bryar; H.Q., Capt. R. D. Milton. The remaining Coys. on the coast were relieved by 5th Devons on October 26th and returned inland.

Early in November the C.O. spent a day with each Coy., inspecting kits; very necessary after months spent in Pl. areas and section billets where "exchanges" are made rather indiscriminately and often without mutual agreement! On the 10th, 56 Div. was transferred from operational rôle to train hard in XI Corps reserve; "recces" were made by officers of all Coys. of positions to be occupied against invasion and "action stations" was practised, whilst air activity continued heavy. Individual training went ahead and the Bn. worked hard, and also played regularly at rugger, soccer, and hockey; all ranks' dances were held to music by the Bn. band. The Bn. took part in a Div. exercise in the Folkestone and Dover area, spending two very cold nights out whilst "mopping up parachutists" and attacking airborne and sea-landing forces, but they were back in time for Christmas dinner, including roast pork, vegetables, Christmas pudding, a free pint and some more beer, cigarettes, and fruit. The Bn. War Diary says training was resumed on the 26th! Each Prisoner of War from 1st Bn. was sent a box of cigarettes through O.C.A. channels, and at about this time Ptes. F. Ford and R. Bailey rejoined the Bn.; they had been taken prisoner with the 1st Bn. at St. Valéry but escaped separately from the marching column at Béthune and hid in a wood. In civilian clothes provided by friendly French folks they each individually crossed German-occupied France, and finally reached Marseilles and then Spain after five months' wandering. Certificates of Gallantry were awarded by the Commander-in-Chief.

CHAPTER VI

ANOTHER YEAR WITH HOME FORCES

JANUARY 1941 opened with heavy snow, and the use of transport was reduced to a minimum and training was restricted. 56 Reconnaissance Regt. was now formed, largely from volunteers within the Div.; and the appointed C.O. selected nearly sixty Kensingtons; and this party well maintained the Bn.'s reputation: C.S.M. Satchwell (D Coy.) straight away became R.S.M., C.Q.M.S. Harold King (B) followed as R.S.M. in 1944, Sgt. Chappell (H.Q.) commanded the A.A. Pl., and 2/Lt. Redmond and Sgt. Allen (H.Q.) formed and ran the transport of this completely mobile unit.

During the last four days in January, with the weather intensely cold, the Bn. were employed on Corps exercise "Tedex" around Brighton, Shoreham, Arundel, and Amberley. Administration was well tested, whilst most Pls. occupied one M.M.G. position and "recced" many more without occupation; tiny convoy lights, shining on the differentials, were used alone for the first time.

All the M.M.G. Coys. fired on Lydd ranges during February and each attended a three-day Div. exercise with an Inf. Bde. On February 22nd, D Coy. came under operational command of 168 Bde. and moved to Romney Marsh area, with Pls. near Dungeness, Lydd, and Greatstone. On the 24th, A Coy., under command 206 Bde., moved into Cheriton and Folkestone, whilst B Coy., under 169 Bde., moved to the area of Port Lympne (adjoining the site of the Bn.'s 1937 T.A. camp) with a Pl. on Lympne aerodrome, and C Coy., supporting 167 Bde., took over Mill House from B Coy. Preparations were in hand to repel any invader "on the beaches".

March came in like a lion for A Coy. H.Q., for during breakfast on the 1st the gymnasium at Shorncliffe was hit by a shell from the German-held French coast; a side of the building was damaged, but early morning P.T. was already over and there were no casualties. And there was a bite in the air for Bn. H.Q. and H.Q. Coy. at Hothfield in the shape of an R.A.F. plane photographing their layout and making adverse comment in the accompanying report. All the forward Coys. reported heavy aerial activity, with bombs and bullets frequently too close to be pleasant; cross-Channel shells arrived occasionally. There were various alarms, and Coys. stood-to 100 per cent.; the normal stand-to now was 60 per cent. during hours of dusk, with the remainder asleep fully dressed, and 30 per cent. by day. When a strong force of Messerschmidts bombed and machine-gunned Lympne aerodrome there were no casualties, but B Coy. Orders (Coy. Comd., C.S.M., escort, and prisoner) dismissed and reformed without any words of command when "black specs from the leading plane grew larger". All the Bn. vehicles took part in a five-hour night convoy drive; as the C.O. said: ". . . we shall not always be defensively static". In turn throughout Coys., an M.G. Pl. enjoyed themselves, demonstrating "M.G. Pl. in action" for the Junior Comd.'s course at XII Corps School. In April, B Coy. H.Q. moved to Drayswood, near Stone Cross, and this became the forward distributing point for all Coys. under Bn. administration. Meanwhile the War Establishment of a M.M.G. Bn. was slightly changed in personnel, arms, and equipment, including exchanges in types of transport; twenty-six tommy-guns replaced rifles in M.M.G. Coys., a long-recommended improvement.

At the beginning of May the C.O. visited Coys. in turn and inspected all kits and equipment. On the 5th, in the afternoon, in one of the very frequent enemy raids on fighter aerodromes, Ptes. G. H. Stevens and J. Flynn of 7 Pl. (B Coy.) were seriously wounded at Lympne, and both died later in hospital; they were buried with military honours at Ashford. On the 8th, L/Cpl. H. Barker was wounded in the shoulder on the same aerodrome, whilst A, B, and D Coys. all reported ammunition expenditure in engaging low-flying aircraft by L.M.G. fire. On May 12th the new Corps Comd., Lt.-Gen. B. L. Montgomery, C.B., D.S.O., soon to be world-famous as "Monty" and later a

Sgt. Thompson instructing on the Vickers Machine-gun at Beaulieu Camp, 1939. (*See Chapter I.*)

TYPICAL M.G. POST, FRANCE, 1940. (*See Chapter III.*)
(*Photo by courtesy of Imperial War Museum.   Copyright reserved.*)

Field-Marshal, lectured to all officers in his Corps at the Odeon Cinema, Folkestone, within shell-range of the Hun across the English Channel, and he preached the defiance he practised. Within Bde. reliefs, C Coy. took over from D, who returned to Iden Green. On May 23rd Bn. H.Q. and H.Q. Coy. moved to Baylisden, near Bethersden.

"Monty" ordered that regular Bn. parades be held in spite of beach defence and 31 officers and 628 other ranks paraded at Hothfield Common on June 15th, the first since April 1940 in Armentières, excepting the Mill Hill parade of those evacuated from B.E.F. Soon afterwards the Div. Comd., Maj.-Gen. M. G. M. Stopford, D.S.O., M.C., spent two days inspecting all Coys. of the Bn. On July 1st, within Bde. relief, D took over from B Coy. in Lympne area, and B moved inland to Townland Farm, with Pls. in huts and billets in Woodchurch. All Coys. spent days at Lydd firing M.M.G. and anti-tank rifles, and using the Gas compound. On the 17th Pte. M. Jackaman was killed in a motor-cycle accident at Bethersden.

The whole 1st Bn. moved on July 22nd to Shorncliffe, with Bn. H.Q., A, B, D, and H.Q. Coys. in Risborough Barracks, and C Coy. and L.A.D. in Napier Barracks; excellent accommodation. Several officers and N.C.O.s departed on courses; Maj. Padfield, M.B.E., was posted to the R.A.F. Regt., and Capt. Wasey, promoted Major, assumed the duties of P.R.I. Capt. I. H. Battye took over C Coy., whilst Capt. Evans assumed temporary command of D. Specialist training cadres were interrupted for frequent drill parades, and from August 4th to 8th the M.M.G. were engaged with Bdes. in Corps exercise "Morebinge". On August 12th, in the company of some O.C.A. Committee members, His Worship the Mayor of Kensington took the salute at a Bn. march-past, and at 11.00 hrs. on the 14th, "Monty" and the Div. Comd. inspected the Bn. and took the salute at the march-past. It appeared that Maj.-Gen. Stopford gave the Bn. such a good report after his earlier inspection that "Monty" wrote upon it: ". . . I am glad to see this excellent report; I would like to see this Bn. on parade one day." In expressing his keen appreciation of the high standard of efficiency and fine bearing displayed by the Bn. he told the officers that they were "fortunate to command such a grand lot of men".

At this stage, Capt. Brown, the doctor, proceeded on embarkation leave and was replaced by Lt. J. Lewis, R.A.M.C. The padre, Capt. Bennett, returned to his parish in Chester, and Capt. Rev. A. J. Radford was temporarily attached. Capt. D. Rae, commanding the L.A.D. since 1939, was posted to Div. Sigs. Towards the end of August Maj. Bryar reassumed command of D Coy. and Capt. Evans took over H.Q. Coy. and the duties of P.R.I. The British Broadcasting Corporation made records of a Pl. firing Vickers guns; these were later heard by the Bn. at a cinema show and broadcast as a feature in a military programme.

Hurried preparation now commenced for a machine-gun concentration which the Bn. was to undergo in October at the Small Arms School, Netheravon. Between specialised M.M.G. training, periods were found for P.T., cross-country runs, and cricket matches, but, considering that over 150 almost untrained other ranks had been received as reinforcements since the end of May, there was obviously insufficient time to bring the general standard up to the top level required by the crack instructors at the S.A.S. So, all too soon, the trucks were loaded and stores checked, and on October 5th the Bn., by road and rail, moved to Bulford, where everyone was under canvas. The thirteen-day programme was completely comprehensive and entailed each Coy. in turn being Duty Coy. in camp daily, whilst the others were due at some map reference on Salisbury Plain by 09.00 hrs. ready to commence battle; this meant reveille before daylight, which was far from fun in tents in October. All ranks, however, worked hard and learnt a great deal, especially so the administrative personnel of H.Q. Coy., who were taught bayonet-fighting, grenades, Bren-gun, tommy-gun, map-reading, stalking, etc., and who had three infantry schemes of their own. The Vickers M.G. programme included all phases (section drill, Pl. drill, battle drill, fire control, range work) of attack, defence, and withdrawal, including safety, map shooting, and night firing, and a very considerable amount of live ammunition was fired. The concentration ended on October 22nd, and the report was disappointing; Coy. Comds. were not altogether surprised, but with machine-guns already unpopular with the highest authorities, who were very Bren-L.M.G.-minded, the uncertainty of how and when the 1 Kensingtons were going to get at grips with the enemy was increased. On October 24th the Bn. returned to the Ashford area; Bn. H.Q. and H.Q. Coy. to Godinton Park, A to Hinxhill, B to Kingsnorth, and C and D to the Industrial School, Ashford. Straight away several officers departed on an Anti-tank Gunnery Course.

Under the new Div. Comd., Maj.-Gen. E. G. Miles, D.S.O., M.C., 56 Div. exchanged areas with the 46 Div., and on November 15th the Bn. moved through Blackwall Tunnel to Brentwood and harboured for the night; Metropolitan Police took control from Bexley Heath to Gallows Corner, groups of twenty vehicles, 2000 yards apart, a wonderful demonstration of how to avoid traffic congestion. And then on to Fornham Park beyond Bury St. Edmunds; a hutted camp not yet completed, almost a sea of mud, so that much work had to be done to huts, roads, vehicle standings, etc., before training could resume. 56 Div. were in reserve with counter-attack tasks in XI Corps area, and probability of recall to North Kent by XII Corps. Officers were out for several days selecting routes, positions, and "liaisoning" with Bdes., etc., and Coys. were frequently away on manning exercises. The Bn. were enemy in Home Guard exercise "Scorch" on December 5/7th; landed at Thorrington, after successfully attacking and capturing Colchester, they fanned out as far as Chelmsford and Cambridge before being wiped out by umpires and returned to billets. On December 9th R.S.M. Nash of the Middlesex Regt. replaced R.S.M. J. Butler, who was posted elsewhere. Working parties from the Bn. gave agricultural assistance to local farmers daily, whilst others struck tented camps in the area, so there was still little training.

On December 12th the Bn. moved to Cherry Tree Camp, Colchester; they found good accommodation in "spiders" of huts, a first-class cook-house, a very useful miniature range, an excellent gymnasium, and a large and very well-run

N.A.A.F.I., so that between Bde. exercises on "approach and contact", and acting as enemy in schemes near Thetford, Christmas dinner with pork, pudding, and beer was very comfortably consumed in Officers', Sergeants', Corporals', and Privates' Messes. P.R.I. and O.C.A. funds provided cigarettes in Germany for those of the 1st Bn. imprisoned there.

CHAPTER VII

MARKING TIME, 1942

On most days the Bn. War Diary reads "uneventful". From early dawn on January 5th there was considerable M.T. activity in reaching harbouring areas in Div. exercise "Swift". During an extremely cold night snow fell and an important item of administration—the issue of a rum ration—was successfully practised, whilst Bde. conferences and moves forward prevented sleep for most. After cease-fire on the 7th, having returned to billets, it was announced that the C.O. had succeeded at last in obtaining authority for the Bn. to be relieved of all outside commitments for one month for the training and testing of all ranks in the arms of the Bn. Thus the remainder of January was spent, and at the end of it twenty-six other ranks were sent on embarkation leave and posted to units abroad. The Comd. of XI Corps, Lt.-Gen. N. M. G. Irwin, C.B., D.S.O., M.C., and the Div. Comd. each spent days with the Bn. watching training, etc.

From February 26th to March 2nd the Bn. was engaged in XI Corps exercise "Repulse", the practising of 3 and 56 Divs. in a mobile rôle in anti-invasion setting. Lt.-Col. F. G. Parker, the C.O., had the unusual pleasure of controlling all units of the Bn. throughout. There was considerable movement, constant dummy air attacks by actual fighter-planes, clever cratering of roads by umpires, often splitting Pl. and section road moves so that junior N.C.O.s and drivers had to find their own detours, a live enemy and close fighting in ambushes and "paratroop" raids, and night patrolling, as well as the occupation of a large number of M.M.G. positions around Stowmarket, Needham Market, River Gipping, Haughley, Lavenham, and Long Melford. Capt. H. A. C. Page had fun commanding a mixed party including some Royal Engineers, Infantry-carrier sections, and two Polish armoured trains in a "death or glory" delaying action.

"THE KENSINGTONS"

Two weeks of Bn. "hardening" followed; days spent by Coys. on Fingrinhoe battle-practice ranges, night occupation of a position involving a long carry over difficult terrain judged in competition by other Coy. Comds. B Coy. marched 22 miles; D marched 20 miles and then each individual cooked his own dinner in the field, and C Coy. marched all night and covered 32 miles; H.Q. Coy marched 15 miles in an evening after normal duties. B Coy then ran a 14-mile cross-country treasure hunt, competitors using both map and compass. Coys. in turn gave their Inf. Bdes. at Fingrinhoe a demonstration of their M.M.G. fire power; the close proximity of overhead support, and nearness of flank protection, and the weight and accuracy of fire surprised many junior leaders. H.Q. Coy. staged a camouflage demonstration for the remainder of the Div., whilst other Coys. were frequently away in the Bde. areas on exercise. Training and fictional films, some most informative and well-prepared lectures given by specialists upon their subject, evening gramophone recitals, and frequent evening passes into Colchester prevented monotony. Officers and N.C.O.s were always away on various courses, and rifle classification was held on Middlewick, whilst all Coys. enjoyed field-firing at Fingrinhoe. "Free days" were introduced and twenty-four-hour passes to London were available, so that the Territorial Kensingtons were able to get home weekly when finances allowed—a wonderful innovation, but one which non-Londoners did not appreciate to such an extent.

At the end of May the Bn. 2/i/C., Maj. de Chimay, became Lt.-Col. in command of 2/7 Middlesex; Major Bryar was appointed 2/i/C.; Capt. Shanks promoted to Major, and the Intelligence Officer, Lt. B. V. C. Harpur, became Capt. and Adjutant. The Coy. lay-out changed considerably: A, Capt. J. W. Doyle; B, Maj. Wasey; C, Maj. Shanks; D, Capt. Evans; H.Q., Capt. H. Page. Capt. and Q.M. E. D. Knight, M.M., was awarded the M.B.E. (Military Division)—a large quantity of Guinness and other alcohol was consumed in celebration. Capt. Rev. A. J. Radford accepted a posting abroad, and the Bn. lost a good padre, and did not receive one in exchange.

On May 28th the Bn. moved right into Colchester to

Hyderabad Barracks, more crowded, but good, solid buildings of pre-war Regular Army standard; early in June D Coy. moved into 168 Bde. area, to Plash Wood near Haughley, and C Coy. to 167 near Nacton, Ipswich. At the end of July an advance party proceeded to Bulford to prepare for the Bn.'s concentration during August; in the later rush of events this was cancelled on August 13th, when all arrangements were complete.

On August 6th Maj.-Gen. Miles confirmed the news that 56 Div. was preparing to proceed abroad, but without its M.M.G. Bn. and Recce Regt. In his farewell speech to all ranks on parade he said:

"Colonel Parker, Officers, Warrant Officers, Non-commissioned Officers, and men of the 1st Kensingtons. We, the rest of 56 (London) Division for which I am speaking, want you to know how much we appreciate the great support you have given the Division. You have been with us for some years and during that time your enthusiasm and efficiency have become well known and appreciated; indeed, very often have I been reminded by other units of the Division of the great feeling of respect for the Kensingtons. Brigadiers have expressed the high opinion they hold of the work done by the Coys. of Kensingtons attached to their Bdes. Now, after all this time together, it has become necessary for our courses to part; the rest of the Division is going away. However, I am confident that no matter whatever happens or whatever changes you may undergo, your very fine spirit, the spirit of your Regiment, and your enthusiasm, will ensure that any job you get to do you will do thoroughly well and with the same efficiency and spirit that you have always shown in the past. I cannot tell, in fact I do not know, what you will be given to do in the future, but I hope that you will be with us again when the Division meets the Germans, wherever that may be. That is all I have to say. The best of luck to you all."

So the temporary unpopularity of the Vickers Machine-gun had apparently robbed the 1 Kensingtons of their immediate destiny, and uncertainty ruled again; would they now fight as Infantry, Anti-tank gunners, or what have you?

Several O.C.A. members attended the Bn.'s farewell party in Colchester, and scores were well below average in some rifle-shooting competitions the following day. On

August 19th the Bn. moved to Westcliff, near Southend. Billeted in odd houses and private schools, trucks at the kerbside, a good deal of cleaning and improvisation was necessary before they could settle in; the pioneers were in great demand and finally did the job so well that red and grey painted signs were still in evidence in 1946! The Bn. was under command of 45 (Drake's Drum) Div. for all purposes, and the Div. Comd., Maj.-Gen. H. de R. Morgan, D.S.O., inspected the Bn. on the 24th. Forthwith the Bn. took over "Bandit" operational rôles on Foulness Island; these meant two Coys., acting as infantry for three-day tours of duty, at thirty minutes' notice in billet with vehicles loaded, and one Pl. at Newhouse Farm near Fisherman's Head for twenty-four hours at a time; the remainder of the Bn. was in mobile reserve. Training concentrated upon pistol, rifle, tommy-gun, aircraft, and tank recognition, street fighting, etc., and officers and N.C.O.s gave frequent instruction to the local Home Guard and Naval personnel. Early in October large parties, over half the Bn. strength, proceeded to Bedford and Fakenham to give agricultural assistance in potato picking and beet "bashing".

The regimental band of the Middlesex Regt. spent ten days with the Bn. and Col. M. Browne stayed for two days; Bn. parades, route-marches, and concerts were enjoyed. Cross-country running and hockey were the main recreations, and the early-morning marches to Southend sea-water baths, followed by a swim and trot back to billets for breakfast, were popular to a degree.

Meanwhile, whilst the Bn. was experimenting at Fingrinhoe with double Brens and double Vickers on radial mountings firing A.A. at balloons, the Eighth Army in the Middle East had found themselves sadly short of light A.A. weapons, mortars, and the sustained and accurate fire beyond 2000 yards offered by Vickers guns. So in October 1942, the higher authorities produced a new War Establishment which was to transform 1 Kensingtons into a Support Battalion. Bn. H.Q. was reduced to a Lt.-Col. as C.O., and a Capt. for Adjutantal as well as Q.M. duties, 2 officers and 7 other ranks only; a Div. Sp. Coy. under a Major, with a small H.Q., a Defence Pl., and four Pls. each with

A.A. guns (20-mm. Oerlikon or Hispano), totalling 6 officers and 187 o/r.; and 3 Inf. Bde. Sp. Coys. each under a Major, with a small H.Q., a Defence Pl., two Pls. of A.A. guns, and three Pls. of four new carrier-borne 4·2-in. heavy mortars. The Bn. to total 38 officers and 812 o/r. The Vickers M.M.G. was to go later to Inf. Bns. on the basis of one Pl. per Bn. The actual copy of the establishment was not received until November 5th, but during October three officers and two Sgts. went to S.A.S., Netheravon, on a heavy mortar course, whilst others received instruction on 3-in. mortars from the Bns. in 45 Div.; refresher cadres for wireless personnel and range-takers were held, and aircraft recognition received considerable attention; on November 1st one officer and four Sgts. went to S.A.S., Bisley, on A.A. course with cartwheel sight. H.Q. Coy. personnel were distributed amongst the other Coys. on November 10th, and there was considerable competition for many first-class N.C.O.s and men; Major Bryar relinquished the appointment of 2/i/C., Capt. Evans was promoted to Major, many N.C.O.s were recommended for higher ranks, and 1 Kensingtons were a Sp. Bn. with effect from November 11th. With the Bn. well under strength and half away farming, the change-over was largely a paper one for the time being. Lt.-Col. Parker received permission to retain temporarily the services of Capt. Knight, M.B.E., M.M., although there was no Quartermaster on the establishment, but Capt. Milton, "Tiny", the M.T.O., joined R.E.M.E., and R.S.M. Nash was posted elsewhere. Church bells, which had been silent since invasion became possible, were again rung on the Sunday following Armistice Day.

During December, 112 other ranks joined the Bn. as reinforcements from MGTC and 1/8th Middlesex, and visits were paid to the Bn. by the Div. Comd., the Corps Comd., and G.O.C. Eastern Command. Some officers and N.C.O.s started attending at Prittlewell Airfield for instruction in 20-mm. Hispano, and training continued on 3-in. mortars, aircraft recognition, carrier-driving, and wireless. The new AFG1098 scale of equipment had not yet been notified, but the transport was being gradually adjusted.

On January 15th, 1943, the agricultural parties rejoined

the Bn., and the L.A.D. (R.E.M.E.) personnel were posted away. Maj.-Gen. J. K. Edwards, D.S.O., M.C., took over command of 45 Div., and Capt. D. B. Tregoning rejoined the Bn. from staff duties with 56 Div. Late in the month all mortar officers and N.C.O.s attended a demonstration by 10 Chemical Warfare Group at Foulness, which included 4·2-in. mortars, and the opportunity was taken to borrow four for training. The Bn. was now promised priority in reorganisation, and with the marking-time phase ending, all ranks were mighty keen to get on with their new tasks; all vacancies on mortar and cartwheel-sight courses were accepted, and with the Bn. all together in Westcliff highly organised training became easier. In an intensive O.C.T.U. candidate drive the Bn. lost several N.C.O.s. Excellent dances were held by all Messes at the Queen's Hotel, and the regimental dance-band was booked most evenings playing for some unit or other, and the P.R.I. funds benefited considerably.

CHAPTER VIII

PREPARE FOR ACTION, 1943

On February 4th the Westcliff billets were handed over to 1 Middlesex, and the next day the 1 Kensingtons moved by road and rail to Dorchester. The 200-mile convoy drive *via* North Circular Road, Northolt, Southall, Staines, Basingstoke, Andover, Salisbury, Blandford, Dorchester, was carried out to schedule, and all vehicles had arrived by midnight. Bn. H.Q., A and C Coys. were in the Main Barracks, used by the Dorsetshire Regt. in peace-time, and B and D Coys. were about 400 yards away in Poundbury Camp; all excellent accommodation. The Bn. was attached to 38 (Welsh) Div. and the Comd., Maj.-Gen. D. C. Butterworth, D.S.O., visited all Coys. whilst training on February 11th. Operationally B Coy. supported 113 Bde.; C, 114; and D, 115; whilst the remainder of the Bn. in reserve formed a "Tank Island" at Dorchester; Coys. were soon engaged in exercise with their Bdes.

February 16th proved a red-letter day. Twenty new 4·2-in. mortars arrived complete with base-plates, and the C.O. received a letter from G.H.Q. stating that 1 Kensingtons would join a permanent Div. of the First Army in North Africa, as soon as adequately equipped and trained, as three Support Groups with a revised establishment including Vickers guns. Lt.-Col. Parker went at once to the War Office in an attempt to clarify the situation, and received instructions to form a Bn. H.Q. and three Sp. Gps. each of Gp. H.Q., Heavy Mortar, and M.M.G. Coys.; A.A. Coys. were to be included, but the existing strength of the Bn. was not large enough to embrace these commitments. On February 22nd the G.O.C. Southern Comd., Lt.-Gen. H. C. Loyd, C.B., D.S.O., M.C., met all officers and saw Coys. training; later, the C.O. addressed all ranks of the Bn. in the dining-hall and explained the necessity and significance of the latest organisation; in the afternoon A

Coy. personnel were distributed amongst the 3 Bde. Sp. Gps., "B", "C", and "D".

At the end of February "B" Gp. moved to Bridport and "D" Gp. to Swanage, to enable the infantry there to move out and take part in exercise "Spartan", which was European-invasion preparation. Training in M.M.G. and H.M. proceeded apace; as the former entailed only revision of the Bn.'s old weapon, personnel were graded according to their standards and the necessary cadres instituted. The new weapon, 4·2-in. heavy mortar (hereafter H.M.) demanded more elementary training, but the drill was rapidly and enthusiastically mastered and small Pl. schemes were carried out. Bn. drill parades were a regular feature, and daily P.T., route-marches, cross-country runs, and after-duty games, including hockey on the barrack square, kept the Bn. fit.

"B" and "D" Gps. returned to Dorchester on March 15th, and in really fine weather great progress was made. In addition to M.M.G. firing at Sydling St. Nicholas, all Gps. fired H.M. for the first time on Studland Battle range on March 17th, which greatly increased the keenness of the Pl. and Sec. teams. The H.M. bomb, weighing 20 pounds, produced a terrific crump up to 4500 yards, and area targets were accurately engaged in most instances. The arrival of twenty-two new carriers enabled carrier learner-driving to go well ahead, but no wireless equipment was to hand, and it was difficult to keep corporal and driver operators interested, and impossible to increase their efficiency or numbers. Many new officers arrived straight from O.C.T.U. without M.M.G. or mortar knowledge; cadres were immediately started to put this right.

The pace quickened still further in April. At the request of the War Office, the C.O. attended when the formulation of a War Establishment was discussed; first, it was decided that Groups should not be self-supporting as Lt.-Col.'s commands, but that Bn. H.Q. should be a practical unit to administer three Groups, instead of a mere figure-head; the make-up of Bn. H.Q. was then thrashed out on the spot, almost at the C.O.'s dictation: C.O. (Lt.-Col.), 2/i/C. (Major), Adj., I.O., Q.M., 5 officers and 58 other ranks, including Provost, m/c orderlies, clerks, pioneers, etc. Also three Support Gps. under Majors, each of Gp. H.Q., Signals Pl., Admin. Pl., H.M. Coy., M.M.G. Coy., A.A. Coy., and F.L. Reinforcements, of 25 officers and 393 o/r. Lt.-Col. Parker was then informed that 1 Kensingtons (and 2/7 Middlesex under Lt.-Col. de Chimay) were to mobilise at very short notice, the Bn. to join 78 (Battle-Axe) Div., fighting in North Africa; right away the Adj. telephoned Dorchester, and Group Comds. having worked out the deficiencies in personnel, vehicles, and probable equipment, the C.O. notified the various branches at the War Office: a total of 80 officers and 1257 other ranks, carried in over four hundred vehicles. 1 Kensingtons assumed this establishment officially on April 16th, 1943, when there were many promotions to be celebrated.

Mobilisation orders were received on April 23rd, and AFG1098 lists of equipment on the 24th; ten days' embarkation leave had commenced with drivers on the 21st, because vehicles would move first. Mobilisation proved arduous indeed; the systematic reception, inspection, inoculation, pay, checking of documents and kit, and dispatch on embarkation leave of the numerous drafts (totalling over six hundred officers and men from over forty other units) which appeared daily without warning, and the fitting of all these unknown persons into the lay-out of Groups, were a gigantic task. Specialist training had to receive particular attention; for example, 12 officers and 146 other ranks passed the driving test during April, and about half this number passed as carrier drivers. Readers will probably be interested to see the approximate lay-out of the Bn. at April 30th:

Bn. H.Q.

C.O., Lt.-Col. F. G. Parker	Q.M., Capt. E. D. Knight, M.B.E., M.M.
2/i/C., Maj. B. L. Bryar	
Adj., Capt. B. V. C. Harpur	R.S.M. Clarke, J. A.
I.O., Lt. J. J. Oliver	R.Q.M.S. Edgecombe, A. R.
	C.Q.M.S. Cook, E. F.

"THE KENSINGTONS"

Bde. Support Groups

	"B"	"C"	"D"
Gp. H.Q.			
		Gp. Comd.	
	Maj. R. Wasey	Maj. E. P. Shanks	Maj. J. J. Evans
		Adj.	
	Capt. R. H. Ellis	Capt. A. W. Pinks	Capt. R. G. Shave
H.M. Coy.			
		O.C.	
	Maj. J. W. Doyle	Maj. D. B. Tregoning	Maj. H. A. C. Page
		2/i/C.	
	Capt. R. D. Hutchings	Capt. R. D. Cohen	Capt. R. May
A.A. Coy.			
		O.C.	
	Capt. I. D. W. Cramer	Capt. B. Silk	Capt. A. R. Newstead
		2/i/C.	
	Capt. D. Underwood	Capt. K. Duff-White	Capt. D. E. M. Piper
M.M.G. Coy.			
		O.C.	
	Capt. B. J. G. Page	Capt. J. A. Nurse	Capt. A. E. B. Foxwell
		2/i/C.	
	Capt. H. J. Holford-Strevens	Capt. C. K. Hopper	Capt. C. E. Cullen
		C.S.M.s	
	Steele, W. J.	Hibberd, F. W.	Dwyer, G.
	Taylor, R.	Smith, J. W.	Young, H.
	Davies, L. A.	Buckland, H.	Gordon, W.
		C.Q.M.S.s	
	Kelk, A.	Morris, H. T.	Headington, F.
	Gerrard, J.	Kluth, F. H.	Dixon, C.
	Upchurch, H.	Soper, G.	Iveson, J.

On May 6th, Lt. Vanderpump left Dorchester with the first batch of forty-six vehicles, and by the 9th all vehicles were on their way to Glasgow, Birkenhead, Manchester, or Cardiff. Major Evans attended a conference at S.A.S., Netheravon, on May 8th/9th, convened to formulate a "doctrine" for use by Brigade Comds. in the handling of Support Groups. Mobilisation was completed on the 11th and the necessary telegram passed to the War Office. Major Tregoning, as Ship's Baggage Officer; Capt. Page, as Ship's Security Officer; Capt. May and Lt. McLean in charge of Bn. baggage party, moved to Liverpool on May 11th/12th, whilst the remainder of the Bn. did their best to improve acquaintance with the many strangers of all ranks who were now Kensingtons, tidied up their personal affairs, and improved the fitting of their khaki drill in between lectures, drill parades, and keeping fit. Many fresh knots were tied in the bonds of friendship with large numbers of O.C.A. members who came especially to wish the Bn. "*bon voyage*". On May 14th the Rev. J. Morrow celebrated Holy Communion for the Bn. at Holy Trinity Church; Maj. Wasey and Maj. Evans marched their respective train parties to Dorchester Station in the late afternoon, and many local friends were present to wave goodbye. Maj. Page, with another train party, followed the next morning, and the final party, including the C.O., left that evening. All personnel of the Bn. were embarked at Liverpool on to H.M.T. *Samaria* by midday on the 16th, and topees and arms were stowed in the hold.

When the *Samaria* cast off and sailed at 18.00 hrs. on May 16th the 1 Kensingtons were technically part of British North African Forces, but next morning found the Bn. anchored in the Clyde basin in fine weather; life-boat drill commenced, the regular Ship's O.C. Troops issued orders, the Captain's inspection took place at 10 a.m. daily, and in a very crowded ship all ranks prayed for fine weather so that maximum hours might be spent on deck. Officers and N.C.O.s endeavoured to get to know their men better, but even movement on deck was greatly restricted by the crush; a small area of deck was reserved for P.T. in turn. The *Samaria* sailed northwards in convoy at 18.00 hrs. on May

19th; about twenty ships altogether, with an aircraft-carrier and several destroyers and corvettes for defence of the convoy. In fine, calm weather, the Irish coast disappeared from view on the 20th. Depth-charges were used by destroyers five or six times on the 21st, and with the Bn.'s A.A. Coys. manning four Oerlikon guns per Group the gun numbers were allowed five minutes' practice shooting; a small storm caused some sickness in the afternoon. In the next few days there were further alarms; all personnel came up on deck for submarine alarms—long buzzes—and all went down below for aircraft alarms—short buzzes. On the 25th, after dark, two west-bound Red Cross ships brilliantly illuminated passed somewhere off Tangiers; after passing Gibraltar khaki drill was worn by order. All ranks were informed that air attack was expected on the 26th, but it had not come when Algiers was sighted just before 07.00 hrs. on May 27th, and in due course disembarkation began, and every officer, N.C.O., and man was going to be glad to find the next two or three days over.

Carriers enter Centuripe after its Epic Capture. (See Chapter X.)
(Photo by courtesy of Imperial War Museum. Copyright reserved.)

The Sangro River with Fifteen Spans of the Main Bridge Demolished. Beyond can be seen the Swampy Ground rising to the Mozzogrogna-Fossacesia Ridge. (*See Chapter XI.*)
(*Photo by courtesy of Imperial War Museum. Copyright reserved.*)

CHAPTER IX

NORTH AFRICAN PRELUDE

MAY 27TH, 1943, was just another burning day for Algiers. For 80 officers and some 1250 other ranks of the Battalion it was a day fraught with bustle and excitement as disembarkation commenced from H.M.T. *Samaria*.

Within ten uneventful days of leaving the United Kingdom, we had found ourselves in North Africa. A mass of people watched us form up on the docks in the heat of the day. We shifted about, adjusted our F.S.M.O., writhed in our new "K.D." and topees, and awaited orders to move, with perspiration and perplexity reflected on every face. By eleven o'clock, toiling and coiling through the cobbled streets, the vast, sinuous column of Kensingtons moved forward.

The sun was furious with our invasion. Its angry heat soon made us cast thirsty looks on the gay French posters which invited us to the cool precincts of the Hôtel Aletti—famed rendezvous of Algiers.

Everything was new to us. For the first time we caught glimpses of that notorious species called the "Wogs", the low-caste Arabs and half-breeds who stalked around with the inevitable long white night-shirt and red fez. We saw a ship near the shore with its bow blown completely off, and listing to port in desolate dejection. We saw Zouaves and Spahis thronging the pavements with other innumerable and unclassifiable nationalities. The sounds, the air, the atmosphere, and the smells were all new.

Eight hours later we were still marching beneath the blazing sun. Scorched arms, blistered feet, and searing pack-straps all contributed to the discomfort. Eventually, the Commanding Officer, at the head of the column, announced that we had reached our destination. It was a place near Rouiba called "X" Reception Camp. Apart from the fact that there was no reception and no camp, the title did attain a degree of relevancy in that the "X" part was very much the unknown quantity.

Here we tottered, by Groups and companies, to isolated farms some distance apart, each of which had an appropriate letter such as "H", "K", "L", etc. We had left Algiers well over twenty miles behind us, and the hard, hot cobbles of the roads had played havoc with the formidable "boots, ankle, pairs".

We settled down in our farms very quickly, despite the fact that there was not even a table under which to get our feet—not that we had any by that time. We slept on concrete floors or on the top of the large wine-vats with which these installations were solely equipped.

For the next fourteen days, unparalleled confusion swamped the entire Battalion. It must be explained that the million odd things from "guns" to "washers", from ammunition to "pants, cellular, short", which comprised the magic expression "G1098" of the Support Battalion, had to be delivered in their entirety to our area. Our mobilisation had been so hasty that huge crates containing all sorts of mysterious packages were sent unopened to the docks in England. Kit-bags by the hundred and a large selection of strange instruments and devices which we had never seen before—but which probably belonged to the "G1098" of some unfortunate Camel Corps of something—also found their way into the central dump at Battalion H.Q.

The Quartermaster, Captain E. D. ("Rocky") Knight, M.B.E., M.M., stood like a Colossus in a desert of debris, perspiring but happy. Anything which lay unclaimed he relegated with a characteristic jab of his pipe to his own precincts. By that time, the Q.M.'s stores were a cross between a bargain basement and Petticoat Lane.

Meanwhile, the transport had not arrived, and the Commanding Officer had to resort to taxis driven by dark-skinned gentlemen to get into Algiers, where A.F.H.Q. was situated, so that this and many other matters could be rectified. Eventually, the vehicles were collected, overhaul and loading trials being the order of the day. But for the constant vigilance of the Commanding Officer, it is doubtful whether the full quota of vehicles and stores would ever have been released. Certainly they would never have arrived so quickly.

Heat and flies were our worst enemies, and the number of cases of "gyppy tummy" and dysentery rose alarmingly. By this time we were firmly introduced to a little yellow tablet called "Mepacrine", which, combined with the use of gauze netting over our beds, gave us malarial immunity. The taking of these precautions became a big and regular event in everybody's life.

One of the major tasks was to provide large and vigilant guards, especially at night, to protect our property against the local Arabs. These shifty customers were reputed to be capable of extracting the gold fillings from your teeth without disturbing your conversation.

Another affliction imposed upon us was the issue of "V" cigarettes. If ever Hitler had a secret weapon, well, this was it. They induced chronic coughing, and in short made smoking a penance. Being manufactured in India, they were dubbed by the troops "Gandhi's revenge".

However, on June 13th, the Battalion started to move from Rouiba to Guelma, some four hundred miles away, where the 78 (Inf.) Division, to which we had been affiliated, was resting after the arduous Tunisian campaign. The carriers were going on tank-transporters, and the remainder of the wheeled vehicles by a very different route.

Apart from seeing Sgt. Sherman (Provost-Sgt.) bore a hole in the ground as he took a "header" from his motorcycle, the most disconcerting thing about the journey was the failure of the A.A. Companies to negotiate adequately any of the prolonged mountain roads. This was not a very happy harbinger. In order to carry the correct G1098 ammunition for the Oerlikons, each truck and trailer was grossly overloaded to begin with, and the weldings on the trailers and guns themselves proved incapable of withstanding the constant buffeting. There was a whole-hearted suspicion that, whereas they might have been tested satisfactorily on the smooth Great West Road in England, they were far from the realms of reliability on the tortuous tracks of Tunisia.

Despite subsequent efforts of the R.E.M.E. service and our much-harassed A.A. Company Commanders (Captain I. D. Cramer, Captain A. R. Newstead, Captain A. Pinks), these defects were never really rectified.

On June 16th the Battalion joined up with the Division, and the Support Groups dispersed to their respective Brigade areas. "B" Group (commanded by Major R. Wasey) went to 11 (Infantry) Brigade, and "C" and "D" Groups (commanded by Major E. P. Shanks and Major J. J. Evans respectively) joined 36 (Infantry) Brigade and 38 (Irish) Brigade. There was a most efficient welcome in every case. Brigadiers visited the same day, telephone lines were run out, representatives of all the services and other Staff Officers called; in fact, it was the first taste of the efficiency and "camaraderie" with which one always associates the 78 Division.

One of the best memories at this time was the reunion of ex-Kensingtons sent to 56 "Recce" Unit in England, which was part of the Division. R.S.M. H. Satchwell and Sqn. S/M. H. King were amongst the familiar faces.

The next day, H.M. the King went through the area, and the cheers of the 78 Division were swollen by Kensingtons also manning the route. An anti-climax was supplied rather unexpectedly by two drunken Arabs, who were seen racing down the road in a tiny cart pulled by a gallant donkey, in hot pursuit of the Royal *cortège*. This unrehearsed incident was wildly acclaimed by the troops.

The Division held conferences with the object of fathoming the employment and tactical handling of Support Groups and their weapons. The new weapon, the 4·2-in. heavy mortar, was fired by respective companies and we succeeded in terrifying the natives. It was rumoured that 2nd/Lt. R. Gray blew up a signal-box 4000 yards away, which was understood to have played havoc with the trains.

Towards the end of the month, we moved with the Division *via* Tunis itself to Hammamet. It was here that our carriers, conveyed on tank-transporters, caught up with us at last, having negotiated the long sea-road route from Rouiba. Once again we tied our bivouacs to the ubiquitous olive-tree, and Brigade exercises (which included the use of mules), night marches, a spot of mountain climbing, "long carries", and other gorgeous distractions peculiar to Army manœuvres took place.

The Mediterranean was close by, and everybody had the finest bathing imaginable. Signal exercises involved the use of a machine like a folding camera, called "Codex", which turned cryptic orders into a mass of nonsensical words. This was calculated to deceive the enemy, but in the initial stages we were a bit mystified ourselves.

On July 1st General Montgomery visited all units of the Division to tell us in effect that, as the 78th had such a great reputation, he insisted on having it in his Eighth Army. He recalled vividly his inspection of the Battalion in Shorncliffe Barracks, Kent, in 1941, and expressed pleasure at having the Battalion in a Division under his command. At the same time the opportunity was taken by the Commanding Officer to have an A.A. mounting and trailer towed to Divisional H.Q., so that General Montgomery himself should be fully acquainted with their defects.

In the evening, he talked for ninety minutes to all officers of the Division, and gave a brilliant lecture without a note or pause—subject: "How I beat Rommel" and "Kill the Italians."

July 3rd was notable for Lt. McLean being wounded slightly when training with a Piat gun, and for a fine act of gallantry by C.Q.M.S. H. Upchurch, who, at great personal risk from falling stones and debris, rescued Pte. E. Brown, who had fallen into a disused well over sixty feet deep. Unfortunately, Pte. Brown subsequently died from the injuries he sustained. The Divisional Commander directed that the act be recorded on C.Q.M.S. Upchurch's conduct sheet.

On July 6th we moved again, through Enfidaville to Sousse, which is memorable for the appalling heat which assailed us *en route*. The Sirocco hit us with all its fury. This burning dry wind punched us about and left us gasping figures in pools of perspiration.

Sousse area was full of olive-groves, which offered us

pathetic protection from the sun, and also provided us with an admirable surfeit of thick dust.

On July 10th we heard that Sicily was invaded, and with the 78 Division standing by for this operation as Army Reserve in case things went wrong, a wave of excitement jerked everybody on to their feet.

Vehicles were waterproofed, and we remained in a state of readiness for a considerable time, which kept us on tenter-hooks.

On July 14th it is recorded that the 2/i/C., Major B. L. Bryar, issued to the Battalion our first beer since leaving England. This NAAFI supply was distributed with "largesse" on the scale of one bottle between two men for a month.

Training, range-firing, and bathing still continued, but suddenly, like a bolt from the blue, the Battalion received the order to embark. This was on July 23rd, and that very morning Major Wasey, with characteristic nonchalance, held "B" Group sports, which, to say the least, was rather reminiscent of Drake and his bowls.

The assembly area to which we hastily moved was called "Blackpool". It was merely a line of olive-groves in which the unit areas were marked with white tapes. After a brief halt, the order to embark arrived.

We accordingly rushed down to the docks in our vehicles, and drove into the giant jaws of the L.S.T.s.[1] Over the huge ramp we climbed and, before we could register much else, the entire embarkation seemed to have been completed. The Quartermaster was nearly left behind, as he had not got the order to move until he had partially completed one of his "foraging" expeditions. However, he raced to the docks, and having told one or two rather highly placed officers not to argue, he secured an assault craft for himself and made his own invasion divorced temporarily from the rest of the Battalion.

That evening, we stole out of Sousse harbour. None of us knew what the future held, except that very shortly we should be in action. We watched the domes and white squat houses of Sousse rapidly recede. Palms nodded to us gently,

[1] Landing Ships, Tank.

and the whole coast-line became swallowed up in the mysterious evening haze. Soon our Armada of little ships was ploughing steadily ahead with nothing but a vast expanse of water all around. Darkness fell and wrote a timely "finis" to our North African chapter.

CHAPTER X

THE SICILIAN CAMPAIGN

THE three Support Groups landed in Sicily in the order in which their respective Brigades were going into action. After less than forty-eight hours at sea, having by-passed Malta, the L.S.T.s ran on to the beach at Avola, on the south-east coast. The Heavy Mortar Company of "B" Group, commanded by Major J. W. Doyle, landed at midday on July 25th, followed by Battalion H.Q. and the remainder of "B" Group. Our eyes were somewhat relieved to note the greenness of the countryside, and the rich vineyards sloping down to the sea, in contrast to the more grim side of the African panorama.

We hastened to an assembly area, where the vehicles were "de-waterproofed". That night we slept under the inevitable olive-tree, with a tattoo of shot and shell in glorious technicolour for a lullaby, as enemy night-intruders met a hail of A.A. fire from near-by Syracuse.

"C" and "D" Groups arrived on July 27th and 29th, 1943, and moved up towards Catenanuova *via* Cassibile, Floridia, Palazzolo, Buccheri, Vizzini, and Mineo. These dirty towns were nothing but irregular plague-spots on a twisting mountainous road. The Sicilian interior had a nauseating similarity in many ways to Tunisia. The heat, dust, and steep spiral roads, which circled the precipitous heights, were all too familiar and imposed a tremendous strain upon the carriers, many of which came to grief.

During our preliminary days, Major H. A. C. Page, who commanded "D" Group Heavy Mortar Coy., went around lecturing everyone on what to expect in the campaign. He was the first member of the Battalion by several days to arrive in Sicily, as he had been sent in advance to join a Heavy Mortar Company of the 2/7 Middlesex Regiment to size up the situation. It may safely be recorded that he proved a very useful visitor to the unit concerned when he ably assisted one of their Platoons which ran into trouble from shelling.

The Eighth Army was held up at Catania, but firmly established along the line of the River Dittano. The rôle of the 78 Division was to force the crossing of the river at Catenanuova, and thrust straight on to Centuripe and roll up the enemy defences west of Mt. Etna *via* Adrano, Bronte, and Randazzo. The breaking of the natural fortress line would turn the enemy's flank, thus inevitably forcing a withdrawal from fiercely contested Catania.

Over a "bull-dozed", dusty track called "Star", the whole of the Division moved up towards Catenanuova. The bulldozer was subsequently to forge many a track and new road for the Division in the long, gruelling months to come.

Gradually the Battalion was initiated in battle. Little dramas were enacted daily which developed our eye for cover, and heightened the sense of self-preservation, particularly of those who had not been to France with the Battalion in 1940.

On July 29th Major R. Wasey and Captain B. J. G. Page, who commanded "B" Group M.M.G. Company, carried out a "recce" on Mt. Scapelli overlooking Catenanuova. Despite their attempts to disguise themselves as flies crawling over the massive feature, an unco-operative German arranged to dust them off with a stream of well-directed shells. The two officers retired hastily.

On July 30th the transport of the Division, winding through the deep defiles, was subjected to air surprise attacks. ME.109's swooped down from nowhere with their guns blazing. A terrifying roar heralded their coming. A few seconds later they were gone. The whole affair would probably last less than a minute, but for those who were not in the fortunate position of being able to shoot back at the marauders, it was an eternity. It was in one of these attacks that our first casualty occurred: Pte. A. E. James, "B" Group, was wounded in the shoulder by a bullet as he jumped from his truck for cover.

Later, a small party consisting of Major J. W. Doyle, Captain J. A. Nurse (commanding "C" Group M.M.G. Company), Pte. Wilshire, and two driver/operators were caught in a traffic block in one of the valleys. At that moment, enemy planes swooped down and the vehicle in which two of the party remained was riddled with bullets, but none of the occupants was scratched. Similar treatment was meted out to a 38 (Irish) Brigade "recce" party which included Major J. J. Evans. The same officer and Sgt. C. Skinner a few hours later actually engaged F.W.110's with a light machine-gun and had the satisfaction of being able to retaliate. On July 31st Sgt. Hodges and one o/r. were wounded, again as the result of one of these air attacks.

The A.A. Companies of each Group came under the command of the Commanding Officer, and were deployed along the line of communications, whence they engaged hostile planes from time to time. There is no record of the success they obtained, but we could see that the shooting was very accurate by watching the Oerlikon tracer shells veering towards their targets.

The Canadians in front of us established a bridge-head over the River Dittano, and 11 Brigade, supported by the M.M.G. Platoons of "B" Group on Mt. Scapelli, went through to capture and hold Catenanuova, despite early counter-attacks. By 04.00 hrs., July 31, the town was firmly in our hands.

With eight guns of "B" Group M.M.G. Company guarding the left flank of the 2nd Bn. Lancashire Fusiliers, and one Mortar Platoon each with 1st Bn. East Surreys and the 5th Bn. Northamptonshire Regiment, the advance continued on to Centuripe. By this time, 36 Brigade, with "C" Group, were rapidly deploying and passing through 11 Brigade.

Perched on a saddle made by several sharp ridges, Centuripe dominated the valley road leading from Catenanuova from a height of between three and four thousand feet. It was unquestionably a most wonderful fortress. Each Group in turn helped to bombard it, and many direct hits were scored on nodal points of the town.

Lieutenant A. Shelley and Lieutenant M. Porter, of "C" Group M.M.G. Company, took Platoons across country on the most gruelling "long carries" and, by dint of rock-climbing, engaged the enemy from unexpected positions.

The former officer was awarded an immediate M.C. for the part his guns played in the final capture of the citadel.

The mortars of "B", "C", and "D" Groups were then combined in one fire-plan to assist the repeated attacks of the three Brigades on the enemy defences, and eventually the final attack, which secured the town at 05.30 hrs. on August 3rd, was carried out by the 6th Bn. Royal Inniskilling Fusiliers with the 1st Bn. R.I.F. This operation was regarded as a masterpiece, and will long live in the annals of military history, as the following extract from a message issued to all units by the G.O.C. 78 Division will show:

> Today I showed General Sir Bernard Montgomery, our Army Commander, around Centuripe, and explained to him how the Division had captured this feature. The Army Commander has asked me to tell all ranks that he considered that the Division had, by capturing the position, performed a wonderful feat of arms, and he doubted if any other Division in his Army could have carried out this operation successfully. This is indeed high praise for the Division for its first battle in the English Army....

The capture of Centuripe—alias "Cherry Ripe"—marked the real beginning of the end for the enemy in Sicily. The difficulties of the Division, however, were by no means lessened. The descent down the other side of the town to the River Simeto was long, winding, and in full view of the enemy, who were now established on the next high ridge. The pursuit was continued, and 1st Bn. R.I. Fusiliers, supported by No. 4 Heavy Mortar Platoon and 7 M.M.G. Platoon "D" Group, managed to reach the bottom of the valley in the evening.

During the next two days, more artillery was deployed and preparations for the bridging and crossing of the Simeto and the attack on Adrano were made. During this time, everything was done by the "Boche" to stop us. His shelling, mortaring, and patrolling increased tremendously. This is not just a general allusion; the "hate" the Boche sent over was experienced at one time or another very acutely and personally by nearly everybody.

August 4th is memorable for the way in which No. 7 Platoon "D" Group sent bullets skimming in and around parties of enemy they saw near a house on Adrano ridge. Cpl. ("Tiny") Waters, in charge of one gun, carried on the war single-handed when he was engaged by a sniper, who achieved some very close "misses". The irate N.C.O. saturated the countryside with some well-directed "swinging traverses", and not content with this expenditure of lead, proceeded to seize a rifle (which somewhat resembled a pencil in his gigantic palm) and fired that as well. It is believed that the sniper died of fright . . . anyway, "Tiny" was not bothered any more.

At this point an order was received to indent for radiator-muffs and skid-chains for our vehicles, which seemed a little incongruous in the burning heat of Sicily.

On August 5th, after giving valuable support to the Royal Irish Fusiliers for two days, No. 7 Platoon "D" Group were moving forward in their carriers to take up fresh gun positions, when they ran into a heavy concentration of shell-fire. One shell killed Sgt. "Bunny" Williams and Cpl. Kinner outright, and wounded Ptes. Horton and Willats. These first casualties came as a shock to "D" Group M.M.G. Company, and especially to No. 7 Platoon and their young commander, 2nd Lieutenant Colin Gunner (then aged nineteen).

The fight was taken up by No. 6 Platoon (M.M.G.), commanded by "D.P." (Lieutenant C. E. Depinna) who, looking through his monocle, evidently found what he wanted, for his platoon had a field day shooting up departing "Huns", with the great approval of 2nd Bn. London Irish Rifles.

Lieutenant A. M. Newton's platoon—No. 5 Platoon M.M.G.—joined the Irish Brigade's battle at 15.00 hrs. This was their first action. Their guns and ammunition were loaded on to two carriers and, with the rest of the troops following on foot, the platoon picked their way forward through a dense orange-grove. The heat was sweltering, and by the time they had reached their gun positions, most men had removed their shirts (like a platoon of "Tarzans", and all contrary to Battalion orders).

Their job was to support, by overhead and flanking fire, an attack launched by the Royal Irish Fusiliers across the River Simeto, and to harass and distract the enemy.

No sooner had the platoon taken up positions on the edge of an escarpment, than numerous "Huns" could be seen moving about in the gardens of some houses about 400 yards distant, and others withdrawing towards Adrano. No. 5 Platoon wasted no time in accelerating the enemy's movement.

This initial enthusiasm was soon damped by a mortar bomb which burst on the gun position and wounded four men, Cpl. Hackfath, L/Cpl. Last, and Pte. Eaton of No. 5 Platoon, and Pte. Price of Lieutenant J. R. Gray's Mortar O.P. Party. After having his wounds dressed, L/Cpl. "Tommy" Last insisted on carrying out repairs to his machine-gun, which had jammed, until he was "ordered off the field" on a stretcher.

The same night, No. 5 Platoon were ordered to cross the River Simeto with the Royal Irish Fusiliers, to consolidate the advance. There were no bridges, so Lieut. Newton had to lead his platoon waist-deep through the fast-flowing river, carrying their heavy loads with them.

Shivering in their wet khaki drill, the platoon spent a highly uncomfortable night listening with the utmost misgivings to noises of gutteral language coming out of the darkness.

The Platoon Sergeant—Sgt. Tobin—also did a fine job on this occasion by organising carrying parties from his stalwarts to carry the platoon's rations and other essentials across the river.

Meanwhile, 2nd/Lieut. G. Smullen and Sgt. F. F. Kendell of "B" Group were sent forward to a rendezvous in an olive-grove not far from the river basin, to help in the vital problems of traffic control. They came under heavy mortar fire at about 22.30 hrs., and Smullen, a fine young officer who had been with the Battalion barely four months, was killed and Sgt. Kendell wounded.

On the night of August 6th/7th, the 11 and 36 Brigades surged through the Irish bridge-head and attacked Adrano. This was preceded by a thunderous barrage of eight Field Regiments and three Medium Regiments, apart from the Mortars and M.M.G.s of the Kensingtons—all co-ordinated into one relentless and scientific blow of annihilation. All night the deafening tattoo of gun-fire continued. The whine of shells, hurtling through the darkness, was endless. The flashes of scores of guns illuminated the sky with a blinding staccato intensity. Adrano was reduced to rubble, but the attack was highly successful and casualties were very light.

It chills the spine a bit to record that, during the barrage, one of our very heavy-calibre shells landed within five yards of the truck where Major J. J. Evans, Major H. A. C. Page, and Lieutenant R. A. Bennett were trying to sleep, but fortunately failed to explode.

The subsequent pursuit round the slopes of Mt. Etna was slow. The enemy fiercely defended every nook and cranny of rock and cliff, in country which was designed for guerilla warfare. This was landscape, not of verdant meadows and rolling downs, but of deep ravines and open stretches of black, larva-strewn rocks. Three or four determined men with a machine-gun could cause innumerable casualties. The Hun flailed the area with his new six-barrelled mortars, the bombs from which suddenly moaned and screamed in flight with paralysing effect. His famous 88-mm. guns snapped back at the least sign of movement.

Lack of room for deployment and bad, narrow roads virtually finished the use of the mortars, which were not easily man-handled. M.T. movement was practically impossible, but "C" Group M.M.G. Coy. enlisted the aid of mules for the first time, and with the rest of the Group supported 11 and 36 Brigades in their successful attacks on Bronte and the important Ravoglio ridge beyond it. On the latter, heavy fire was met, and one salvo from a multi-barrelled *Nebelwerfer* exploded in the trees above "C" Group Mortar Company H.Q., with the result that L/Cpl. Guscott was immediately killed and Lieut. W. A. Impey's right arm was smashed, thus putting an early finish to the fighting career of a popular young officer. Pte. Keen of the Group's M.M.G. Coy., was also wounded at the same time, and two days later (on the 11th) Cpl. E. Husher of the same company was killed by further shelling of the Ravoglio ridge. During this period C.S.M. Hibberd and his driver escaped by a miracle when their truck, crammed with mortar bombs, took a full toss from an "88" shell, and one night four of the six trucks of 3 Platoon were put out of action by shell-fire. However, the advance continued when the Irish Brigade captured Maletto and pushed on to Randazzo on the night of August 12th/13th, where the Americans, swinging in from the west, took over the impetus of the attack.

By this time the enemy had been forced off Mt. Etna and Catania had been evacuated. 78 Division and the Americans swept round the west side and rear of Etna, which constituted a tangible threat to the enemy forces sandwiched in the corridor between the east slopes of the volcano and the sea. A hasty evacuation from the island was accomplished by the Hun across the Straits of Messina.

The Sicilian campaign was virtually over when the Battalion concentrated between Bronte and Adrano, August 13th and 14th, and shortly afterwards the following newspaper extract showed that we had hit the headlines:

"KENSINGTONS IN ACTION"
(*Reprinted from* The Times, *September 20th, 1943*)

Among the troops who fought in Sicily were the Princess Louise's Kensington Regiment, who left North Africa for the first campaign on European soil late in July. They took part in the operations on the central front, and distinguished themselves in the actions in the Centuripe area which ended in the capture of the mountain stronghold on August 2nd. Later they were in action to the west of Mount Etna, and helped to capture Adrano and other towns in the difficult country on the lower slopes of the volcano.

The Regiment now forms part of the Middlesex Regiment. It has a great reputation and fought gallantly with the 51st Division. The Kensingtons have been associated with the Highlanders from the early days of this war. They fought with them in France, in the actions which ended at St. Valéry. They were in the line in the Metz area from May 1st to the 15th, when, after engaging the enemy in hard fighting, they were withdrawn. Few units can have been engaged in more travel during their brief campaign. From May 21st to 31st they moved from St. Arivaux Chenes through Hautecourt Vitry, Liancourt St. Pierre to Foucarmont, where they came into divisional reserve. Three days later, they were with the Black Watch, defending the line of the River Bresle, and were heavily involved when the Germans attacked the entire divisional front. Day after day the Kensingtons withdrew towards Le Havre, putting up a fierce resistance against prodigious odds as they fell back. They finally left France on June 12th, embarking at Cherbourg.

Some things about the Sicilian campaign we shall never forget, apart from the first warning "swish" of bomb or shell. There was the ghastly, torrid heat; the irksome "one-way" timing for traffic on the one and only road which constituted the Divisional axis; the lack of cigarettes in the early stages, which made us welcome the infamous "V" variety; and the long intervals between issues of mail. The fetid stink of German flesh decomposing in the sun, the same nauseating, rich, sickly smell of dead mules with their inevitable swarms of flies, and the black patch on the road beside a burnt-out vehicle, can never be forgotten. Again, the grapes that were plucked from vineyards just off the cratered roads, the enormous, dry river basins, the pathetic train of dirty peasants returning to their broken homes when the tide of war had passed, and the narrow, gaily painted Sicilian carts with their enormous wheels some seven feet in height, will be equally remembered. All these were an essential part of the kaleidoscopic background.

The A.A. companies, in protecting the lines of communication, had, eventually, a thankless, boring job and returned to their various Groups when the Battalion was concentrated.

Our casualties had been extremely light, and in all amounted to five killed and nineteen wounded.

R.S.M. Clarke had a bad spill from a motor-cycle and the nature of his injuries precluded him from returning to the Battalion. His place was taken by R.Q.M.S. A. R. Edgecombe, who was promoted R.S.M. on August 20th, and C.Q.M.S. Headington became R.Q.M.S.

Next followed a period of reorganisation, of which cleaning and checking of stores and re-allocation of personnel took priority.

Amongst the officer changes, Captain B. V. C. Harpur ceased to be Adjutant and was posted to "D" Group to command the M.M.G. Company, replacing Captain A. E. B. Foxwell, who took over the Heavy Mortar Company.

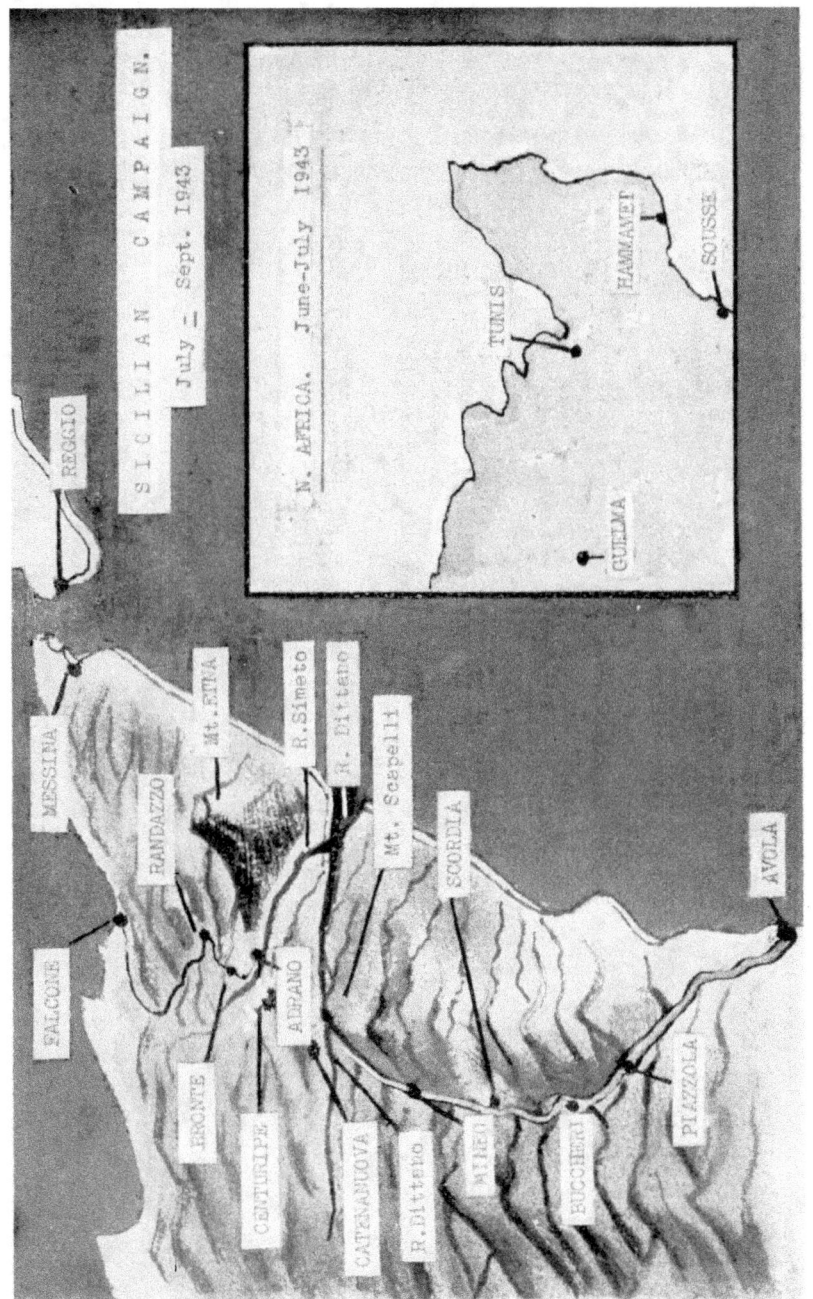

Sicilian Campaign, July–September 1943. (See Chapter X.)

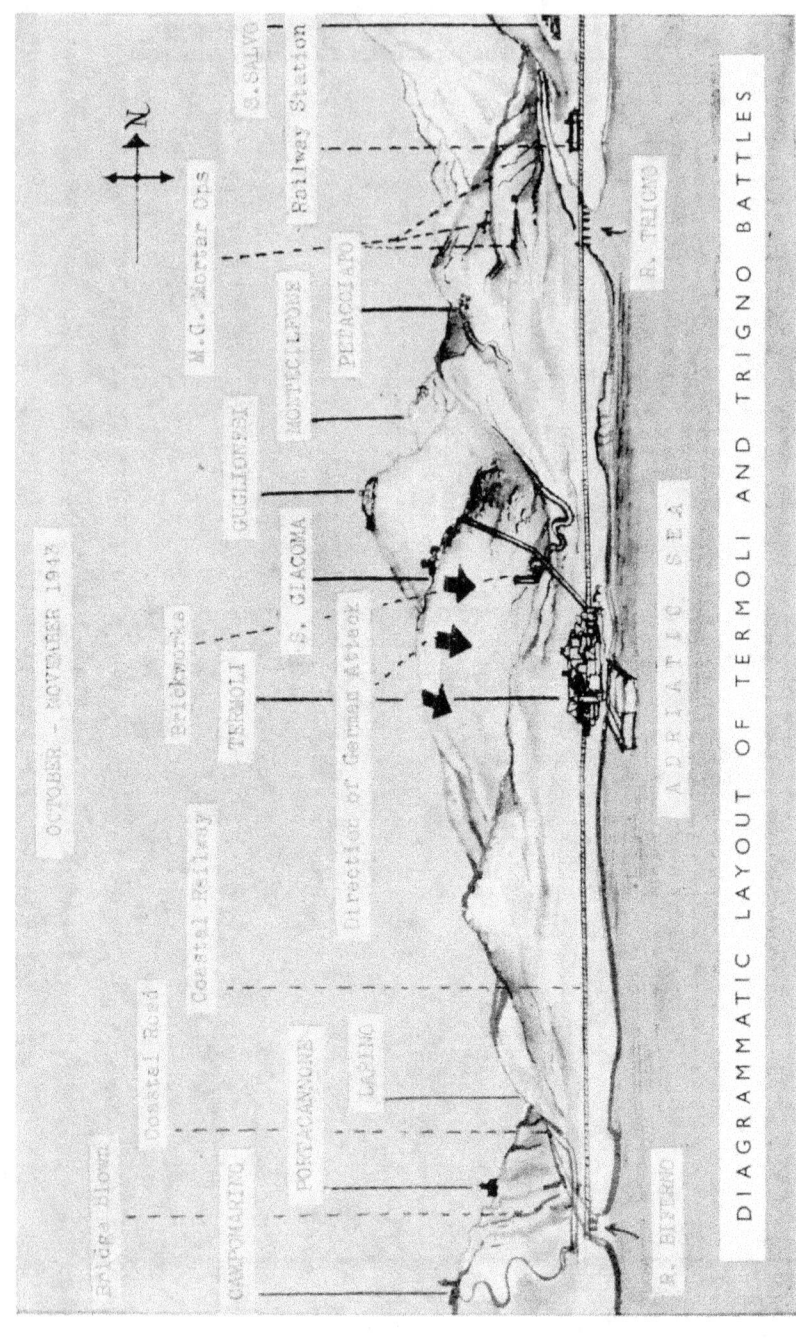

Diagrammatic Layout of Termoli and Trigno Battles, October–November 1943. (*See Chapter XI.*)

[81]

Captain R. D. Hutchings left "B" Group to occupy the adjutantal chair. The second major in each Group relinquished command of the Mortar Company and went to Group H.Q. This was done in order to ensure that the 2/i/C. was not operationally committed unnecessarily, thus minimising the chances of the Group Commander and 2/i/C. becoming casualties simultaneously. As a matter of general interest, Battalion Order No. 72 of August 14th, 1943, is reprinted below to show the main disposition of officers at the time:

OFFICERS—DUTIES AND APPOINTMENTS

"B" Group	"C" Group	"D" Group
	Group Command	
Major R. Wasey	Major E. P. Shanks	Major J. J. Evans
	2/i/C.	
Capt. J. W. Doyle	Major D. B. Tregoning	Major H. A. C. Page
Heavy Mortar Coy.		
	Coy. Command	
Capt. J. A. Nurse	Capt. G. E. K. Hopper	Capt. A. E. Foxwell
	Coy. 2/i/C.	
Capt. D. J. Underwood	Capt. R. G. Shave	Capt. R. May
M.M.G. Coy.		
	Coy. Command	
Capt. B. J. Page	Capt. R. H. Ellis	Capt. B. V. C. Harpur
	Coy. 2/i/C.	
Capt. H. Holford-Strevens	Capt. D. E. M. Piper	Capt. C. E. Cullen
A.A. Coy.		
	Coy. Command	
Capt. I. D. W. Cramer	Capt. A. W. Pinks	Capt. A. R. Newstead
	Coy. 2/i/C.	
Lt. M. Griffiths	Capt. K. Duff-White	Capt. B. E. Silk

Capt. R. D. Hutchings will report to Bn. H.Q. forthwith to act as assistant Adjutant.

On August 18th the C.O. held a conference at which the lessons of the campaign were discussed with Group Commanders, and afterwards a dinner was arranged for all, which was the first the senior officers of the Battalion had eaten together since leaving England.

On August 20th, at precisely ten minutes to two o'clock in the morning, a message was received ordering 50 per cent. of us to go to the seaside immediately and "rest". Less than an hour and a half to dress, pack up, and cross the start-point for the run down to the coast was given. This is quite the usual sort of thing in the Army, and with our usual *sangfroid* we accomplished it—and squeezed in a bit of breakfast, too.

There were only eighty or ninety miles to cover, *via* Randazzo, Castille Umberto, Naso, Cap d'Orlando, Patti to Falcone, which was our specific area. Thus we anticipated reaching our destination before midday at least. However, all the convoys got mixed up with the 51 Highland Division moving operationally to Messina, and then, to ensure that the deadlock was clinched, the Americans joined in the fun.

We sweltered in the sun all day, glued to our vehicles—except for an occasional dash up a hill for grapes. In some places we were averaging less than a mile an hour. Eventually, we struggled into our "rest" area about eight o'clock in the evening, having spent about fourteen hours in all on the road.

The bathing at Falcone, and the sheer delight of doing nothing for a couple of days, came none too soon. The memory of that sparkling azure sea, girdled with the warm sands, will remain for ever vivid. Fruit there was in abundance—apples, figs, grapes, plums, and pears being munched with great avidity. "Sing-songs" and impromptu concerts, stimulated by frequent resort to the potent "Vino" bottle, took place nightly.

On August 23 the first party returned to Adrano, and the following day the other half of the Battalion moved *en masse* for their share of rest at the seaside resort. However, they did not return, because the whole Division moved into the north-coast area and we concentrated, very conveniently, as a Battalion at Falcone on August 29th.

We were all living in bivouacs, tied to the inevitable olive-tree. The day started with much clamour and confusion as enormous Sicilian washerwomen roared through our lines, balancing baskets precariously on their heads and screaming with strident, ringing voices: "Lavare! Sapone! Lavare!" This was their invitation to us to present our "smalls" for cleaning. They achieved this by bashing the linen violently against a river rock for about an hour. In exchange, we gave them a bit of soap or chocolate.

It was later revealed that the casualties from malaria in Sicily were higher than all the battle casualties put together, and the whole Division was put on special quinine treatment.

News of the invasion of Italy on September 3rd found the Battalion as a whole taking it easy on the beaches. The bathing and sun-bathing were occasionally interrupted by such training as was necessary, and every opportunity was taken by the mortars to rid themselves of the bad training ammunition.

One of the Bofors detachments which had been installed to protect the airfield which had appeared almost overnight on our doorstep was rather shaken when one of these bombs, destined to mutilate the waves some thousands of yards from the coast, suddenly arrived (heralded by that frightening drone so well known to those who attended the early Netheravon courses) in the middle of their cook-house, luckily without exploding. Rather than interfere with it, it was decided to move the gun detachment.

While all this was going on, the "powers that be" were working out our immediate future. The rôle of the Division as a whole had not been clarified, but it seemed as though the chances were that we should be required to carry out an assault somewhere on the southern shores of Italy. To protect any such landing from air attack, it was decided to employ the A.A. Companies on the beaches, but this brought up considerable problems of haulage, as the trip across Africa and Sicily had demonstrated that our trucks left much to be desired when employed in that way. Further experiments carried out on the beaches at Falcone proved beyond any shadow of doubt that, unless some other method of towing could be found, the Oerlikons would serve no useful purpose.

So, mysterious things were done with carriers, and after considerable improvisation on the part of the R.E.M.E. resources, an answer was found. Then the problem arose of finding carriers for all the guns, and after many conferences between the Commanding Officer and the Group Commanders, the first of our own special "War Establishments" was produced. This allowed for one of the platoons in the M.G. Companies to be carried on trucks, and their carriers were used in the A.A. Companies.

About this time, at an exhibition of shooting by the Divisional Artillery, "B" Group used both its mortar platoons under the direction of Major Doyle to illustrate the difference between "normal" and "streamlined" bombs. The difference was most marked, as the latter were far more accurate, and the demonstration was an "eye-opener" to the Divisional spectators.

On September 8th the surrender of Italy was announced, which happily coincided with a concert given by "D" Group, and there was much elation and gaiety.

Meanwhile, no definite information was forthcoming as to our ultimate task. Eventually, a fortnight after the Italian invasion, orders were received, and all the plans for combined "ops" and our "composite" companies went overboard. The Division had been given the task of consolidating the gains of the Airborne Division in Taranto and Brindisi.

The Divisional Commander had been given command in that area, and it appeared to him that the German forces known to be advancing southwards would soon be met there.

CHAPTER XI

TARANTO TO THE APENNINES

ITALY (*September–December, 1943*)

THE Battalion swarmed into Italy by divers routes and in fragments, which makes any orderly survey of the movement very difficult.

On September 17th, Battalion H.Q., very much enlarged, with "B" Group M.M.G. Company went across *via* Messina, Reggio, Crotone, Taranto, leaving Major R. Wasey behind to command the remainder of the Battalion.

Sixty-eight carriers of the Battalion with Captain B. V. C. Harpur in charge—many towing Oerlikon guns—struggled over the mountains on September 19th to Catania *via* "Sun Track", Randazzo, and Adrano. The journey took two days, and the colossal strain on the carriers, as they wound over the enormous mountains with their heavy loads, proved almost too much. Some had to be abandoned *en route* for workshop repairs. L.S.T.s awaited at Catania to carry this party direct to Taranto. Thereafter, the direct 230-mile road route to Taranto, *via* Reggio, was followed by the rest of the Battalion, which moved off in their trucks from Falcone in small sub-units, as follows :

Sept. 20th......................."C" and "D" Groups, M.M.G. Coys.
Sept. 21st........."C" Group, A.A. Coy.—"B" Group, H.M. Coy.
Sept. 22nd..............................."C" Group, H.M. Coy.
Sept. 23rd..............................."D" Group, H.M. Coy.
Sept. 24th...............................Remainder of Battalion.

Battalion H.Q. and "B" Group M.G. Company had an enjoyable run across Calabria. Half-way round, they met the first Kensingtons to land in Italy. This party (consisting of Major D. B. Tregoning, Captain A. E. B. Foxwell, Captain A. Oakes, Lieutenant J. A. German, Pte. G. Ware and Pte. R. Kemp) was responsible for the running of a 78 Division Staging Area at Crotone.

On arrival at Taranto it was found that the situation had changed, and instead of sitting around a perimeter outside the port, it had been decided that the forces available should sally forward to make contact with the enemy, and secure the airfield and port of Bari.

The streets in all the towns and villages were lined with the cheering populace. The carriers were bedecked with flowers, and it was hard to decide whether this was a mobile force seeking the enemy or a wedding procession. The one thing which was never in doubt was the direction which we should take. The onlookers steadfastly foiled any attempt to take any side turning which would not bring us speedily into the enemy's lines.

Eventually, we arrived in Bari *via* Massafra and Capurso. The road was delightful after Sicily. As far as the civilians were concerned, things were very much as normal. At the level crossings, a railway official decided to lower the barrier in the middle of the convoy immediately in front of the truck bearing the insignia of the Quartermaster. Captain Knight then proved once more that it is the way you say a thing and not what you say that matters, with the result that our convoy was allowed to proceed, leaving behind it a completely disorganised Italian railway system, and an official whose ancestry had been traced for several generations, to the delight of the listening troops.

At Bari airfield the column was greeted with the same lack of understanding, but this time the Commander of the airfield was the obstructionist, and he chose for himself a formidable combination of opponents in the persons of Captain B. J. Page and the Commanding Officer. The gates swung rapidly open after the latter had addressed a few sharp words to the Italian commander, the convoy rushed on to the landing-ground, and Bari with its airfield was ours. Road blocks were soon established on the Termoli road and around the aerodrome.

The morning following the capture of Bari brought with it new orders. These had been expected and eagerly awaited. Consequently, when the Signals Officer, Lieutenant

C. G. Stuttard, was aroused in the middle of the night with a double-transposition cipher message, he tackled it with as much enthusiasm as could possibly be mustered by anyone awakened at such an awful time. His disgust and rage were unbounded when, after hours of hard work and eyestrain trying to decipher the almost illegible writing by the dim light provided in the wireless truck, his final answer proved to be a message from Division asking whether they might borrow our water-cart the following morning. Apparently a junior staff officer had been subjected to the hospitality of the local inhabitants to a degree to which he was not accustomed, with the result that he signed a message form in the wrong place.

After daylight, however, the Commanding Officer was called to an Order group at which it was decided that the elements of 78 Division available should be split into two columns and push ahead as far and as fast as possible along the coast road and an inland route to Termoli. The column to negotiate the latter was commanded by Lieutenant-Colonel F. G. Parker and consisted of some "25-pounders", some A/T guns, a squadron of "Recce", and the 1 Kensingtons, of which, at this time, the only fighting element to have arrived was "B" Group M.G. Company.

The immediate object was to secure the bridges across the river which joined the sea just north of Barletta, and the two columns pressed on against minor opposition. Armoured cars of the "Recce" caught a lorry-load of Germans completely unawares as their vehicle was taking them back to their camp, and one German D.R. who was mending a puncture by the roadside glanced up from his work to find himself looking down the barrel of a tommy-gun wielded by an enormous British sergeant. The surprise was so great that he burst into tears, and was led sobbing into captivity.

That evening found the two columns half-way to the objective, and it still appeared as though the enemy hardly realised that British troops were operating in their area. However, during the night, the sentries from the platoons reported large explosions and fires ahead.

At first light the following morning the pursuit continued. Unfortunately, fast as our advance had been, it had not been fast enough to prevent the enemy from preparing demolitions. The result was that as the carriers and "Recce" cars approached the objectives, bridges collapsed into heaps of rubble, and we had our first experience of the obstacles and demolitions which we were to come to know so well.

These were too complete and too well defended by small-arms fire for an immediate crossing by the "Recce" troops to be effected. The position was therefore consolidated, and "B" Group M.G. Company bore the initial brunt of this consolidation, as they were the only infantry troops available. In the evening moderately heavy shelling came from the enemy. During the night of September 22nd patrols were sent out from the "Recce" on the inland road, while on the coast Lieutenant Steadman, who was commanding the platoon there, was asked by the force commander to carry out an impossible patrol some five or six miles over the river just north of Canosa, in addition to maintaining a protective screen behind which the remainder of the column might retire with some feeling of safety for the night. This was one of the occasions, few in number, when the Regiment was incapable of performing all the tasks asked of it.

During the evening, "Parker Force" was strengthened by the arrival of the other two M.G. Companies. "D" Group M.G. Company carried out a night occupation on the River Ofanto, north of Canosa, their vehicles running in very slowly in top gear to prevent any noise being communicated to the enemy. "C" Group M.G.s were deployed in rear and to the flanks, guarding A/T guns and road blocks, to counter any threat which might be forthcoming from those directions.

The following morning brought additional strength to the force by the arrival of tanks from the Third City of London Yeomanry, and the Brigadier commanding the 4 Armoured Brigade took command of the two columns.

The river was crossed without opposition, and the advance continued with all speed to the next water obstacle. Here the same procedure was repeated, but resistance was stiffening, and the enemy inflicted numerous casualties on other elements, but not on ourselves.

On September 25th we passed through Cerignola and,

brushing aside the inevitable excited crowds, went all-out for Foggia. On the way, Lieut. J. Corbridge, commanding 7 Platoon "B" Group, successfully accelerated the pace of the enemy who were withdrawing towards Cerignola. His guns caused casualties at long range, and were more successful than the German sniper who had a shot at the Commanding Officer the next day at a distance of about 50 yards, and who fortunately missed. The surprise was so great, however, that the miscreant made good his escape before the compliment could be returned.

The M.G.s were employed for the most part at this stage in flank protection. A report from civilian sources came in that a German regiment was advancing to attack on our left. In the middle of a freak thunderstorm, during which everyone was soaked to the skin, arrangements were made to receive our unwanted visitors with unexpected warmth. "C" and "D" Groups M.M.G. Companies took up positions at a small road centre called Ortanova. Some confusion still seemed to remain in the minds of the civilians as to the present state of affairs. There was no doubt that, for the most part, they were terribly glad to see us. So much so that the Ortanova band had turned out to entertain "D" Group M.M.G. Company as they sat in the new positions which they had toiled all night in the torrential rain to occupy, and for the concealment of which particular care had been taken. The brass band eventually retired in disorder to the scenes of drunkenness and revelry with which the villagers were heralding their liberation. When it was apparent that this flanking threat was removed, bivouacs were untied, the guns were dismantled, and the chase continued.

Foggia gave some idea of the drastic effects of our bombing, and no one wanted to linger among the scenes of desolation there. Officially, Foggia had been the ultimate objective in this push, but exploitation was the order of the day, particularly when patrols reported no signs of the enemy. "D" Group M.M.G. Company found themselves in the van of the advance when detached in support of the 5th Bn. Northamptonshire Regiment, and their carriers stormed Serracapriola practically unaided.

It was in this town that symptoms of the Hun's devilry were first blatantly evinced. They left time-bombs all over the place, which exploded at irregular intervals, killing and wounding none but civilians, including some little children. "D" Group M.M.G. Company personnel did great work in rendering first-aid.

On October 2nd the advance from Serracapriola was continued. By nightfall, Portocannone was reached, with the platoons of "D" Group M.M.G. Company consolidating the gains.

This was a hectic day, which started with an air attack on Serracapriola early in the morning by twelve enemy fighter-bombers. This was directed at troops and transport concentrated behind the town, of which XIII Corps—coming rapidly forward with the rest of the 11 Infantry Brigade—formed part. A hail of small-arms fire prevented the planes from doing much damage, and the timely arrival of some Spitfires ensured the hasty retreat of the marauders, two of which were shot out of the sky. No casualties were sustained by us, fortunately, although one or two vehicles were hit.

Next a profusion of mines and wrecked bridges was met at every conceivable point, and the impetus of the attack was slowed down as we struggled across country.

Then it started to rain. Heavy showers fell which marked both the beginning of the wet season and acute discomfort.

The main road from Serracapriola to Termoli was subjected to sudden "straffing" from the air very frequently. In one of these raids, on October 3rd, C.S.M. A. Kelk was unfortunately wounded.

During the night of October 2nd the Commandos stormed Termoli, which they captured by surprise tactics, having landed from the sea.

By this time the Battalion had more or less all arrived in the same place. The headlong rush of the Kensingtons at their appointed intervals from Taranto to the Termoli area was over.

However, it must be recalled, before going any further, that on September 28th, during the run to Termoli, Corporal

E. C. Stanbridge performed an act of gallantry which was recorded by direction of G.O.C. on his conduct sheet as follows:

A lorry loaded with 5,000 rounds of Oerlikon shells and the vehicles reserve petrol, caught fire, and Corporal Stanbridge, who was riding in a following vehicle, rushed to the burning truck and with the help of a few others started to unload it. Some of the forward boxes began to smoulder. Corporal Stanbridge continued to unload with exceptional energy, and complete disregard for his own safety, although he knew full well the nature of the ammunition. Three boxes were fully alight, and were thrown into a ditch where they exploded, some fragments piercing the side of the truck. However, through his action, only six magazines were destroyed, and more serious damage was undoubtedly averted.

During the night of October 3rd/4th, 36 Infantry Brigade made an amphibious landing near Termoli, and the Battalion took up positions on the high ground to the west of the town.

In the evening of October 3rd, "B" Group M.M.G. Company went over complete to join Termoli's garrison, which included the Lancashire Fusiliers, part of 56 "Recce" Regiment, and a battery of 132 Field Regiment. One of "B" Group's H.M. Platoons, commanded by Lieutenant L. Matthews, was put in support of the Royal West Kents at request of 36 Infantry Brigade, and the remainder of "B" Group H.M. Company was some miles inland supporting 1st Battalion East Surrey Regiment in the attack on Larino.

The only way the forces coming up from the south by land could reach Termoli was by a hastily constructed bridge over the River Biferno, just north of Campomarino, which replaced the bridge blown on the main road. Having allowed five tanks to cross, this collapsed. Then it started to rain spasmodically, which made it fantastically difficult for our vehicles, harbouring in woods and fields, to become mobile once more.

Enemy air activity increased, and innumerable hit-and-run raids were made everywhere. Special attention was directed at the "diversion" on the Biferno, where the gallant Sappers were working as usual against time.

Suddenly, in the morning of October 4th, the "fluid" situation was solidified in the most alarming manner. Switched unexpectedly from the Naples front, tanks of the crack German 16th Panzer Division, supported by infantry, rolled over the Guglionesi–S. Giacomo feature just west of Termoli in a gigantic and concerted counter-attack.

The first intimation of this development was inadvertently garnered by Captain B. J. G. Page, who proceeded, together with his "Recce" party and a section of Lieutenant Steadman's No. 6 Platoon, to take over a road block at S. Giacomo—purporting to be manned by our own troops. The Germans, however, had relieved it first.

Captain Page deployed the guns with him to cover the approaches leading from the village, but before they could dig-in properly, enemy tanks rumbled forward and shot up the section with high-explosives and overran it. The carriers were knocked out one by one, and serious casualties resulted as 5 o/r. were wounded and 6 o/r. were taken prisoner. Captain Page had to shoot his way out in traditional fashion with his pistol. He killed or wounded three Germans, who had left their tank, at point-blank range, and made a daring escape, bringing with him the vital news of this enemy thrust. He was awarded an immediate M.C. for this very gallant work.

At first light on October 5th Captain Page put a second platoon into action in an excellent position on the left of the 2nd Bn. Lancashire Fusiliers, and successfully engaged the enemy throughout the day. During the night of the 5th/6th, when the position was critical, and Termoli was threatened by German tanks and infantry, Captain Page remained with the platoon in action although the infantry support had been withdrawn. On the morning of the 6th, this platoon engaged with success German attacks on the Lancashire Fusiliers.

Meanwhile, L/Sgt. A. E. Harvey, commanding the other section of 6 Platoon, was also creating history by directing the fire of his guns on the advancing Huns with the same cool "aplomb" he evinced when singing "Roll on my seven".

During the morning of October 5th his section (which included Corporal K. R. Broom, Pte. E. Taylor, Pte. Radcliffe, Pte. Swain, Pte. J. Morgan, and Pte. Hickin) was in action with No. 6 Tp. 3 Commando near the brickworks west of Termoli. About 10.00 hrs., an enemy tank with one company of infantry appeared on the high ground to the west. They were engaged at a range of 1650 yards, casualties were inflicted, and the enemy withdrew into dead ground.

Later in the afternoon, following a tank battle, the M.G. section was heavily shelled and machine-gunned, and enemy infantry moving forward were continuously engaged by L/Sgt. Harvey, who inflicted heavy casualties. The infantry on the left of the M.G. position were subjected to heavy mortar-fire and withdrew; nevertheless L/Sgt. Harvey continued to engage the enemy and, owing to the clever use of ground, he was constantly able to move his guns.

Finally, about fifty enemy infantry appeared less than 200 yards away. These he successfully engaged with several belts, using the swinging traverse with sights down. Shortly afterwards, the Commandos withdrew and L/Sgt. Harvey brought his section out of action after burying the locks—which he subsequently recovered. Throughout the day, this N.C.O. and his section fought with great skill, courage, and determination, and assisted the Commandos to hold the enemy until dusk, which was at least an hour longer than the Commando officer estimated that he could hold out. This officer expressed great appreciation of the work done by L/Sgt. Harvey and his men, and L/Sgt. Harvey was awarded an immediate M.M.

On the morning of October 5th, "B" Group main H.Q. came over the river, and some hours later retired in undignified haste. Afterwards, when the battle got uncomfortably close, "C" Group M.M.G. Company and H.M. Company were hastily deployed along the high ground from Campomarino to Portacannone overlooking the river, to give covering fire should a general withdrawal become necessary.

The situation was now extremely serious. The garrison had been forced to retire temporarily from the high ground with their backs to the sea, which was in some cases less than half a mile away. Sappers worked like madmen to make the

Biferno crossing really reliable, so that our tanks and A/T guns could come over to the assistance of the hard-pressed infantry.

Despite shelling of the harbour, 38 (Irish) Infantry Brigade landed throughout the evening, and rapidly took over defence of the small perimeter around the town. The crossing of the Biferno was made, and tank support increased accordingly.

In the early hours of the morning of October 6th, "D" Group Tac. H.Q. and H.M. Company arrived. The latter was deployed in the town to support the Irish battalions in the counter-attack which started about 11.00 hrs. Our mortar-fire was directed primarily on the enemy strong-points around the brick factory with a tall chimney a little way outside the town on a junction of the main road. Many direct hits were recorded, the Hun stretcher-bearers waving white flags could be clearly seen trying to attend to their casualties. Another M.M.G. platoon of "B" Group, commanded by Lieutenant Corbidge, was in a good position also to support this attack, which it did with effect by means of overhead fire.

At 11.30 hrs. "D" Group M.M.G. Company arrived complete, having left the 5th Bn. Northamptonshire Regiment at Portocannone. Platoons were immediately sent after the Irish battalions, and "prepare for long carries" was the order.

4 Platoon of "B" Group's Heavy Mortars had temporarily taken up position near the road to Campobasso, and had retreated to the Biferno when our infantry were knocked back. The platoon went forward again, only to be told by an infantry battle patrol that they were in front of the F.D.L.s, and so once more hastily withdrew.

Just about this time No. 4 Platoon "D" Group in Termoli were annoyed considerably by some accurate shelling and sniping. It was subsequently discovered that this originated from a German O.P. party left behind in the church tower near by. As a result, Major H. A. C. Page was seriously wounded in the face by a shell fragment. He was rushed to a dressing-station, and although he sustained the loss of an eye and was for some time on the "dangerously ill" list, he managed to survive, but never rejoined the Battalion despite his innumerable efforts to do so. We all felt the loss of this gallant officer very much. We have a definite feeling that had he been able to talk at the time of his misfortune, he would have pulled out a well-thumbed little note-book in which innumerable wagers were recorded, and said : "Betcha ten to one I'm back within a week."

The Irish Brigade attack was highly successful, and the next few days were spent licking our wounds and reorganising in a gentle way.

"D" Group M.M.G. Company were deployed along the ridge from the brickworks to S. Giacomo, with the mortars just behind, now in the care of Major A. E. B. Foxwell, who replaced Major H. A. C. Page.

"B" Group drew back to Campomarino for rest and refitting, less "Nurseforce", which consisted of an M.M.G. and H.M. Platoons supporting the 1st Bn. East Surreys with conspicuous success in the Larino operations some fifteen miles west of Termoli. On October 4th the commander, Captain J. A. Nurse, was wounded in the thigh from shrapnel, and Sergeant Meehan and Corporal S. Saunders were also casualties at the same time. The 2/i/C., Captain Underwood, then took charge.

At this point we were very sorry to lose Major B. L. Bryar, our 2/i/C., who was posted in the same appointment to the 6th Bn. Inniskilling Fusiliers. At the same time our bustling, energetic, and keen-witted commander of "B" Group, Major "Ronnie" Wasey, was sent as 2/i/C. to the 5th Bn. Northamptonshire Regiment.

Major E. P. Shanks was appointed Battalion 2/i/C., and command of "C" Group then devolved on Major D. B. Tregoning, and that of "B" Group on Major J. W. Doyle, who had Capt. B. V. C. Harpur sent to him as his 2/i/C.

The Commanding Officer was then forced to review the organisation of the Battalion, with the result that the A.A. Companies were reduced to one complete company of guns and a nucleus of one platoon and Company H.Q. retained from the others. Vehicles and personnel from the latter went to offset the deficiencies of the rest of the Battalion through casualties and sickness. Since leaving England there had been no replacements, and the only new faces to be seen were those of some officers and o/r. from the 5 Mahrattas (Support Battalion of the new 8 Indian Division), who were attached on October 13th to the Battalion to get battle experience.

Meanwhile 36 Brigade with "C" Group were carrying out an operation to occupy Guglionesi and Montecilfone. The former town was quickly taken, and on consolidation No. 7 Platoon of "C" Group M.M.G. Company, commanded by Lieutenant J. S. McKay, engaged an S.P. gun at about 3000 yards range, causing the crew to become inoperative. Some "Tiger" tanks, however, took up the challenge and fired some "H.E.", which resulted in Sergeant T. Jones being wounded.

The misfortunes of this platoon were really chronic when, on October 18th, whilst supporting the Royal West Kents in the operation to take Montecilfone, one section were almost all casualties, which included Pte. A. Dewey being killed, when their vehicles were blown up by some "Tellermines". The same day the other section was subjected to a full-scale attack by the Hun. The infantry had to retire, leaving the section "in the air", and the M.G. position was surprised from the rear and overrun. The calamitous result was that Sgt. L. W. Bird, Cpl. C. Hall, Cpl. A. Davies, Ptes. F. Butler, G. Bolton, D. Carroll, E. Hooper, D. Hooper, D. Porter, and A. Russell, were all captured. The Platoon Commander himself shot one fanatical German officer with his pistol, when only about two or three yards away, and managed to escape. A counter-attack very soon afterwards, in which Lieutenant J. S. McKay assisted, restored the loss of ground; the two guns were found intact, although one had been damaged by Spandau fire in the initial stages of the enemy thrust.

The following night one of the mortar platoons of "C" Group H.M. Company was subjected to rough treatment. A large enemy patrol cleverly infiltrated in the darkness through the Royal West Kent's positions, and surprised the mortar platoon. In the confused fire of grenades and small arms, Lieut. J. Etchells and 6 o/r. were wounded (including Ptes. A. Brown and H. Coward, who subsequently died),

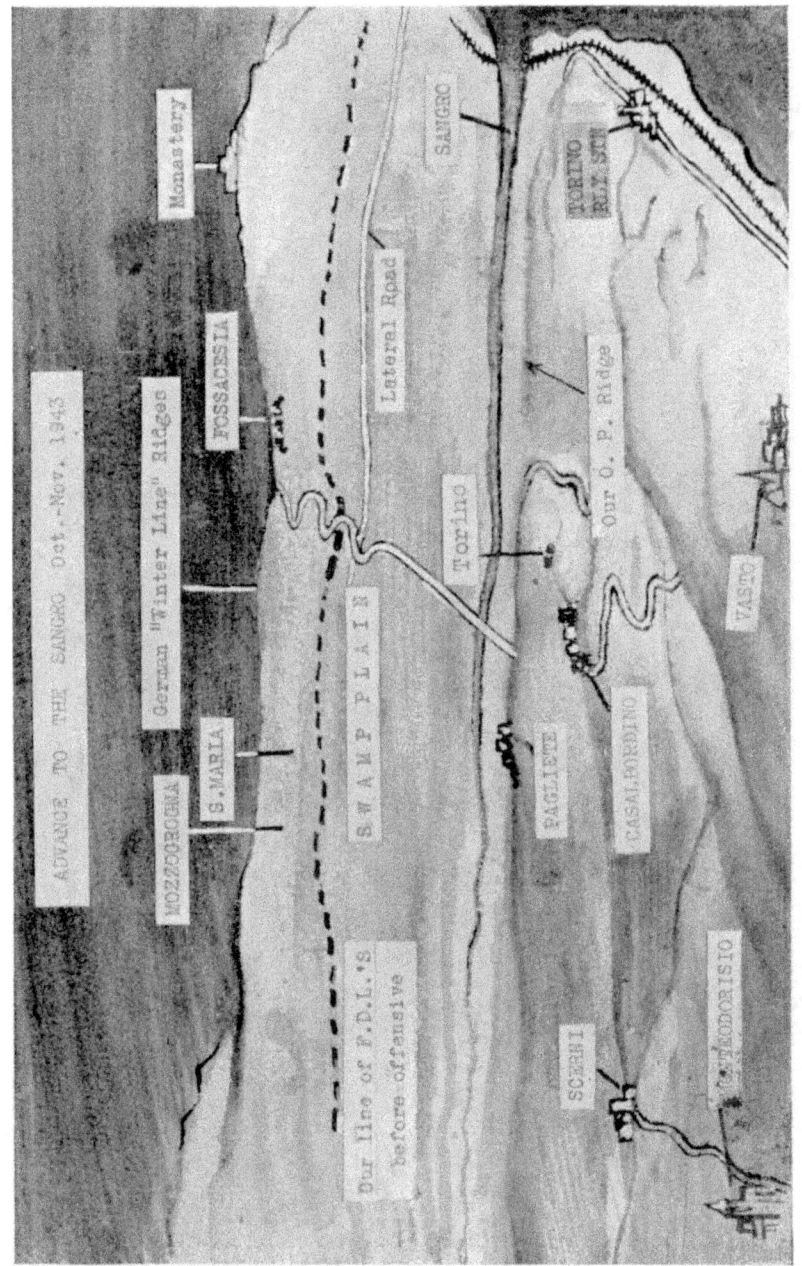

Operations in Advance to the Sangro, October–November 1943. (*See Chapter XI.*)

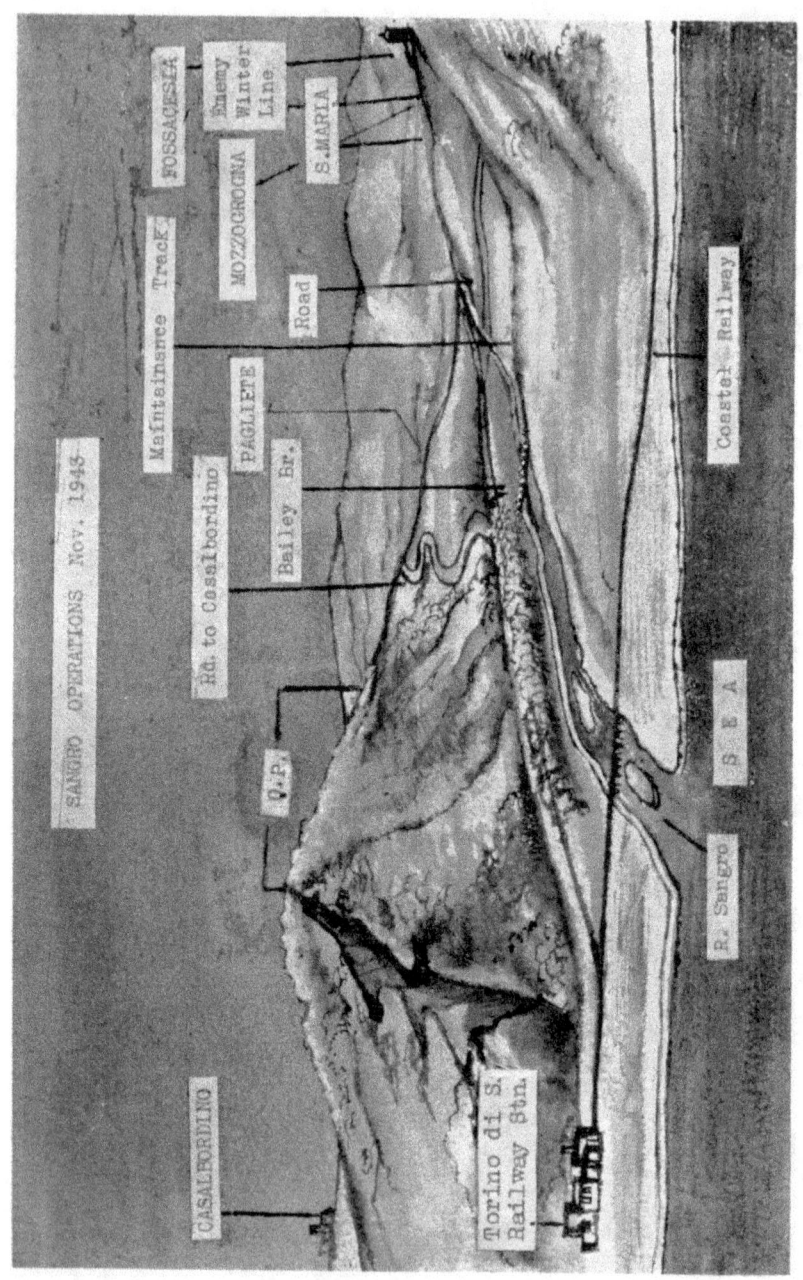

SANGRO OPERATIONS, NOVEMBER 1943. (*See Chapter XI.*)

and Ptes. Rivers and Arthur Worsop were taken prisoner. Although several of the trucks were damaged, the mortars were fortunately unharmed, and it was possible next morning to reorganise the platoon. The Platoon Commander himself (Lieut. P. Chesterton) was in his O.P. at the other end of the village, and it was Capt. R. G. Shave who started to restore order and remove casualties when he and C.S.M. Kluth arrived with rations at 03.30 hrs.

The offensive was resumed on October 19th, when Petacciato was captured by 38 (Irish) Brigade, with "D" Group in support around the high ground farther north. Four days later, when assisting the Royal Irish Fusiliers in operations to clear the ground beyond the town, Ptes. Howard and E. Smith, of 7 Platoon "D" Group, were badly wounded by shell-fire, and died whilst being evacuated.

At this point the Division was beset by an onslaught of jaundice, which appeared to be confined solely to the officers. Lieutenant J. Corbidge and Major J. W. Doyle, to mention only two of the victims, were affected, and in the absence of the latter, Major B. V. C. Harpur took over command of "B" Group for the whole month of November and early December.

The Division's next task was to cross the River Trigno, which required a lot of bloody fighting and a full-scale attack. For ten days the whole Battalion in support of respective Brigades was subjected to severe mortar- and shell-fire; punctuated by frequent air attacks. Above all, the extreme discomfort will be remembered, as it poured incessantly with rain. The country was turned into one enormous field of mud, in which the carriers and trucks churned with futile fury.

By the end of October the whole Division, with 11 Brigade on the right next to the sea, was deployed along the high ridge overlooking the Trigno, on which there were many excellent O.P.s for observing the town of S. Salvo, and also the high ground beyond on which the enemy were well dug in for some considerable depth.

The Irish Brigade went across first, and made a limited bridge-head after sustaining many casualties. The Sappers toiled to get crossings organised. A profusion of mines and mortar-fire was met everywhere. It was decided to put 36 Brigade through subsequently to capture S. Salvo, and for this purpose "C" and "D" Groups reverted to under command of the Commanding Officer to provide a large volume of fire on the left flank. This, it was hoped, would lead the enemy to believe that an attack was coming in from that direction, whereas in reality it was only a feint. Two platoons of Oerlikons were added to the Kensington cocktail of fire power, and the whole gigantic fire-plan was due for ignition at midnight on November 2nd/3rd.

Division H.Q., however, sent through a message postponing the shoot until one o'clock in the morning. This arrived very late, and after much excitement, frenzied 'phone calls, and madly dashing dispatch riders, the message was got to the guns with only two minutes to spare.

The Vickers guns fired altogether nearly 100,000 rounds, and the 4·2-in. mortars over 1500 bombs. The whole show was a complete success, and the sight of German defensive fire falling on the areas where they thought our attack was developing was watched with great glee. The only mishap was when the enemy deposited about a dozen of their mortar bombs on the lines of a "C" Group Mortar Platoon. One o/r. was wounded, but otherwise no real damage was done.

"B" Group on the right, next to the sea, fired a considerable amount in support of 11 Brigade. The final touch to this thunderous background was the continuous roar of the ubiquitous Artillery—and broadsides from our naval units, which helped to flatten Vasto's communications. At noon, two platoons of "C" A.A. Coy. engaged twelve enemy aircraft, and were delighted to see that several were well and truly damaged and one, in fact, was brought down.

All through the day of November 3rd, the battle for S. Salvo town waxed fierce and long. The infantry, supported by tanks, were meeting very strong opposition. Our M.M.G. and H.M. Platoons seized many opportunities to engage parties of the enemy, which helped considerably. The whole battlefield was spread out before our eyes, and we could see German tanks winding slowly down the long precipitous descent to S. Salvo where our own "big boys" fought them to a standstill and won the day.

On the right the Lancashire Fusiliers were attacking S. Salvo station, and eventually captured it despite mines, booby-traps, machine-gun fire, and all the "dirt and derision" which the angry Hun could fling over.

By November 4th the situation was well under control, and a fierce exploitation was inaugurated.

11 (Inf.) Brigade with "B" Group moved on to take Cupello, Monteodorisio, over the River Sinello to Scerni, and once more over the River Osento on to Paglieto. This was a magnificent advance, during which the infantry covered in less than three days about thirty miles of country, fighting bitterly all the way. The M.M.G. Platoons performed fantastic "long carries" of seven and eight miles at a time, with infantry carrying-parties to help—and the Heavy Mortar Platoons were leap-frogging forward in constant support of the battalions. In the same way "C" Group supported 36 Brigade on the coastal road and surged through Vasto, so that a rapid advance to the Sangro River via Casalbordino and Torino was made.

The bad weather by this time had made mobility a thing of the past. Carriers were strewn all round the countryside up to their hulls in mud. Teams of six to twelve oxen were requisitioned in some cases to pull out vehicles. "C" Group's platoons were all deployed on the high ridge overlooking the Sangro, and with the support weapons of the infantry under command of O.C. "C" Group a fire-plan was worked out to rest, as far as possible, the 36 Bde. infantry on their wide front. "D" Group remained in reserve with the Irish Brigade. "B" Group concentrated near Casalbordino a week later. From then on, the stage gradually became set for one of the biggest sagas of the war—the battle of the River Sangro—where the Germans had established their "stay-put" winter line.

The Sangro was wide and fast-flowing. Rain and snow from the distant mountains made its depth vary with terrifying rapidity. A rise of three to six feet in a couple of hours was not unusual. A swampy and heavily mined carpet of flat country led up to the Fossacesia–S. Maria Ridge, on which the enemy weapons bristled. The descent on our side was most precipitous, but we had excellent O.P.s all along the ridge. The long bridge which had linked the main road either side of the river was completely demolished.

Battalions of 36 Brigade, supported by two M.M.G. Platoons of "C" Group, were first over the river, and vigorous patrolling ensued, in which ascendancy was quickly established over the enemy. It was subsequently learnt from a captured document that the Hun considered chaining his machine-guns to keep them from being removed by our men, which happened on several occasions.

Lieutenant McKay's M.M.G. Platoon of "C" Group was in position on the high ground behind the river, about 300 yards from the sea, and Lieutenant G. A. Laver's Mortar Platoon was sited farther inland on the same ridge. The latter had an excellent O.P. with a cunningly constructed covered approach. As a result, innumerable "visitors" went there to gaze out on to the enemy territory, amongst whom was numbered the C.-in-C. of the Eighth Army—then General Sir Bernard Law Montgomery.

A few days later the whole of "B" Group deployed. One M.M.G. Platoon, commanded by Sergeant B. Meehan, went over to "C" Group. The 4·2-in. mortar platoons occupied the same area as Lieutenant McKay's M.M.G. Platoon, which was in a very deep and narrow defile—a stone's throw from the beach.

Gradually the technique which spelt "Offensive" was developed throughout the Division. More and more artillery deployed in "Gun Alley" behind the foremost ridge. Any other precious space that could be found off the road and between the cliffs and chasms had a gun promptly dumped on it. Stocks of food, "ammo", petrol, and all the other necessities, appeared like mushrooms overnight along the line of communication from Vasto to Casalbordino.

Aircraft flew in from the sea, and kept dropping heavy bombs on the Hun with relentless precision and regularity.

The infantry of 36 Brigade, hanging on desperately to their waterlogged slit-trenches between the Devil and the Sangro, were eventually relieved in part by battalions of the 11 Brigade. The situation at this time is well summarised by the following extract from a popular newspaper:

From Eric Lloyd Williams, Reuter's Special Correspondent. With the Eighth Army, Friday, November 28th, 1943.

The British 78th Division, veterans of Tunisia and Sicily, and heroes of such hard-fought battles as Longstop Hill and "Cherry-ripe", were mainly responsible for the crossing of the flooded Sangro River.

When General Montgomery said recently that "British soldiers have risen to great heights" he was referring to men of the 78th Infantry Division—men from London and the Home Counties, and from the Highlands, Lancashire, and Irish Regiments.

Under what General Montgomery described as "the most appalling weather conditions", they established a vital bridge-head over the Sangro and held it in face of furious German attempts to drive them into the river.

Montgomery signalled to them across the river: "Stand fast at all costs." They stood fast. Attacked continually by German infantry and artillery and in driving rain, the 78th held firm, fighting in mud-filled holes in the ground, going for days without changing their sodden battledress—without being able to brew up their beloved mugs of tea.

They stood fast, well knowing that with the fast-rising river already over their shoulders, it was unlikely that supplies would be able to reach them, that their anti-tank guns might never get across, that their ammunition might run out, and that they were unlikely to be able to send back their wounded.

We could see these British infantry from a high ridge south of the river. We could see mortar bombs exploding, hear the rattle of machine-guns, and see smoke clouds where German shells were falling.

We knew these men were going through hell, but when we reached them they were in the highest spirits, and a steady stream of German prisoners was coming back across the river.

To-day their stand is almost another 78th Division legend.

Enemy patrolling, counter-attacks, shelling, mortaring, and air attacks occurred on a heavy scale every day. The worst thing, perhaps, was the mud, which dried a bit during fine spells only to be turned into a filthy liquid glue almost as soon as a cloud approached. Vehicles churned about helplessly in its grip anywhere off the main road. A good picture is given by the following newspaper extract:

APPALLING MUD

When I read in England of battles slowed down by mud, I am afraid that, like many other people with pictures of "sunny Italy" in my mind, I did not realise the appalling conditions in which our men are fighting.

The mud here is equal to anything I ever saw in France in the last war. One slip off the centre of most of the roads and you are calf deep in mud so sticky that you can hardly pull your foot out after each step. The fields beside the roads are quagmires. Cars and trucks without four-wheel drives could not move in them. I have even seen tanks bogged down in them. The moving of traffic after an hour or two of rain becomes a matter of the most extraordinary difficulty.

With the usual infantry protection parties in attendance, the Sappers cleared mines and got crossings over the river, employing Bailey bridges from island to island.

By night the Kensingtons moved farther forward, right up into the infantry F.D.L.s. "B" Group's two mortar platoons took up position under the lee of the ridge on which the enemy uneasily sat. The O.P.s remained behind them on the high ground south of the Sangro.

Lieutenant Trott, a new officer who had joined the Battalion only a few days previously, carried out a very fine daylight "recce" on the far side of the river. He brought his platoon across and took up position just on the far bank, whence he could shoot on to the high ground in front, and at the same time protect the vital river crossing should the enemy infiltrate. His platoon lay so skilfully concealed for many days in full view of the enemy that not a single casualty resulted.

Over the crossing made farther inland went Lieutenant Munsey and his M.M.G. Platoon, and Lieutenant Smith with his Mortar Platoon, from "C" Group.

The Sangro was proving very difficult to negotiate. Its crossing each night by the traffic necessary to maintain our troops on the far side was indeed hazardous. One never knew how deep it would be or how fast it would be flowing. Frequently the Bailey bridges were washed away and the fords blotted out in a swirling mass of icy water. Constant shelling made the game of chance even more exciting.

Sergeant Axten of "C" Group was awarded an immediate M.M., which was gained by his great coolness, courage, and devotion to duty when getting machine-gun kit across the

Sangro under shell-fire on the night of November 25th/26th, and in negotiating the equally hazardous return journey, when one N.C.O. (Corporal T. Moran) was unfortunately swept away by the torrent and lost.

The Commanding Officer established a forward H.Q. to help administer the Groups. This was sited just off the main road on high ground near a village called Torino di Sangro. It was frequently shelled, and on one occasion, on November 25th, Sergeant Lombardi, the Battalion Orderly-room Sergeant, Corporal Gabriel, and Pte. Birmingham of the Regimental Police were wounded. The former subsequently died of wounds—a loss sorely grieved by all. Sergeant Lombardi was extremely popular. His ready wit and brilliant drawings and cartoons under the title of "Leo" had become a permanent institution in the Battalion.

The plan to break through the Winter Line was imparted to Commanding Officers at Vasto by General Montgomery himself.

8 Indian Division would pass to capture Mozzagrogna and S. Maria. Then the Irish Brigade would exploit this gap and turn right towards the sea, rolling up the defences from the flank. This in turn would create a space big enough for wholesale exploitation and pursuit to the ultimate objective—the port of Pescara.

The date for the attack was postponed day after day with maddening regularity. The reason for this was, of course, due to the weather, which could not make up its mind to stay fine.

However, circumstances were eventually propitious. With the whole of the M.E. Air Force, six Field Regiments of 25-pounders, three Medium Regiments and other Artillery, and some four hundred tanks, in addition to the normal Divisional resources—the attack went in on December 1st. Fierce and prodigious resistance was met all along the line. The attack by the 8 Indian Division on the two towns was a bloody and prolonged affair, and 17 Indian Brigade met flame-throwers for the first time at Mozzagrogna.

Our artillery concentrations were tremendous, and the enemy replied with everything he had at his disposal, including many multi-barrelled mortars, which flailed the ground on which our troops were trying to consolidate.

"B" Group mortars and M.M.G.s fired defensively for the Northamptons, who, in position with the sea as their right flank, were subjected to several attacks.

"C" Group similarly blazed away with their M.M.G.s and mortars, which had been got over the river previously.

38 (Irish) Brigade went over the Sangro and on December 1st, with tank assistance, started their part of the plan. Whilst waiting near the river the previous day to support the "Irish", "D" Group mortar and M.M.G. platoons were bombed by enemy aircraft. Casualties unhappily resulted, and Cpl. J. Brett was killed. At the same time five others were wounded, including Pte. R. M. Flint, who later died.

To deceive the enemy and make him think a frontal attack was coming in near the coast, a battery of Artillery, a Company of the Northamptons, and the whole of "B" Support Group fired everything they had for one hour in the direction of the Monastery just east of Fossacesia. The success of this "Chinese" attack was tremendous. For over an hour the enemy fired his "D.F."s in the direction from which we hoped he would think the attack was developing. The net result was that the Irish Brigade, riding along on the tanks from the flank, found the "Krauts" almost to a man facing the wrong way.

Sudden enemy air attacks caused casualties amongst both men and vehicles. Mortaring and shelling were still experienced on a reasonably heavy scale.

A platoon of "D" Group had the additional job of rounding up and escorting prisoners, and they were kept busy. One German C.S.M. tried to incite some of his subordinates to escape, and was promptly shot by the Platoon Commander, who experienced no further trouble.

The Winter Line was shattered, and even after the tide of war had passed beyond, little German monstrosities kept crawling pathetically out of their funk-holes in twos and threes, and thankfully surrendered.

Practically every tree, bush, and house on the whole of the Winter Line ridge was blasted to hell by our fire power and bombing. Enemy vehicles and guns could be found abandoned, and innumerable items of his equipment and ammunition could be seen everywhere.

Enemy dug-outs were very deep and large, and furnished with proper beds, clocks, chairs, tables, and even had wallpaper on the walls—all looted from the local Italians. A network of "trenches de luxe" and specially reinforced weapon pits testified to his thoroughness. The approaches not covered by his direct observation and fire were so heavily mined that a mouse could hardly get through without setting something off.

The Irish Brigade with "D" Group mortars and M.M.G. platoons firing in support, continued to chase the Hun as far as the River Moro, five miles beyond, whilst "B" Group consolidated on Fossacesia.

At this point the Division was relieved at last by 1 Canadian Division, and the Battalion trooped back to a village called S. Marco near S. Severo, a distance of some 120 miles from the battlefield, and about one hundred miles from the rest of the Division at Campobasso.

The following special order of the day was then sent to the Division by Lieutenant-General C. W. Allfrey, C.B., D.S.O., M.C., commanding V Corps, and well summarises the operations to date:

78th Division is now leaving this Corps again, and is going to rest. I would like to convey to all ranks in the Division my appreciation for the splendid way in which you have fought. You have been fighting the enemy continuously now for over two months and pushing him back. You have three successful battles to add to your laurels—the battles of Termoli, the Trigno, and the Sangro.

You have broken through the main enemy Winter Line and have done it quickly and with few casualties. You can go out to rest knowing that you have done a fine job and added to your reputation, of which you are entitled to be extremely proud. For the present: Good-bye and Good Luck.

On arrival, a horde of officers and some o/r. reinforcements awaited us. This involved a large-scale readjustment of personnel throughout the Battalion. Major J. W. Doyle, for example, having recovered from his jaundice, resumed command of "B" Group, and Captain I. H. Battye, posted from the staff of 56 Division, took command of its Mortar Company.

Unfortunately, within forty-eight hours of their gaining the sanctuary of the rest area, "B" Group were turned out, "lock, stock, and barrel", to support 11 Brigade in the central Apennines, some twenty miles north of Isernia. The Brigade went into the line to relieve elements of 5 Division for a task on the coast. The rôle was one of constant vigilance and active patrolling.

By December 6th, "B" Group H.Q. was established in a village called Forli. The platoons were dispersed between Montenero, Castel di Sangro, and Rionero. The latter towns were blown into a heap of rubble by the enemy, who then placed little notices all over the stones, enquiring kindly:

"How do you like your winter billets, Tommy?"

The whole of the country, some 4000 feet altitude, occupied by the Group was dominated by enemy-held Monte Greco, which was some 3000 feet higher.

Occupation of the lonely platoon positions and O.P.s was a very eerie business. When darkness or one of those strange Apennine mists fell, anything could happen. On December 17th, "anything" did, and Sergeant M. Hunt of 4 Platoon of "B" Group H.M. Company, after telling his mortar-line men that he would rejoin them from the O.P. as it was so misty he could not see, was never seen or heard of again. It was subsequently learnt that he had been captured by a party of the enemy who had suddenly loomed out of the snow.

The discomfort of the men was aggravated when several platoons were unable to secure billets of any description, and had to be accommodated finally in their small canvas bivouacs. It was extremely cold, and a biting wind swept down from the ice-capped peaks. Mules were constantly in use for taking up supplies to the forward sections.

The remainder of the Battalion moved to S. Giuliano, near Campobasso and the rest of the Division. "C" Group occupied another small village near by called Cercipiccolo.

December 25th was celebrated in great style. The Q.M. and his staff had not only scrounged enough real turkeys for the whole Battalion, but had worked wonders transforming a dingy hall into a banquet-room for Battalion H.Q., with proper tables, chairs, and decorations. The Christmas fare was excellent, and included all the traditional ingredients. Truly, "Rocky" Knight and his R.Q.M.S. deserved a special vote of thanks.

The Commanding Officer visited every Mess-room and saw the whole Battalion except "B" Group, who were a very considerable distance away and in action.

"B" Group, standing-to in their battle positions, could meanwhile do nothing except listen to the Huns singing in the distance the beautiful carol "Holy Night", and dream about their celebrations to come, for which the turkeys and other extras had been saved.

Hard on the heels of the Christmas Day "orgies" came an order for "D" Group to move into the line on the right of "B" Group to thicken up the fire of 56 "Recce" Regiment, which had been constantly troubled by enemy fighting patrols. These operated all along the front and constituted a very grave menace, as often skilled mountain troops were employed.

At the end of December, "B" Group hoped to be relieved so that they could have their belated Christmas dinners. One or two platoons were scheduled for early withdrawal, but suddenly the weather took a hand.

On New Year's Eve snow came down over the whole area on a tremendous scale. Sheets were "borrowed" hastily from the Forli inhabitants to provide camouflage for the weapon pits. Drifts from three to twenty feet deep were piled up in the driving wind.

A biting blizzard heralded in 1944.

CHAPTER XII

"WINTER FIGHTING AND CASSINO"

ITALY *(January—April, 1944)*

ON January 1st snow again fell very heavily throughout the whole of the night in the Divisional area. A depth of three feet in the hills was reached, whilst a wind of gale force whipped the loose snow into drifts, in some cases as deep as twenty feet.

No. 6 Platoon "B" Group M.M.G. Company set out from Vandra carrying what rations they could in large packs in an endeavour to relieve No. 5 Platoon. In many cases, this party had to dig their way through six feet of snow and eventually reached Rionero almost exhausted, having taken over ten hours to cover a distance of some five to six miles, and still being only half-way to their destination.

On January 2nd the platoon again set out early, carrying six days' rations on their backs. After digging their way through drifts for many hours, they finally reached 5 Platoon, who then commenced the long hike back to Rionero.

"C" Group, completely snowed up in Cercipiccolo, mobilised all available help for snow clearance, and finally got three carriers into Campobasso for rations. "D" Group H.Q., in Carovilli, spent an arduous day in digging out their transport.

The conditions for some of the outlying platoons under bivouacs were extremely bad indeed. So far no real winter or snow equipment had been issued. The absence of snow-camouflage clothing made movement amongst the forward positions impossible by day. Thus, all rations had to go up by night on mule trains.

"B" Group, with a home-made toboggan loaded with rations, endeavoured to get through to the mortar platoon at Montenero, but were forced back by the deep drifts still existing on the road past Rionero. Captain I. H. Battye himself was marooned at Rionero organising this relief.

On January 3rd, "D" Group moved into action in the Carovilli sector and platoons were deployed in the neighbouring towns of S. Pietro and Pescopennataro. During the following night, 4 Platoon (Mortars) from "D" Group relieved "B" Group's mortar platoon at Montenero with the aid of mules.

On January 4th, small parties of officers and o/r. were able to enjoy three days' well-earned rest at the Divisional Rest Centre in Campobasso, where entertainment and canteens, etc., had been established. A serious tax had been placed on the Battalion by the task of providing officers and o/r. to staff these rest camps, and the constant provision of wireless sets and personnel to man the communication of the road posts. On January 4th, also, it was unhappily learnt that L/Cpl. Harvey and Pte. R. Bailey, of "D" Group, had died as a result of injuries received in a vehicle accident. The latter will be particularly remembered for his daring escape from France in 1940.

Each day brought fresh problems, but the unrelenting background of enemy patrols, blizzards, and the threat of hunger was ever present. Those unprotected from the whirling snowstorms, in particular, knew the cold. There were times when the embrace of the icy winds sapped the vitality almost completely. One just had the desire to fall on the inviting snow and sleep, being but dimly conscious that to do so would mean no earthly reveille. There are many who served at this time who, despite the passing of the years, will never obliterate the memory of the unequal contest with the elements.

The Battalion had none of the equipment, resources, or training of a "Mountain Battalion" which would normally be assigned for operations in this type of terrain. There were no special warm clothing, skis, or camouflage equipment for snow warfare, without which the rigours of an Italian winter cannot be adequately faced, especially for those living in exposed positions.

It might not be inappropriate, therefore, at this point to record our everlasting thanks to the Women's Guild, Mill Hill (under the direction of Mrs. Booth), and to Mrs.

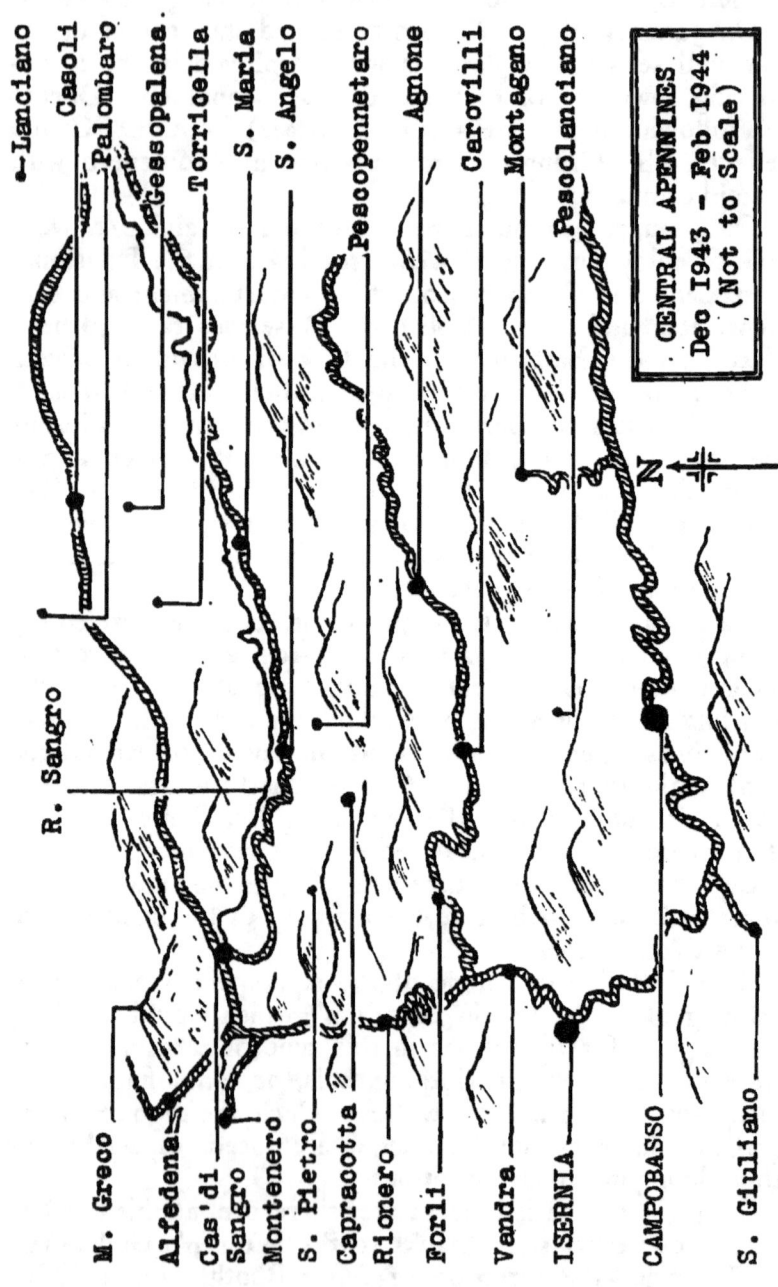

Parker, the wife of the Commanding Officer, by whose wonderful efforts innumerable woollen comforts were sent out and distributed to the Battalion.

By January 7th the ration situation with 6 Platoon, "B" Group, was chronic, and the telephone line was "dead". A relief party of thirty men culled from all parts of "B" Group, staggered through the snow carrying six days' rations split up in "big packs". After many hours they managed to force their way through, and having dumped their rations on the bewildered platoon they returned immediately to Rionero. The whole journey involved a distance of some twelve miles across country in the most appalling conditions.

The serious ration situation at Capracotta and Pescopennataro, where "D" Group was holding out, was finally eased by aircraft dropping supplies.

One of the less serious features of this "snow warfare" was the amount of kit "lost" through navigating avalanches and drifts. The Q.M. regularly got messages of compasses, binoculars, watches, etc., being "mislaid", the inevitable excuse being that they were lost in a snow-drift. This did not deceive the "Q" department, as the following verse from a poem by R.Q.M.S. Headington will show:

> The Q.M. of the Kensingtons, by the Clothing Regs he swore
> That the soldiers of the Kensingtons should flog their kit no more;
> By the Clothing Regs he swore it, vowed, "I'll make the blighters pay";
> Soon messages in triplicate were speeding on their way:
> "For losses due to battle, Sirs, a write-off there may be,
> But boots lost in a snow-drift, why, that cuts no ice with me."

With "D" Group side-stepping to their left, "B" Group less No. 6 Platoon were relieved and went back to Isernia to rest and reorganise. At the same time, just to show how elastic our organisation could be, "C" Group A.A. Company, under Captain A. Oakes, changed themselves into an infantry company of four platoons each with three Bren-gun sections. By January 9th, just as "D" Group were establishing themselves in the "B" Group sector, this "infantry company" moved to Capracotta and, marching the last three to four miles of their journey, relieved a company of the Royal Inniskilling Fusiliers commanded by Lieutenant-Colonel B. L. Bryar, our former 2/i/C.

In mid-January, Major E. P. Shanks, our 2/i/C., left for a staff course in England. He was succeeded by Major J. J. Evans, who handed over his command of "D" Group to Major P. D. H. Marshall who, in turn, had joined the Battalion as 2/i/C. of "C" Group in December. Another one to leave for a staff course at Haifa, after a very brief posting to the Battalion, was popular Captain I. H. Battye, who had been Signals Officer to the Battalion in France and who had commanded "B" Group H.M. Company during the Forli days just reported.

Corporal H. Gabriel produced and devised an excellent concert party in Isernia theatre, called "Kens-a-poppin' ", which had all the gay madcap variety of the film counterpart "Hellz-a-poppin' ". The artistes were mostly raked out of the Q.M.'s store, where so many good things could be found. "Butch" White, L/C. Starr, Pte. Ormes, Sgt. West, Sgt. Powis, Sgt. Clayton, Pte. Hickey (leading lady), and the Ware Brothers formed the nucleus of this band, with Sgt. Rothwell bringing up the rear in a spirited and superb imitation of Harry Champion at his best, even down to the top-hat and "old watch chain".

"C" Group moved eventually to Casoli, and by January 15th No. 3 Platoon (Mortars) and 5 Platoon (M.M.G.) were up to their necks in snow in the Gessopalina area, whilst the other platoons deployed in the Polambaro area, where Lieut. J. S. McKay installed his machine-guns on the balcony of a house. Captain A. W. Pinks got his majority, and took over the duties of Group 2/i/C. The Group subsequently engaged many targets, including the Torricella church tower, which was known to be an enemy "O.P." When the town was later occupied by the Royal West Kent's, the effect of their mortar-fire was seen to have been deadly.

Meanwhile "D" Group were having their own excitement, and No. 4 Platoon used up a considerable amount of bombs in engaging suspected enemy positions.

Convoys grind Tortuously into the Apennines. Typical of the Routes negotiated by the Battalion in many parts of N. Africa, Sicily, and Italy. (See Chapter XIII.)
(Photo by courtesy of Imperial War Museum. Copyright reserved.)

Activity on the Mortar Lines of "B" Group near Ronchi—in the Valley immediately behind our F.D.L.s. (See Chapter XV.)
(Photo by courtesy of Imperial War Museum. Copyright reserved.)

On January 19th, Corporal Colquitt and Pte. Spencer of the same Platoon were wounded when one of the sections got mixed up in a sharp fight between men of the London Irish Rifles and sixty enemy who launched a surprise attack behind our lines at breakfast-time.

The same day, 6 Platoon, "B" Group, was at long last relieved by 7 Platoon, "D" Group, using some twenty mules.

At this time, also, the Commanding Officer of the M.G. Battalion of No. 3 Carpathian Division (Polish Corps) paid our Commanding Officer a visit to study our methods and dispositions in our sector. The Poles were scheduled to relieve the Division early in February. Towards the end of the month, in order to ease communication problems, Montenero was abandoned, which necessitated "D" Group re-allocating its fire-power farther back to thicken that of the infantry. First news was then received that the "Support Battalion" as such was going to be reorganised as an "M.M.G. Battalion" of three companies of M.M.G.s and one company of four platoons of 4·2-in. mortars. The change-over was not to take place, however, until we were relieved of operational commitments.

On January 30th Battalion H.Q. and the remnants of the A.A. Companies moved to Montagano, which was about fifteen miles north-east of Campobasso.

The main subject of discussion at this time was the possibility of the landing at Anzio menacing Rome. This bridgehead now seemed, however, as static as it was dangerous.

One high-light of January on the social side was the leave facilities offered in Campobasso, which stood out as a rosy, gay metropolis of wine, song, and electric light in the mountainous wastes of snow and icy desolation. Many lucky members of the Battalion spent three days (that included travelling time) there. There was a cinema, an ENSA show —Leslie Henson appeared for a few days—and perhaps a dance.

The Royal York, officers' hotel, gained an unparalleled and unprecedented reputation for its parties, in which every unit of the Division was represented. A melodious background of "Lili Marlene" and "Arriva la Banda" was supplied by the Italian orchestra, whose repertoire was perforce expanded to suit all tastes after instruction each night from a horde of officers who insisted on conducting in turn.

On February 1st, "B" Group moved to Lanciano, where they stayed in a disused tobacco factory ready to support the rest of the 11 Brigade there.

On the way, however, a most unfortunate accident occurred which threw a blanket of acute depression over everybody for days to come. A carrier, negotiating the spiral road near Gissi, overturned on the precipitous edge and fell upside-down on marshy ground not far below. Lieutenant H. Trott, who had served with such distinction during the three months he had been with the Battalion, was killed. Pte. Woodard, a very popular old Kensington, was also a fatal casualty, and of the other two members of the crew, Pte. Barrow sustained serious injuries and Pte. Robbins escaped more or less unhurt, though very shaken, by burrowing his way out from under the vehicle.

At this point, two new officers, Lieutenant J. Oldland and Lieutenant J. Wimbury, and 60 o/r. joined the Battalion as sorely needed reinforcements, although most of them were untrained in our weapons.

"D" Group handed over their sector to the Poles with tears of thankfulness, although the relief of one platoon commanded by Lieutenant J. J. Oliver, situated in a cemetery in the area of S. Pietro, was considerably delayed as they were icebound.

On February 4th, "C" Group's A.A. Company was looking forward to abandoning their infantry rôle, but in a matter of hours heavy snowstorms and blizzards sealed off the road to Capracotta.

The next few days everything went haywire. It snowed and snowed until the roads almost creaked under the weight. Freezing winds blew down trees and telephone wires, and piled up drifts as high as thirty feet in some places. The whole of the 78 Division came to an abrupt standstill.

Battalion H.Q. was isolated at Montagano. A pathetic message from "C" Group A.A. Company managed to come through, which said: "Not relieved yet, and now impossible to get out."

"D" Group, concentrating, after their relief by the Poles,

in Campolieto, were separated from the outside world for some days, until Major A. E. B. Foxwell, the Group 2/i/C., coaxed a bull-dozer to forge a path to them which reached the garrison about five o'clock in the morning, having rescued an ENSA party *en route*. What Major Foxwell did with the latter has never been recorded in our official archives.

Messages and operational orders arrived two days after their amendments had been received. Groups and platoons lived an almost hand-to-mouth existence, as the trickle of rations varied according to the mood of the weather.

However, out of the maze of difficulties, orders, and counter-orders, moves and counter-moves, one fact became clear: the Division was going to move very secretly to the Fifth Army front in the Capua area half-way between Naples and Cassino, where the Americans were being held up.

On February 12th, "B" Group moved from Lanciano and reached Pignataro in the new area some five days later, having had to negotiate a long and circuitous route. This involved going back to Vasto, then on to Termoli, Campomarino (where the carriers were left for conveyance on transporters), S. Severo, Casalnuova, Motta, Volturara, and Alife—in all, a distance of some 270 miles. Eventually more roads were cleared of snow, and on February 16th, "D" Group left Campolieto and reached their new area early the next day. "C" Group by this time had already moved from Casoli back to Montecilfone, their former unlucky battle-ground. They continued the journey *via* Lucera, and on February 19th completed their last lap of the journey from Isernia, having negotiated the icy roads and hazards of the weather along practically the same route which "B" Group had been forced to take.

"C" Group A.A. Company left Capracotta in six three-ton lorries, having been relieved at last by the Poles. Unfortunately, when only two miles outside the town, a fresh blizzard blew drifts across the road again. The first three vehicles did manage to get through to Montagano, but the remainder were soon snow-bound and personnel once more were forced to return to Capracotta. By this time, the

Mayor began to suspect that the Kensingtons were going to be permanently domiciled there.

Battalion H.Q. the same evening finally gained the sanctuary of their new area, having had the grim experience of being more or less shut up in Montagano for nearly fourteen days.

So by February 21st, with the A.A. Companies safely installed near Battalion H.Q., all the Kensingtons were properly concentrated out of action for the first time since leaving Falcone in Sicily in September 1943.

Billets were very scarce, and many found themselves living in their bivouacs once again among the olive-groves. Special attention was paid to the transport, which by this time was reaching a deplorable state. Ever since leaving North Africa, every vehicle had more than done its job. The opportunity was also taken, of course, to overhaul all weapons, kit, and their accessories, as well as re-allocating personnel among the Groups.

Before moving up into the line with 11 Brigade on February 23rd, "B" Group managed to squeeze in a couple of excellent concerts for all ranks—organised by the officers only on one night, and sergeants only the next. Both were histrionic "direct hits." It also appears that Lieutenant J. Oldland and Lieutenant Bob Mitchell were a staggering success, as the forelegs and hindlegs of a mule, respectively.

11 Brigade moved up just west of Cassino, where the East Surreys had taken over a slice of the line on the River Rapido. "B" Group, almost submerged by the most appalling rain and mud, was forced to harbour in a cemetery near Mignano, whence the railway line to Cassino had been torn up by the Americans and converted into quite a decent road called "Speedy Express." The sojourn of "B" Group in their cemetery was very brief. Perhaps the sight of the cadaverous Group Clerk (Cpl. R. J. Dodwell) setting up his typewriter on a tombstone, coupled with the macabre menu of the cooks which advertised "Bone Soup", proved too unnerving. Anyway, a new area farther forward was quickly found, which was a mile or so beyond Mignano and just off "Speedy Express".

On the next day, February 24th, 7 Platoon "B" Group

moved their guns up behind Mount Trocchio to assume a counter-penetration rôle. The remainder of the Mortar and M.M.G. Platoons were occupied in surveying the land and digging positions in the East Surrey's area, for subsequent occupation. Very heavy rain continued to knock morale about, and hard standings to keep the vehicles from disappearing in a sea of mud were most difficult to find.

At this point a balloon was sent up by Division H.Q. in the form of a suggestion that all the Groups should come under Brigades entirely for all administration except "A" matters. The Commanding Officer quickly shot that one down after a visit to the G.O.C. and the Brigadiers.

"C" Group moved up on February 26th into the Mignano area, where they stayed until such time as 36 Brigade was used.

By the end of February, "B" Group had positions ready for full deployment in support of the Brigade offensive. Ammunition was ferried forward, for which purpose Captain G. A. Lavers borrowed an American six-wheel-drive truck to get bombs over the muddy tracks. Group H.Q. was moved up beyond Mignano, just off the "Speedy Express". Telephone lines were laid to all platoons and O.P.s and H.Q. by the indomitable Signallers. The central exchange for this lay-out bore the romantic name of "Harpic"!

To celebrate the one day which comes only every fourth year, 7 Platoon, "B" Group, carried out a harassing shoot on a little town on the enemy bank of the River Rapido, called S. Angelo, when movement of Boche transport was heard by our forward listening-posts. February 29th was also noted for the timely arrival of some new transport for the Battalion. Many a truck driver gave a weary sigh of thanksgiving when the news was circulated.

The first two muddy weeks in March passed quickly. Lieutenant C. E. Depinna, with 5 Platoon, "D" Group, went over on the heavily shelled left sector of the S. Angelo front with 56 "Recce" to help guard the left flank of the Division and garrison O.P.s for use subsequently when an offensive started.

"B" Group had now laid twenty miles of cable, to ensure

that their communications were "teed up". At this point Major J. W. Doyle devised a system for dealing with enemy mortars at the instigation of the 1st Battalion East Surreys. Using No. 3 and No. 4 Platoons alternately, positions were occupied by the 4·2-in. mortars at night, generally in the area of a disused railway cutting. As soon as the forward troops reported that they were getting mortared—which happened almost invariably on a heavy scale every night—our mortars retaliated on prearranged areas, each of which had a code name known to the infantry. The point is that these areas were carefully selected as being the most likely to be occupied by the enemy, and our speedy answer to anything they put over proved most effective. Time and time again the Surreys reported that things had quietened down after we had unleashed our own little "hate". The infantry were most enthusiastic and heartened by this success. This was to mark a new era in "counter-mortar" work. A special organisation was set up within the Division, to deal with enemy mortars on the same lines as our long-established "counter-battery" had been doing with their artillery.

Following a visit to the 11 Brigade, the Commander of Royal Artillery at Corps expressed the opinion that the interest in reporting enemy mortars from flash and sound bearings, etc., and the methods employed to deal with them, were by far the best he had noticed on the whole of the Corps front.

Meanwhile "C" Group carried out training, which even included a run in P.T. kit in shivering weather, led by Major Tregoning to the top of the famous Monte Cammino near-by.

"D" Group were also busy, and executed "long carries" around the countryside, pausing occasionally to nip over the River Volturno in assault boats and rafts. These were to be the means of conveying our men over the River Rapido when the big assault on Cassino warranted exploitation on the plain of which Highway 6, the main road running through Cassino, was the right boundary.

The enemy held the "Gustav Line" in great strength. The right flank was nailed down by Cassino Town, the Monastery which dominated everything, and Monte Cairo, which dominated the Monastery. The left flank was nicely secured by the formidable Arunci mountains. Joining these bastions from east to west was the River Rapido, wide and fast-flowing. In addition, the enemy had broken lock-gates and flooded vast areas. The defence position was superb and, indeed, military experts have alluded to it as such over hundreds of years.

The gigantic assault on Cassino by 2 New Zealand Division and 4 Indian Division was disguised under the code name "Bradman". Owing to the reactions of the ground to the fluctuating moods of the weather, the attack was ordered and cancelled with regularity.

However, on March 15th, 1944, the offensive started. At 09.00 hrs., wave after wave of enormous bombers lazily appeared from behind the mountains with wing tips and fuselage flashing silver in the sun. Our troops in Cassino quickly withdrew from the town, and very soon afterwards bombs hurtled down on the Huns who were left. Dark spirals of smoke billowed up which were visible for miles.

For some hours the tremendous crump of bombs echoed around the mountains and shook the ground. Then some six hundred guns fired a barrage and the infantry went in and started to clear the town. Unfortunately, the demolitions prevented the tanks from getting through. Heidrich's parachutists recovered sufficiently to make things very difficult with their machine-gun fire from heavily defended posts. By nightfall, it was obvious that with only part of the town and Monastery Hill, including the Castle, in our hands, exploitation was not possible, and so 11 Brigade were not asked to force the crossing of the River Rapido.

Fierce fighting continued on the 16th, but very little progress was made.

A state of checkmate ensued, and "C" and "D" Groups were held at short notice to move.

Enemy shelling and mortaring, which had been very heavy for twenty-four hours a day for the past month, increased to new violence spasmodically, and 5 and 6 Platoons, "B" Group, suffered casualties as a result on March 17th. As light relief, an enormous railway gun of French origin trundled up on a single track at Mignano, and loosed off an occasional round on the doorstep of Main Division H.Q. The scene rather resembled Charlie Chaplin with his big gun in the opening stages of the film *The Great Dictator*. The result was that the Hun retaliated by sending a few shells into Main Division H.Q., which was not at all popular.

Meanwhile, in the rear areas, the A.A. Companies were more or less disbanded, and formed into what was known as "R" Company to form a pool of trained reinforcements for the Groups. In addition, the G.O.C. asked that two battle patrols and some snipers be drawn from "C" A.A. Company for subsequent use on a Division level. The former were quickly made up from volunteers, and under Lieutenant Wilding and Lieutenant Orchard repaired to "D" Group for training under 38 Brigade. The Oerlikons were handed over to the Division R.A.S.C. Companies.

Enemy patrol activities and counter-attacks in Cassino became more and more offensive in every sense of the word. Lieutenant Depinna, with his private army, over on the extreme left of the Division, had his share of excitement. Raked out from the dusty archives, we come across his description of an episode fraught with excitement which words cannot really impart. This is as follows:

We are using the foremost half-shelled house as an O.P., and we are withdrawing at night into the house behind, where we sleep together with the Assault Section. We have laid "S" mines in front of the O.P. and booby-trapped the approaches with rattling cans for night alarm. According to intelligence reports, German patrols visit Palumbo village regularly at night and early morning.

No offensive action is to be taken without my orders. On no account are we to reveal our presence in the village. Two days later, on March 19th, at 00.05 hrs., the guard upstairs aroused me by touching my shoulder, whispering: "Boche patrol is outside the front door". The orders given to me emphasise that "No offensive action will be taken *except in self-defence*". I creep softly up the stone stairs in stockinged feet (nobody being allowed to wear boots in the house on account of noise). The second "Recce" guard has the safety-pin withdrawn from a grenade which he is suspending through the peephole over the heads of three entirely oblivious Huns, sombre clad, with dark faces, great-coats, and their collars turned up. They are covering the threshold of the front door with Schmeisser automatics. Meanwhile another three of the party work their way round to the rear of the house. One of these can be seen in the subdued glare of his electric torch groping on the ground and fumbling for some ten anxious minutes. It is not possible to see what he does. Thereupon, they all pass noiselessly through the village. An hour later they return, tripping over trip-wires to the accompaniment of a rattle of tin cans and "Hsst" from their evident patrol leader. Finally they assembled near the O.P., call the roll—then pass on their way through the mine-field, while we strain our ears in vain for the inevitable explosions.

Dawn at last. It is necessary to collect observation reports and to examine the antics of our "Boche" visitors. They had passed through the "S" mine-field, carefully immobilising the mine trip-wires by the ingenious insertion of a short twig under the drop lever. A yard of cable has been cut out of our O.P. telephone wire.

The "B" Group mortars were constantly in action every day and night, engaging enemy positions and replying viciously to those of the enemy with speedy and unprecedented results. Major J. W. Doyle was accordingly handed over the whole of the Brigade counter-mortar responsibilities and told to organise all the infantry 3-in. mortars for this purpose as well.

On March 20th, "C" Group started to come into the picture in a big way with the committing of the 6th Bn. Royal West Kents and 5th Bn. Buffs in the Cassino contest. 5 Platoon, under Lieutenant W. H. Scott, moved up in the evening into the station area. Major Tregoning moved his Tac. H.Q. with that of 36 Brigade under the Porchia ridge. 7 Platoon was put at two hours' notice to move.

Thus, more and more Kensingtons were gradually being caught up by the maelstrom of fire and shell in the vortex of Cassino, over which the Monastery presided in majestic and dominating isolation.

On the same day our Commanding Officer left us. Lieutenant-Colonel F. G. Parker had commanded us with immense distinction for four vital years. It would be impossible to describe adequately his personal achievements which went into the making of the Battalion. It may suffice to say that without his characteristic drive, cheerfulness, clear thinking, and leadership we could never have acquitted ourselves as well as we did when the real testing-time in France and in subsequent battles arose.

His final order of the day is printed here, and needs no further comment:

SPECIAL ORDER OF THE DAY

by

Lt.-Col. F. Gordon Parker

A period of four years has now elapsed since I assumed command of this Battalion, and the time has now arrived when I have to leave you and take up another appointment.

To me, personally, it has been an exceedingly happy four years, a period that I shall always look back upon with pride at the privilege of commanding such a magnificent body of Officers, Warrant-Officers, Non-Commissioned Officers, and Men.

During the difficult and anxious times in France, all ranks were ever cheerful and confident and always ready for any call that was made upon them.

At home between 1940 and 1943 by your loyal efforts and hard work the Battalion won the reputation of being one of the finest and best-disciplined units in the Army. Your exemplary behaviour whilst stationed at Ashford, Shorncliffe, Colchester, Southend, and Dorchester won the respect and admiration of the civil authorities and the inhabitants alike.

The sudden change-over in organisation from a Machine Gun to a Support Battalion was accomplished with efficiency and enthusiasm and without fuss.

In Sicily and Italy the 78th Division soon learnt to appreciate your sterling qualities and invaluable assistance rendered to the Infantry.

At the time of the Sangro battle the Divisional Commander told me how very pleased he was with the Battalion and that you had set a fine example and had won the admiration of the whole Division.

Your success throughout has been due in no small way to your pride in your Regiment and its good name—Keep it up, Kensingtons.

You have made my task light by your constant loyal support and devotion to duty, and for that alone I thank you all from the bottom of my heart.

I know you will give the same support to my successor.

Over 80 per cent. of the Battalion are now members of the

Kensington O.C.A., and in wishing you good-bye and good luck it is my earnest hope that we may all meet again at a great re-union after the war.

You may rest assured that I shall follow your fortunes in the coming battles with interest and pride.

God bless you all.

(Signed) F. GORDON PARKER,
Lt.-Colonel.

In the Field.
20th March, 1944.

It was typical of our good fortune that his successor, who arrived the same day, should be none other than Lieutenant-Colonel B. L. Bryar, fresh from his command of the 6th Bn. Royal Inniskilling Fusiliers. As the oldest of Kensingtons in the Battalion, we knew we were in safe hands and returned to the fray with renewed vitality.

By March 23rd the whole of "B" Group had been relieved by "D" Group, with 38 Brigade taking over the commitments of 11 Brigade. "B" Group withdrew to Mignano.

The same evening, 7 Platoon, under Lieutenant J. S. McKay, moved into Cassino station itself to increase the M.M.G. support for the Buffs. Battalion H.Q., with the attendant "C" A.A. Company and "R" Company, moved forward to the Mignano area.

The enemy varied his intense artillery and mortar-fire with hit-and-run raids from small numbers of aircraft, which zoomed out of the blue from behind Monte Cairo at unexpected intervals.

Meanwhile 7 Platoon, "C" Group, in the station was having a fair proportion of sleepless nights. Lieutenant J. S. McKay has written the following laconic description of what twenty-four hours there could mean. The Commanding Officer and Major Tregoning made the hazardous journey forward to visit the two platoons, and can testify to the nerve-racking situation :

ONE DAY IN CASSINO STATION

Just before first light, after an anxious night of continuous peering into the darkness and straining our ears for the next enemy shell to land, we crept outside the protection (more moral than material) of "our house" to attend to the needs of nature. This being done, we watched the battered town of Cassino grow clearer as the morning mist lifted. To our right and rear lay the town, such as it was, a mass of crumbling buildings, with Castle Hill towering above it. In front of us was "Baron's Castle", a strong enemy position, once an impressive building. On our right was the notorious Monastery Hill, with the Monastery itself on top and the Amphitheatre at its foot.

After an anxious half-hour of broad daylight, whilst the four New Zealand tanks in the station appeared very naked—especially the one against the rear of our house—a smoke screen was laid down by the Gunners and slowly the town and vicinity disappeared from view.

After an *ersatz* breakfast, and putting two men on look-out duty, we lay down on the floor and hoped for the best.

Five minutes of this and one of the sentries reported enemy movement on Route 6 about 300 yards ahead. The smoke screen had lifted slightly, and two "Tiger" tanks and about a dozen Boche could be seen moving along the road into the town. We could not engage them with our own M.G.s, as they were too far to the right, but our tanks opened up on them with armour-piercing shot and M.G. fire. The "Tigers" were missed, but some of the Germans were seen to fall.

The rest of the day our area was mortared and shelled continuously, and planes dropped some light anti-personnel "butterfly" bombs about a hundred yards from us, but luckily no casualties except for two shell-shock victims. Pte. Jones had a narrow escape when a direct hit on our "house" knocked yet another hole in the wall and a piece of "dead" shrapnel about six inches in length pierced his trousers and shirt and badly bruised his stomach.

The only other movement seen during the day was a party of stretcher-bearers carrying wounded from the town along Route 6.

After nightfall, M.G.s under Sergeant Daniels took up a position under a pile of rubble about fifty yards from the house, to harass Route 6 and stop enemy movement there. Early in the evening some Gurkhas, who were being withdrawn from their perilous position on "Hangman's Hill", wandered into our position. These brave soldiers were cheered on their way back for a well-earned rest with a tall tot of rum.

Shelling and mortaring increased during the night, and some of our own 25-pounders started to fall short into our area. Most unpleasant! After two direct hits on his position, damaging the M.G.s and badly shaking the occupants, Sgt. Daniels was forced to cease harassing fire and come back to our battered house.

The infantry suffered heavy casualties in the night, a Company

Commander and many personnel being killed or wounded. About three o'clock in the morning, enemy shelling ceased. We then had a message from the infantry warning us that an enemy patrol was in our area. Straining our eyes and ears, we waited further developments. The only sound to be heard was the continual croaking of frogs in the flooded plain of Cassino and the occasional bursting round us as the odd smoke-shell landed, screening the movement of our supply columns, which, owing to the moon, would be visible to the Hun. And so we waited until dawn came and happily no enemy patrol had materialised.

The infantry later reported counting over a thousand enemy mortar bombs and shells landing in our area during that period of twenty-four hours.

After five such days and nights we were withdrawn and the New Zealanders, who took over the commitment, decided that it was not possible to occupy our house.

Postscript: Forty-eight hours after we left, the Germans crossed the river in force, occupied our "house", and knocked out our tank.

"D" Group Mortar Platoons were constantly blazing away on counter-mortar work in the same manner as their predecessors, "B" Group. The latter sent out "Recce" parties on March 25th to S. Michele area, where 11 Brigade were getting ready to take over from a Brigade of the 4 Indian Division.

March 27 was a busy day for all. The whole of "B" Group moved across to this new area. 7 Platoon, with the help of jeeps under Lieutenant V. McLean, had been installed in an uncomfortable position on the lower slopes of Monte Castellone, north-east of the Monastery, the evening before. Main Group H.Q. moved into a leafy grove near S. Michele, whilst both Mortar Platoons took up positions near an old farm-house bastion, dubbed the "Plasterers' Arms" because of the unfailing but unfortunately hostile attention one got at this wayside inn. 6 Platoon, "C" Group, with the help of a carrying-party from the Mortar Company, went forward to support the Royal West Kents, which was again too much in the immediate vicinity of Cassino itself. However, in compensation, 5 and 7 Platoons were withdrawn from the station area, an operation which *mirabilis dictu* was accomplished without incident, with the aid of a carrier-party led by Lieut. Leonard.

At the same time "D" Group had withdrawn completely from the S. Angelo sector and accomplished a gradual infiltrated deployment in the Cairo village area. "Recces" had been carried out with the aid of French guides, of whom, it is rumoured, the Group Commander inquired if "the pen of his Aunt was still in the jolly old garden." The French troops in the area handed over completely with many a heartfelt *merci* to the Irish Brigade.

By March 29th Battalion H.Q. had moved to S. Pietro behind Cervaro, which was the village between the former and S. Vittore. All these little villages, like Cassino itself, were just skeletons, reminiscent of those of the last war when fighting had taken place for years in one locality.

"D" Group's 4 Platoon was in action in the shadow of Monte Cairo, and reported that their arrival coincided with that of two hundred shells from the Boche during the night.

The end of the month was ushered out by a tragedy, when, on the 31st, "B" Group's 7 Platoon suffered casualties as an almost inevitable result of the continual shelling. Corporal Ames and Private Payton were killed and Private Baxter badly wounded. He subsequently died. This rather offset the good luck enjoyed by 6 Platoon, "C" Group, when one of the guns received a direct hit without harm to the personnel.

By this time the mortars of the Battalion were constantly being used for counter-mortar activity. The Division had now instituted, with Artillery representatives, a larger counter-mortar organisation.

One great asset which must be recorded was a marked improvement in the weather, which made living in slit-trenches covered by bivouacs almost reasonable.

The general appreciation of the Battalion as it embarked upon its second gruelling month in the Cassino area is well reflected in the official description from the War Diary, as the first few April days will show:

Battalion H.Q.: The month opens with the Battalion fully committed to the ground N. and N.W. of Cassino, where the fighting has reached a stage of very active patrolling by both sides and heavy artillery and mortar counter-fire. Now, as never before, the 4·2-in. mortars have given an excellent account of their fire-power, and every gully of the ground in front of the Division sector is covered by at least one platoon of 4·2-in. mortars. To maintain the Division in its present sector is a feat in itself, for all supplies must go up by night along tracks barely a few feet in width, and continually harassed by enemy shell-fire. A few jeeps and trailers have been secured by the Groups for conveying bombs to the mortar lines, but supplies to the M.M.G. Platoons sited farther forward in the Infantry "F.D.L.s" must go up on mules all the way from S. Michele, a distance of some 7–8 miles each way, the journey taking practically the whole night to complete.

Unfortunately, the limit of twenty-four rounds per mortar per day, as the maximum which may be fired, still is in force. It is understood that at the moment there is an acute shortage of 4·2 ammunition in this theatre of war, due to a snag in production.

With the assistance of aerial photographs, flash and sound bearing apparatus, etc., all known enemy mortar positions, gun positions, and paths used by the enemy in maintaining forward troops have been plotted and labelled with a code-name, the mention of which is sufficient to bring fire to bear on that area without the constant repetition of data. So numerous have been the mortar shoots today that it is impossible to list them.

April 3rd. Battalion H.Q.: It has now become apparent that Oerlikon A.A. Companies as such in a Sp. Battalion will shortly cease to exist. In view of this, the Commanding Officer held a conference at Battalion H.Q. today finally disbanding "C" A.A. Company, whose rôle will be that of a training company providing reinforcements for the remainder of the Battalion. The remaining Oerlikons are still on charge to this Company, although at the moment twelve have been handed over to the 49 L.A.A. Regiment for deployment in the forward areas.

We would like to say a word about our A.A. Companies, which had finally reached the twilight of their existence. Records do not in any way illustrate their real efforts adequately. Perhaps of all the elements in a Battalion undergoing change after change throughout the weary months, they were the most victimised. The lonely Oerlikon posts, dotted around the countryside with their tiny, pathetic teams, engulfed in a sea of mud, but ever vigilant, were not always appreciated. The men of the A.A. Companies showed unstinting devotion and amazing versatility. They were asked to lead mules over long, hazardous journeys; they acted as infantry, they volunteered for patrolling, they went forward as carrying parties; the companies and platoons were chopped and changed about according to the needs of the situation, almost as regularly as were their vehicles. From the very start in N. Africa they had special and unique difficulties, which were additional to the cross the others had to bear owing to the inadequacy of their equipment. Nevertheless, they stiffened up the A.A. defence of the Division in no uncertain manner, and the Oerlikons were used also as ground weapons firing indirect in some of our major battles to great effect. They did a grand job and were of tremendous value to the Battalion. The men who subsequently joined the other Companies quickly adapted themselves to the new weapons and proved wonderful material. Truly, the Mortar and M.M.G. Companies were lucky to have them as their reinforcements.

The Battalion was next called upon to form a composite company to provide supporting fire for the 1 Guards Brigade and No. 2 Ind. Para. Brigade in the Liri Valley sector, which the Division had just vacated.

This was duly formed on April 4th, and bore the nomenclature of "X" Company. Commanded by Captain G. E. K. Hopper, and with Captain I. D. W. Cramer as 2/i/C., it consisted of 4 Platoon, "B" Group, 4 Platoon, "C" Group, as mortar elements; in addition, 5 Platoon, "C" Group, took over the current rôle of the latter on Pt. 225 to prevent any enemy break-through until April 9th, when this possibility was deemed to be obsolete.

For three weeks the mortars of the Battalion fired incessantly. Every day and every night each Group reported curtly in their twelve-hour situation reports: "Mortars in action as usual."

"D" Group kept referring constantly to the prodigious number of shells that landed in the area of "Sandbag Villa", their Group H.Q. near Cairo village. It would appear that Major Marshall had a team of accountants conscientiously recording the arrival of each missile.

It is true to say that every platoon area and every H.Q. area of every Group was harassed continuously by enemy shell- and mortar-fire. Unless more than a hundred shells or bombs fell in the vicinity during a period of darkness to

Against a Panorama of Mountainous and Desolate Terrain, a Mule Train plods forward through the Snow near Rionero. (See Chapter XII.)
(Photo by courtesy of Imperial War Museum. Copyright reserved.)

Cassino shrouded by Smoke from Enemy Shellfire and our own Screens. Emerging on the Left is Monastery Hill, and Right—Snowcapped M. Cairo. (See Chapter XII.)
(Photo by courtesy of Imperial War Museum. Copyright reserved.)

daylight, then practically no reference was made to it except to send back a "shell-rep." for Counter-battery or Counter-mortar to handle.

The War Diary was enhanced day by day with little dramas, of which, in the interests of brevity, extracts are quoted.

April 5th. "D" Group—00.30 hrs. Enemy patrol approached "D" Company, 1st Bn. Royal Irish Fusiliers. Section of 7 Platoon M.M.G. fired on fixed lines. Enemy withdrew. Blood-stained tablecloth found in area, but no bodies—two belts used. 4 Platoon fired C.M. tasks. . . .

April 6th. "D" Group. Counter-mortar Office completed by 214 Field Company R.E. until ground-floor room of house represents fairly good dug-out. O.P. occupied by 17 Field Regiment and Sergeant Paul of Mortar Company heavily shelled at 11.00 hrs. and had to be evacuated.

April 7th. "D" Group. Dead mules in area now smelling beyond all description. Impossible to bury owing to rocky nature of soil. Urgent demand for quick-lime sent to Main H.Q.

April 9th. "C" Group. 6 Platoon M.M.G.—3000 Rds. Mk. VIIIZ belonging to this platoon were destroyed during a period of heavy shell-fire on the platoon area.

April 10th. "B" Group—20.40 hrs. 5 Platoon M.M.G. reported movement of German tanks in front of platoon positions.

April 11th. "B" Group—09.45 hrs. 6 Platoon M.M.G. report two women passing through their positions—taken to Brigade for interrogation.

Enemy mortars were dubbed by "B" Group in terms of alcoholic drinks, of which "Brandy" was appropriately most in demand. Very often "Brandy" and "Soda" were shot together, although on occasions the Boche had to take the former "neat"! The War Diary continues:

April 11th. "C" Group—16.50 hrs. 3 Platoon mortars report one casualty on mortar line caused by large boulders, loosened by the recent heavy rain, rolling down the hill-side into their position. "D" Group track caved in as a result of recent heavy rain. "X" Company mortars in action.

April 12th. "B" Group—00.10 hrs. Through close liaison of the three Group Counter-mortar Officers, "B" Group Tac. H.Q. were able to shoot "Brandy" with twelve mortars from the Group, one

Platoon "C" Group, and the 3-in. mortars of the Lancashire Fusiliers.

April 13*th.* Battalion H.Q. Night of 12/13th, Commanding Officer I.O. and S.O. visited "D" Group M.M.G. Tac. and "D" Group H.Q. Anxious moments were experienced on the return journey, when the Jeep caught fire in Cairo.

[This happened in full view of the Monastery. The party, with Captain C. E. Cullen dancing in attendance (fire extinguisher in hand—found to be empty), rushed around in a frenzy to put out the conflagration. All ears were cocked simultaneously for the warning "swish" of an enemy shell. A most nerve-wracking experience, which fortunately ended without further incident. Pte. Fullegar, the Commanding Officer's driver, drove away from the spot in no leisurely manner.]

"X" Company. Captain Cullen took over command of the company this evening. Lieutenant Orchard was sent from "S" Company to assist at the Company's Tac. H.Q.

April 14*th*. "B" Group—Night 13th/14th. 7 Platoon M.M.G. relieved 5 Platoon M.M.G. Relief very difficult to carry out, since tracks were now in a very poor state following a day of torrential rainstorms. "C" Group—17.00 hrs. to 19.00 hrs., approximately 110 shells fell in area, cutting the telephone line from 3 Platoon mortars to the Group Exchange. "D" Group—12.00 hrs. Very heavy shelling in area of Group Tac. H.Q. Signal Exchange received a direct hit. No casualties. 18.30, ammunition dump set alight by enemy shelling. Captain May, assisted by Lieutenant Gray and four o/r. from 4 Platoon, attempted to get the fire under control.

The full story of this hazardous undertaking of Captain May and party is given below in the citation which the Divisional Commander directed be recorded on their conduct sheets.

At 18.00 hrs. on the 14th April, 1944, track junction was heavily shelled and mortared by the enemy. At this track junction there were dumps of 3-in. and 4·2-in. mortar H.E. and smoke bombs and numerous other dumps of American 60-mm. and 81-mm. mortar bombs, American smoke grenades, S.A.A. and six boxes of T.N.T., which were later discovered under the S.A.A. This ammunition dump caught fire in several places. When the fire was first seen H.E. bombs were heard exploding, and the smoke bombs were being scattered in all directions.

At 19.00 hrs. Captain May set out to investigate the fire, as it was feared that it might hold up the nightly Brigade Maintenance train. He was unable to get very near to the dump as the bombs and S.A.A. were still exploding. At 20.00 hrs. Captain May tackled the many fires which were still burning and smouldering, by throwing earth on to them and pulling the remaining bombs out of the stacks and hurling them off the road. He was seen doing this by Lieutenant J. R. Gray, who appeared on the scene at approximately 20.15 hrs. with five other ranks, Pte. Firth, E., Pte. Honour, C., Pte. Donelly, C., Pte. Smith, D., and Pte. Hooper, E., all carrying shovels.

As Lieutenant Gray approached, he saw two 4·2-in. mortar bombs explode about 30 yards away from Captain May, who at the time was trying to smother the remnants of a dump of 4·2-in. smoke bombs. The two officers, an N.C.O. who joined the party, and the five o/r. worked hard to extinguish the remaining fires. Their task was a most dangerous one as many bombs were still red-hot, also the road and ammunition boxes were covered with burning phosphorus from the smoke bombs. At 20.50 hrs. the fire was under control and the jeeps and trailers of the Brigade Maintenance train were able to proceed, supervised by Captain May, who remained at the track junction until all the jeeps had passed through.

One of the events which will assuredly be discussed *ad nauseam* through the years to come will be the excitements experienced in the nightly journey to the forward platoons. Almost everybody at one time or another put on his moral armour and sallied forth to do battle with the terrors of the night. The procedure was very much the same for each Group.

As dusk slowly enveloped the countryside and the baleful Monastery was dimmed from view, half a dozen jeeps and trailers on loan from the R.A.S.C. would pull in at the Group "A" Echelon near S. Michele. Bombs, rations, water-cans, mail, bundles of laundry, N.A.A.F.I issue, a mortar base-plate, rum, repaired boots, machine-gun barrels, precious extra tea, sugar, and milk, would be loaded on in neat array, all blatantly labelled for easy identification on arrival. Perhaps some men coming back from hospital or leave would be included, and would take their places in the spare seats beside the drivers. The officer or N.C.O. whose turn it was to be in charge would sit in the leading jeep. The little column would then drive out to the start-point, almost invariably a medley of tracks called "Clapham Junction", where it would take its turn to go forward in the thronging mass of jeeps and trailers which formed the rest of the Brigade Maintenance train.

The A.P.M., Major Roy Pearson, or his representative, would call out: "Kensingtons—righto, off you go", and the curtain was up for an all-night drama. The following account reveals the incidents of such a journey:

The last flicker of natural light behind the sullen Monastery has already been replaced by the flash of exploding shells and bombs. The little jeeps race forward, twisting and turning along the "Inferno" road. Suddenly one jeep bounces in and out of a shell-hole and almost shudders to a standstill. The driver swears and mentally registers the location. That shell-hole had not been there the night before. The driver and companion at his side strain in nervy concentration to catch the first sound of the inevitable shell. A strident whistle passes close enough overhead to be heard above the noise of the engine, and is followed by a "crrrrrump" some hundreds of yards behind. This is followed by another, and another. Instinctively the driver lowers his head and steps on the accelerator. Somebody behind has probably "copped it".

The corner into the "Mad Mile" is turned and the perilous journey continues. A string of red lights curves a graceful arc high above, which slowly melt one by one into the darkened void. The Boche are firing tracer into Cassino. Flares go up over Monastery Hill and Monte Cairo, and seem to hang in the air as if suspended by an invisible wire. They throw out enormous light. The jeep convoy, racing grimly along the cratered road, feels naked. The "stonk" which must assuredly come is awaited.

Suddenly a thousand devils are let loose. Without the slightest warning an inhuman cacophony of sound is unleashed. Whining and sobbing overhead, the "moaning Minnies" from the multi-barrelled *Nebelwerfers* flail the air. It is too late to stop, anyway there are mines on the sides of the road and in the ditches. Almost in unison, angry "crumps"—short staccato "crumps" break out away to the left.

Prayers of thankfulness go up simultaneously from the jeep column. Things always sound so much closer at night.

"Hell-fire Corner", with its ever-growing fence of shattered

"WINTER FIGHTING AND CASSINO"

vehicles, is turned. The road has narrowed, the track junction by the old Italian barracks is now approached. This is a favourite target for the *Kraut* gunners.

Suddenly an enormous screech reverberates through the valley. Instinctively, all heads go down and the jeeps jump forward. A shell lands in the barracks they have just passed.

Again prayers ascend. The whine of a shell or mortar bomb as it screams through the valley is magnified enormously by the echoes from the mountainous confines. Knowledge of that fact makes no difference whatsoever to its paralysing effect.

Grinding up the little track just wide enough to take a jeep, the racing engines blot out almost every other sound. This is no place to halt to sort out a traffic block. A dark mass looms out of the night to our left. It is the "Plasterers' Arms". Stores and rations are unloaded quickly. Conversation, cigarettes and written messages are exchanged with the "Residents". Half an hour later the return journey commences. The trailers this time bear empty water-cans, and the kits of one or two men going back on leave or going "sick".

The Advance Dressing Station and Dannert Wire Corner, with its stench of dead mules, are passed. The hazardous run through Cairo Village is navigated between the pauses in shelling. Flares, tracer bullets, and shell-flashes illuminate the route. Some time between midnight and four o'clock in the morning the jeep column straggles into the "A" Echelon area.

Mule trains went forward regularly through the same dangers to reach the more inaccessible platoons. Their story is the same, except that they had the added discomfort of walking all the way there and back. Controlling mules and hysterical native muleteers during constant shelling demands courage, humour, and initiative of the highest order. Fortunately, Thomas Atkins has it all, and the rations got there.

The "Plasterers' Arms" was accepted universally throughout the Division as a landmark of supreme importance. Its thick walls harboured "B" Group's Tac and Company H.Q. Switchboards and wireless sets were massed in formidable array around the only habitable room. Personnel from every unit wandered in and out on various missions, and the house stood up like a Colossus under the hail of shell- and mortar-fire—perpetual refuge for those fortunate enough to be near it.

Captain G. A. Lavers and Captain D. E. M. Piper exploited the humorous side of their hostelry by inaugurating an "Innkeeper's Diary" and Visitor's Book. Corporal R. J. Dodwell was the first to sign the latter, and amongst the others Captain J. A. Nurse testified to his enthralling visit by adding: "I got simply plastered".

The Diary is a work of art, and amongst the many contributors the following entries are rather typical:

THE DIARY OF TWO INNKEEPERS

by myne hostes—D. E. M. Piper, Esq., and G. A. Lavers, Esq. (with apologies to John Fothergill and "The Spreadeagle", Bill Shakespeare, S. Pepys, Adam Bede, Julius Cæsar, and anyone else you like).

YE PLASTERERS' ARMS, MUCH MORTARING, 1944

April 6th. I arrived at this sumptuous inne—how well appointed —with cold water, two minutes from the Station (Alight here for the Casino) and every moderne inconvenience. A quiet night. The empties were collected. Were visited by Brian the Harpur and Nod the Shepherd (Major J. W. Doyle), with fiery countenance, bushy mustachio, and chest heavings. Heap big war palavar and wompum talk between these twain.

Overheard at dinner:

Ye serfe: "Can I shell you some monkey-nuts, master?"

Ye diner: "Thank you, no, I prefer them mortared."

April 7th. A night of musick. Master Chaston performed upon the Italian spinet and delighted our ears with the "Refrain" from Spitting, and the third movement from "Paying the Rent". We were then entertained by Spit and Cough, the Phlegmish comedians. John the Nurse departed.

21.30 hrs. My Lorde Edwardes arrives.

21.31 hrs. Shell from Teuton arrives.

21.32 hrs. My Lorde Edwardes departs.

23.00 hrs. Hobden the Hydra (Lieut. P. Hobden) appeared and partook of much spirit. Much singynge from ye Common Bar. Atmosphere resemblant of the Wild West in the "Roaring Forties".

The next extracts were inserted by Captain B. J. G. Page, M.C., who chanced upon "The Diary" whilst awaiting the relief of his platoons by the Poles. He was obviously too harassed to try and emulate the "Olde Worlde" style of his predecessors.

"WINTER FIGHTING AND CASSINO"

April 14th. Muchmore was relieved from his post on the rocky crag and the mule train to 5 Platoon ran into Jerry "fixed line", causing considerable alarm and despondency, and the prompt retreat of the "muley wallahs". The muleteer with the rations was last seen heading for the enemy at full tilt, but the "Naafi" (weekly supply of cigarettes and chocolates) was saved—praise be!

April 15th. A brief visit by Honest John (Major J. J. Evans) brought us news of the outside world. D.P. (Captain C. E. Depinna) was with him and didn't say "no" to a gin. Where does Lavers get all this gin? I must look into it.

April 16th—12.20 hrs. Visibility is excellent, which is unfortunate, as I want to visit our latrine, but must wait until night or a mist descends upon us. Early this morning G.L. (Geoffrey Lavers) visited the mortar line to do something about a bomb stuck in the barrel. A loud bang was heard, but I hadn't even started to go through his kit when he walked in, safe and sound.

April 19th. C.Q.M.S. Upchurch came up with the rations, and Corporal Johnson (R.A.S.C.) brought a sandbag full of monkey-nuts, and the floor was soon covered with the shells. Pte. Cooper of 3 Platoon phoned at 03.00 hrs. to say that the mules which had brought him back from the O.P. had sat down at Gimes Corner and refused to move. They had brought the kit down from there themselves, and tied the recumbent mule to a piece of signal cable. I told them to go up before first light and see if it had changed its mind. They did this, but it had gone.

One of the best things that happened during these weeks was the organisation of leave on a proper basis. The Division took over a place called Maiori on the coast south of Naples Bay, where truly the scenery is breath-taking. This little town, former tourist Mecca, was dubbed "Axeminster"; it was entirely devoted to leave parties from the 78 Division and was well organised by Captain R. Ellis, an officer of the Battalion. The Battle-axe sign predominated. The Officers' Club was known as "Hatchetts", and that of the o/r. as the "Golden Chopper". The recipe for rest included bathing, sunshine, magnificent scenery, and good food as the chief ingredients. A seasoning of signorinas (add "vino" to taste) could be mobilised for the palate of the gourmet.

There was also a Division rest camp at Quattraventi, where relaxation could be had for forty-eight hours. Day passes to Naples were also popular, where the sight of real shops for a change evoked a desire to "see Naples and buy".

On April 23rd advance parties from the Polish Corps went forward with the Group Maintenance trains. The Poles were going to take over from us at last.

This relief was unforgettable. The Kensingtons and their Polish counterparts wrestled with all the intricate problems through a medium of broken English, with Italian and French thrown in at random, with surprising results. The guns, stores, rations, water-cans, etc., to be handed over, would be discussed interminably in varying pitches of exasperation. The date, time, and method of relieving "X" Platoon, 1 Kensingtons, by "Y" Platoon of the Polish Support Battalion invoked more talk and resignations than a meeting of Foreign Secretaries.

However, and may it stand to the eternal credit of the United Nations—one determined to get out of Cassino, and the other equally determined to get in there—the relief was effected.

How it was done and all the dramas that attended it were consigned to oblivion in the joy of reaching the rest area near Caiazzo, where peace and rehabilitation were found amidst scenery not unlike that of the English countryside.

By April 28th, whilst the Commanding Officer was conducting a "recce" for positions which the Battalion weapons could reoccupy to support 8 Indian Division in their attack on S. Angelo, the whole of the Battalion was concentrated. By April 30th Miss Fenwick (Y.M.C.A.) had started up a Canteen for all o/r. called "The Clarendon", Shades of Hammersmith Road! The second "Kens-a-poppin'" show was performed under the capable direction of Corporal Gabriel, resulting in another score of pounds for the P.O.W. Fund, and all Groups were "smartening up" and wallowing in a paradise of green fields, undulating hills, and woods; in fact, a Garden of Eden, less apple, serpent, and Eves.

CHAPTER XIII

SUMMER OFFENSIVE

ITALY (*May–July*) 1944

ALTHOUGH the whole of the Battalion was at the disposal of the 8 Indian Division for the "Gustav Line" offensive, only the two Mortar Platoons and two M.M.G. Platoons of "C" Group took up positions in the first few days of May, whence their fire-power could be brought to bear on a strip of ground called the "Liri Appendix". 8 Indian Division then asked for more mortars, and so both platoons from "B" and "D" Groups went forward on May 8th. This "C" Group force, commanded by Major A. W. Pinks, thus consisted of six 4·2-in. Mortar Platoons and two M.M.G. Platoons— enough fire-power to create havoc reminiscent of the aftermath of a Sergeants' Mess party.

Over 3600 bombs were dragged, carried, and "wheeled" on to the mortar lines. The Commanding Officer set up a control post near the Tac. H.Q. of the 5 Mahrattas (M.G. Battalion of the 8 Indian Division) to co-ordinate the fireplan. A little farther back, the acting Q.M.—R.S.M. A. R. Edgecombe—inaugurated a composite "B" Echelon for the maintenance of the "force". Telephone lines were laid, and the whole organisation was set to kill *Krauts* in the best Kensington traditions.

All this time the remainder of the Division was resting. It seemed to be the fate of the Kensingtons to be "pulled out of the line", then told to go back in again just as the stores had been unloaded and the latrines completed.

On May 3rd the departure of Captain E. D. Knight, M.B.E., M.M., to be Q.M. of the New Army Rest Camp directed by our former Commanding Officer, Lieutenant-Colonel F. G. Parker, is recorded. Words cannot describe adequately the depth of our loss.

Beginning as R.S.M., "Rocky" eventually administered

magnificently the needs of the Battalion for close on a decade, as its indomitable and undisputed Quartermaster. The life, character, and activities of our beloved "Rocky" are subject for a separate history. It will suffice to say that, even in the twilight of our memory, our reminiscences will be perpetually enriched by the thought of this Grenadier Guardsman who ruled his stores with a rod of iron and a heart of gold, who initiated us into the ceremonial mysteries arising from the custody of King George's Keys, who perpetuated for ever in our midst the rollicking rhythm of the "Old Grey Mare", who adorned the Regimental pages daily with diatribes and incidents as colourful as the rows of ribbons on his chest, and who subordinated every impulse and interest which might detract from his unflagging devotion to the Regiment. It was a sad day for the Battalion when "Rocky" packed his kit and decided to "get on that truck" to which, it will be remembered one day at Hothfield (Kent), he had so ruthlessly consigned all and sundry who happened at the time to be passing near his sacred office. Those of us who knew this Old Soldier, will never fail to think of him without an accompanying surge of vast and happy memories.

On May 8th the Commanding Officer divulged to all officers the secrets of the gigantic assault on the "Gustav Line", which had hitherto been masked under the code name of "Honker".

At 23.00 hrs., May 11th, the greatest artillery barrage since Alamein heralded the beginning of the attack which became the cynosure of the eyes of the world. Three-quarters of an hour later, 8 Indian Division commenced crossing the river in assault boats. The staccato thunder of a thousand guns continued until 04.00 hrs., May 12th, as part of the prearranged fire-plan, but for days and days to come some guns were firing somewhere for somebody every minute of every hour.

Toiling and sweating through the night, the Battalion fed their voracious mortars and machine-guns, and fired their part of the barrage with precision. Ammunition, which had been laboriously piled up in readiness for days and days beforehand, was now expended in the same number of hours.

Initially, two thousand bombs and a hundred thousand bullets sufficed to engage the areas allocated.

We cull from the War Diary a glimpse of the early stages of the battle, which is as inadequate in describing the Wagnerian dramas of the moment as it is brief :

04.30 hrs., *May 12th*—Battalion H.Q.—News received from "C" Group force that mortar and M.M.G. barrages have gone according to plan. Slight trouble was experienced with mortar base-plates, which in most cases had to be constantly re-sited after firing a few bombs. However, such difficulties were quickly overcome and did not interfere with the programme as laid down. Despite the fact that such a large number of bombs were fired, all platoons report no retaliation from the enemy.

05.00 hrs.—First news of 8 Indian Division attack received. The swift current of the River Gari, and an exceptionally heavy mist throughout the night, made the crossing of the river extremely difficult. Forward Battalions are reported as being down to one boat per Battalion, remainder having been swept away by the very swift current. However, despite these hazards, elements of the Division have now managed to get a foothold on the western bank, and, despite heavy enemy shelling and mortaring, have been able to stay there.

08.00 hrs.—A temporary tank bridge has now been erected allowing considerable armour to cross and deploy to screen foremost troops.

By dusk this evening, assaulting troops, although pinned down in a number of cases by enemy fire, were nevertheless across the river, which had remained an obstacle for the last seven months.

"C" Group force continued their good work by sending over a constant stream of well-directed harassing fire, and on May 14th, with the battle situation improving, orders were received to rejoin 78 Division, now forming up to crash through from the bridge-head.

"Getting out of position" is one of those expressions which sounds as easy as "falling off a chair", but here it necessitated a "long carry" of much heavy mortar equipment for over a thousand yards and the use of a meagre allocation of jeeps for ferrying material back to the main collecting point. The long, arduous task was accomplished just in time for the platoons to reach their respective Groups before joining in the offensive.

"D" Group, concentrating with 38 (Irish) Brigade behind Mount Trocchio area on May 15th, were soon in action across the River Rapido. 6 Platoon had their guns with the Royal Inniskilling Fusiliers, whilst 7 Platoon assisted 2nd Bn. London Irish Rifles. But it was the third Machine-gun Platoon (5 Platoon) which suffered the first casualties, when it was heavily mortared by *Nebelwerfers*. L/Sgt. Hebbard, Corporal Tucker, Privates A. Gray, S. Chapman, and A. Kanharn were killed, and two men wounded.

Both the Mortar Platoons were very busy engaging large numbers of real live targets and scored a direct hit on an S.P. gun which they had engaged at the request of the Inniskillings, who reported it as "a mass of flames". Most unfortunately, one of the O.P. parties was shelled trying to get into position—Pte. L. Gray being killed, and Corporal King and one other man being wounded.

The same day, "B" Group started to deploy on the far side of the river in support of 11 Brigade. 5 Platoon M.M.G. stayed with 5th Bn. Northamptonshire Regiment, and 7 Platoon M.M.G. with 2nd Bn. Lancashire Fusiliers. "C" Group moved up with 36 Brigade again behind our old friend, Monte Trocchio.

On May 16th, with the Irish Brigade as spearhead, the Division launched its first main attack from the bridge-head, preceded by a colossal barrage. All the Platoons of "D" Group were in position well forward to support the Battalions—in fact, 3 Platoon had rather an anxious time because of their proximity to the Hun. The enemy developed a counter-attack from Cassino, which appeared to be on the point of enveloping the mortar position, and Captain C. E. Cullen had to scrape together "odd bodies" to form a local defence platoon in front of the mortar line. L/Cpl. Sharples, accompanied by Pte. Parsons—the Group boot repairer—who had gone "just for the ride", arrived on the scene with the water-cart from "B" Echelon only to find themselves impressed without argument to stop a counter-attack.

By dusk, however, the threat seemed to have disappeared, and although there was a "stand-to" throughout the night nothing actually happened. Early the same morning heavy shelling around the Main H.Q. of "B" Group caused casualties. L/Cpl. W. Worrall was killed and two others were wounded.

The progress on the 17th was still very slow, as enemy resistance was extremely formidable. 36 Brigade, with "C" Group in attendance, was flung into the offensive near Puimerola, where there was room to commit only 5th Bn. Buffs with 5 Platoon (M.M.G.) and 4 Platoon (Mortars) at their disposal.

The shelling throughout the day was intense. The cook's truck of "B" Group 5 Platoon (M.M.G.) was completely destroyed by direct hits. One enormous shell landed three yards from a "C" Group M.M.G. carrier, but fortunately Corporal Outten and the other occupants were well ensconced in a slit-trench and were not touched. "D" Group stalwarts were also forced to spend a generous portion of their time in seeking refuge in their slit-trenches, but nevertheless were always at hand to answer the frequent calls for defensive fire. The day was rounded off by a large-scale enemy air attack one hour before midnight. All the Group areas were subjected to heavy bombing, but once again the Battalion was one of the few units in the Division which did not suffer a single casualty. During the course of the air attack, millions of fireflies took off from the swamps and made countless sorties over some parts of the Division area, switching their rear lights on and off in massed defiance of the "black-out" regulations.

On May 18th, however, the capture of Cassino and the Monastery marked the beginning of solid victory.

36 Brigade took up the main impetus of the Division attack, and by the end of the day, with the constant support of "C" Group platoons all the way, a dramatic advance was triumphantly concluded with the capture of Aquino airfield.

For the next four days the Division more or less marked time near the town of Aquino whilst waiting for the Canadians to loosen up the next line for further exploitation.

The whole of this period had proved a tremendous testing-time for organisation and morale. The movement along "bull-dozed" tracks, to which the whole of the Division was almost virtually confined, was a triumph of planning and opportune judgment. The narrow boundaries in which we had to operate made things very congested and difficult. Smoke canisters were constantly in use to screen our activities from the Boche O.P.s on our right. Above all, the shelling, mortaring, and mines were put down on an enormous scale. Fortunately, the Battalion casualties were absurdly light, and were not in the slightest way commensurate with the risks and the dangers faced during the ubiquitous operations in support of every unit in the Division.

On May 20th, "B" Group reported that one truck of 4 Platoon had received a direct hit from a shell which went through the gear-box but did not explode. This is just one of the many problems which our M.T. staff took in their stride.

On May 21st, R.S.M. A. R. Edgecombe was appointed Lieutenant and Q.M. of the Battalion, and his place was taken by C.S.M. W. Steele.

With 11 Brigade being the next in turn to assume the offensive, "B" Group, on May 23rd, were now in evidence, and assisted the Canadians first of all by firing on ten different targets for them, all grouped under a fire-plan known as "Elephant's Breath". On the other hand, "C" and "D" Groups were trying to get a well-earned rest not far from Piumerola.

Aquino, garrisoned by crack German Paratroopers, still required clearing by May 24th, and "B" Group mortars constantly harassed the northern end of the town as well as successfully fighting out duels with *Nebelwerfers* close by, whose presence was revealed by their tell-tale flash.

However, pressure by our old friends 6 Armoured Division carried the "mailed fist" up to the River Melfa on one flank of the Boche, and Aquino was hastily vacated. This allowed the Northamptonshires and "B" Group to move forward some miles to support the armour.

On May 26th the same Battalion, supported by the whole of "B" Group, advanced to fill the narrow corridor between 8 Indian Division on our right and 6 Armoured Division on our left. One of the platoons of "B" Group found a *Nebelwerfer* battery complete some miles beyond Aquino, of which one weapon was fully loaded and ready for discharge. During the night of May 25th/26th a heavy air attack was developed against parts of the Division area, and the enemy dropped high-explosive, anti-personnel, and "butterfly" bombs in profusion. When they ran out of these missiles, they circled in the darkness and machine-gunned the countryside liberally. We, almost as usual, had no casualties, although a number of "B" Group vehicles were riddled by bullets and shrapnel, and a Heavy-mortar Company vehicle of "C" Group was hit by a "butterfly" bomb.

During the next few days objectives were given to the Division, but the increasing rate of advance by other formations jostling each other between narrow boundaries resulted in our objectives being taken for us.

However, on the capture of Ceprano by the Canadians and Arce being sealed off by 6 Armoured Division on the right flank, 36 Brigade commenced at first light on May 29th a further exploitation along Route 6.

The 36 Brigade advance was hampered all the way by craters in the road, mines, shelling, and counter-attacks. Amidst all the hazards enumerated, it is almost bathos to record that these were nought but repetitive high-lights in the life of every H.Q. and platoon. One is apt to be blinded in the glare of more obvious dangers and to lose sight of the little domestic dramas which stud our memory of the daily routine.

For instance, there were the unfortunate incidents on May 29th, when Pte. Thomas, of "C" Group's 4 Platoon, had his foot crushed by the base-plate of a mortar "bedding-in", and the jeep in which Captain Holford-Strevens was delivering rations overturned in a "blow" on the road, with injuries to the driver.

However, 36 Brigade stormed on towards Frosinone, meeting resistance which necessitated one Battalion attack after another to seize the high ground on either side of Route 6. These attacks were supported once again by "C" Group's mortars, with additional fire coming from the M.M.G.s whenever required. 4 Platoon (Heavy Mortars) and 7 Platoon (M.M.G.) appeared to have been the most prominently used at this period.

On the last day of the month, 36 Brigade, by-passing Ripi (now in the hands of the 2nd Bn. London Irish Rifles), slogged across country towards Castel-Massino beyond Torrice, a few miles from Frosinone. The O.P. party of 4

Platoon, "C" Group, was going forward to join the Royal West Kents when their carrier was shattered by a teller-mine on Route 6. Lieutenant R. Smith, Sergeant G. Axten, M.M., and Pte. Sawyer, although not seriously injured, were all badly burned and had to be evacuated. The formation and dispatch of another O.P. party from the meagre Group resources were accomplished with speed and efficiency.

It is a good opportunity at this point to pay a tribute to the Mortar O.P. officers and their gallant parties. One officer, with anything from four to seven men, would go forward carrying all the heavy paraphernalia of their trade—a wireless set, batteries, rations, etc.—and keep pace with the most forward infantry. They walked miles and miles, sweated up hill and down dale, had almost invariably more than their fair share of danger, coupled with acute discomfort, and yet all the time were relied upon to get back information, engage targets, and support the infantry with well-directed fire whenever the opportunity and need arose. If we just mention by name the prominent O.P. officers at this time, all those wireless operators and men who formed their "parties", and others who at one time or another acted as O.P. officers, are, of course, included in this inadequate tribute.

For "B" Group we had Lieutenant "Bob" Mitchell and Lieutenant "Peter" Hobden. "C" Group employed Lieutenant R. Smith and Lieutenant N. F. Leonard, and "D" Group had an indomitable team in Lieutenant "Dicky" Gray and Lieutenant Harvey Shillidy.

On June 1st the Canadians cleared Frosinone, and "C" Group's 4 Platoon supported the Royal West Kents and the Argyll and Sutherland Highlanders from a mortar position beyond the town. But little firing was done, and the speed of the advance of the formations on both flanks reduced the need for employing the machine-guns in consolidation rôles. Alatri, a large town about ten miles north of Frosinone, was taken by 36 Brigade, and Lieutenant W. H. Scott and the M.M.G. Platoon Commander of the 5th Bn. Buffs were "captured". These two officers had gone forward on a "recce", and on looking behind them from the hill on which they were standing they saw our infantry walking with their rifles at the "high port" and preceded by a mass of tanks all swinging their guns ominously in their direction. Lieutenant W. H. Scott, having been shelled by our own tanks by mistake the night before, was taking no chances, and refuge was sought in a cellar until they and the objective were taken. That afternoon, a stray shell exploded on the dump of mortar bombs being used by 3 Platoon for firing on Alatri. In the ensuing firework display Lieut. Brown and a sergeant were wounded.

On June 3rd, 78 Division had been "squeezed" out of the picture and were told to rest for a while as Corps Reserve. The whole Battalion concentrated in the Frosinone area for a well-deserved pause, in which sleep took top priority.

By this time news had spread throughout the Groups regarding the epic capture of a prisoner by Battalion H.Q. a few days before. Without detracting from this contribution to victory we would point out that, owing to Lieutenant H. Vanderpump (M.T.O.) placing (erroneously, we believe) a "reserved 64" sign somewhat *in front of the forward defended localities* when reconnoitring the next site for Battalion H.Q., the Orderly Room with its attendant administrative tentacles was established on uncharted territory. So one *Kraut,* skulking in the undergrowth, took his chance and stepped smartly forward into captivity.

On June 5th we heard that the Americans, bursting out of the Anzio bubble, had taken Rome. The next day, this wonderful news was put in the shade by an announcement that the Second Front had opened in Normandy. Our spirits and morale soared even higher than ever before. At the same time, Major D. B. Tregoning received a message of congratulations and thanks from Lieutenant-Colonel H. Taylor, M.C., in command of 8th Bn. Argyll and Sutherland Highlanders, for all the fine work the Group had accomplished in supporting this Battalion during the hectic weeks that had passed.

On June 7th, "C" Group officers gave a party to which many officers from the Battalion and 36 Brigade were invited. At this event "Kens-a-poppin'," edition No. 3, was performed, producing yet another score of pounds for our P.O.W. fund.

The following day the Brigade Groups were ordered forward to resume the offensive. We stayed, first of all, at Rignano, to the west of the Tiber, on Route No. 3 some twenty miles north of Rome, of which we had no time to get more than a glimpse as we passed. A more satisfactory tour of the Eternal City came later. "D" Group Mortar Company occupied S. Oreste (Capena), which had a wonderful O.P., being situated on top of M. Sarrate, in which Kesselring had installed his G.H.Q. in long, deep tunnels impervious to air attack. The souvenirs that were obtained from this enemy H.Q. included boxes of brand-new Iron Crosses!

Civita Castellano, Fabrica, and Viterbo were the next big towns on our route cards. We then pushed along minor roads *via* Castiglione until we struck Route 71 near Orvieto, with its high walls and lovely cathedral. All this time we harboured almost every night in a separate place. The weather was reasonably fine, and sleeping under bivouacs attached to trees or trucks presented no real hardship.

Units of the Division deployed in turn to engage the enemy *en route*, with the platoons of the respective Groups in support, but practically no opposition was encountered. The enemy was on the run, and our quick advance made it difficult for him to make a stand.

However, on June 15th, with 11 Brigade and "B" Group in the van of the advance, resistance was found to be a little firmer around a small town called Ficulle. This delayed the advance some hours, during which the mortar platoons had some good shoots.

On the next day the advance continued *via* Faiola, where we were "strafed" by the R.A.F., who could not believe that our fellows had got so far—fortunately without casualties.

During the afternoon the enemy defence crystallised around the town of Montegabbione. The 5th Bn. Northamptonshire Regiment was meeting unexpected resistance from the defenders. Enemy shell- and mortar-fire increased, and "B" Group's 5 Platoon had a machine-gun and dial sight damaged by a mortar bomb. There were no casualties. To assist the attack on the town, 5 Platoon fired some fifteen thousand rounds and 3 Platoon over two hundred bombs on observed targets. An S.P. gun was set on fire, and the "Boche" suffered casualties from this miniature bombardment. During the night the Germans withdrew, and the chase continued at first light on the 17th with "B" Group's platoons firing a considerable amount of ammunition, as they "leap-frogged" forward in support of the hard-worked infantry.

Over the whole area shelling had now increased noticeably, and snipers were much in evidence; in fact, one of these gentlemen nearly hit Pte. B. Slade, who was driving Captain B. J. G. Page, M.C., in a jeep—but a miss is as good as a mile, and no harm was done.

On June 18th the Argyll and Sutherland Highlanders, supported by "C" Group, were sent to outflank Citta S. Pieve. The Mortar Platoons fired on several counter-mortar tasks, and got heavily shelled for their pains, during which 4 Platoon suffered four casualties, one of which was Sergeant Perry, the popular Platoon Sergeant, who sustained shrapnel wounds in the neck. An hour before midnight the Machine-gun Platoons harassed the road from the town along which it was thought the "Boche" might withdraw. This actually happened, and the Buffs occupied it early on the 19th despite severe mortaring. Some enemy dead were found by Captain P. Holdstock in the area of the Group's shoot the previous night.

In the meantime, 11 Brigade column, still supported by "B" Group, had gone through Piegaro, and later the Mortar Platoons of "C" Group and 5 Platoon M.M.G. helped the Buffs and the Royal West Kents to attain further objectives in a manner which solicited from the Brigade Commander a personal message to Major D. G. Tregoning, asking him to tell both Mortar and Machine-gun Platoons how pleased he had been with the support the Group had given.

"B" Group carried out some good observed mortar shoots on parties of the enemy attempting to get away along the main road, and very shortly afterwards Panicale was occupied—a town which had a dominating position overlooking Lake Trasimeno and the undulating country to the west of it. "D" Group, still in reserve, as 38 Brigade had not yet been committed, moved into Tavernelle some five miles behind Panicale.

On the 20th, 11 Brigade, dogged by good luck, and "B" Group moved down the forward slopes from Panicale and reached Sanfatucchio—a little village not far from the shores of the lake. "B" Group concentrated everything—including "B" Echelon—at Macchie near-by, where the Mortar Platoons once again deployed for action.

Meanwhile "C" Group's mortars were embroiled in firing D.F. tasks for the 8th Bn. Argyll and Sutherland Highlanders, punctuated by giving a flanking barrage for the Buffs. Good results were recorded, and the Divisional Commander happened to meet the Group Commander at an O.P., where he expressed his pleasure at the good work all the Kensingtons' mortars were doing. "C" Group's M.M.G. Company area was at one point subjected to heavy shelling from 150-mm. guns, but fortunately again no casualties were caused.

In the evening the Lancashire Fusiliers made repeated attacks on Sanfatucchio, but tremendous resistance in the town precluded a break-through, and only about half of it was occupied. These attacks were supported in full measure by "B" Group, who found some excellent "live" targets to engage.

On June 21st things became a little more hectic. "D" Group came into the picture, as 6 Platoon brought forward their guns to support 2nd Bn. London Irish Rifles in an attack simultaneously with the 2nd Bn. Lancashire Fusiliers upon Sanfatucchio. Both the Mortar Platoons went into action near the brickworks in the Macchie area, and, together with those of "B" Group, were called upon to give close support continuously.

After very heavy fighting, the town was captured and 6th Bn. Royal Inniskilling Fusiliers went through to seize the next group of buildings about a mile beyond, called Puccierelli, which they achieved in the evening. 5 and 7 Platoons of "D" Group were then moved forward to consolidate, and all the guns were sited in houses on the outskirts of the two villages. At night the forward areas came under very heavy shell-fire and the mortars of 3 Platoon, "D"

Group, were moved to an alternative position, having previously engaged an S.P. gun which, needless to say, did not fire again once the bombs had found the target. Throughout the day, "C" Group mortars had fired a thousand bombs on various targets at the request of the Royal Artillery, of all people!

By June 22nd shelling and mortaring had greatly increased, and the number of mines which had now been located made it clear that the Germans were determined to stay. This increased activity made it necessary for "B" Group's Echelon vehicles to be withdrawn to Tavernelle, near Battalion H.Q. "C" Group received orders that, on 36 Brigade being relieved by 28 Brigade of 4 (British) Division, they would hand over to 2nd Bn. Royal Northumberland Fusiliers.

However, the high-light of the day was an episode which will long be discussed, particularly by those in "D" Group.

In the early hours of the morning a strong German counter-attack was put in against our forward positions in Puccierelli, where "D" Group platoons had consolidated. As the enemy appeared to be trying to enter the town from the left, 5 Platoon, who were in some houses on the right of the road, "stood-to" with their guns. The platoon's position then came under heavy fire from enemy mortars, small-arms, and S.P. guns. All weapons of 5 Platoon opened up on enemy infantry who were seen to be advancing along the street, and Sergeant Ganley showed great courage in carrying on firing throughout the action with complete disregard to his own personal safety. The enemy approached very close to the house, and so grenade exchanges took place. One grenade thrown by M.M.G. Company Commander Captain Cullen, recoiled off a window shutter and fell back into the room, slightly wounding one o/r. Meanwhile, more enemy infantry had infiltrated through the corn to 4 Platoon's mortar positions. 4 Platoon took cover and engaged the enemy with small-arms fire. During this action, Pte. Topham was unfortunately killed at close range by a *schmeisser* bullet. The German counter-attack had now lost momentum, and by 10.00 hrs. the enemy had withdrawn to his original position. Throughout the remainder of the day there was heavy mortar- and shell-fire on the Group's positions, with slight casualties to five more o/r. Captain Cullen was himself wounded slightly by shrapnel, but remained at duty.

An extract from the *Union Jack,* one of the Army newspapers, shows how this "D" Group battle was reported from the journalistic viewpoint:

HAIRBREADTH ESCAPES AT CLOSE RANGE

There was a lot of "close fighting". That phrase often occurs in the communiqués lately. Sometimes it means that the bayonet has been used. More often it suggests grenades or small-arms fire from point-blank range—from one side of a street to the other, for instance.

Take the Support Group of a Brigade which I happened to run into recently when for a change they were brewing tea instead of tanks. They were involved in the German counter-attack at Puccierelli, and it was not until the enemy was 150 yards away that the Support Group knew anything about the counter-attack.

Then they learned fast. The counter-attack came in from the west flank, and got in with an S.P. gun from close range. Then the Germans worked round until they reached a thicket only five yards from the house, in which the Support Group had two M.G.s operating from the first floor.

A "Victor McLaglen".

In the words of L/Sgt. E. Mount, of 114 Marlborough Road, Bowes Park, London: "Sgt. Paddy Ganley had done a 'Victor McLaglen' with an M.G." He was assisted by Captain C. E. Cullen, who fed him the belt.

When the fighting became most bitter round the beleaguered house, L/Sgt. Mount did a bit of a "McLaglen" himself—as did everyone else inside it.

At one stage the Support Group was letting go with M.G.s, rifles, pistols, and grenades, and getting heavily sniped in return. Captain Cullen heaved one "Mills memento", but it struck the side of the window and rebounded into the room.

They looked at it with "thoughts too deep for words", but when it went off it caused only a few scratches—"Nothing but self-inflicted wounds", as the O.C. of the Support Group put it.

At one stage two of our men were lying in wait for a couple of Germans who were trying to get away. Before they could reach our men, Pte. Murphy F. rushed out with his tommy-gun and cut them down in front of the astonished eyes of the would-be ambushers.

While L/Sgt. Mount was firing his M.G., it was put out of action by a burst from an M.G.42—but he received only the sort of scratch on the face that you get from a rough shave.

Some idea of the intensity of the fighting can be got from the fact that they fired 3700 bombs in two days, and then transformed themselves into infantrymen when they saw the Germans coming for them out of some corn only 150 yards away.

It may be noted that the first decoration to be awarded to a member of "D" Group (but not the first to be deserved) was an award of the M.M. to Sergeant Ganley for his display of gallantry on this occasion—an honour shared by the machine-gunners of "D" Group who fought with him in that hour.

The next day "C" Group were relieved by their counterparts from the 2nd Bn. Royal Northumberland Fusiliers, and went forward to support 36 Brigade, who were scheduled to take over the 38 Brigade sector just to the left of Route 71.

"D" Group were still having a rather trying time. At 12.30 hrs. the enemy began to shell and mortar the forward machine-gun positions. This was brought on by three Sherman tanks, which pulled into the open. 5 Platoon in particular experienced very heavy shelling for three hours, during which time five direct hits were sustained on their building, wounding five o/r., two of them, Ptes. Murphy and Everson, very seriously. One carrier belonging to this Platoon was also knocked out by a direct hit from a *Nebelwerfer*. After this the rest of the day passed rather quietly, with some slight mortar fire during the evening. The H.M. Company Commander, Captain Hutchings (who had been succeeded by Capt. R. G. Shave as Adjutant), went forward to visit a new area, but his jeep unfortunately hit a shell crater and overturned. Captain Hutchings sustained a broken collarbone, and both the driver and Cpl./Operator were injured. The Group Commander then arranged for Captain Silk to take over the command of the H.M. Company.

On June 24th, 36 and 38 Brigades launched a further attack across the small River Pescia towards a village of the same name, and Ranciano, which constituted another 2000 yards advance. All Mortar Platoons of both "C" and "D"

Groups fired a tremendous amount of ammunition, mingled with harassing fire from the machine-guns to assist the infantry—and by dusk the objectives had been taken and consolidated. Heavy rain which had fallen during the day put "C" Group's 4 Platoon out of action, as they were established on low ground and the base-plates were under water. This broke the magnificent spell of fine weather, which had been enjoyed for the past month, in no uncertain manner, but fortunately it did not last long.

The following day, all Groups reported widespread mortaring and shelling which by this time was, to put it mildly, getting beyond a joke. Major J. H. Doyle handed over the tactical command of "B" Group to Major B. V. C. Harpur, so that he could get in a few days' well-deserved rest.

The H.M. Company H.Q. and both Mortar Platoon areas of "C" Group survived an unpleasant dose of shelling without casualties, although many near misses occurred. One shell, in fact, demolished half the house in which the Company Commander had sited his O.P.

The Mortar Platoons of "D" Group were subjected to the attention of the *Kraut* gunners also, and when two heavy-calibre shells exploded near the mortar line of 3 Platoon, Sergeant Paul was seriously wounded in the back, and considerable damage was done to the platoon equipment.

The 26th of June was monopolised almost entirely by incidents in "C" Group. News was received that Brigadier James, Commanding 36 Infantry Brigade, had been killed by shell-fire. Anxiety about Lieutenant J. S. McKay and Lieutenant A. Shelley, M.C., commanding 7 and 6 M.M.G. Platoons respectively, was evinced when they had failed to return from a "recce". They had set off in a carrier at 09.30 hrs. the previous morning to contact the Argyll and Sutherland Highlanders, and since then had not been seen. However, twenty-four hours later, Major Tregoning got news of their safe return. Apparently, having accidentally overshot the F.D.L.s at La Bandita, an enemy A.P. shell passed right through their carrier. Both officers, and Ptes. Purdom and Bridgeman who completed the party, took cover in a ditch and later in a farmhouse. The area was then shelled very heavily, and the carrier received a couple of direct hits which set it completely aflame. The party was unable to leave the farmhouse at all during the day, owing to enemy M.G. fire, but eventually managed to leave under cover of darkness, returning to the Group "B" Echelon. Lieutenant A. F. D. Shelley was later admitted to a dressing-station suffering from shock.

This good news was rather offset when it was learned that Pte. Eyles of 5 Platoon had been killed by shell splinters in the neck when Pescia had been heavily shelled.

In the evening, "D" Group withdrew to Tavernelle, less 3 Platoon, which remained to support two companies of 2nd Bn. London Irish Rifles in Ranciano. 38 Brigade were by now concentrating in the rear, preparatory to a move completely out of the battle zone. This was the first real intimation that we were going out for a rest, although we knew that Major J. J. Evans had already left with advance parties to organise an area at Tivoli, near Rome.

At dawn on June 27th, 6 Platoon, "C" Group, came under considerable shell-fire. Two shells landed alongside Sergeant Nicholson's section, one of which buried Corporal Powell in his slit-trench. They were all shaken, but luckily unhurt. The mortars and machine-guns fired on many targets during the day, and things were much quieter until 18.00 hrs., when a large shell landed close to the cook-house of "C" Group's 3 Platoon. The platoon was just drawing its well-earned evening meal at the time, and tragedy resulted. Sergeant Holloway and Ptes. Coulson, Graham, and Ravenscroft were killed outright, and Ptes. Cotton, Parker, and Greenwood were wounded—the latter dying later in hospital from the wounds he had received. Pte. Hawthorn had a lucky escape, and he summoned Major Tregoning and Capt. P. Holdstock from the Mortar Coy. H.Q. in the next house; they did what they could for the wounded whilst waiting for the ambulance.

The day was rounded off when "B" Group withdrew platoons supporting 1 East Surreys in the La Villa area, where they had enjoyed much good shooting, and the whole outfit was concentrated behind Badia to support the 2nd Bn. Lancashire Fusiliers. Badia had previously been taken by the Irish Brigade, and the Fusiliers' next objective was the town, a mile beyond, called Flatvecchia. During the night all mortars harassed the objective and "softened" it up for the attack the next day.

At 04.00 hrs. on June 28th, news came from "B" Group that positions had been found for the mortars of 4 Platoon immediately behind the town of Badia, through which access was gained to some high ground for siting the guns of 6 and 7 Platoons. All three platoons moved to these new areas and were in action by 07.00 hrs. The Lancashire Fusiliers soon got as far as Flatvecchia, and as their forward elements reached the line of the main road at Stoppa ridge, increased enemy mortar- and shell-fire reached such a large scale as to imply an enemy counter-attack. 3 Platoon was immediately pushed forward into the valley in front of Badia with their mortars, and 7 Platoon got into position despite heavy shell-fire on the forward edge of the next hill immediately north of the town. By 11.00 hrs. it was ascertained that two German counter-attacks were under way from the north-east and north-west supported by tanks, the apex of the two attacks converging on the lightly held Stoppa ridge. At the repeated request of the Lancashire Fusiliers, the mortars fired on enemy likely forming-up places, and got off over a thousand bombs in record time. At 13.00 hrs. the forward infantry companies reported large parties of Germans digging in about 400 yards away. Mortar-fire was again called for and was corrected by the forward infantry using No. 18 wireless sets. This proved such a success that the constant cries for "repeats" resulted in a shortage of ammunition and some abuse when the demands by the enthusiastic infantry had to be refused temporarily. It is known that quite a few of the enemy were killed by the mortar-fire.

The delighted Commanding Officer of the 2nd Battalion Lancashire Fusiliers insisted on showing Major B. V. C. Harpur the cratered ground on which our bombs had fallen with such accuracy. There was no doubt that this shoot, brilliantly directed by Lieutenant "Bob" Mitchell, had completely disorganised the enemy.

However, further disheartening news trickled in from "C" Group, in whose area, after a fairly quiet morning, the enemy shelling and mortaring increased. At about 14.00

hrs. No. 6 Platoon M.M.G. got rather badly shaken by shells which landed very close to them. 5 Platoon M.M.G., who were right in the area of the mortaring, had one bomb which exploded in the trees and wounded L/C. Cross and Ptes. Hawkesworth and Cash, who were repairing a carrier. L/C. Cross died shortly afterwards in the R.A.P. The house in which 7 Platoon M.M.G. had a gun mounted suffered a direct hit, but apart from a few sheep being killed by the collapsing of the floor, no other casualties were suffered.

The next day the 1st Bn. East Surreys took over the advance on the 11 Brigade sector, with "B" Group's platoons concentrating in Flatvecchia area to give support. 6 Platoon M.M.G. was sent back, however, to Macchie, where the Group "B" Echelon was once more established, for rest and reorganisation. This included the repair of four of their vehicles and a motor-cycle, which had been badly hit in Badia the previous afternoon when the town had been heavily shelled for two hours. Within twenty-four hours, these vehicles were on the road again, which speaks volumes for Lieutenant J. Downes, Sergeant Shaw, and others of the M.T. staff.

On the 36 Brigade front the enemy were withdrawing along Route 71, which had been suspected, owing to M.T. movement being heard the night before. "C" Group stood by to consolidate the gains of the Battalions with 3 Platoon (Mortars) and 6 and 7 Platoons M.M.G. The rest of the Group was withdrawn for a rest, but this was thwarted by enemy aircraft, which, about an hour before midnight, dropped anti-personnel bombs all over the place, and machine-gunned lateral roads and scattered areas lining Route 71.

At this point it is pleasant to note that congratulatory messages were again received by "C" Group for their good work from the Brigadier of 36 Infantry Brigade and Lieutenant-Colonel H. Taylor, M.C., commanding 8th Bn. Argyll and Sutherland Highlanders.

On the last day of the month, 3 and 4 Mortar Platoons, "B" Group, were so well forward in support of 1st Bn. East Surreys that only two companies of this Battalion were in front of them, and small-arms fire, shelling, and mortaring required much avoiding action. Directed by Lieutenant Peter Hobden, 4 Platoon did some good shooting very close to our F.D.L.s, where enemy movement had been seen. The close nature of the country precluded any proper use of the machine-guns, and 5 Platoon, commanded by Lieutenant H. Sandford, was kept as mobile reserve, should an emergency arise, some way back in a farmhouse. During the course of the universal heavy shelling, the roof sustained a direct hit. As fate would have it, some of the platoon happened to be in the top room just at that time, and Corporal H. Chappell and Pte. W. Burt were killed outright, and Ptes. Yellam and Sollinger wounded. An amazing escape was experienced by C.Q.M.S. H. Upchurch, who had entered the room simultaneously with the shell. He was carried some distance by the explosion blast but emerged alive and unhurt.

Over with "C" Group, 6 Platoon M.M.G., when assisting the 8th Bn. Argyll and Sutherland Highlanders, had their Platoon H.Q. area heavily shelled, which succeeded in wounding Pte. Perkins slightly and severely damaging one truck. In the evening the Group concentrated for a rest in the village of Piano, which was close to Castiglione, a large town situated on a promontory overlooking Lake Trasimeno. 11 Brigade commenced to take over the 36 Brigade sector at the same time.

Fine weather with brilliant sunshine had brought back the dust upon the tracks. Parts of these in the more forward areas were often under observation, and although one felt inclined to negotiate these particular bits as fast as possible, to do so would be to advertise one's presence with a cloud of dust, which invariably drew heavy shelling. The alternative, which was more nerve-racking but not so hazardous, was to reduce speed to about 5 m.p.h. and hope for the best.

The opening of July found "C" Group taking over from "B" Group. Thus "C" Group had barely twenty-four hours for their so-called "rest". The relief was completed during the night without undue trouble, and by early morning on July 2nd "B" Group had concentrated complete at Macchie, whilst "C" Group the same day helped 36 Brigade in the pursuit as far as the River Spina, having made very little contact with the Hun.

Bn. H.Q., followed by "D" Group, at this time left Tavérnelle on the twelve-hour run to Tivoli, near Rome.

By July 4th the last section of 6 Platoon, "C" Group, having been relieved after their support of the 6th Bn. Royal West Kents, who had advanced quickly to a few miles south of Cortona, the remainder of the Kensingtons were ready to retrace their steps to Tivoli, where "B" Group had already arrived.

"C" Group concentrated about five miles south of Castiglione, and all officers with twenty o/r. attended a parade where General Sir Oliver Leese, Commanding the Eighth Army, spoke to them for about fifteen minutes and expressed especially his appreciation of the magnificent fighting 78 Division as a whole had performed.

This brought down the curtain on the memorable battles around Lake Trasimeno, of which the words of Eric Linklater in a B.B.C. broadcast may express a true reflection. These were recorded in *The Crusader* of July 8th, 1944, the Eighth Army's Sunday newspaper, and the following extract sums up the battle incidents as :

> An illuminating picture of how closely and stubbornly they had fought in their battles, these men of the 78th Division. All the soldiers in that neighbourhood of cornfields and little woods and rolling hills, on the western shore of Lake Trasimeno, belonged to the 78th, and so great have been the achievement of their Division that I hope they realize, and you also, how much of history they have been making, and how fine a name for themselves, in this land where great names and long tradition are a natural growth.

The high regard in which the Battalion was held by the rest of the Division is characterised in a splendid tribute received by Major J. W. Doyle from Brigadier R. K. Arbuthnott, D.S.O., M.C., commanding 11 Brigade, after coming back to the rest area. The letter reads :

Dear John,

I would be grateful if you would tell all ranks of "B" Support Group how much I—and I know I can also speak for all C.O.s too

—appreciate the excellent work performed by the Group since the Division came over from the Adriatic coast last February.

Your Mortar Platoons did sterling work on the Rapido and Monastery Hill, and I am sure their counter-mortar fire did much to keep down casualties in the Brigade during those two months.

During the advance from the Gustav Line, there have been many calls on the Group, and I know that at times they have been asked to operate for days and nights on end without rest.

There is no doubt that on occasions their fire has had a direct and decisive effect on the course of the battle. In particular, I remember the losses inflicted on the enemy who attempted to re-occupy the ridge opposite the 1st Surreys to the West of Sanfatucchio and the attack by the 2nd Lancashire Fusiliers at Stoppa.

I am glad casualties were light, and this I attribute to good selection of positions by officers and good training on the part of the men.

Again many thanks for your good work,
Yours sincerely,
(Signed) R. K. ARBUTHNOTT.

7th July, 1944.

With "C" Group finally catching up with the remainder of the Battalion, the whole of the Kensingtons were wholly concentrated by July 5th.

For the next few days the real *pièce de résistance* was a visit to Rome. This beautiful city, with its wide, clean streets, its large, modern hotels, its statues and varied architecture, its gems of historical interest such as the Coliseum and St. Peter's, proved a miraculous contrast to the many Italian towns and villages through which we had passed. Our eyes feasted on the shops, the cinemas, the flowers, the parks, the gardens, and the gay dresses of the "chic" Roman ladies—in fact, everything which smacked of the civilisation we had left some fourteen months before.

However, within a week, the face of the Battalion had changed dramatically. The War Establishment Sword of Damocles suspended previously by the operational thread had fallen, so the change-over to the new M.G. Battalion organisation, which had been in the air since early in the year, had at last become a reality.

The Mortar Platoons were withdrawn from Groups and formed into "A" Company, commanded by Major P. D. H. Marshall. "B", "C", and "D" Groups dissolved into "B",

"C", and "D" Companies, each consisting of just the three M.M.G. platoons. These were commanded by Major J. W. Doyle, Major D. B. Tregoning, and Major A. E. B. Foxwell respectively.

Many personnel were unfortunately surplus to the War Establishment now, and these were concentrated into a mythical "R" Company before being dispatched to No. 1 I.R.T.D. In this way we unfortunately lost scores of individuals who had rendered sterling service to the Battalion, and with whom we had great ties of comradeship cemented by the common dangers and duress shared on the field of battle.

Another important event which happened at this time was the handing over of our vehicles, weapons, and equipment complete to the 6th Bn. Cheshire Regiment [the M.G. Battalion attached to the 56 (Black Cat) Division with which we had formerly enjoyed such a long association in England]. The Cheshires' advance party had arrived very shortly after our concentration near Tivoli—just in time, in fact, for their officers to join a poker party in the Battalion H.Q. Mess, where, under the auspices of Captain J. A. German and the Commanding Officer, they were well and truly "fleeced".

On July 13th, the day before our reorganisation became official, a gigantic audience attended "Kens-a-poppin'" production No. 4. This once more proved a first-class show, under the guidance of Corporal Gabriel, and was the last presentation he was to make, as he was one of *les misérables* who had to leave the Battalion.

Captain B. J. G. Page, M.C., at this point got tired of being reorganised, so he left the Battalion to join the Paratroops. The next we heard from him was some months later, when he was wounded in Greece. We were very sorry to see him go, as he was a very old pre-war Kensington, and had served in No. 7 Platoon, B Company, as platoon runner in France. His military career was nearly as distinguished and varied as his unusual arsenal of enemy weapons and bags of "loot".

On July 14th the Battalion, commanded by Major D. B. Tregoning (Lieutenant-Colonel B. L. Bryar had already flown by air to Cairo), entrained at Rome's Prenestina Station and, pausing to view shattered Cassino and the Monastery with very mixed memories, finally reached the tented camp at Taranto before midday on the 16th. This journey took 2½ days in "box cars" of the " 20 *chevaux*/40 *hommes*" type.

On the 17th, having passed the disembarked 56 Division on the road, we selected a big, sturdy ship called *Empire Pride,* which became our quarters for the voyage to come.

At midday on the 18th we sailed out of Taranto harbour, with no regrets.

CHAPTER XIV

EGYPTIAN INTERLUDE

July 22nd–September 16th, 1944

THE Battalion landed at Alexandria in the evening of July 22nd, after an uneventful voyage, although several false air-raid alarms had broken the quiet routine. Once again the atmosphere, smells, sounds, colours, and people of a country new to most of us provided much excitement and interest.

Natives stalked up and down the quays and platforms hawking a comprehensive variety of wares. We were cajoled and beseeched in the most aggressive manner to purchase articles ranging from watches that did anything but tell the time, to bottles of coloured water purporting to be champagne. However, one commodity which required no sales talk was the banana. This almost legendary fruit, a relic of the piping days of peace, was bought in vast quantities.

As dawn broke on July 23rd we reached our destination. This was a canvas city in the middle of nowhere called Qassasin. Thousands of tents were regimented in close array and were encircled completely, as far as the eye could see, by nothing but desert. There were a few wood and stone buildings which subsequently turned out to be the hospital, Officers' and Sergeants' Clubs, and NAAFI canteens and cinemas. The latter had stood the test of time since the close of World War I. The metropolis was cut into segments by good tarmac roads, which we suspected must lead somewhere.

We settled down very quickly. Major J. J. Evans, with his advance party, had everything well organised. For the next ten days we were completely re-equipped. Stores, weapons, and vehicles were drawn from large Ordnance Depots. At the same time, leave parties were sent off to Cairo, Alexandria, and Ismailia. This resulted in a chronic and universal shortage of cash. Leave was an expensive business, because, apart from high prices, the natives had a nasty habit of walking off with your wallet if you did not have it on a chain.

Early in August we got orders to prepare to move to Southern Palestine, but this served only as a breeding-ground for first-class rumours, and our emigration never happened.

On August 11th the Battalion moved *via* the "Sweet Water Canal" road to Beni Yusef, in the shade of the Pyramids. Once again we were in tents, erected by Major D. B. Tregoning's advance party.

Perched precariously on a tiny sand dune near-by was a little wooden hut, where it was rumoured the Commanding Officer slept. This desirable residence was faintly reminiscent of Hitler's hide-out in the "Eagle's Nest" at Berchtesgaden, although the view of the camp was not perhaps so inspiring as that of the Bavarian Alps. The H.Q. and Company Offices were installed in wooden huts which faced each other at the entrance of the camp, and the road separating them was immediately signed up as "Kensington High Street".

A spate of training was inaugurated within range of the phlegmatic Sphinx, whose smile must have been a trifle more "inscrutable" when Major D. B. Tregoning allowed his M.M.G. Platoons on one occasion to fire over the heads of himself and Lieut. W. H. Scott, in order to demonstrate the accuracy and safety of the guns.

About the middle of August he left the Battalion to take up a staff appointment. His departure was viewed with regret on all sides, for "Trigger", as he was irreverently dubbed, had both by the nature of his character and by his intrepid leadership assumed a permanent place in the affection of the Battalion.

Major B. V. C. Harpur was then ear-marked to take over command of "C" Company, which was left temporarily in the care of Captain A. W. Pinks, as the former had "B" Company on his hands when Major J. W. Doyle left earlier in the month to command the advance party of the whole Division back in Italy.

On August 28th a queue of august personages arrived to

have a look at us and our training. General Sir Bernard Paget, C.-in-C., M.E.F., our new Div. Commander, Major-General D. C. Butterworth, who used to command 38 (Welsh) Division when we were at Dorchester, and Brigadier R. K. Arbuthnott, D.S.O., M.C., commanding 11 Infantry Brigade, made a tour of the camp, accompanied by hordes of A.D.C.s and other minions. Apart from Captain R. G. Shave, our Adjutant since May, who complained bitterly about the mass of paper work which seemed to emanate from the gallant G.H.Q., the procession proceeded without incident, and the compliments to which we were accustomed were handed out liberally before the party left.

By this time our vehicles had been leaving for the docks each day, and by the end of the month we were lucky to have a bicycle between us. This did not prevent us from having a gay social life, which rapidly sabotaged our purchasing power.

The social centres of Cairo, such as Mena House, the Continental and Shepheard's Hotels, the Gezira Club, the Alamein Club, not to mention other weird places, provided a constant source of entertainment, punctuated by the odd visit to Groppi's Restaurants for an enormous slab of ice-cream. One of the more select rendezvous was the Club de la Chasse, where on one occasion Captain C. E. Cullen gave a spirited if inebriated rendering of "Come to me, my Melancholy Baby" at the microphone, for the benefit of King Farouk. The last day of August saw the promotion of Sergeant F. F. Kendell to Signal Officer of "A" Company mortars. He had been awarded an immediate commission.

On September 6th the Commanding Officer sent off a congratulatory telegram to the 51 (Highland) Division, when it was learnt that they had captured St. Valéry-en-Caux, in France—scene of their last stand in 1940, when we lost two of our companies when supporting this famous formation.

On September 9th we entrained at El Giza station, and embarked the same day on S.S. *Monarch of Bermuda* at Port Said. Our piastres were changed into B.M.A. currency, and early on the 10th our voyage began.

Held off-shore for twenty-four hours, the Battalion eventually disembarked at Taranto on September 16th.

No mention of our Egyptian tour would be complete without reference to a famous riot which took place there early in August. One evening a mass of "unidentified soldiers" evinced their displeasure by turning Cairo upside-down. Much havoc and damage were sustained by the native hostelries as a result, and an enormous bill was submitted to the authorities for compensation. As a riot it appeared to have put Cassino in the shade and, believe it or not, 78 Division was somehow connected with it. Of course, this allegation was easily refuted when, as the outcome of Courts of Inquiry held in all units, it was established that every man in the Division who had entered the town had quietly spent the entire evening, by some strange coincidence, at the pictures.

CHAPTER XV

INTO BATTLE AGAIN

September–December, 1944

THE Battalion was installed in large olive-groves on the outskirts of Taranto, and a bivouac existence ensued.

For the next ten days the time was devoted to administrative work, coupled with occasional sorties to the respective Brigade areas for tactical exercises. The addition of two extra Mortar Platoons was considered advisable over and above the four platoons authorised on the establishment. The Commanding Officer vanished on mysterious missions and very shortly the extra weapons appeared, together with some reinforcements to man them. The latter included many of the men who had left us at Tivoli prior to the strenuous Cairo campaign!

During our sojourn a most unfortunate accident occurred, when Pte. J. A. Lane, of H.Q. Company, was killed in a motor-cycle crash when completing one of his normal duty runs.

38 Brigade was the first to leave the Divisional area, and "D" Company went off with them on September 24th and 25th. The remainder of the Battalion commenced the 500-mile long journey in convoy to the north of Italy on September 27th. All our carriers were sent off separately and were, in fact, transported most of the way by train. By this time the great Gothic Line had been broken and the Greek Brigade was fighting at Rimini, the eastern gateway to the valley of the Po.

The first staging area was at San Severo, and thereafter the coastal road along the Adriatic was followed until Fano was reached on October 2nd. The journey had been interrupted at several points, as some of the bridges had been washed away by tempestuous rains.

The Battalion had no sooner concentrated at Fano than it was decided that Rimini was not to be our battle-ground.

The Division was destined, instead, to join XIII Corps in the central Apennines. The convoys hastily evacuated the area on October 3rd and 4th, and the companies consequently struggled out of their muddy encampments to join in as far as possible with their respective Brigades.

The first staging area was the romantic little town of Assisi, and appropriately enough a large part of the convoy arrived there on St. Francis's Day. Many were thus able to see the pageantry and festivities which the inhabitants (clad in quaint medieval garb) had organised for the occasion.

On resumption of the journey, progress became more erratic as the roads were transformed into water-ways at several points due to the spasmodic but very heavy rainfall. The time-table of "C" Company and Battalion H.Q. was retarded in particular, but nevertheless the advance *via* Montevarchi and Scarperia was relentlessly carried out. Eventually the convoys spiralled over the vast mountains towards Firenzuola.

By October 12th both "A" Company and Battalion Tactical H.Q. were established in Castel del Rio. This was the town from which 78 Division was debouching to take over the commitments of the 88 U.S. Division. It was frequently shelled by heavy-calibre guns, especially on the open road at the northern end, and many daring runs by vehicles were timed between the explosions.

By this time "D" Company was already in action in support of operations made by 38 Brigade, and a section of mortars under Lieutenant "Bob" Mitchell was assisting a Guards Brigade in the mountains just north-east of Castel del Rio. In addition the mortars of 5 Platoon, "A" Company, were put into position near a village several miles north-west of Castel del Rio called San Appolinare (not long captured by the Americans), and Major J. W. Doyle's "B" Company had Nos. 7 and 8 Platoons with their machine-guns committed in the same muddy and unwholesome area. A section of the latter platoon was moved forward on foot to a cluster of farm buildings called La Morea, from which a good shoot to support an East Surrey's attack on Point 508 could be obtained. The equipment and ammunition for this section was "humped" forward in packs and "Everest" carriers by night, for which purpose every man in the platoon had to play his part.

It must be explained here that Pt. 508 was a massive conical feature of rock which dominated the entire area. The closest outpost to this objective was a shell-shattered village called Gesso, from which a narrow strip of ground, running eastwards, joined up with the feature. This was the only plausible approach for attacks on Pt. 508 and was well covered by the enemy, as well as being strewn with a large variety of mines. Consequently repeated attacks, first by the Americans and subsequently by the British, resulted in there being very heavy casualties and virtually no success.

As this succession of gallant but abortive attempts to capture Pt. 508 demonstrated more and more its importance to the enemy, so the activities of the Division in devising new ways and means of taking it increased. The operations of the Division became more complex as a result, and were based almost entirely on the Appolinare and Gesso areas, which were being gradually taken over from the Americans.

During the initial deployment of the Battalion, a suspicion harboured by Major J. W. Doyle was confirmed quite independently by the Divisional Commander, namely, that the new organisation was not proving as successful as that which had been evolved and tested during the early days of the Italian Campaign, when we operated by Groups with both weapons under unified command. The magnitude of the impending battles lent a sense of urgency in favour of reversion to the former organisation, and this the Commanding Officer immediately adopted. The reorganisation was made to conform as far as possible with the original layout. As all the companies were in action this entailed considerable trouble, but the change-over was made as circumstances permitted, and the internal upheaval was not allowed to disrupt the efficiency of our answer to the calls from outside the Battalion.

Each M.M.G. Company disbanded one platoon, and the personnel and vehicles thus released were "pooled" to provide two extra Mortar Platoons for which, it will be remembered, the weapons were obtained whilst at Taranto.

The Companies were renamed "B", "C", and "D" Groups, being the nomenclature to which the whole Division was thoroughly accustomed. "A" Company was disbanded, and when all the Mortar Platoons had been re-allocated, each Group consisted of two platoons of each weapon, and the platoons in each case were operated in battle by a Captain (with a small staff) who in turn came under the direction of the Group Commander. Many of "A" Company personnel amalgamated with those of H.Q. Company to form H.Q. Group, which became the administrative focal-point for the entire Battalion, as heretofore.

After much juggling and many headaches, the distribution of platoons, which were retained as far as possible in the Groups to which they were formerly allotted, finally emerged as follows:

	M.M.G.	4·2-in. Mtr.
"B" Group (Major J. W. Doyle)	7, 8 Pls.	5, 6 Pls.
"C" Group (Major B. V. C. Harpur)	9, 10 ,,	1, 2 ,,
"D" Group (Major A. E. B. Foxwell)	11, 12 ,,	3, 4 ,,

By the middle of October the demand for the machine-guns and mortars of the Battalion was prodigious. The latter were particularly valuable, owing to the mountainous nature of the terrain. As the innumerable ridges around Gesso and Appolinare were under constant enemy observation and shell-fire, movement by day was confined to the valleys and "dead" ground. The tracks, however, ran along the tops of the ridges, and so all rations, ammunition, etc., had to be brought forward at night when the mules could make use of them unobserved.

At this point, the operations of the Battalion become so complex that it is impossible to do justice to them by describing them collectively. So, hereafter, the activities of each Group will be recorded separately, to cover the period from the middle of October to the end of December, 1944.

B GROUP

Firstly, "B" Group in support of 11 Brigade started to make redispositions on October 16th. 8 Platoon at La Morea was relieved by a section of 11 Platoon, "C" Group, commanded by Lieutenant B. Munsey. This was accomplished just in time for the new section to help repel a German counter-attack, during the course of which Sergeant Bradley managed to get his men away without loss of kit or casualties to Appolinare. 7 Platoon was also withdrawn for a very brief rest. A section of this platoon, together with the whole of 8 Platoon under command of Lieutenant A. Sandford, which had been out of the line for only two days before being reinstalled on the ridge above Appolinare, moved sideways with the help of mules to another ridge on which were perched two well-built farmhouses about 200 yards apart, called La Strada and Vigna. Here they took over from "C" Group and supported an attack by the Royal Irish Fusiliers on Little Spaduro, which was a curving neck of high ground running from the rear of Pt. 508. This shoot by the six Vickers guns lasted all night, despite the appalling rain which flooded the gun positions and soaked everybody to the skin. The same day, the remaining section of 7 Platoon under Lieutenant C. Mole moved to the H.Q. of the East Surreys, overlooking the Ripiano valley, where it carried out many harassing shoots.

On the night of October 23rd, despite a blinding rainstorm, 11 Brigade made a series of successful attacks to gain further high ground. Indirect shoots, which demanded much precision because of safety problems in connection with our own troops, were carried out by both platoons from the positions already described.

By this time the men of 5 Platoon had almost wearied of feeding their voracious mortars, as they had been in constant action near Appolinare for many days. The calls for their fire never seemed to end, and the bomb expenditure was enormous.

On October 24th an inexplicable lull in the operations afforded the opportunity for clothes and equipment to be dried out, and for an attempt to obtain something which approximated to sleep. This did not last long, however, as the order to move was given, so that the platoons could conform to the new infantry gains. Owing to the terrible weather conditions, only mules could carry equipment. The uncertain temperament of these animals, coupled with the shelling of the supply routes, rendered every journey a fantastic nightmare. Lieutenant C. Mole got both his sections concentrated at La Strada and subsequently moved forward to Ripiano. Here Lieutenant A. H. Sandford had already one section of 8 Platoon well installed in a large house, whilst the other section was in position on the high ground above Ripiano (Pt. 298) ready to support further attacks.

During the last week of October the newly formed 6 Platoon brought their mortars into action near San Clemente, where close liaison with the Americans was necessary as they had control of the area in which the mortars happened to be sited. Here the platoon remained under constant enemy shell-fire until October 30th. Then, despite the elements, it was moved over the San Clemente ford to join up with the mortars of 5 Platoon in Ronchi house, where there was more protection from the torrential rains and the continuous shelling.

The supply of the two Mortar Platoons at Ronchi and both the Machine-gun Platoons based on Ripiano presented chronic difficulties. This was mainly due to the uncertainty of the depth of the fast-flowing water at the Clemente ford, coupled with the accurate harassing fire of the enemy on the muddy routes. On occasions, the River Sillaro became so hazardous at the Clemente crossing that mules and vehicles were swept away.

The following account by Sergeant J. Tuvey (5 Platoon) of a mule supply train well illustrates and is typical of the problems and chaos experienced by all the Groups at one time or another, in the matter of administration.

We gathered at the mule point at Appolinare in the afternoon. Captain C. E. Cullen was in charge of our train, which consisted of forty mules, twenty Italian muleteers, five British soldiers, and myself. We loaded the animals with bombs, M.G. ammunition, rations, wireless spare parts, etc., and, most important of all, RUM! There was another mule train also waiting near by, which was to leave before ours. In addition there were several other mule trains at Sassaleone which were to use the track to Ripiano as well, so timing was of the utmost importance.

We started about 16.05 hrs. Great, heavy clouds hung overhead, and any minute we expected our daily downpour. Far in front we could see the other mule trains crawling like ants over the mountains. The going was very hard in the mud, but we were making fairly good progress, and I had high hopes of eating in Ronchi by 19.30 hrs. No one spoke, and the only sounds were the jingling of harness and the squelching of the mud. Then, suddenly, things began to happen. It was just about dark and the rain was starting, when there was a short whistle and a "crrump", then another, then another, and we realised that the first mule train was being well and truly "stonked". Captain Cullen immediately halted the column and we took the opportunity to adjust our gas-capes as the rain was sweeping down in great gusts. The shelling didn't last long and in a few minutes we had started, bending forward against the rain.

Immediately, we began to descend into Ripiano valley, I realised that nothing we had gone through so far was going to compare with what was to come. The mud got thicker and deeper, until in parts it reached up to my thigh. As darkness was now well and truly upon us, black as ink, I couldn't see farther than the mule in front of me. First one mule, then two, got stuck in the mire, and in their frantic efforts to free themselves they threw their loads. One man who got waist-deep in the ooze was pulled out minus his boots, socks, and gaiters! I, at the rear, had only a vague idea what was going on from the shouts and yells. I had previously fallen over the dead bodies of both Germans and Americans at the top of the ridge; what with those and the driving rain now worse than ever, coupled with the terrific job of getting one foot in front of the other, I realised that the Italian muleteers wouldn't stand very much more and would be deserting at any moment.

I decided to go forward and give Captain Cullen a hand. By great luck I soon stumbled into him and he told me that he was going to try to find an alternative route. Many of the mules were now belly deep in the mud, and in the pitch darkness and rain it was impossible to know how many we had lost. As I was floundering around trying to reorganise our column, I was suddenly confronted by a mule train coming the other way. In vain I tried to stop it running into ours. They just merged, and to add to the confusion the original train, which had set out before us, had now collected its scattered forces and was even now up to the rear of our lot. So there were about a hundred mules and men, feet deep in mud, in a horrid tangled mess on a pitch-black night in driving rain. To this was added the fear of further shelling. It was just then, when things looked really grim, that I had my second stroke of luck. I stumbled into Captain Cullen once more, who told me that he had found a new way down the hill to the stream in the valley.

Mules were lying everywhere, their kicking had shot the loads off all over the place, and one mule, I remember, had fallen into a disused slit-trench with only its saddle supporting it on either side of the hole. We started to sort all this mess out, first collecting our own men and leading them on to firmer ground, and then by grabbing any Italian we saw and forcing him to follow. Finally, after what seemed an age, we got under way again, and I still had the RUM!

On reaching the river at the bottom of the hill, we again ran into further trouble. The rope across was still there, but the first step that Captain Cullen took into it covered his thighs. We managed to pull him out and I suggested a good swig of rum. This did the trick, for he made the other side first time. Then after endless trouble we got everyone else across and got to Ripiano without further incident.

There, we started to sort out the mules with the M.G. kit and those with the mortar kit, as Captain Cullen had still to go down the valley to Ronchi with the latter. You can therefore imagine our astonishment when we found that we had six mules over and above our original number! The Italian muleteers had simply decided to follow the main party wherever it was going.

Torrential rain ushered in November. It was also on the first of the month that the enemy began to shell the Ripiano–Ronchi valley by night. This was followed on the 2nd by the shelling of the Mortar Platoons by day as well, when a dozen missiles exploded squarely on the site. Fortunately two of these arrived before the others and gave a timely warning. As a result only one man, Pte. Jarvis of 6 Platoon, was wounded, and he was able to be evacuated quickly.

Thanks to the courageous efforts of those bringing up the mule trains, and of the jeep drivers when the conditions allowed them to operate, fair stocks of ammunition accumulated during the next few days. But for this the increasing demand for mortar and M.G. fire could not have been met to the same extent.

On November 8th the first person from the Group to go on leave to England (Sergeant Graves) had an extremely bad night for his departure, as the route was being heavily shelled. However, after the jeep scheduled to take him had delayed its departure until things subsided, he got away in safety.

On November 9th snow fell for the first time, and the pattern of days that ensued was virtually the same. Each night the battle of administration was renewed. The dangerous Clemente crossing was negotiated by the jeeps quite regularly, and the nightmare journeys of the mule trains continued, which ensured somehow or other that the supplies got through. Daily the machine-guns and mortars harassed the enemy, and daily the enemy returned the compliment. Snow, slush, and mud played their part in turn in making life difficult. Positions were constantly strengthened, and the sight of Corporal R. Marks and L/Cpl. Young with their signal colleagues trying to repair a succession of broken lines in all weathers was not unusual.

The only movement recorded at this time was when the Group Main H.Q. came forward on November 11th to occupy a battered house just off the main road between Sassaleone and Clemente. Here Corporal R. J. Dodwell, the doyen of clerks, optimistically set up office in the back of his truck and prepared to file anything which might be found in his baskets. Also, by this time, Captain C. E. Cullen had been appointed 2/i/C. of the Group, in place of Captain A. W. Pinks, who unfortunately had to be evacuated due to illness.

On the afternoon of November 22nd Ronchi house was heavily shelled and set on fire. Lieutenant Peter Hobden and Lieutenant A. Edwards gave orders immediately for the evacuation of all kit on to the mortar positions. Ammunition and petrol belonging to the tanks near by started to burn and explode. All night the task of removing the stores continued feverishly, and by the morning not only had this been done, but the fires had been extinguished. The only casualty was Pte. Jones, of "D" Group, who was wounded, and this is nothing short of miraculous when one considers that the area was constantly shelled whilst everybody had been moving backwards and forwards in the open.

Additional dug-outs were made after this on the mortar positions, in order to provide accommodation for the homeless crews, and a Group signal exchange was set up which was dubbed "Embassy". The other Group exchange at Ripiano was called "Windmill", which is most appropriate when one recalls that the theatre of that name in London was the one that "never closed".

However, on one occasion, on November 25th, "Windmill" exchange was in fact temporarily out of order, when some very accurate shelling hit the house. One shell entered a room where a R.A.P. was established and claimed a score of victims, amongst whom, fortunately, there were no Kensingtons. All the lines were broken, and L/Cpl. Young with Pte. Beasley and others had a nerve-racking time in effecting the repairs.

Towards the end of the month Captain L. W. Matthews arrived at the Group, and was sent forward by Major Doyle to take charge of the mortars and also co-ordinate those of the infantry.

The whole of December was spent in very much the same way. If anything the enemy harassing fire increased; suitable retaliation was difficult, as the shortage of bombs throughout the Battalion made rationing a necessity. Being wise in the ways of self-preservation, and having an intimate knowledge of the habits of the enemy in regard to shelling, it is satisfying to record that there was an absence of casualties. Nevertheless chance played its part, and illustrative of the good luck enjoyed by the men of the Battalion in general is an episode which occurred on the 16th of the month. It happened to be fine that day, so the men of "B" Group emerged in the open to do some belated washing of clothes on the mortar and machine-gun lines. This was done quite happily and without incident. Three days later, when precisely the same conditions reigned, a very large shell burst on 6 Platoon's position. This knocked out two mortars and set fifty bombs on fire. But there were no casualties, as everybody was under cover. Had this shell arrived at the same time three days earlier, when everyone was out and about attending to their cleanliness, tragedy must have resulted. As a happy conclusion, it must be added that the burning bombs were quickly dealt with, and again without mishap.

December, with its daily repetition of such incidents, gradually drew to a close. Christmas Day was not celebrated in traditional fashion, as the platoons were to have their festivities at a later date when they could be safely withdrawn from the line. It was marked, however, both by a cessation of hostilities on both sides, which produced an eerie silence among the snow-clad mountains, and by the distribution of pork between the Machine-gun Platoons as the result of the timely discovery of an unsuspecting pig.

On New Year's Eve enemy activity flared up, particularly in the sector to the right of the Group, but, like the Old Year, it had petered out by midnight.

"C" GROUP

The story of "C" Group during the same period will now be told.

On October 15th the Group started to deploy in order to support attacks by 36 Brigade on Pt. 508. Being the last of the Groups to be committed on this occasion, it had enjoyed several days' respite in a pine-girdled encampment south of Firenzuola which was originally built by the enemy on the old Gothic Line. However, when the order to move arrived, things happened quickly, and by October 16th the whole Group was in action.

10 Platoon, under Lieutenant W. H. Scott, took up an indirect fire position with their machine-guns in the lee of the solid farmhouse at La Strada. Lieutenant J. S. McKay had the guns of 9 Platoon installed near Vignia house to cover a valley on the left flank of the Argyll and Sutherland Highlanders, who had relieved the American troops at Gesso. A section of 11 Platoon, under Lieutenant Basil Munsey, was also in action in the exposed position at La Morea, as already related. As the Mortar Platoons allocated to the Group from "A" Company due to the reorganisation of the Battalion were already sited conveniently in the Appolinare area, they did not have to move, and the Group Tactical H.Q. was placed on the Brigadier's doorstep in the village itself.

On the night October 15th/16th, an O.P. party for the mortars had to be got forward to link up with the Argylls at Gesso. Captain C. E. Cullen readily volunteered to take charge, and thus solved the problem of finding an O.P. Officer which, because of the shortage of officers and the strain imposed on those who were left as a result of the non-stop activity of the past few days, was extremely acute.

After many anxious moments when Major B. V. C. Harpur, who was acting as guide, had led the party astray in the mist, Gesso was safely reached about midnight, although further delays occurred due to some heavy shelling and the somewhat perilous negotiation of a tiny track which ran through a large mine-field. Because of the mist and rain which subsequently set in, this party had to resign itself to firing only a few ranging rounds and getting thoroughly soaked and shelled during the next few days.

On the night of October 18th, 10 Platoon carried out a big harassing shoot on Pt. 508, assisted by the section of 11 Platoon at La Morea, and the feature was captured at last, together with the ridge to the right of it. During this operation the Mortar Platoons plastered the enemy's line of withdrawal.

The section at La Morea was now no longer required, and so the opportunity was taken on the 20th to send it back to join the other section at Group "A" Echelon near Pezzolo. 11 Platoon was then sorrowfully disbanded in accordance with the reorganisation.

At this point Captain R. May left his duties as instructor at the Training Centre at Benevento, near Naples, and joined the Group for a few days to brush up his knowledge in the hard school of experience. Before he could fill his pipe he found himself uncomfortably ensconced on the top of Pt. 508, and directing the fire of the Mortar Platoons. He was relieved in every sense of the word when Captain J. A. Nurse took over this unhealthy post a few days later.

By the 21st the Argylls had swept across the narrow neck of land (later known as the "Causeway") connecting Pt. 508 with the next high feature, called Monte Acqua Salata.

On the same day a catastrophe befell 10 Platoon, which came as a great shock to all the Battalion. Some shells from our own artillery fell short in their harbouring area on the high hillocks north of Appolinare, generally known as the "Twin Tits". As a result, Pte. Newman and Pte. Owen were wounded, fortunately not fatally. However, Corporal J. D. Cox also got hit, and died at an Advanced Dressing Station. The tragedy was heightened by the fact that his father, who was a Sergeant in a Mortar Platoon, had paid a chance visit to have a chat just as the shelling began. Thus, not only did he witness the whole affair, but he helped to evacuate his son, who died in his arms an hour later. Words cannot express the sorrow which this awful incident provoked.

The close of this lamentable day saw 9 Platoon struggling into position on Pt. 374 with the help of mules, in support of the infantry in the sector to the right of Pt. 508.

Not least of our memories at this time was the spectacle of the enormous casualties in and around the shattered village of Gesso. There seemed to be a dead body in every slit-trench, and on the ground there lay a profusion of dismembered corpses which bore witness to the presence of the tiny but dread *"Schu"* mines and the spate of heavy-calibre shell- and mortar-fire. Even the most hardened veteran felt sick at the sight of this carnage, which testified so irrefutably to the futility of war.

During the next few days the rains became more insistent. Mules replaced vehicles entirely in the forward areas for the carrying of stores. In handling the administration of the Group at this stage, Captain G. A. Lavers, assisted by C.S.M. F. Kluth and Sergeant Jones, nearly had apoplexy. However, hard work and the genius for improvisation will not be denied, and the supplies of food and ammunition got through. The one thing delivered regularly was rain, so there was no difficulty in maintaining that "100 per cent. reserve of water" so fondly advocated by the administrative moguls in the rear areas.

On the night October 23rd/24th the Group supported the attack of the Royal West Kents on Monte Verro, which was the next high feature beyond Acqua Salata. This was successful, but it was the last movement by any unit in the Division for some months which helped to bring us nearer to Germany.

No. 1 Platoon found a position for their mortars to support this attack in the ravines at the base of Pt. 508. In the absence of Lieutenant D. Blizard, who had been carrying out the dangerous duties of O.P. Officer with his operators in the van of practically every attack on Pt. 508, and who was, in fact, still away with the Royal West Kents in the same sleepless and hazardous rôle, the activities of 1 Platoon were excellently directed by Sergeant C. E. Bland, for which he was awarded the American Bronze Star many months later.

After carrying out difficult harassing shoots from the area of the "Twin Tits", 10 Platoon was sent over the treacherous "Causeway" to help consolidate the gains of the 6 R.W.K. However, no suitable position to occupy could be found, and as the weather became so appalling, the platoon was withdrawn. Nevertheless, this platoon had more than done its share in supporting the infantry by its series of shoots during the previous nights. These were carried out from behind a hump on the ridge, ominously near the Gesso cemetery, which offered little protection either from the rain or from the shell-fire. Lieut. W. H. Scott spent sleepless nights floundering through the mud and mine-fields trying to find alternative positions. He kept his gallant men in great heart, and discharged his duties so efficiently and courageously, when everything mitigated against it, that he was awarded an immediate M.C.

Tempestuous rains, which transformed the countryside into one vast mud-patch, now became our enemy. The "Causeway" was just a ribbon of clawing mire some 2–3 feet deep. 1 Platoon found their mortars being covered by an avalanche of slime, from which they just managed to save their equipment after hours of frantic work.

By the end of October, to make matters worse, the enemy had inaugurated a system of harassing fire. From Carre House and "Dead Cow Gulch" at the far end of the "Causeway" right back to Castel del Rio, shell-fire mixed with "airbursts" was encountered. As a result, Pte. Cockerill and Pte. Benson were wounded and evacuated from Acqua Salata, where the Group had loaned a section to man the machine-guns of the infantry. Chiefly because of the terrible mud, it took some eight to ten hours for casualties to be brought back to Appolinare, a distance of only two miles. It was, indeed, a disturbing sight to see stretcher-bearers, who were relieved in turn by other parties every two or three hundred yards, staggering slowly through the mud with their precious human burdens.

The men leading the nightly mule trains to the platoons, who included Corporal Kershaw, Corporal Garrad, and Ptes. Davy, Dickson, English, Measures, amongst others, showed consistent gallantry in getting their teams to their destinations despite the shelling, mine-fields, and mud. Largely because of the indomitable spirit of such men as these, the Group, on at least two occasions, was the only unit in the Brigade which managed to get supplies through to the platoons in the forward areas.

The task of Lieutenant J. S. McKay with 9 Platoon on Pt. 374 was eased by the fact that they were under cover in a house which was also shared by men of the 56 "Recce" Regiment. There he was joined by Captain D. E. M. Piper, as Mortar O.P. Officer, who controlled the fire of a section of 1 Platoon which was installed near by at Casa Gualdo under Sergeant Coles and Sergeant Furzeland. Captain Piper showed remarkable efficiency in spotting and engaging odd parties of the "Boche" who were unwise enough to reveal their presence on the Penzola ridge.

The first few days of November brought no change either in the weather or in the rôle of the Group. However, with regard to the latter, several moves became imminent when it was learnt that 36 Brigade was to take over from the Irish Brigade about the middle of the month. This meant that the Group would have to be deployed for a while on a two-brigade frontage, as the process of changing over from one area to another was necessarily slow.

From November 11th onwards the platoons and sections, with their ammunition and equipment, were transferred by stages from one position to another, an operation which involved the use of hundreds of mules and the greatest skill in planning and administration. Finally, the outcome was notably successful, and all the combatants of the Group had good positions for their weapons, coupled with a house near by in every case, which is a feat in itself when one remembers that a roof over the head at this time was a priceless thing, and every unit in the Division was competing furiously for the very few buildings that were left.

By the end of the month, 1 Platoon had their mortars excellently sited on the side of a ridge at Casa Salara, covering the Piano Nuova valley. No. 2 Platoon had a section with a reserve mortar behind Pt. 508, and the personnel of the remaining section alternated in manning the position with the forward one from a house, some distance behind, at La Morea. Under Sergeant Axten and Sergeant Isaakson, the site behind Pt. 508 was gradually improved by the addition of proper sandbagged dug-outs, although the base-plate positions themselves were difficult to maintain because of the mud. No. 10 Platoon had their guns trained to cover Comaggio, and valleys to the west of it, from an excellent position hewn out of rock at Pt. 401, which was in the shadow of Pt. 508.

No. 9 Platoon had a section of guns on an exposed position on Pt. 387, which alternated with the other section based on "Peterhouse". This was a nice, secluded farmhouse by a little stream down in the valley behind.

Sergeant Peacock and L/Cpl. Bailey, together with the Group H.Q. and indomitable platoon wireless operators, transformed the communications into a well-knit entity. A control exchange dubbed "Myra" was set up in a little house at Pt. 248, and another at Casone house, where the forward infantry Battalion H.Q. was situated. Lines radiated in every direction over vast distances, and required considerable maintenance. For this purpose Ptes. Ambrose and Hawthorn withdrew into the privacy of a house off the beaten track at Pt. 408 (behind the Gesso ridge), and were lost to the sight of mankind for weeks on end. They had a special mule to deliver rations to them, and so gallantly and conscientiously did they discharge their duties, despite the constant harassing fire on the Gesso ridge, that not once did the exchanges have to report "lines dead".

Although these changes were the main preoccupations, there were many other incidents which were woven into the pattern of the daily routine. On November 15th and 23rd further casualties occurred at Main Group H.Q. near Pezzolo, where firstly Ptes. Purdom and Downer, and later Pte. Corderoy, had the ill-luck to be wounded as the result of shell-fire.

On November 18th the section behind Pt. 508 was heavily shelled in particular, but fortunately the only damage was that incurred by the reserve mortar and base-plate.

A few days later both this section and the machine-guns on Pt. 401 fired a tremendous amount at the repeated and urgent request of the infantry, who sustained fierce enemy attacks on November 22nd and 25th. No ground was given, and the infantry Battalion Commanders involved congratulated the Group on their prompt and accurate fire which did so much to help in the dispersal of enemy concentrations.

On November 23rd the Brigadier ordered that the entire responsibility for the counter-mortar work within 36 Brigade should devolve upon the Group. This meant that the existing organisation set up for this purpose by the Royal Artillery came under our orders. To the vast resources which this Counter-mortar Organisation had behind them, was added the fire-power of the infantry 3-in. mortars, apart from the mortars of the Group itself. This extra responsibility was regarded as a great compliment to the efficiency of the men of the Group, especially when one remembers that it was previously the task of the Royal Artillery and that the Brigadier who made this decision was himself a "gunner". The rationing of mortar bombs was proving most irksome, in view of the constant demands for support by the infantry. The problem was partially solved by organising "scrounging" parties, who retrieved the odd bomb from the numerous mule tracks where it had been discarded by an irate mule in some nightmare journey of the past. Many were discovered and reconditioned. In this work Pte. King was particularly successful. It was not unusual to see him cheerfully returning with a bomb under each arm and dragging an unhappy mule behind him festooned with cases of the same deadly cargo.

On November 29th we were sorry to lose Lieutenant R. C. F. Perry to "D" Group. He had joined the group a week previously with a "distinguished" report obtained on a mortar course at the Army Training Centre, Benevento. He had kept Lieutenant W. H. Scott company as Mortar O.P. Officer on Pt. 401. However, we were equally glad to have Lieutenant W. Duff, who rejoined us at the same time to replace him.

Early in December the officer strength was increased by the arrival of Lieutenant Wilson and Lieutenant Ball, who were followed later by Lieutenant "Smudger" Smith, who was transferred from "D" Group. These officers had joined the Battalion from a disbanded A.A. Unit of the Division, and although they had only brief instruction in mortar work, they quickly showed an appreciation of the Battalion spirit in general, and a capacity for hard work with the Mortar Platoons in particular.

The main task of the Group in December was the support of the Brigade attack on Commagio and Sconcola ridge. This involved much preparation, not least of which was the organising of effective counter-mortar measures because the enemy mortars were not only numerous but extremely active. On December 13th the attack went in, with a tremendous barrage to support it. All the Group weapons without exception were in action, and their fire became increasingly important as the hours dragged on and covering fire for our infantry was needed to help their withdrawal. The attack was unsuccessful, chiefly because of the appalling rain which, starting just before zero hour, made movement almost impossible. It is gratifying to record, however, that for the first two hours, which was one hour longer than the assault was timed to take, there was no mortar-fire from the enemy. This was doubtless due largely to the thoroughness of the Group's counter-mortar arrangements, whereby the likely enemy mortar areas were soaked with fire on a round-the-clock schedule. At a conference afterwards the Brigadier expressed great appreciation of this effort.

After this, preparations were put in hand for the Christmas festivities. The administration of the Group was now chiefly in the capable hands of Captain C. G. Stuttard. He had taken over earlier in the month from Captain G. A. Lavers, who was packed off ostensibly on a course but actually to get a truly well-earned rest. Captain C. G. Stuttard, however, revelled in the difficulty and complexity of his duties, which he discharged with rare energy.

On December 21st we learnt that 36 Brigade was being withdrawn from the "front" so that it would be free to enjoy Christmas in comfort. The Group, much to its chagrin, was not included in this, however, and so became resigned to being permanent tenants of their fortress position.

Just before Christmas it became extremely cold. Snow started to fall again. The water in the machine-gun casings froze up. Tracks were covered with ice, and mules slipped so badly on the treacherous surface that on occasions the maintenance trains were abandoned and food reserves were opened.

Each platoon made the best of their lot on Christmas Day. There was no need to dream "of a White Christmas" because it was a reality. No. 1 Platoon supplemented their rations by the addition of a pig which, we are told, met a gallant death after leading his pursuers a merry dance practically into enemy territory. There was much feasting also at Pt. 401 and "Peterhouse", where No. 10 and No. 9 Platoons respectively testified to the goodly fare served by the platoon cooks. At La Morea No. 2 Platoon even had a dance, to the strains of Pte. Stewart's accordion. Somehow or other the Italian family whose farm they occupied was kind enough to furnish several daughters of a suitable age for the occasion. This in a wilderness of men was regarded as nothing short of a miracle.

The last few days of December drew uneventfully to a close, but not before another tragedy occurred. On the 28th, a Brigade from 8 Indian Division came to take over the positions in the Pt. 387 area which included our M.G. post. These troops of the Royal Fusiliers, unused to the ground and being new to the area, exposed themselves, and the enemy shelled and mortared the ridge. Pte. A. Powell was killed in his trench by a direct hit. This was all the more unfortunate in view of the fact that, ten minutes later, the machine-gun position was relieved.

"D" GROUP

The story of "D" Group has been contributed by Major A. E. B. Foxwell himself, and the authors deemed it wise to have it reproduced verbatim because it scintillates with many a "Foxwellian" phrase and in fact reflects the gallant qualities of the Commander as well as doing justice to the doughty deeds of the men. Major Foxwell unfolds the saga in his own inimitable style, thus :

"On 19th October, 36 Brigade captured Monte La Pieve (Pt. 408), which was the cue for the Irish Brigade to attack Monte Spaduro. Accordingly the 1st Bn. Royal Irish Fusiliers took up positions just forward of Pt. 408, ready for their assault on Spaduro that night.

"The Brigadier was particularly keen to have our mortars in support. This was real mortar country: the bombs in their vertical descent could get right into the enemy's gullies: the gunners couldn't do the same thing because of the crest-clearance problem.

"Lt. Dick Gray—O.C. No. 4 Platoon (Mortars)—found a mortar position, a deep gully just behind Gesso. The Platoon moved out of their position facing Gaggio and occupied their new positions by 20.00 hours, about half an hour before the attack was to go in. Meanwhile Dick Gray and his O.P. party, consisting of Cpl. Dennis, a wireless operator, 2 mules and 2 wireless sets, went off to join R.H.Q. of the Faughs at Pt. 416. They had a nasty trip beyond Monte La Pieve, groping their way along a white tape through a mine-field and being 'stonked' all the way. They eventually arrived intact.

"No. 4 Platoon gave supporting fire in the attack which the Faughs pressed forward with great gallantry. They reported the capture of Spaduro at 05.15 hours on 20th October. At 06.00 hours the enemy counter-attacked in strength. The two leading companies of the Faughs fought stubbornly and heroically but against superior odds and they fought to the end until they ran out of ammunition. Spaduro was yet to be won. The Brigadier ordered the 2nd Bn. the London Irish to take it on the night of the 20th. For this purpose our other Mortar Platoon was required. No. 3 Platoon took up a position near No. 4 Platoon. Dick Gray now came under the orders of the London Irish and controlled the fire of both platoons.

"No. 12 Platoon (M.G.) joined the London Irish for the attack. They took up positions on the hill at Pt. 410. On the way, the platoon's wireless set was deposited in a mine-field by the mule which was supposed to be carrying it. With somewhat foolhardy gallantry Sgt. Waters retrieved it (much to the annoyance, no doubt, of the operator, who thought the mule had given him a temporary relief from his labours).

"After the previous night's battle, Jerry's gunners had turned the heat right on. No. 4 Platoon (Mortars) had three mortar bombs on their mortar position. Luckily nobody was hurt. The chaps dug deeper into their holes and hoped for the best.

"The London Irish attack went in at midnight 20th/21st October with the limited objective of Little Spaduro—Hill 387.

"As in the Faugh's attack, the enemy at Spinello House caused trouble. The London Irish by-passed this strong-point and pressed on towards their objective. There they were pinned to the ground by the Spinello garrison and by the enemy on Hill 387 itself. All day on 21st October they remained unable to move. At dusk they continued the attack, but they were withdrawn by their C.O. six hours later without dislodging the Hun from Hill 387.

"All day on the 21st the London Irish called upon No. 3 and No. 4 Platoons to 'stonk' Hill 387, and the section of 'C' Group Mortars on Pieve joined in at fifteen minutes' notice to help. At their request too, No. 12 Platoon (M.G.) shot up Spinello House and Hill 387 from their direct-fire positions on Hill 401.

"Lt. Norman Wimbury's M.G. Platoon (No. 11) had a job that evening. Under cover of darkness, they went forward with twenty mules to relieve one company of Lancashire Fusiliers on a spur sticking 600 yards out into no man's land in front of Gesso. They had Brigade H.Q. Defence Platoon under command. We called the position Wimbury Pimple. During the two days they were there, they fortunately had a fairly quiet time.

"The 22nd and 23rd October were devoted to an all-out hate by both sides. In this all our four platoons took an active part.

"A new plan to capture Spaduro was made—a two-brigade, four-battalion affair. No. 11 Brigade was to attack Spaduro itself while the Irish Brigade was to capture Little Spaduro (Hill 387).

"The assault by the Skins (the 2nd Bn. Royal Inniskilling Fusiliers) was timed for 22.30 hours, but a lengthy approach march down a river-bed with mules necessitated starting out at 16.30 hours. In order to cover up their noise, the London Irish were ordered to start cleaning up Spinello at the same time. This was a bit tough, as it meant a direct daylight assault on the garrison which had been the cause of upsetting two Battalion attacks already.

"Lt.-Col. Bredin of the London Irish sent a patrol out to Casa Spinello with the objective of bringing back a prisoner who might give information of the enemy's lay-out there and on Hill 387. Upon the success of this patrol depended everything, from their own lives to the success or failure of the four-battalion attack that night.

"It was certain that once the Hun noticed them the patrol would be extremely lucky to make the return journey of 400 yards to our F.D.L.s. Among other precautions, Lt.-Col. Bredin told O.C. No. 12 Platoon that he wanted an M.G. section jacked up and ready to take on Spinello as soon as they opened fire. Whether Sgt. W. Taylor was given the job or whether he prevented anyone else from doing it, history doesn't relate; in any case it was right up his street.

"He decided not to use his normal direct-fire positions in case they should be made the target for Teuton gunnery for ever after. He found another position where, with Cpl. Henshall as his No. 2, he mounted his M.G., watched like a hawk and waited.

"The patrol crawled stealthily forward and reached Spinello unnoticed. They pounced on a slit-trench; shot two Huns, and collared the third. The surprised garrison opened up with all they had got—so did Sgt. Taylor. A personal duel ensued between Sgt. Taylor and two Spandaus in the house. Sgt. Taylor silenced one Spandau and kept the attention of the other until at last the patrol came back complete with its prisoner.

"The Hun talked. His information was invaluable. It included the defences of Spinello and the general set-up of the enemy on Hill 387. The information came just in time for the London Irish main attack which started at 16.30 hours. It was accompanied by a weighty artillery fire programme and innumerable juicy 'crumps' from our two mortar platoons directed by Dick Gray. Once again Sgt. Taylor took on his Spandau.

"The London Irish got Spinello, at a price, and were able to hold it against three counter-attacks. This accomplished, the other three battalions were able to start their assaults at 22.30 hours. The attacks were costly but all were successful, and all our immediate objectives were won. Lt.-Col. Bredin expressed his great appreciation of the work done by both the mortars and the M.G.s during the three days 21st–23rd October. Sgt. Taylor received an immediate award of the M.M.

"With the capture of the new positions, Wimbury Pimple was no longer sticking out into no man's land. So No. 11 Platoon (M.G.) were given the new job of thickening up the defences of the newly-won positions of the Skins. Twenty-two mules were brought forward to move the platoon's kit. They floundered and slithered on the slimy mountainside; it was all the platoon could do to reach their new positions. Norman Wimbury spent most of the next day chasing up six mule-loads of kit that had dropped off on the way.

"On the 25th, No. 3 Platoon (Mortars) were ordered to move round to Ripiano on the left flank to give D.F. fire to the Skins. They had to borrow twenty men from the Faughs to help dig up their base-plates and move their kit on to the road. Six R.A.S.C. jeeps and trailers started to ferry them off to Ripiano, where they shared a house with No. 5 Platoon, 'B' Group. The platoon's move coincided with the beginning of torrential rain, which continued without a stop for forty-eight hours. The route to Ripiano crossed the River Sillaro at the San Clemente ford. When the first convoy crossed, the water was a foot deep. Two hours later when the second convoy came to cross, the river was a raging torrent and the ford three feet deep. It was by then pitch dark. As all Kensingtons know, the ford was a favourite 'stonking' ground for the Jerry gunners. Sgt. Walder made a game attempt to take the first jeep over, but as soon as it went into the water it was swept down the river with trailer, bombs and all the rest. Sgt. Walder and the driver managed to scramble out of the water. This half of No. 3 Platoon was stranded at San Clemente in the haunted houses for the next three days.

"Lt. Dick Gray, Cpl. Dennis and their O.P. party were relieved on the 25th, having been at Pt. 416—R.H.Q. first of the Faughs and then of the London Irish—since the 19th. They had had very little sleep during those six days. The enemy's shell-fire had been so incessant that they hardly dared to go outside to relieve nature. Communication with the mortar position had been a constant problem. They were lucky if the telephone cable lasted half an hour before being cut by shell-fire. Their No. 22 Wireless Set had been put out of action during a 'stonk', but they managed to scrape along with their No. 18 Set when the telephone went 'dis'.

"Their relief was Lt. Harvey Shillidy and his O.P. party. They went to R.H.Q. of the Skins. Just as they were about to set off, one of their two mules collapsed and died, without having the decency to give a warning murmur of complaint. Mules were like that. This incident merely serves as a typical illustration of the sort of frustrating things which were continually happening to everybody.

"It was on this rainy day that No. 12 Platoon were ordered back to Appolinare for two days' rest. They arrived at dusk—all soaked to the skin and thoroughly worn out after six days and nights under heavy fire. Two of them were sick, but they could not be evacuated as the Divisional maintenance road to the rear had fallen away in a landslide. Appolinare, a tiny village of about ten houses, was already choked with 36 Bde. H.Q. and the Irish Bde H.Q. Half the platoon were squeezed into a stable already filled with other soldiers. An inch of water stood on the floor. There was no question of dry clothes. The best that could be done was to light fires inside the stable; huddle closely together; and hopefully hang socks over the fire on sticks. O.C. 'C' Group—Major Harpur—had a little outhouse for his H.Q. about 12 feet square. With fellow-feeling for these gallant and exhausted Kensingtons he allowed fifteen of them to sleep on his mud floor—beautiful dry mud. They slept on it with grateful hearts, oozing water like sponges.

"Sgt. 'Tiny' Waters was the Platoon Commander and, believe it or not, he had no trousers; they had been washed off the mountain in the deluge. Prompted by a desire to maintain Regimental prestige, the Group Commander lent 'Tiny' his denim trousers (and he never got them back).

"The 26th dawned. Icy rain was still pouring down; it had now been raining continuously for twenty hours. At 10.00 hours Sgt. Shoobert—acting Mortar Position Officer of No. 4 Platoon—reported that their once dry gulley was now a raging torrent; one of the mortar base-plates was under water; the slit-trenches had filled in; the men's kit was swamped; and soil was falling down the side of the gully. At 11.00 hours Sgt. Shoobert reported that one of the mortars had only one inch of muzzle showing above the water; the torrent had risen three feet; the whole mortar position was being swamped by water and landslides; he had only one mortar above the water-level. He was ordered to keep his one mortar in action and to salvage the other mortar sights and any other equipment he could. At 12.00 hours wireless and telephone communication with the platoon ceased altogether. An hour later, Cpl. Gladding reported to Group H.Q. that one of the mortars had been completely buried in a landslide and that the last remaining mortar had to be dismantled to save it from a similar fate. When he left the platoon the men were working as hard as possible to salvage what kit they could. He said it was all he could physically do to get himself out of the gully.

"Capt. Depinna—O.C. Mortar Company—went off to help salvage his platoon. By diligent searching he found an isolated house about half a mile away. He managed by degrees to get the platoon into it that day. Every man was completely exhausted and numbed with cold and wet. If they had not found that house, the whole lot would have been hospital cases. For instance, Cpl. Sewell was dazed for days afterwards from his magnificent feat in maintaining vital communications for five days and nights without relief.

"On 27th, No. 11 Platoon, clinging to Hill 387, were

even worse off. There was no shelter whatever; if they tried to dig a slit-trench it immediately filled with water; there was nowhere to sit except on the muddy slope at an angle of 45 degrees. Ten of their number collapsed with exposure or trench foot and had to be evacuated as sick. Cpl. Simmance invented a system whereby two men, crouched under their gas-capes, lit a small No. 3 petrol cooker, brewed up some tea, and tried to keep warm at the same time. The only snag was that there was only one cooker per ten men and a great scarcity of petrol. The man who preserved the rest of the platoon from hospital that day was the self-appointed cook—Pte. Adshead—who, by some miracle, brewed up a dixie of tea. Lt. Norman Wimbury told the Group Commander with Lancastrian directness that unless something was done there would be no No. 11 Platoon in twenty-four hours : there would just be a heap of bodies. The only platoon to relieve them was No. 12 Platoon which was 'resting' in Appolinare. They were completely unfit. All were suffering from trench foot in some degree; in thirty-six hours at Apollinare they had not even got dry. All that could be said was that they had had a decent square meal cooked by the Group H.Q. cook, Topper Brown. The whole thing was fantastic; but for the fact that the rifle battalions had suffered great casualties and, like us, large numbers were sick, we would have said with excellent reason, that the thing was 'not on'. So that night, with boots as heavy as lead, No. 12 Platoon went up to relieve No. 11 Platoon with the Skins on Hill 387. Just before the relief, Sgt. Ganley's section carried out a harassing fire shoot at the Skins' request.

"The only place for No. 11 Platoon to go was a dirty, poky, partly demolished house in view of the enemy just in front of Gesso; they thought themselves very lucky to get it. It was only half a mile from their gun positions but they were so exhausted, their feet were so sore and the mud was so appalling that it took some of them four hours to walk it. When taking stock of the Platoon the next day it was found that fifteen men had trench foot or 'flu; but from then on they began to dry out gradually.

"First No. 12 Platoon on the 25th, then No. 4 Platoon

on the 26th, and now No. 11 Platoon on the 27th were all exhausted to the limit of endurance. They all knew that no relief was possible and that they must stick it out somehow. The whole thing was a nightmare.

"All the platoons wanted socks. The Battalion wanted socks. The Division wanted socks. The whole of the Eighth Army wanted socks; but we were told that there were none in Italy or even in England. We didn't get the socks. Shortly afterwards, this scandal was reported to a visiting M.P. He cabled the Prime Minister and quite a lot of socks turned up rather smartly.

"The nightmare was not confined to the platoons. Capt. Alf Oakes—the Group Second-in-Command—had one every minute. Every hour of every day he was bombarded with demands from the platoons: to send up a petrol cooker here; a M.G. tripod there; insatiable demands for socks, foot powder, gas-capes, great coats, battle dress, clean clothes of all kinds, to say nothing of rum, rations, and ammunition. Every bit of it had to be loaded on a mule.

"There was no more noble work done in the Group than by the driver mechanics (now muleteers) who piloted the mule trains which were supplied by an Italian mule company. Night after night, through the Spaduro battles and the rains that followed, they groped their way along, climbing the steep, muddy ascent out of Appolinare—avoiding the swamp where a dozen mules had sunk by Gesso cemetery—passing the bogged-down tanks on the way to Gesso—picking their way through the mine-field—quickening the pace through the ruins of Gesso to avoid the almost inevitable 'stonking'—floundering along the nightmare track of interminable length to Hill 387—arriving after a four-hour journey at Sgt. Ganley's section at the very end of the world, only to find that some vital sandbag had dropped off a mule. Then the same procedure going back—getting very hungry—perspiring with the effort of squelching along in the mud—flopping into it to avoid a shell screaming down—stumbling into a shell-hole that wasn't there on the way up. At last, back in Appolinare, the muleteer got his well-earned one-twentieth bottle of rum and fell into some straw to sleep. It was lucky for us that the man in charge of mule trains from Appolinare forward was Sgt. John Bowley. There was no more efficient and energetic soldier in 'D' Group—qualities which were entirely eclipsed by the fact that he was our Secret Weapon against despair—our private Tommy Handley. We loved his non-stop comment which made for us, and us alone, such ordinary things as a cigar-smoking G.I., an unshaven Italian gentleman, or a dusky Indian muleteer, objects of ribald mirth.

"At the end of the Spaduro battles Brigadier T. P. D. Scott, D.S.O., Commander of the Irish Brigade, sent out a personal message to the Brigade in which he congratulated each Battalion in turn, describing the achievements of each. Referring to 'D' Group, he said, 'I have, too, a special word of praise for the close support given by the Kensingtons D Support Group who were in the thick of it all.'

"Further offensive operations were impossible because the whole front was one colossal morass, and battle casualties and sickness had taken a huge toll. All our efforts were needed to keep the forward troops supplied with the barest essentials. During the next three weeks the four platoons were engaged on M.G. and mortar-harassing fire tasks. These were strictly limited by the amount of ammunition that could be brought forward.

"On 18th November the Irish Brigade side-stepped to the left to take over a brigade sector from 5 Division. The area was in the hills below Monte Grande to the left of San Clemente. In some respects it was not so bad as the place we had left. The platoon areas were much less muddy. Admin. problems were easier because rations could be taken up in daylight, except to No. 12 Platoon at Casa Luca.

"The Casa Luca position was an evil and isolated spot from the beginning. The day that No. 12 Platoon occupied it, they were heavily mortared. Pte. Ward was wounded. One bomb burst in the cooking department—Pte. Adshead narrowly missed being sent for a six. The place was always being 'stonked'. The platoon just had to live underground in a state of tension. One night L/Sgt. Ridgeway left his tin hat outside his dug-out; next morning it was riddled like a cullender.

Typical Scene of this Period. Transport Awaits Road Repairs near Sassaleone, but the Mule Trains Plod on through the Mud. (See Chapter XV.)
(Photo by courtesy of Imperial War Museum. Copyright reserved.)

Medium Machine-guns of a "D" Group Platoon firing from a house in support of the Infantry during the Senio Attack. (*See Chapter XVI.*)
(*Photo by courtesy of Imperial War Museum. Copyright reserved.*)

"Bitterest loss of all was on 2nd December. Lt. Harvey Shillidy and Cpl. Lee were killed there by a mortar bomb just as they were leaving their O.P. at dusk. Harvey hadn't missed a battle since the campaign started. He, like Dick Gray, was so famed in the Irish Brigade for his reliability and mastery of the 4·2-in. mortar, that no Irish Battalion ever went into action without demanding either 'Harvey' or 'Dick'. Expressions of grief at his loss came from all Battalions, but to us his loss was more personal. Harvey was a brother in our family and we loved him for his charming qualities no less than we admired him for his gallant conduct in battle over a very long period. Cpl. Lee was one of those quiet, efficient chaps who was also extremely popular, and we felt his loss very keenly indeed.

"No. 12 Platoon occupied this position for two months without relief. It was one of the nastiest places imaginable. Owing to the shortage of officers it was commanded during most of this period by N.C.O.s, notably C.Q.M.S. McGowan and Sgt. Ganley, backed up by such seasoned and indomitable warriors as Cpl. Simmance, Cpl. Thomas, and L/Sgt. Ridgeway. Ridgeway took command of the platoon for a short spell; instead, he ought to have been in hospital: his tummy couldn't digest anything at all, but he flatly refused to report sick.

"No. 11 Platoon—now commanded by Lt. John Young —occupied a position near the Battalion H.Q. in that area. It was not nearly so bad as the Casa Luca position, but it had its full share of trouble. The place was like a rabbit warren; everyone lived in huge slit-trenches which, being sandy, kept reasonably dry and clean.

"If John Young wasn't swanning on the sky-line with some wild Irishman—teasing the Tedeschi—he was stirring up his platoon or roundly castigating some poor, innocent soldier, or being severely ticked off himself by his own batman. Alternatively he would sit in his slit-trench listening to the B.B.C. on his No. 18 set—sipping from some secret hoard of vino and drafting some vitriolic signal to Group H.Q. demanding to know why his platoon never got enough food or indeed any food at all. John was a constant source of entertainment to his platoon and the Irish Brigade as well. Brigadier Scott wrote in his diary: 'There was John Young—a great enthusiast who fired his weapons on any and every possible occasion and provocation.'

"Quoting further from the Brigadier's diary, it is recorded that on the evening of 26th November, No. 11 Machine-gun Platoon did a very good shoot on Cereto which obviously had results, as Sgt. Callinan (infantry listening-patrol commander) heard screams afterwards. On that day also a mortar 'stonk' (from our mortars) on Tamagnin coincided with the entry of a Hun ration party, so it was probable there was a bag. There were certainly some results that day, as at dawn the next day German stretcher-bearers and an ambulance were seen busy at their A.D.S.

"But the 'stonking' was not all on one side. The Group Commander's diary contains the following entries:

> *Tuesday, Dec. 5th.* Considerable enemy H.F. with heavy mortars in forward area. Both sections of 11 Platoon received 'stonks'. Cpl. Henshall was badly wounded in the chest. Pte. Hogg and L/Cpl. Edwards were wounded at the same time. Pte. Lee of the other section was also wounded. Pte. Shackall was deafened by blast but he remained at duty.
>
> *Wednesday, Dec. 6th.* Very foggy in the morning in the F.D.L.s. More than one enemy patrol entered F.D.L.s under cover of fog at 07.15 hours. Skins had one man taken prisoner from O.P. about 75 yards from the nearest 12 Platoon position. Both M.G. Platoons had 100% stand-to all day. No. 3 Platoon (mortars) fired D.F. at call of Faughs.
>
> Slight H.F. on 11 and 12 positions during the night.
>
> *Thursday, Dec. 7th.* 11 and 12 Platoons harassed by enemy mortars all day. Enemy H.F. continued during the night. No. 1 Gun, No. 1 section, 11 Platoon, was hit by mortar shrapnel. The barrel casing was punctured beyond repair.

So it went on with the M.G. Platoons day after day. Little wonder that tempers got frayed and nerves became screwed up to bursting-point. For instance, there was the occasion when Sgt. Ganley was furious with rage when his sentry at Casa Luca fired his M.G. at three Germans 200 yards away and killed only one of them.

"While No. 3 Platoon were at Ripiano, the mortar line

stood 100 yards in front of their house. The intervening ground was usually 1 foot under water, as the River Sillaro was always flooding. When there was a call for D.F. the platoon, with the mighty Cpl. Searle in the lead, would go roaring away to the mortars attired in martial dress, less trousers plus shoes, canvas, pairs, 1. They left their boots and trousers high and dry in the house. When No. 3 Platoon's house at Ripiano was hit on 22nd November, Sgt. Bryan organised the salvage of nearly all the platoon equipment. In the face of exploding tank ammunition, it was a very fine achievement. Luckily, the only casualty was Pte. J. Jones, who got some shrapnel in his leg. After that, the platoon had to live in muddy dug-outs on the mortar line.

"They later moved to the valley behind the San Clemente valley, where they built mud and bomb-case igloos to live in. Soon after, there was a big snowstorm followed by a thaw, with the result that (*a*) the igloos collapsed,. and (*b*) the language was something awful. The platoon then moved to the San Clemente valley and they were careful to build their houses on rock this time.

"In the San Clemente sector No. 4 Platoon had a position in the valley just above the mule point. It was a dirty, muddy place. Any digging just filled up with water, so it was a case of building up sort of igloos out of empty bomb cases and mud to keep the wind out.

"About this time we were issued with two welcome items :
"(*a*) *New Officers*.

"Capt. Reg. Perry, whom we had known in England, took command of the M.G. Company. Lts. Basil Rogers, 'Smudger' Smith, and Frank Dixon came to the Mortars. In a short time they became staunch Kensingtons and they were a great help to us.

"(*b*) *Winter clothing*.
  (i) Coats, Duffle, White.
  (ii) Caps, Ski (Teuton style).
  (iii) Suits, Ski (these were sort of huge denim pyjamas with a hood. We called them 'Zoot Suits'.)

The huge figures of 'Smudger' Smith and Sgt. Knapp looked as funny in their Zoot Suits as John Young and Cpl. Fitzgerald looked dashingly romantic in their duffle coats.

"No. 4 Platoon's mud igloo position got rather unhealthy on account of harassing fire, so they moved further down the valley. They were given the parts of a Nissen hut and told to build it. They did.

"By now things were settling down to a winter siege; although there was always talk of a big offensive next week, it never actually happened.

"No account of the San Clemente set-up would be complete without a reference to 'Bowley Lodge', so called after mine host, Sgt. John Bowley. This was a peasant's cottage about half a mile up the San Clemente valley, conveniently close to the mule point. We had two rooms in it; the rest was used by alternating Irish Battalions—no doubt 'lo Patrone' with his wife 'casa mia' were lurking about somewhere. The one room downstairs was filled with John Bowley and his mule boys. The one room upstairs was 'D' Group Signal Centre and M.G. Coy Tac H.Q. It was called Bowley Lodge on the Bde. Signal Diagram and by this name it was known to all.

"John Bowley himself, assisted by other senior N.C.O.s and half a dozen of his stalwart drivers, organised the mule trains for the two M.G. Platoons. As always, John Bowley's sense of humour deluded his soldiers into supposing that war wasn't too tiring after all.

"In conclusion, it may fairly be said that the soldiers of 'D' Group, in enduring the torments of hell day after day and in the lonely watches of the night from October to December 1944, had grown to the full stature of manhood.

"Nobody said as much, but each man felt in his bones that England had summoned him to Her service and each knew that there was only one course open: that was to stick it out.

"There was among them a code of discipline not to be found in King's Regulations. Each man had to give all he had got; there was no truck with passengers. In return he enjoyed the sublime blessing of the absolute loyalty of his fellow men—without which he would have been blown away like a leaf in the wind, if he didn't go mad first.

"If he had fought his last battle in this seemingly endless struggle, each man was entitled to feel that he had been put to the highest test and had passed with honours. If he ever went home again he could confidently look his neighbour in the eye—not arrogantly, but tempered with the knowledge that this was not only a soldiers' war; news from home, however reassuring, could not conceal the fact that it was everybody's war."

CHAPTER XVI

STATIC WARFARE AND THE FINAL OFFENSIVE

January 1st–May 2nd, 1945

ONLY one minute of the New Year's Day had elapsed when every conceivable gun in the Division fired one shell simultaneously on the village of San Martino. This enormous salvo was by way of being our greeting to the Hun Paratroopers.

The snow was thick on the ground everywhere, concealing the dismal, devastated tracts of mud and shattered landscape in a soft white cloak.

On January 2nd, shortly after midnight, three civilians were caught by "C" Group in the Pt. 508 area and sent back under escort, as they were suspected to be enemy agents trying to penetrate our lines. The same evening the "Boche" launched a big attack on Monte Verro preceded by a colossal barrage which included the Gesso—Pt. 508 Ridge. A deadly mixture of fire from every type of weapon on which the enemy could lay his hands produced these massive "stonks". Very shortly afterwards the Coldstream Guards sent an urgent appeal to "C" Group to harass the "forming-up" areas. An answer was swiftly forthcoming, and eventually the situation was restored after the Guards counter-attacked, supported by our mortars and machine-guns. The Commanding Officer of the 2nd Battalion Coldstream Guards subsequently thanked the Group Commander personally for the "speedy aid" delivered at a critical moment.

The whole of January was spent by the Battalion in freezing conditions. The daily routine was taken up almost entirely in trying to keep warm and improving weapon-pits and dug-outs. Snow had to be cleared away constantly from the ammunition dumps and equipment. "Anti-freeze" mixture was put in the barrel casings of the Vickers guns. Wooden stakes, corrugated iron, wire, and sandbags by the thousand were laboriously brought up by the gallant mules, which slipped every ten yards on the icy slopes.

Every evening, whilst the magnificent maintenance trains were plodding forward with the rations, oblivious of the spasmodic shell-fire and snow, the warming crackle of the machine-guns would echo across the mountains as they harassed the enemy's supply lines. The vicious cough of the 4·2-in. mortars could be heard as bombs were sent hurtling into the enemy areas at the request of the Infantry or Brigade Counter-mortar Officers.

The abysmal weather conditions and precipitous terrain precluded any activity on the part of the "Boche" except patrolling and the continual pounding of our F.D.L.s and supply routes.

Throughout the months the discomfort and tasks were very much the same for each Group. The guns of "B" Group on the Pt. 298 Ridge and their mortars in the snow-bound valley behind were constantly in action harassing the enemy on Monte Merlo escarpment and answering calls for counter-mortar fire. Supplies were brought up mainly by jeep across the treacherous and much-shelled S. Clemente ford—but mules had to be used to reach the M.M.G. Platoons.

"C" Group sector also had a lot of attention from enemy shelling, particularly along the Gesso ridge and Pt. 401. The Canadian tanks stuck in that area after supporting infantry attacks the previous October were responsible for drawing a lot of fire. The new shell-holes could always be recognised by the dirty black patches dotted about on the virgin snow. The men of 9 Platoon were constantly in and out of positions relieving the infantry machine-gun sections on the exposed Pt. 387 feature and Little Spaduro House, which was nothing but a mass of rubble surrounded by hundreds of shell craters. The mortars and M.M.G.s were constantly firing D.F.s for the infantry and putting down counter-mortar fire. Targets were also registered by "C" Group mortars from aircraft loaned by the R.A., which proved very successful. Owing to the deep chasms and valleys, where many bombs were lost, observation from these "flying O.P.s" made correction much more satisfactory.

"D" Group M.M.G. Platoons, perched precariously on the lower eastern slopes of gigantic Monte Grande, also contributed to the general "hate" with well-directed harassing fire. 12 Platoon was very noticeable for the summary way in which they dealt out death to the odd parties of "Boche" which came into their arc of fire.

On January 3rd, 1945, Royal Irish Fusiliers planned a platoon attack on a heavily defended enemy house called "Tamagmim", which was situated about 300 yards in front of the forward localities. C.Q.M.S. McGowan's platoon then occupied a particularly nasty position on the slopes of Monte Grande that constantly received the enemy's attention.

Their job on this occasion was to engage any "Huns" that might escape from Tamagmim House as a result of the attack. To do this, it was necessary to move their guns forward, in order to have a field of fire down the slope of the mountain. Such a position was necessarily in full and unrestricted view of the enemy's nearest position, only 200 yards away.

C.Q.M.S. McGowan decided to use two machine-guns. He ordered Sergeant Ganley to take charge of one gun and he took the other himself. With one other man each the N.C.O.s took their guns forward, with four belts of ammunition, before daylight on January 3rd, to positions they had previously reconnoitred.

They remained motionless until 10.00 a.m., when an extraordinarily daring and successful attack on Tamagmim was made by the Royal Irish Fusiliers. A terrific exchange of small-arms fire ensued, and out of the back door of this wasps' nest poured forty "Jerries" running towards Germany like scalded cats. Machine-gunners have seldom seen such a target 250 yards away, and rarely has any target been dealt with by such cool and capable machine-gunners. The slaughter was horrible.

During this action, an enemy sniper's bullet went clean through a tripod leg of C.Q.M.S. McGowan's gun, but luckily not through the gallant C.Q.M.S. as well. A smoke-screen put down by 2nd Bn. London Irish Rifles enabled the two gun teams to withdraw.

The same platoon had an unpleasant experience when on the last day of the month a small enemy patrol slipped around them in the darkness and engaged the Platoon H.Q. with small-arms fire, but fortunately there were no casualties. "D" Group mortars in their frozen valley were constantly in action, and in fact hardly found time to build themselves "igloos".

During these January weeks, the shortage of 4·2-in. mortar bombs made us cast envious glances at our American neighbours, who had stacks of ammunition, as well as having a type of 4·2-in. mortar which appeared more accurate than ours. Our Commanding Officer, who had been constantly walking himself off his feet in determined visits to the platoons along the whole of the Divisional Front, decided that we might acquire some of these weapons. So we sent off officers from each Group on attachment to the American Mortar Battalion; they came back with glowing reports. However, we did not reap the fruits of our private "lease-lend" scheme until later.

No record of this January would be complete without reference to the magnificent Divisional pantomime "Cinderella", which played to packed houses for weeks in Castel del Rio, and then went off proudly on tour. Many of its all-male cast were drawn from the Kensingtons.

The Battalion Rest House at Castel del Rio was also in great demand by the platoons of "B" and "D" Groups for holding very belated but none the less spirited Christmas parties.

"B" and "C" Groups had tiny houses for their "A" and "B" Echelons, and transport some way back from the front line on the main road from Castel del Rio. "D" Group was not so lucky, as their lot was an open field subsequently improved by the addition of a couple of Nissen huts. In these Echelon areas the Quartermaster-Sergeants and their staffs, the clerks and drivers, cheerfully tackled all the administrative problems with a conscientious fortitude which was as admirable as it was efficient. It was here that a million worries were sorted out. It was here that the precious mail, dry socks, boots, rations, rum, ammunition, spare parts, clothing, NAAFI issues of cigarettes, razor blades, soap, etc., were checked, labelled, and ferried forward for final delivery to the equally indomitable addressees.

Major J. J. Evans, Capt. J. Downes (M.T.O.), Lieutenant and Q.M. A. R. Edgecombe, and R.Q.M.S. F. Headington and their staffs, working in primitive conditions on the side of the road some miles north of Firenzuola, produced the goods and the answers with a precision which set the highest standard for our whole "Q" department from Battalion H.Q. down to Platoons.

From the operational viewpoint, the first few days in February were spent very much the same as the previous 120 days. "C" Group busied themselves firing D.F.s for men of 56 "Recce" Regiment who had an outpost at Ca Salara house, which was constantly attacked by enemy patrols supported by shell-fire which invariably landed on the ridge behind, where a section of 9 Platoon was established. This never deterred Pte. "Wag" Knight, who always placed a large sandbag on the back of his neck to prevent any shell splinters coming in from the tradesmen's entrance. "B" Group were summoned as a last resort on one occasion to silence a harassing Spandau post, which they promptly proceeded to do with their mortars, much to the delight of the infantry.

A change in the weather brought down heavy mists on the mountains, of which enemy patrols took full advantage. "D" Group platoons in particular had an anxious time, constantly "standing-to" in anticipation of trouble which never came.

All Groups had occasional opportune shoots on parties of the "Boche" who were revealed by sudden lifts of the mist, whilst moving about on their positions. The "Boche" at the time started to increase his machine-gun harassing fire, doubtless taking a leaf out of our book, and casualties amongst the infantry and mule trains resulted.

During the first ten days platoons were surprised to see odd representatives from the 1st Bn. Royal Northumberland Fusiliers suddenly appear at their positions, and very shortly the "latrine telegraph service" produced a rumour that at last—at long last—we were to be relieved by the 10 Indian Division. This was actually no rumour, but a delightful reality.

However, just to remind us that the elements also had a relief system, a deluge of rain came on February 9th to replace the snow. Very soon tracks and roads became quagmires. The snow started to thaw and the icy Sillaro river became a raging torrent which made the S. Clemente crossing most hazardous. The sides of the mountains, pitted with little channels of gushing water, started to slide. A section of "C" Group's No. 1 Mortar Platoon, which was now in position behind the shattered village of Gesso, found their mortars being quickly enveloped in an avalanche of seething mud.

"D" Group's vehicles, in their "A" Echelon area, were sinking up to the axles. Dug-outs, gun positions, and slit-trenches all over the front, which had taken months to construct, were crushed by landslides or filled with water as the walls slowly crumbled. Mule trains splashing up the supply routes, went through all the horrors once more that had been experienced when the rains came the previous November.

However, by the middle of the month, the relief was in full swing. Masses of stores and clothing were evacuated by jeep and mule. The mountains of winter equipment, such as white sleeping-bags, skis, duffle coats, and camouflage smocks, were amassed gradually in the rear areas. Ammunition and weapons were left behind for the Northumberland Fusiliers to take over.

On February 12th, 13th, and 14th, dirty personnel of the platoons straggled wearily out of the "Line" and slumped on the waiting transports for conveyance to the new area. Most of the platoons had been in position continuously for nearly 130 days.

The familiar road to Castel del Rio and the Utopia beyond was traversed for the last time. This one and only road had been kept open by the unflagging work of the "Sappers" and Pioneer Corps recruited from Africa. The sight of dark-skinned boys from Basutoland huddled over miserable fires beside the road, their black faces ashen with cold, was a daily reminder of the loyalty commanded by the Mother Country.

An amusing incident was once witnessed by Lieutenant-Colonel B. L. Bryar when returning from one of his visits to the forward localities. His jeep was following an enormous American truck, driven with reckless nonchalance by a big Negro from the States. The truck halted just beside one of the unfortunate Basuto natives, who was shovelling snow as fast as his petrified hands would let him. The big "buck nigger" pushed his head out of the cab of the truck, flicked his cigar ash with marked disdain, and greeted his African brother with : "Hello, Savage—where's yo spear?"

By February 15th, the whole of the Battalion was concentrated around Florence. Most personnel were accommodated in nice villas. Words cannot express our happiness on reaching this pleasant stretch of Italy. Florence offered civilised attractions, from which we had been severed for nearly seven months. There was no mud. The climate was warmer, and there was both hot water and electric light.

However, just as the outer layers of dirt were being scrubbed away, we moved within four days across the Apennines once more on to the Eighth Army front, where our final Rest Area was found amongst the flat fields near Cesena. This was a town of considerable size some fifteen miles from the perimeter of our bulge in the fiercely contested Po plain.

Whilst navigating the precipitous and tortuous pass over the mountains, a "C" Group carrier went over the side of the road and fell some forty feet. Pte. F. Saunders and Ptes. Inglis and Prince were seriously hurt, and later Pte. Saunders died of the multiple injuries he sustained. This was a tragic conclusion to what was otherwise a very successful and uneventful convoy movement.

By February 20th the whole Battalion was installed in innumerable small farmhouses, and feverish cleaning of vehicles, stores, and clothing was immediately inaugurated, punctuated by drill parades. The Divisional Commander was going to visit us on February 23rd, which gave us just three days to present the glittering façade of the parade ground, which had been completely neglected during the previous six months.

Everybody worked overtime, and by the appointed day we were not ill-pleased with ourselves. The General inspected all the men, slowly and meticulously. We then marched proudly past the saluting base to the skirl of the Irish Pipes loaned from the Inniskilling Fusiliers. A close examination of our billets and transport followed, and darkness had fallen before our distinguished visitor, who was obviously delighted, left the Battalion area. The Commanding Officer then issued the following message:

Major-General R. K. Arbuthnott, C.B.E., D.S.O., M.C., Commanding 78th Infantry Division, at the conclusion of his inspection of the Battalion, asked me to convey to all ranks his congratulations on the splendid turn-out and bearing of the Battalion on parade. He also said he was most impressed with the cleanliness of the billets and said what a pleasure it was to see transport looking so clean and in such good condition. He also enjoyed very much meeting a number of you and talking to you.

I would like to add my own congratulations for the magnificent achievement in cleaning up and reaching such a high standard of soldierly smartness in such a short space of time, after the appalling conditions under which the majority of you have been living for the last four months. I have no doubt that the high standard reached will be maintained in the best tradition of the Regiment, and that each one of us can justifiably feel proud to belong to the Battalion with the full knowledge that our joint efforts have made it one of the finest in the British Army.

(Signed) B. L. BRYAR, Lt.-Col., Commanding
1st Bn. P.L. Kensington Regiment.

During the next few weeks we trained, we took part in Brigade exercises, we carried out mortar and machine-gun shooting in valleys especially allocated for this purpose near by, and we played inter-Group football matches. The Officers' Mess of each Group gave prodigious parties in turn, culminating in a mammoth dinner organised by Captain J. A. German, when all officers of the Battalion came into Battalion H.Q. to partake of wine and food. An old friend, Captain and Q.M. E. D. Knight, M.B.E., M.M., was present, and the quiet of the early hours was shattered by the inevitable rendering of "The Old Grey Mare".

The "Clarendon" Restaurant, under the guidance of Miss Kay Sheard, who had been with the Battalion during the dire days of Castel del Rio, was reopened. There were a cinema and more canteens at Cesena, and further entertainment could be obtained from the neighbouring town of Forli.

This period out of action came as a blessed relief, and as the weather was good we had no discomfort. The only incident to offset our enjoyment was when it was learnt on March 1st that Pte. W. Robson, of "D" Group, was killed as the result of an unfortunate accident when cleaning his rifle.

The beginning of March also saw a team of officer sleuths from an Inspectorate Board visit the Battalion to find out if we were holding equipment to which we were not entitled. Perhaps we can divulge, now that our Commanding Officer has joined the civilian ranks, how it was we concealed from the expert prying eyes our immense collection of "extras". These were absolutely invaluable for rectifying deficiencies in our G.1098 stores.

The Inspectorate passed pathetic little "German graves" complete with wooden cross and helmet. Bits of land marked "Foul Ground", or roped off with the menacing notice "Beware—Mines", were also carefully avoided. Only the privileged minority knew that in such "graves" and areas was buried our treasure. One storeman had dug so many little "caches" that he had to compile a comprehensive chart showing landmarks, distances, and compass bearings, so that there was no fear of one being overlooked when the "all clear" was sounded and excavation commenced.

All good things come to an end, however, and by March 11th, "C" and "D" Groups found themselves in the "line" once more. 56 Division was relieved by our Division, and the 6th Bn. Cheshire Regiment had nice, cosy areas for us to occupy. Compared with winter conditions in the mountains, this proved to be an absolute picnic. Every platoon had a nice, big farmhouse to itself, with mortar and indirect M.M.G. positions practically on the doorstep.

The nature of the country made it possible to get even to the most forward positions in daylight by truck or jeep.

Large wine-vats were found, which made excellent bath-tubs, and the fact that some were full only meant that platoons could dispense lavish hospitality. Visitors were lucky if they could "do the rounds" without returning in an alcoholic stupor.

The Senio sector, in which we found ourselves, was a mass of trees and vines intersected by a maze of narrow tracks and roads and small dykes. The country was as flat as a pancake, and visibility in any direction was restricted to about 200 yards. Thus shooting had to be done entirely by calculations from a map.

The Sen o itself was about thirty yards wide, flanked by two enormous flood-banks, each of which was wide enough at the top to allow a truck to be driven along it. We held the southern flood-bank except for a few short stretches where the enemy had outpost positions. The proximity of our troops to the "Boche" led to a constant exchange of small-arms fire and marathon grenade duels. During daylight, things were normally fairly quiet, but in the evening and at night constant enemy machine-gun fire swept the whole of the area, making movement very hazardous, and sentries had to keep their vigil from look-out positions indoors. Gun-fire was quite light, but the "Boche" used his mortars and *Nebelwerfers* on an unprecedented scale to counteract this deficiency.

"C" and "D" Groups devised elaborate M.M.G. harassing programmes which were calculated to catch the Hun with his trousers in an awkward position at odd times throughout the day. Cotignola and Lugo, the two big towns opposite us, were subjected to liberal doses of lead, as they were reported to be full of enemy.

"C" Group carried out the registration of many targets with the use of flying O.P.s and the pilot on one occasion broke the rules of wireless security when, at the conclusion of a particularly accurate display by their mortars, he enthused over the ether: "Oh, good shooting—very good shooting!"

All platoons busied themselves daily with improving positions, and organising local defence schemes. The latter included the laying out of trip wires for igniting flares—

but 9 Platoon, "C" Group, took a dim view of this, when they found one of their flares set off by a stray wild cat. The poor animal in question was cornered the following day and massacred.

On March 20th our opponents on the other side of the flood-bank, 98 Infantry and 26 Panzer Divisions, showed a little more spirit. From 22.45 hrs. onwards grenades, mortar bombs, and rocket shells were fired into the right-hand forward company of 8th Bn. Argyll and Sutherland Highlanders with some intensity. At 23.00 hrs., the platoons were withdrawn under cover of smoke, and an attack appeared to be imminent. "C" Group received the order to "Stand to", and at 23.10 hrs. all D.F.s were called down. A good deal of confused noise was heard the other side of the flood-bank, but no Germans appeared. Enemy fire gradually decreased, and by 02.30 hrs. "Stand down" was given. It was subsequently learned, from a deserter, that the attack had formed up on the "home" side of the flood-bank, according to plan. However, after a little reflection, the redoubtable Grenadiers decided unanimously that this was not really a healthy proposition after all, and promptly organised a "go-slow" strike.

The enemy varied his fire from time to time by sending over rockets, and "D" Group, on March 24th, reported that a vast quantity of these missiles had landed in their area mixed with oil incendiary shells.

In turn both Groups' Mortar and M.M.G. Platoons kept harrying the Hun every day with "all round the clock" programmes. "C" Group carried out operation "Whackit". This was a co-ordinated heavy fire programme of all supporting arms, designed to give the enemy a night of "horrors". Accordingly, "C" Group fired smoke-screens, M.M.G. barrage shoots, heavy concentrations of mortar-fire, and even attempted a little fire-raising in Cotignola. Altogether a most unpleasant night for our opponents.

Meanwhile, Battalion H.Q. had established themselves comfortably in a little town called Russi, about a couple of miles behind the forward Groups. Here a depleted Battalion football team took the field against the town eleven, and were promptly beaten five goals to three by the fast

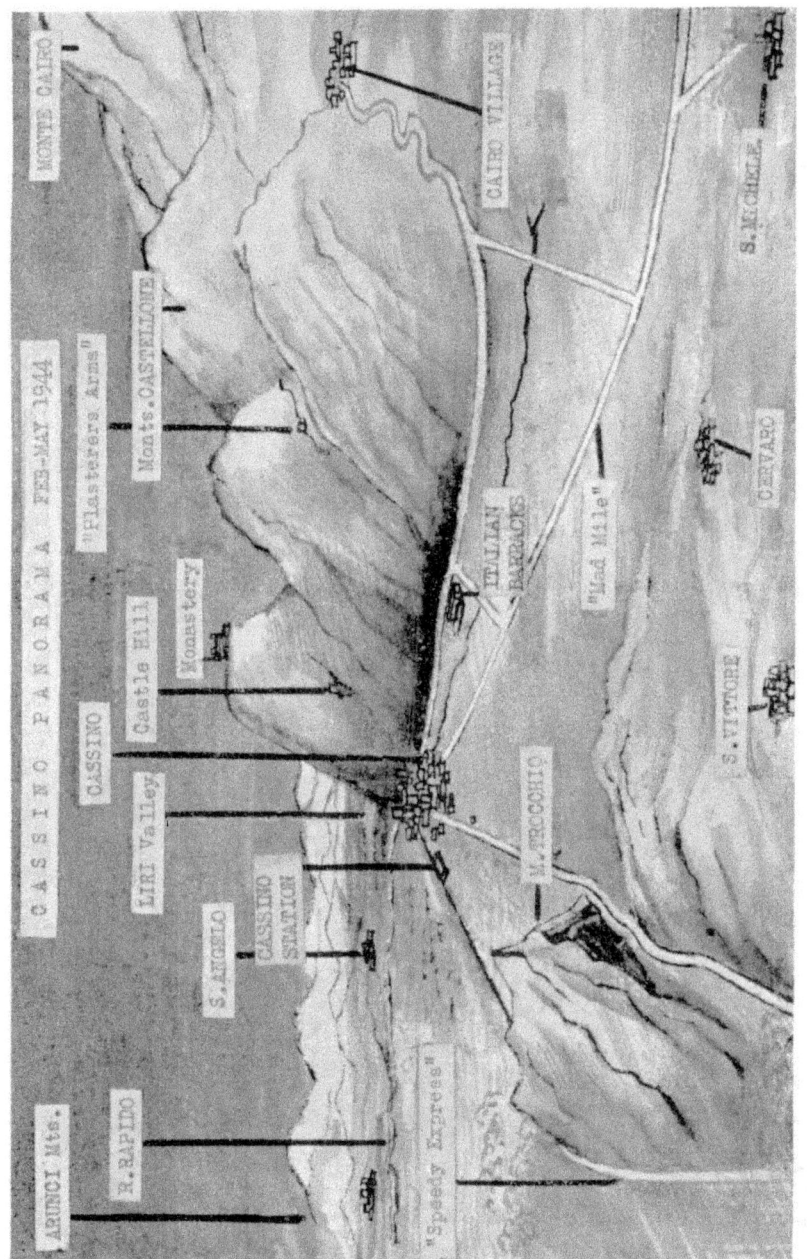

Cassino Panorama, February–May 1944. (*See Chapter XII.*)

Diagram of Trasimeno Operations, June 1944. (*See Chapter XIII.*)

Italian stalwarts. Our respect for the "Eyeties" increased slightly as a result.

On March 28th, "B" Group, who had been busily training whilst in reserve, took over "D" Group's sector. Major J. W. Doyle then went up in a Flying O.P. himself, and saw his mortars register targets for the first time from this unusual position.

By the end of the month, stacks of ammunition and dumps of stores had appeared. Gun-pits and tracks were multiplied. Whispers and rumours became rife. We felt we were on the eve of some great offensive. Indeed, a long series of orders and instructions had already started to arrive under "Top Secret" cover, heralding the approach of a gigantic operation called "Buckland".

By the second day of April, "B" Group side-stepped to the right and ousted "C" Group, who came back to S. Pietro to commence their training with the American mortar. It must be recorded that by this time the whole Battalion had been equipped with this new weapon. We felt that it was a signal honour for us to be the only British Support Battalion to be allowed to adopt the American mortar, especially as we were told that we could have the whole of the American ammunition allotted to the Eighth Army, which constituted an initial supply of some 87,000 shells. Such an amazing monopoly could not have been secured had not our ability to exploit the use of the 4·2-in. mortar been fully appreciated.

On April 3rd, the Commanding Officer gave out a few of the secrets regarding "Buckland". The object of this plan was to smash the German armies south of the River Po by the combined assault of the Fifth and Eighth Armies. Put briefly like that, it all sounds rather pleasant, but that is precisely what had been attempted with varying degrees of success for the past twenty months—and this time the Army was without the French and Canadian Corps.

We were not surprised when we were told that we would have to support the 2 New Zealand Division on our left and the 8 Indian Division on our right as well. "C" Group's Mortar Platoons were assigned to look after the "Kiwis", and those of "D" Group prepared to go into position on the north side of the town of Bagnacavallo, to support the Indian Division.

Under the supervision of American officers, loaned from No. 100 Chemical Warfare Battalion, U.S. Army, our training proceeded at a prodigious pace. This was a necessity, because time was only too short before the offensive began.

Simultaneously, feverish work went on to ferry up enormous dumps of ammunition and prepare the positions for occupation in support of the flanking Divisions. Miles of signal cable were laid to ensure our communications by telephone, reconnaissances were being made constantly, and all officers and men were "briefed".

On April 6th the Commanding Officer made a tour of the Battalion's "lay-out" on the ground. Everyone was found to be hard at work improving gun-pits and eagerly awaiting action. "D" Group Mortar Platoons moved up into position in the 8 Indian Division's sector. Many old members of the Battalion had rejoined us. These included Captain Hutchings from M.E.F., and Lieutenants McLean, Porter, Oldland, and Meehan from No. 2 C.R.U. Later, Lieutenant Blizard arrived back from the U.S. Army dump at Leghorn, bringing with him aiming-circles, protractors, and other much-needed instruments.

All day long the front had been comparatively quiet, but from approximately 18.00 hrs. onwards enemy gun-fire increased until it seemed almost certain that our opponents were about to launch a major offensive. The whole Divisional front was saturated with the most intense barrage we had experienced for many months. Over 4000 shells were fired on one sector alone. It was later discovered from P.O.W.s that this operation, known to the Germans as "Leonidas I", had three main objects : (1) to break up our concentrations of troops and materials; (2) to destroy our gun-lines; (3) to cover the withdrawal of troops and equipment.

By April 8th, although every effort was made to keep the general appearance of the front normal, there was an unmistakable air of tension in the forward area. Everything was ready for "H" hour, and the period of waiting was found to be trying. Later news was received that all officers could be informed that "D" day, for what we believed would be the Eighth Army's last great offensive of the war, was April 9th, 1945. At 18.00 hrs., the Commanding Officer and I.O. went up to the Battalion Command Post where all available officers were collected. The Commanding Officer then gave a summary of the forthcoming operations, and explained Fifth Army's part in the plan.

On April 9th every weapon was ready to commence firing, and it remained only to wait until the programme was due to start. Promptly to time, the first shell-bursts appeared in the cloudless sky. For a few minutes nothing further happened, then a steady drone could be heard from the south, and soon squadrons of bombers were passing overhead. They swung south, and a little later a dense, light-brown cloud, accompanied by a heavy rumbling, could be seen rising over the tops of the trees. For the remainder of the afternoon, the whole area shook with the concussion of bombs, shells of every calibre, and cannon fire from the hundreds of fighter bombers swarming over the Senio. At last there was silence, whilst the flame-throwers drenched the far flood-banks and the assaulting infantry formed up for the crossing. Then, as darkness fell, the barrages for the attack proper commenced. No reports were received for almost an hour, and then news began to trickle slowly through. The New Zealanders were well over and going strongly against stiff opposition. Over three thousand P.O.W. were taken within the first three-quarters of an hour. On the right, 8 Indian Division had made a bridgehead over the river in the teeth of fierce resistance and were consolidating it. The advance continued steadily, and, in the early hours of the morning, all initial objectives, except the town of Lugo, had been successfully taken. The much-vaunted "Senio Line" was a thing of the past. Throughout the whole of the operation, all platoons were firing almost continuously.

At first light on April 10th the advance continued. After heavy fighting, 8 Indian Division cleared Lugo by midday, and continued to press on towards the Santerno river. South of them, the New Zealanders were fighting steadily onwards. Meanwhile, back on the Senio, the Lancashire Fusiliers were mopping up enemy who were still holding out in the flood-banks, and the East Surreys had the privilege of clearing the town of Cotignola, long a thorn in our side. "B" Group's platoons remained in their positions, but "C" Group and "D" Group concentrated in the Bagnacavallo area. The remainder of the day was spent in checking over the mortars and their equipment. Much useful experience was gained from recent shoots, particularly as regards the preparation of proper base-plate positions. The new equipment itself stood up to an unfair battering extremely well, and very few breakages occurred.

During the morning of April 11th, "C" Group moved forward to their Brigade concentration area on the western outskirts of Lugo. It was expected that the Division would shortly be required to thrust through the 8 Indian Division. Later in the day, news came back that the Santerno defences had been stormed, and that heavy fighting was in progress on the other side of the river. Surprised by the speed of our advance, and being caught on the wrong foot by an armoured thrust from an unexpected direction, the enemy was forced to abandon a large part of the Santerno Line intact. "D" Group moved forward from their concentration area to Lugo, where they were at short notice to join the battle in support of 38 Brigade. Battalion H.Q. also moved up into the same town.

The fighting across the river went well on April 12th. No. 2 New Zealand Division had pushed forward south of Massa Lombarda, and was then menacing the town itself. The 8 Indian Division had consolidated a substantial bridgehead, and was pushing slowly on. At midday, 36 Brigade was at last ordered to pass through 8 Indian Division and to swing north towards the formidable Reno river. Both Mortar Platoons of "C" Group crossed the Santerno with them, and were soon in action supporting the Argyll and Sutherland Highlanders and Royal West Kents. By last light the village of S. Patrizio had been taken—an extremely good advance.

First light on the 13th brought the splendid news that 36 Brigade had advanced again during the night, and were in possession of half of Conselice. The enemy was reported to be holding on determinedly, in spite of the bomb concentrations that Nos. 1 and 2 Platoons, "C" Group, were bringing down on them. During the night, 38 Brigade, with "D" Group in support, crossed the Santerno, and at dawn commenced the advance up the western bank of the river. This force made good progress, and by nightfall Lavezzola was reached. A little later, the leading troops succeeded in getting over the Reno river by means of an imperfectly blown girder bridge. They received a very warm reception, however, and had to return to our side. During the course of the morning advance, the Infantry Company nearest the river bank was sharply counter-attacked. Mortar-fire was called for, and many casualties were inflicted on the enemy by Nos. 3 and 4 Platoons.

Starting early in the morning of April 14th, Battalion H.Q. moved up to La Frascata on the 36 Brigade front. "C" Group's platoons were still in the same positions. They experienced a busy night harassing the Sillaro river banks and the approaches to it. Conselice had now been completely cleared, and the enemy in this sector appeared to have withdrawn to behind the river. Germans who were overrun by our swift advance were still being collected, many from areas far behind the line, and the Division's total swelled daily. During the afternoon No. 1 Platoon bombarded a party of enemy who were digging on the far side of the Sillaro. After two ranging rounds, a concentration was dropped directly on the trenches being engaged. No further movement was seen.

April 15th marked the beginning of the Division's major part in the "Buckland" plan—the forcing of the Argenta Gap, whence the enemy's series of defence lines radiated. Dependent on the success of this operation lay the issue of whether the Eighth Army would realise its objective or not —the destruction of the German Tenth Army south of the River Po. By April 16th full deployment was made, and all the platoons of "B" Group were committed in support of 11 Brigade. Pushing on steadily against heavy resistance, the village of Bastia was cleared in the morning, having been given a good softening up by No. 6 Platoon beforehand. Keeping up a strong pressure, the advance was maintained throughout the day, and by last light the town of Argenta itself was under fire. The enemy's determination to hold on to the Argenta Gap was made very clear by the fierce opposition encountered, and also by the identification of two of his reserve Divisions in the line.

During the night the 2nd Bn. Lancashire Fusiliers carried out an assault on the Fossa Marina, a canal running due east of Argenta town. The obstacle was bitterly defended, and both of "B" Group Mortar Platoons were called on continuously to fire D.F. tasks. The assault was eventually successful, and the infantry afterwards reported many enemy dead in areas known to have been engaged only by the mortars of "B" Group.

Dawn of April 17th found the battle for Argenta still in full swing, and the assaulting companies of the 5th Bn. Northamptons were eventually covered into the outskirts of the town by the guns of 9 Platoon at a range of 900 yards. Inside the town the fighting raged from house to house, and it was not until 21.00 hrs. that the town was proclaimed as being in our hands. Earlier in the day, 36 Brigade crossed the Reno and moved up behind 11 Brigade, preparatory to thrusting through them. At dusk, Nos. 1 and 2 Heavy Mortar Platoons of "C" Group occupied positions to support this break-through.

On April 18th, after another good night advance, 36 Brigade got to Boccaleone, and pushed on astride Route 16. Both "C" Group Mortar Platoons had fired almost continuously throughout the night. During the afternoon Battalion H.Q. moved across the Reno river, and was soon re-established in S. Biagio.

At last light, 36 Brigade was reported to have reached Consandolo, some six miles farther up Route 16. At this point, however, a counter-attack on the Brigade's exposed left flank brought the advance to a halt. After a good deal of firing at a very short range, Nos. 1 and 2 Platoons were given the "Stand-down", and were informed that the attack had been beaten off. On the right flank, 56 "Recce" Regiment made a sensational advance, and by evening had established a foothold in Portomaggiore. Meanwhile, "D"

STATIC WARFARE AND THE FINAL OFFENSIVE

Group remained back in the Argenta area with 38 Brigade, who were awaiting their turn in the pursuit.

Starting early in the morning of April 20th, Battalion H.Q. moved forward again, this time just south of Portomaggiore. All along the front the enemy now resisted with the utmost bitterness, the Canale di S. Nicolo being the obstacle he had chosen to stem our advance. Several small bridge-heads were made during the day, but little progress had been reported by them. All "B" Group's platoons were in action, and were finding it hard to meet the many calls made on them by the Infantry Battalions. Then "D" Group moved up in the evening, as 38 Brigade prepared to attack.

Despite stiff resistance throughout April 21st, better progress was made and a substantial bridge-head was formed. During the night 38 Brigade crossed the canal, and pushed forward in a north-easterly direction. "D" Group's platoons were soon in action with their respective Battalions, and were kept hard at work. In particular, No. 12 Platoon had a "field-day". At 10.30 hrs. the platoon guns were put in position to give right-flank protection to the Inniskillings. On arrival at their position they surprised a party of enemy only a few hundred yards in front of them. A rapid engagement followed, during which the Germans lost several of their number before they hurriedly withdrew. A few minutes later, the whole area was subjected to severe enemy shell-fire. The platoon wireless-set and a motor-cycle were badly damaged and one of the guns received a direct hit. Shortly afterwards, the platoon moved to a further position where a company of Germans was observed, apparently forming up for a counter-attack. This target was engaged and heavy casualties were inflicted on the enemy before they withdrew in disorder. Again the gun-line received unwelcome attention from enemy artillery, and Pte. Pupworth was unlucky in being wounded by shrapnel in the back, fortunately not seriously. No. 4 Platoon also had a most strenuous day, occupying three different positions and firing some 280 shells.

By last light the situation improved considerably. Unable to withstand the strong pressure against them, the enemy began to falter. Taking advantage of this our Armour forged ahead in a sensational dash and reached the Po di Volano. On April 22nd fighting continued towards the Diversivo di Volano, and the line of this obstacle was reached later in the day. Other troops of 36 Brigade succeeded in getting into the outskirts of Ferrara, but were held up there. The next day the enemy now appeared to be trying to hold us off from the Po crossings for as long as possible. Everywhere resistance was heavy, and only limited advances were made. In particular, the area around Baura was strongly defended and was engaged many times by "D" Group Mortar Platoons. "C" and "D" Groups busied themselves with flank-protection rôles, as the situation was very "fluid". News was later received that elements of the 6 Armoured Division on the left had succeeded in reaching the Po.

Better progress was made against the enemy's rearguards on April 24th. Early in the morning Baura was cleared, and the advance continued throughout the day to reach a point well beyond Saletta. "D" Group platoons had a somewhat quieter time, although both Mortar Platoons occupied three different positions during the advance, and No. 11 M.M.G. Platoon had the satisfaction of shooting up an enemy vehicle which was rash enough to try to make a dash from cover. Late that night information was received that 36 Brigade might be required for an assault crossing of the Po, and subsequently the Battalion 2/i/C., Major J. J. Evans, was instructed to report to the G.S.O.1 at H.Q., 78 Division. There he was informed that he would be Beachmaster on the north side of the Po if the assault crossing was made. After a short "recce" with the G.S.O.1, a conference was held at which all arms were represented. A provisional plan was agreed on; however, later in the day 36 Brigade was given the "Stand-down" order, as it was reported that elements of the Army had got a foothold over the Po already on our left.

Morning of April 25th found only a few remnants of the enemy south of the Po who still wished to offer resistance. A short-lived stand was made in the area of Ruina, but was well and truly dealt with by Nos. 3 and 4 Platoons of "D"

Group. Some 370 shells were fired, and subsequent inspection showed the village to have been indeed well named. By evening there was no fighting south of the river.

With the close of the fighting south of the Po, the rôle of the Division changed to one of holding the southern banks of the river. For this purpose, Groups remained under command of Brigades, and all platoons remained in their present positions for the time being. Most platoons spent the day checking equipment, and prisoner drives were organised. Many hundreds of Germans were combed out in this way. The reason for the enemy's stubborn resistance on the approaches to the river was now very obvious. The whole southern bank was strewn with a vast mass of abandoned material. Over two thousand vehicles, tanks, and S.P. guns were counted, and the area swarmed with army horses, much to the gratification of the local Italian population. From April 25th onwards, the Division "marked time".

The chronicle of events just enumerated really gives a very inadequate glimpse of the ubiquitous operations of the Battalion. Relentless pressure was exerted on the enemy every minute of every twenty-four hours. Tanks and infantry were just as accustomed to pushing on by night as they were by day. Our advance surged forward like some gigantic tidal wave, crushing the dykes of resistance by infiltration through some hole which allowed a trickle to become an irresistible deluge. Our jabs and thrusts, re-registered hourly on the map, resembled long, tenuous fingers sprawling through the enemy lines. Our flanks were often exposed, and it was not unusual for pockets of enemy to appear in our rear echelon areas, so quickly had our battle columns passed them.

For days and nights without end our mortars and machine-guns were rushed along the dusty roads in ceaseless support. They were no sooner deployed than requests for fire from the infantry were being answered, punctuated with a little private shooting at errant parties of "Boche" which had escaped attention. When one platoon was in action, another would be on the move ready to harass the Hun as soon as the advance carried the profusion of targets out of range of the former. Officers and men had little or no sleep in ensuring that the enemy had none at all. But the spirit and excitement of the chase was in the blood, and morale rocketed to an unprecedented height.

The breaking of the Argenta Gap, on which the whole enemy defence was hinged, offered the most formidable task. It was a narrow gap between Lake Comacchio on one side and flat marshes on the other. Several river defence lines converged upon it, and thus, once the gap was pierced, they were all out-flanked at one blow. Mines were laid in profusion everywhere. Entrenchments, pill-boxes, and entanglements in considerable depth testified to the Hun's determination to stop any break-through in this vital sector.

It needs little imagination to realise that this might have become another Cassino battle with a large cemetery "in lieu" of the Monastery. But our swift advance and preliminary shattering blows left the Argenta defence without sufficient German "cannon-fodder" to make it secure. After forty-eight hours' bitter and bloody fighting, in which the Battalion was well and truly enmeshed, the gap was opened. The Division had come through just in time to prevent the German reserves, frantically rushed from the north, from bolstering up their faltering lines. One indication of the enemy's confusion was that they had not even time to remove the *Achtung Minen* notices which surrounded their maze of mine-fields, and we accordingly knew of their existence without learning the "hard way".

The last few days of April were spent in "cleaning up"— how often that phrase occurs in the battle lulls—and we disported ourselves by examining abandoned enemy equipment, and riding around on horses, of which the enemy had allowed hundreds to run loose. The Division, entering into the spirit of things, organised a highly successful Gymkhana, and, even in this unwarlike direction, the Battalion participated with some distinction. Pte. Harrison, riding his charger "Dog Support", took second place in the first race!

In the meantime, the noise of battle had long since receded, as the "Kiwis" and 6 Armoured Division, jostled by the Fifth Army Americans, made a headlong rush for the Northern Italian boundaries.

On May 2nd, 1945, we had scarcely started to celebrate the fall of Berlin before the news of the final German collapse in Italy came through. Someone had intercepted a broadcast, in the early evening, which announced that the whole of the German Southern Group of Armies had capitulated.

Suddenly the sky became lurid with the flash of tracer ammunition, flares, and Verey light stars as far as the eye could see. That victory firework display by the infantry will always be remembered.

A certain elation was indeed shared by all, but nearly every one of us realised that we were in no way experiencing the tremendous emotion which we thought would engulf us when envisaging the end of our war in the preceding years. It was as if the final curtain had fallen violently on a drama so great, that the audience applauded only instinctively because their minds were still in the sphere of unreality.

However, in assessing events one fact which is abundantly clear is that casualties were very light, despite the large part taken by the Battalion throughout this bitter campaign. They total 350 all ranks, of which 48 were killed in action, 281 were wounded (including 120 injured as result of battle accidents), and 21 were accounted for as prisoners of war. It is interesting to compare these figures with the number who were evacuated to a Casualty Clearing Station or hospital on account of illness, for the latter amount to 187 officers and 1801 other ranks. If those who were treated at the R.A.P. and Medical Dressing Stations were added, the figure would be incredible.

Amongst the many congratulatory messages received by the Battalion from all strata of Army society on the conclusion of hostilities, tributes from the people with whom we had fought, of which the following, addressed to Major A. E. B. Foxwell, Commanding "D" Group, are typical, gave us the greatest satisfaction:

Dear Foxy,

You will, no doubt, have received the messages of congratulation sent out by the Army and Divisional Commanders.

I would like to add, that so far as credit may be due to the Irish

Brigade in these operations, we are pleased and proud to share it with you. Our partnership is now of such long and tried standing, that nothing we achieve is done without the invaluable contribution which you always give. Please, once again, thank all your soldiers. . . .

(Signed) T. P. D. SCOTT,
Brigadier, D.S.O.

To Major A. E. B. Foxwell,
Commanding "D" Support Group, 1st Kensingtons.

From Lt.-Col. D. L. Shaw, M.C.,
2nd Bn. The Royal Inniskilling Fusiliers.

Sunday, 29th April, 1945.

Dear Foxy,

I want to express to you my admiration for the terrific good work your boys have done for me. No job was too hard or too much for them. I am truly grateful. Will you convey to all the admiration of the Battalion, and I can only hope that we may have them with us again if we go forward.

(Signed) D. L. SHAW.

Major A. E. B. Foxwell,
Commanding "D" Support Group, 1st Kensingtons.

On May 5th we moved to Pordenone, sixty miles northwest of Venice. Three days later we chased Cossacks and Georgians, who had been fighting for the Germans, through the Alps, whilst Italian Partisans, with red scarves and a comprehensive arsenal in their belts, made an opportune, but mainly belated, appearance.

On May 8th we passed through Tolmezzo, and spiralled over the enormous Monte Croce pass into Austria, just as Mr. Winston Churchill was broadcasting the news of the final surrender of all German forces. We had no "V.E." Day celebrations. We were too busy blinking our eyes in baby astonishment at the veritable fairyland of Carinthia, with its grandiose scenery of pine-girdled mountains, verdant valleys, and picturesque chalets. The pretty towns of Mauthen and Kotschach, so neat and clean with their red roofs and gay paint, gave us a foretaste of the lovely country which we were to occupy. There was no more suitable territory in the whole of Europe that could have been chosen for our "Journey's End".

CHAPTER XVII

A GLIMPSE OF THE AUSTRIAN AFTERMATH

May 1945–April 1946

FOR the first few weeks in Austria, everybody worked harder than had ever been anticipated. We were in a beautiful country, but what a mess!

Events are recorded hereafter day by day merely as a factual and superficial record, which will only hint at the underlying chaos and complexity of the situations with which we had to cope.

May 9th. Overnight and throughout the day the remainder of "C" Group moved forward to join Group H.Q. at Ober Drauberg. From there the whole Group moved on again to Sillian. The area was found to be swarming with displaced persons and P.O.W., as well as refugees of all nations and descriptions. On arrival at Sillian, a spontaneous parade for the Group Commander was held by the French ex-P.O.W. who had been doing forced labour in that area, and were now liberated. Road blocks were established, and a collecting camp was set up. "B" Group spent the day finding billets in Mauthen, and "D" Group continued their task of organising the hundreds of stragglers who were continually drifting down the roads towards Udine, in Italy. An advance party, consisting of Major J. J. Evans and Captain J. A. German, left for Austria to "recce" an area for Battalion H.Q. and H.Q. Group.

May 10th and 11th. Collection of arrestable persons in "C" Group area continued. Information was received that two Gestapo agents were hiding in a house at Arnbach. A party was dispatched to arrest them, but unfortunately they committed suicide before this could be effected.

"D" Group left Udine area and, after a long run, staged for the night about five miles east of Klagenfurt.

"B" Group, at Mauthen, spent a pleasant day at the swimming-baths just outside the town. Late at night, however, they received orders to stand by at two hours' notice to move.

May 12*th*. During the early morning "B" Group left Mauthen and proceeded to "Longstop" Barracks, Villach. "C" Group, at Sillian, reported no change in their hectic situation. "D" Group continued their march to the east, and were eventually established at Wolfsberg. Later in the day, half of the Group moved back to Griffen, and immediately started light armoured patrols against the Bulgarian irregulars who were reported to be ravaging the district. It was found that there were about five thousand Bulgars in the area, and these were gently but firmly shepherded back across the Yugoslav border.

May 13*th*. "B" Group, having settled into "Longstop" Barracks, now established road posts. These posts checked and marshalled the remnants of the German Armies streaming back from the eastern front. Meanwhile, in the barracks, "B" Group H.Q. did everything possible to make the allied ex-P.O.W. they held there as comfortable as possible.

"C" Group reported work continuing, and there was no change in the situation in "D" Group area.

May 14*th*. The flow of P.O.W.s, etc., into Villach showed no signs of abatement, and the ration strength now reached an average figure of two thousand daily. For their recreation "B" Group had been lucky in finding Madelenensee, a beautiful little lake in the middle of the pine-woods near the barracks. "D" Group were still maintaining their carrier patrols and were very busy keeping Tito's troops on the right side of the border. The Commanding Officer visited "C" Group in the Sillian area, and inspected the camps they had established there. Major J. J. Evans proceeded to Treffen, and was engaged in inspecting billets when a message arrived informing us that the Commanding Officer was appointed Area Commander, Spittal area, and Major J. J. Evans as Town Major. For the remainder of the day a hurried "recce" of Spittal was made, and a preliminary take-over was arranged for the following day. The Town Major already there was found to be none other than Major R. Wasey!

May 15th and 16th. Organisation of the Spittal area proceeded. The Commanding Officer and the Town Major established their H.Q. in the main square, and all offices were flooded by thousands of people of all nationalities from opening until closing time. The Town Billeting Officer (Capt. J. Oliver) spent a very busy day finding better accommodation for our troops. There were several large internee camps just outside the town, and these were used to house the different categories of people to be detained. "C" Group held a large-scale interrogation of the P.O.W. they were holding.

May 17th. The Commanding Officer attended a conference at H.Q. 78 Division to discuss and co-ordinate the present lay-out for disposal of enemy personnel.

On the other side of Austria, at Griffen, two of "D" Group's patrols, under the command of Lieutenants Dixon and Wimbury, had the honour of disarming some four thousand Cossack soldiers who had been fighting for the Germans. This unique experience was marred by an unfortunate accident in which Lieutenant Dixon was shot in the leg. Then further bad news revealed that the Battalion had lost Pte. J. W. Wonfor, who was killed in a tragic carrier accident in "D" Group area.

May 18th. Having collected in all stray displaced persons and prisoners in their immediate area, "C" Group organised a drive to comb some of the mountain villages near by. A wide sweep was made and many local arrests resulted. In the afternoon "D" Group received a warning order to be ready to move from Wolfsberg and Griffen at short notice. All equipment and kit were hastily packed up. In Spittal, despite an excellent staff of interpreters, the Town Major was an extremely harassed man. There appeared to be no end to the number of people who wanted interviews. Late in the day the Commanding Officer was visited by a delegation from the International Red Cross Committee. The deputation consisted of four Counts—a Frenchman, a Swiss, an Italian, and an Austrian. They were well pleased with what they saw.

May 19th. Early in the morning, "D" Group received orders to move off to Tarvisio, Italy. On arrival there, this order was countermanded, and the Group was routed back to Villach instead. This "Kits on—Kits off" procedure was characteristic of the bedlam in Carinthia.

The now familiar sign of the "Clarendon" once again made its appearance in the afternoon. A large restaurant in the centre of the town was taken over fully furnished, and was converted into a very excellent Battalion canteen.

May 20th. "D" Group established themselves in an ex-German Ordnance depot just outside Villach, and stood by for a possible operational rôle against Tito's Yugoslavian forces. As far as could be understood, a political deadlock had been reached and considerable tension had resulted.

May 21st. "B" Group found life a little easier in Villach. The number of Germans who passed through their hands remained undiminished, but an organisation for dealing with them more rapidly was set up, and all ranks started to get a little more spare time. In the town, cinemas and other welfare amenities were opened and were much appreciated by those who were able to get an evening off duty. "C" Group held an inter-platoon sports meeting, and "D" Group were still standing by in the Villach area.

May 22nd. During the morning Major E. Grant, G.S.O.2 78 Division, visited "C" Group. After his inspection he remarked that he had been instructed by the G.O.C. to endorse strongly the Divisional Commander's congratulations of a few days previously. "C" Group were still collecting in arrestable categories, and, in addition, also had many Cossacks in their area. "D" Group started to move up to Spittal. They were to be accommodated in the Lieser Caserne, a very roomy but then dirty barracks at the entrance to the town. Thanks to the untiring efforts of Captain J. A. German, H.Q. Group sat down to their meals at tables, and had them served completely on china-ware.

May 23rd. Owing to an impending large-scale movement of P.O.W., "C" Group were to have a representative force in the town of Lienz. An advance party left Sillian to find billets for the platoons who were required to go there. Meanwhile, at Sillian, the Group football team played H.Q. 36 Brigade and won by two goals to one, after a hard game. The Battalion was glad to welcome back Captain R. May,

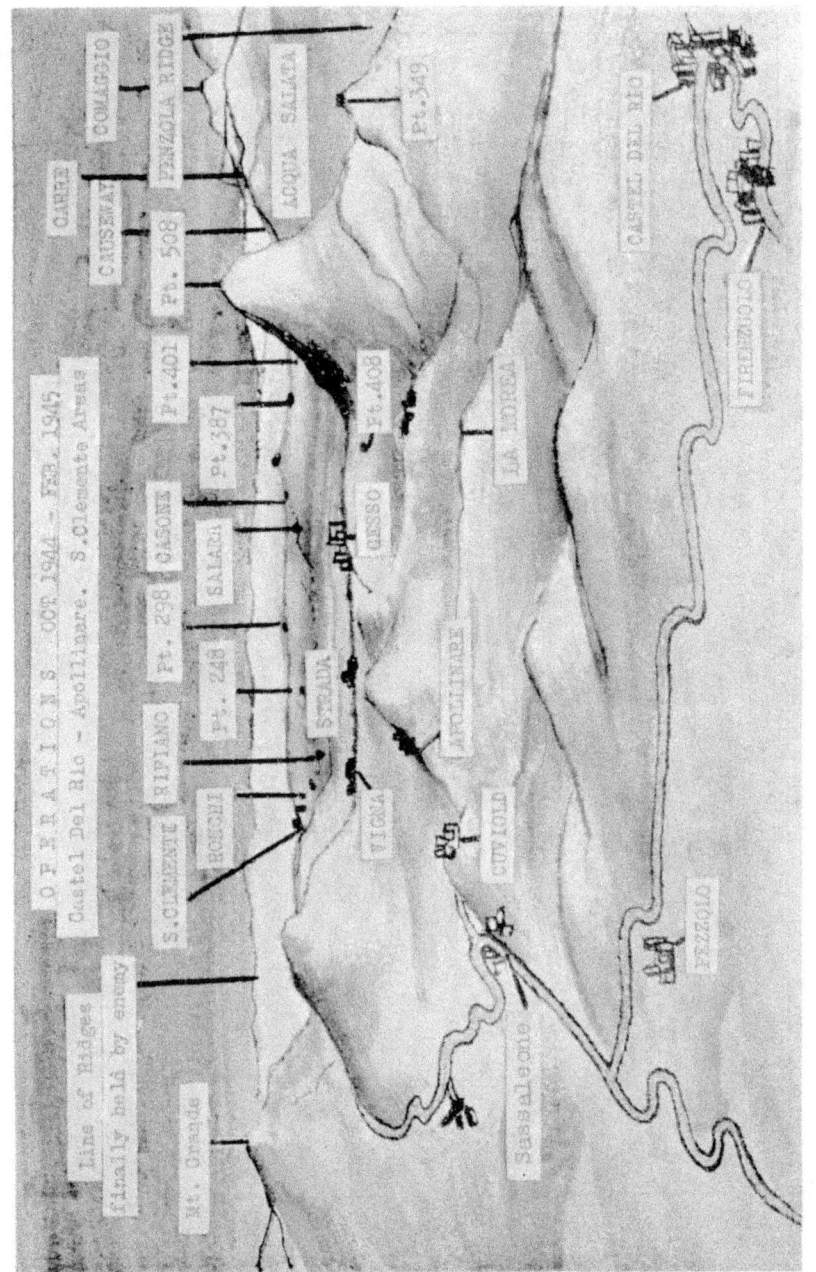

OPERATIONS, OCTOBER 1944–FEBRUARY 1945. (*See Chapter XV.*)

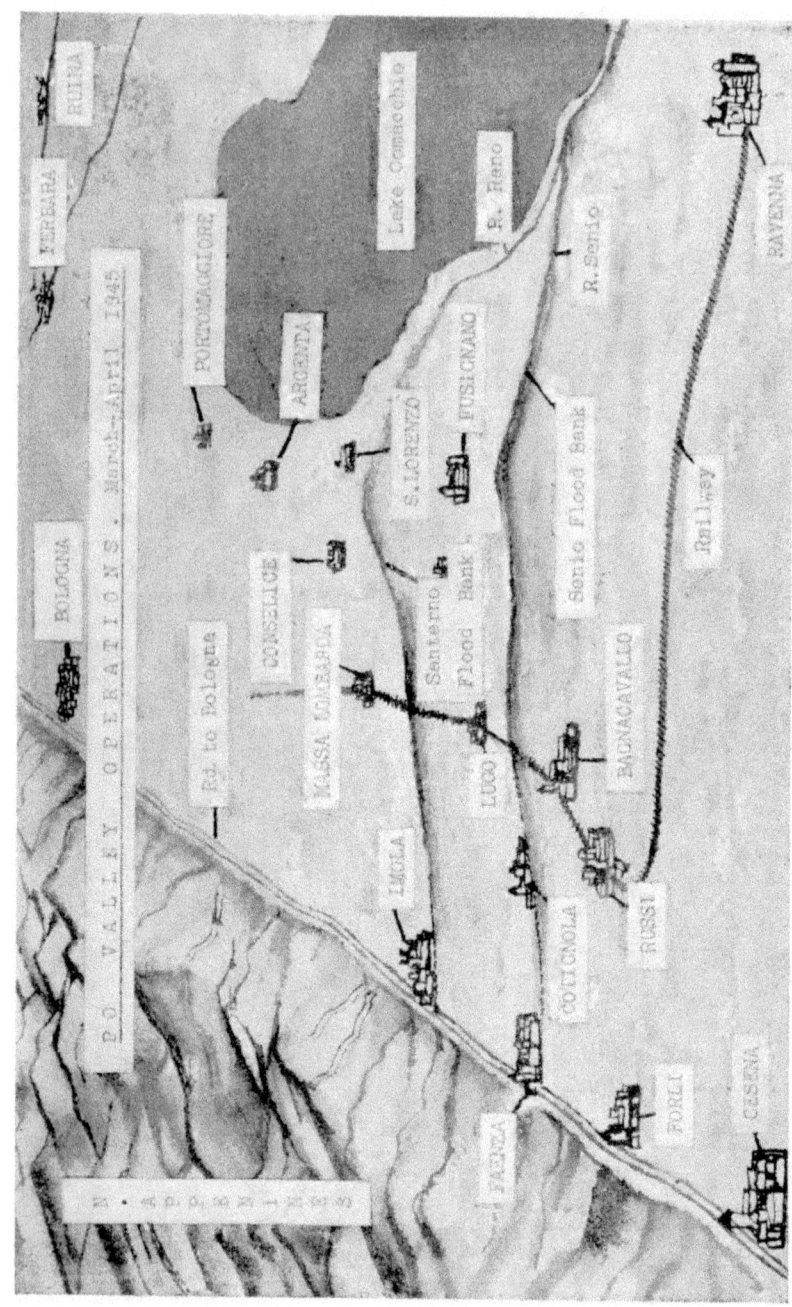

Po Valley Operations, March–April 1945. (*See Chapter XVI.*)

who returned from the C.M.T.C. He was posted to "C" Group. The remainder of "D" Group moved into the Lieser Caserne during the morning, and immediately started the task of cleaning up the barracks.

May 25th. Visits and inspections came to the fore in "B" Group's barracks. Lieutenant-General Sir Richard McCreery, K.C.B., D.S.O., M.B.E., M.C., G.O.C. Eighth Army, accompanied by Commander of V Corps and the Divisional Commander, carried out an inspection of the French ex-P.O.W. The parade was drawn up in the middle of the barrack square, and, after the inspection, an address was read to General McCreery by one of the French Officers. General McCreery replied suitably. The Guard of Honour was supplied by "B" Group. "C" Group continued their "recce" of Lienz, and "D" Group were still making very heavy going of cleaning up the Lieser Caserne. The Stables which Hercules was meant to tidy up had nothing on these barracks. The Battalion was visited by Mrs. Dorothy Thompson, the celebrated American columnist, who was touring the area.

May 26th. Group H.Q. and the two M.M.G. Platoons of "C" Group were to move to Lienz the following day, and the remainder of the day was spent by them in packing up.

May 27th. During the morning "B" Group were given a lecture by Lieutenant C. Belsom, a French Officer and ex-internee. The subject of this most moving and instructive talk was "German Concentration Camps", with which subject Lieutenant Belsom had had plenty of first-hand experience. "C" Group H.Q. and two M.M.G. Platoons accomplished their move to Lienz satisfactorily. The task of cleaning the Lieser Caserne still continued to occupy "D" Group fully!

May 28th. The reason behind "C" Group's move to Lienz was now apparent. 78 Div. Operational Order No. 6 was received which explained the terms of the Yalta agreement recently concluded with the U.S.S.R. Under this agreement, Soviet Nationals were to be returned to Russia, and the two thousand-odd officers of the Cossack Division concentrated in 36 Brigade area were to be the first to go from this sector. Return to the U.S.S.R. was the last thing in the world that these people wanted, and it was anticipated that there might be considerable trouble in getting them moved. The Commanding Officer convened a conference and explained the responsibilities and Guard duties which would be necessary, at the same time emphasising the need for extreme caution in handling these Cossacks. Meanwhile, in the 36 Brigade area, the Cossack officers were informed that they were required to attend a conference, and were in due course embussed and brought to Spittal. On arrival they were admitted to camp under a strong guard. The Commanding Officer then sent for General Dominoff, and gave him orders regarding discipline and routine while in Spittal camp. The General was also informed of the eventual destination of the Cossack Division.

May 29th. After a good deal of trouble, the Cossack officers in the camp were embussed early and moved off on the last stage of their journey. During the night there were three attempted suicides, one unsuccessful....

"B" Group moved up to Spittal, and took over "Knightsbridge" Camp from 255th A/Tank Battery R.A. "C" Group continued their patrols in the Sillian area, and more "arrestables" were brought in daily.

May 30th. Having congratulated ourselves on finishing a most unpleasant business, the Battalion was somewhat irritated to find that a further batch of Cossack officers had been sent to Spittal. They arrived on May 29th, approximately seventy in strength, and the same procedure was carried out as for the first batch. Meanwhile, reports continued to come in of disturbances and demonstrations in the Cossack camps in the "C" Group area. Several "sit-down" strikes had to be forcibly dispersed, and many of the camps were hung with black flags and posters bearing the slogan: "Hunger and Death before return to the Soviet Union."

May 31st. The last of the Cossack officers were dispatched without incident, except for one unsuccessful attempt at suicide. After a week of hard work, "D" Group now had the Lieser Caserne well under control, and the building began to approach peace-time barrack standards. "B" Group was comfortably housed at "Knightsbridge", and Battalion H.Q. and H.Q. Group, after a few changes of billets, were well placed in the town itself. Now that the initial flood of work was over, more time was available for recreation. A string of a dozen horses were kept by the Battalion, under the supervision of Captain C. E. Depinna, and was always in great demand. Parties were also sent daily to Millstattersee, a very beautiful lake about 8 km. outside the town. The cinema in the town was opened, and also a theatre, where evening entertainments of all descriptions were planned.

As we said, these brief daily accounts disclose just a few of the problems which the Battalion had to tackle. There were thousands of Displaced Personnel of all nationalities, each of whom came daily to us with his individual requests and complaints. In addition, the work of rounding up Nazis, "S.S." men, and other arrestable categories went on continuously, punctuated by a few hours of recreation occasionally.

The efficiency, enthusiasm, and smartness of the Battalion is well reflected in the following typical tribute from the Acting Brigadier of H.Q. 36 Infantry Brigade, on the occasion of "C" Group rejoining the Battalion from Sillian early in July :

Dear Bryar,
Now that "C" Support Group has returned completely to your care, I would like to express the appreciation of myself and the rest of the Brigade for all the work they have done for us since we have been in Austria. They were given a large and difficult area. Because of the distances involved, they had to do all the work of organisation and "cleaning up" with very little help from outside. They encountered, and solved, many problems ranging from frontier control to liaison with the Americans. Everything they have done—and they have done a great deal—has been done efficiently and expeditiously. Brian Harpur's organisation, and that of his successor, has produced an area which is as "tidy" as any in the Division. Brigadier Musson said, at a conference a week or so after our arrival in Austria, that the turn-out and saluting of the men of "C" Group was the best in the Brigade Group. I am sorry that they have left us, and I would be grateful if you would thank them all for their excellent work.

We found the Austrian civilians on the whole very

friendly, and even more so when the fraternisation ban was lifted in the early autumn. As the weeks progressed, Spittal, with its familiar red and grey signs announcing such nostalgic landmarks as "Hyde Park Hotel" (Officers' Mess), "Kensington Gardens" (the local park), "Wormwood Scrubs" (the local gaol), "Adam and Eve" (the local pub), and "Kensington High Street", became more and more like a little London.

Enormous guards had to be supplied from Groups to look after dumps and "S.S." camps, for which men had to be found from ever-dwindling strengths, as parties on U.K. leave and on release were dispatched daily.

Trickling through "the usual channels" came many belated awards and decorations to men of the Battalion won in previous months. The full list, totalling about a hundred awards, can be found in the Appendices.

Mention has already been made as to how some of these were earned. It is regretted, however, that it has been found impossible to allude to all the incidents which gave rise to the citations, because their inclusion *in toto* would simply have meant the omission of events essential to the Battalion story as a whole, due to lack of space.

After the first chaos, the Battalion soon settled down to a rather care-free existence. The summer proved to be excellent, and not interrupted by so many of those spasmodic thunderstorms which we knew so well in our Italian days. There was an air of unreality about everything which was engendered primarily by the beautiful scenery of almost fairylike nature, but there was also an artificial atmosphere about all activities, which somehow seemed to make people concerned more with the social aspect of life than with the realities of an occupation army.

A great occasion came on July 6th, when Lieut.-Gen. Sir Richard L. McCreery, K.C.B., K.B.E., D.S.O., M.C., doughty Commander of the Eighth Army, inspected the 78 Division at Spittal. This parade—noted for its clockwork precision, we take some pride in saying—was organised by Major J. W. Doyle, M.C., who had been posted to Divisional H.Q., it seemed, expressly for this purpose. Under a blazing sun, surrounded by towering peaks, all the units of the Division were massed in serried ranks for the last time. Memories of the past three years surged to the mind, and when it was also remembered that many of the comrades standing there that day would soon be dispatched to civilian life, the occasion became fraught with an intensity which only great emotion can bring. When the inspection was over, the troops marched past their Commander-in-Chief and also the Divisional Commander and then swung down Spittal High Street, watched by many thousands of the Germans whom they had helped to defeat. That parade, never to be forgotten, marked the final phase of the great and gallant trek from Algiers to Austria.

Within a matter of days men in the first release groups were saying good-bye, and the autumn of the Battalion had set in. For those who remained there was only a routine of minor inspections and constant wood-cutting. The latter was introduced because this valuable fuel was needed in great quantities for dispatching to Vienna where the many thousands of inhabitants badly needed a substitute for coal during the coming winter months.

By the end of August the Battalion was firmly installed in the Spittal area, and Groups were dispersed as follows:

"B" Group (Commanded by Major C. E. Cullen), in a village north of Spittal called Radenthein.
"C" Group (Commanded by Major R. May), at Edling Camp—near Spittal.
"D" Group (Commanded by Major R. D. Hutchings), in the famous barracks in Spittal itself.

The only incidents which were unusual were the organisation of security patrols which went up into the mountains every week to round up suspected Nazi sympathisers. These patrols ensured that a good quota of the Battalion became hardy mountaineers, but they seldom produced results as regards catching their prey.

In September the first major changes in the Battalion took place, when the Commanding Officer and the Second-in-Command, Major J. J. Evans, left for England on release. In their absence Major A. E. B. Foxwell took over command until the arrival of Lt.-Col. J. B. Worton, followed by the arrival of a new Second-in-Command some months later, namely, Major Gilbert.

The departure of Lt.-Col. B. L. Bryar and Major Evans was viewed with great regret, and when finally Major Foxwell took the same road for "Blighty" a sense of loss most grievous was felt, which the many bibulous farewell parties did naught to assuage.

Fortunately Lt.-Col. J. B. Worton and Major Gilbert were of the calibre to meet the needs of the situation. By their tact, understanding, and supremely soldier-like qualities they quickly won the devotion of all those who served under them.

As the winter months drew on, preparations were made to exploit ski-ing, and when snow actually fell the Battalion very soon had large programmes under way.

The Christmas of 1945 will long remain in the memories of the Battalion. Apart from the traditional effort of the Kensington Administration to provide suitable fare in the form of turkeys, snow began to fall at midday and continued right throughout Christmas night, so that "Dreaming of a White Christmas" was in fact a reality once again.

By this time also, of course, the miseries of the thousands of displaced persons in the area did not seem so urgent, and time was even found to provide a gigantic Christmas party for the Austrian children in the Town Hall, for which, quite voluntarily, everybody had forgone a day's rations. Capt. "Gerry" German, commanding H.Q. Group, played no small part in making these Christmas arrangements.

It remains only to be said that the festivities, tinged with a certain amount of regret because so many of the faces at the previous Christmas celebrations were now missing, were nevertheless a great success.

The first three months of 1946 were chiefly taken up with training and ski-ing, and also with the training of small drafts of reinforcements taking the place, inadequately to begin with, of those who had left. Suddenly, on April 8th, Lt.-Col. J. B. Worton received news that the Battalion was to convert to the rôle of the infantry and move by rail to the Naples area. This involved a tremendous amount of reorganisation. The problem was greatly complicated by the fact that so many of the more experienced members of the Battalion were on the verge of demobilisation. Towards the end of April, however, the Battalion moved south to the Naples area of Italy in accordance with orders.

CHAPTER XVIII

GRECIAN TWILIGHT

April 1946–September 1946

SHORTLY before sailing to Greece, Capt. Hemming arrived with the rearguard from Spittal, having finally got rid of the last of the vehicles and stores, and on April 20th, leaving behind Major May, Lieut. Shimield, Lieut. Kendell, and a small party who were shortly due for release, the Battalion embarked at Naples. About midday the ship cast off, and as evening approached, the glow of Stromboli could be seen to starboard.

Fortunately the intensity of the sun in April was not too great to make life between decks unbearable, but nevertheless the quarters were cramped, and so, as the ship steamed slowly into Piræus on the morning of the 23rd, the majority were glad to think that they would soon be on land again with some freedom of movement.

From Piræus harbour we were transported by truck to 30 Reception Camp in the north-western suburbs of Athens, where further reinforcements joined us. Like a snowball, we had been increasing in size all the way from Austria to Greece, and by now the Battalion was almost up to strength.

The following day the transport was collected, and on the 27th the Battalion headed for Patras, on the north coast of the Peloponnese at the mouth of the Gulf of Corinth.

The camp there bordered the seashore and stretched to within ten yards of the water's edge. It was situated about a mile from the centre of Patras, on the north-eastern outskirts of the town. The area included four houses and their gardens and some open land, on which had been erected a number of Nissen huts and a similar-shaped but larger hut as a dining-hall.

Owing to lack of room in the camp "C" Company had to be billeted out in a school a mile or so along the road to

Corinth, but were fortunate in one respect, in that their billets remained fairly cool during the heat of summer, whereas the Nissen huts in the main camp acted as enlarged versions of Aldershot ovens and the atmosphere inside them became unbearable, especially as there was little or no breeze during the heat of the day.

On arrival the Battalion became fully engaged in guard duties. Not only had guards to be provided for the Brigade petrol dump and other stores, but there had to be a guard of no fewer than 12 N.C.O.s and 64 o/r. to protect the Battalion camp alone from the designs of the "klepsi-wallahs", who were capable of removing stores and equipment with even more adroitness than the Egyptian "wog". The triple Dannert wire surrounding the camp had to be inspected and often repaired daily. The thieves would approach the shore silently by night in a rowing-boat, put through the wire a small boy who would raid a billet or store, run to the wire and throw the kit over to his waiting confederates. The boy would often be caught, but the kit would be gone. Brigade H.Q. authorised the use of harmless booby-traps and trip flares, but to counteract these the "klepsi-wallahs" would send dogs through the wire or stand by day outside the Dannert and throw stones over at any visible trip wire. Against such sport there was no remedy, as we were not allowed to touch one of our "Allies" unless caught inside W.D. property.

The strictest guard had to be kept on explosives, as high prices were offered by fishermen for such bait. Fishing with explosives was forbidden, but if caught the penalty was only small and was many times offset by the resultant large catch of fish.

Infantry training for any men not on guard was the next priority. A field-firing range was taken over in a small open valley behind the town, and there platoon exercises took place. A battalion shooting competition was held in preparation for the Divisional competition in July, and the Divisional competition itself was held eventually on the slopes of Mt. Hymethus, south-east of Athens. At the end of a hot and tiring day the Battalion teams in the various events finished second.

Meanwhile the Battalion was sending "Show the Flag" patrols across the Gulf of Patras. A few trucks and a small party about platoon strength would be transported in L.C.T.s across the water to Messolonghi, Byron's resting-place, and then would set out on a circular tour in the mountainous area to the east. The local population always seemed pleased to see the British Army, and when the patrol halted for the night a village would often roast a sheep for them.

To these outlying districts U.N.R.R.A. supplies had not penetrated, and although food was not short, medical supplies were in great need. Many of the children would be found suffering from impetigo and other skin diseases. It is to be hoped that the reports of these patrols were passed on to the right authorities and that the much-wanted supplies did eventually find these obscure villages hidden in the depths of the mountains.

Anti-malarial precautions in the Patras area were carried out on an imposing scale. U.N.R.R.A. planes sprayed the swamps, and parties from the Battalion cut down acres of reed and rush. Every house in the district was sprayed with D.D.T., with the result that Patras, which a year or so before had been one of the worst malarial areas in Greece, was left almost free of the scourge.

The Battalion had been only a short time in Patras when Lt.-Col. Worton returned from England and resumed command. Capt. Scott received promotion and took over "D" Coy., handing over the duties of Adjutant to Capt. McKay, who, after a short time, passed the job on to Lieut. A. Cosgrove, the latter relinquishing the appointment of Quartermaster on the arrival of Capt. (Q.M.) P. F. Newman, of the Middlesex Regt. Capt. Bennett also received his crown and remained in command of H.Q. Coy.

One week-end in July Patras was visited by the Royal Navy in the shapes of H.M.S. *Mermaid* and H.M.S. *Magpie*, two sloops from the Mediterranean fleet. Lt.-Col. Worton, acting as Commander 179 Brigade in the absence of the Brigadier, headed the reception committee, which immediately received a broadside of hospitality under the awnings of the *Mermaid*. In the few days during which the

Navy remained at Patras, inter-service rivalry in the way of entertainment reached unprecedented heights, and it is to be noted that as H.M.S. *Mermaid* steamed out of the harbour on the Tuesday morning and came opposite the Battalion camp a message was flashed by Aldis lamp to our signallers at H.Q. The message read, "Refer to Book of Job, chapter 18, verse 9"; a hasty reference to the Bible revealed the sentence, "The gin shall take him by the heel..."!

Inter-service relations also flourished with the R.A.F. At Araxos, twenty miles to the west of Patras, 252 Squadron, R.A.F., was stationed on an airfield built by the Germans during the war. To the airmen there it might have been in the middle of the desert, except that the sea was only a short way off and there were always plenty of turkeys. Hardly had the Kensingtons got to hear of 252 Sqdn. than a cricket match was arranged; in fact, that match was to become an almost weekly event, one Saturday afternoon at Araxos, the next at Patras, and often the visiting teams would spend the night with their hosts, returning on Sunday morning.

Despite the scorching heat, it was impossible to stop Kensingtons playing football, and a series of inter-platoon matches was arranged. The pitch was in the stadium not far from the camp. Often the spectators had more idea of the way the ball was going than the players, as every time it was kicked there was a vast cloud of brown dust enveloping all.

The loss of Sgt. Edmeads, the Battalion Medical Sgt., was a deep blow to the Battalion. It had been arranged that several sergeants should go over to the R.A.F. at Araxos and be taken for short trips in Beaufighters. Unfortunately one of these planes, in which Sgt. Edmeads was a passenger, flying parallel with the south shore of the Gulf of Corinth about half a mile out over the water, crashed and sank immediately.

The summer passed with no lessening of the guard commitments, and as August drew to a close and more men went on release we heard that the Battalion was to be disbanded at the end of September. We had seen Territorial units disbanded all around us and we, being one of the last survivors, realised that our turn could not be far off.

On September 15th, 1946, we were put "in suspended animation". Stores and equipment were crated and prepared for delivery to Egypt by Capt. (Q.M.) Newman. Ten days later the Battalion was taken by train, on the recently repaired Patras to Athens narrow-gauge railway, to 30 Reception Camp on the outskirts of the capital. There, on September 29th, the Kensingtons as a military unit ceased to exist. Those who had originally sailed with the Battalion for North Africa were shortly due for "Python", the home posting after $3\frac{1}{2}$ years overseas, and remained in the camp for a month before boarding H.M.T. *Durban Castle* for home. Regulars in the Middlesex Regiment were sent to join their parent regiment in Palestine. The remainder were sent to units all over Greece, many joining 4 Inf. Div. in Salonika.

The move of the remnants of the Battalion to Greece, so briefly described, and its final disbandment there, puts an end to the story. It has concerned primarily the three fighting Groups, but we feel that the solid base on which the success of all our operations was founded was made up by the cheerful and indefatigable "Private Tommy Atkins", just as much in evidence in H.Q. Group and Battalion H.Q. as anywhere else.

We can never forget the sterling work performed in difficulty and in danger by those "unknowns" who always got the work and never got the glory. The "Q" staff in H.Q. Group saw to it that we never lacked for rations, and that our million needs were always satisfied. The H.Q., M.T. staff, with their Light Aid Detachment, worked hard and incessantly, and produced results which were second to none. The Signals Section and those of the Groups had this tribute paid to them:

> Under the cover of "General Signal Routine" there was always a tapestry of gallantry and unselfishness and a sense of responsibility which enabled the Battalion to repeat at all times—"Signals, Strength 5"....

There were also the drivers, who manned our vehicles and drove them all those thousands of miles from Algiers to the Alps with such habitual efficiency and bravery that we are afraid we rather took them for granted.

Then we had those "doyens" of the Battalion who formed the background of our routine, and because of them it was a routine which could never be dislocated. We speak of the cooks, who summoned us regularly to the cook-house with a valiant "Come and get it"—despite the rain of shells or just the rain; and of the storemen, the sanitary men, the orderlies, and the indomitable clerks.

We can do no more than conclude by quoting the words of Major-General R. K. Arbuthnott, C.B., D.S.O., M.C., when, in a written message to the whole of his Division in the first issue of the Divisional newspaper, *The Battleaxe Weekly*, he said:

> ... the infantry will, I know, like me to say a special word of praise to those who have provided the supporting fire in our operations ... the 1st Kensingtons. It is my belief that it would not be possible to find ... a better Support Battalion in any Army in any theatre of war. ...

He has reaffirmed these sentiments on several occasions since the war, and when it is remembered that he commanded the Division which was commonly mooted as being the finest in the British Army, such a tribute assumes added significance. However, it is probably best to regard it merely as some evidence of the success achieved on the part of the 1st Battalion in its attempt to live up to the tradition so gloriously forged by the Kensingtons who have gone before.

CHAPTER XIX

"QUID NOBIS ARDUI"—THE CAPTIVE KENSINGTONS

HAVING read of the exploits of the 1st Bn. throughout several years, let us now return to France in June, 1940.

Whilst Battalion H.Q., H.Q., "B", and "C" Companies were being evacuated from Le Havre, the survivors of "A" and "D" Companies were being herded together by shouting Germans on the morning of June 12th. Already everyone had rendered useless personal arms and destroyed any documents that might be of value to the enemy, but the Germans, confronted with the task of searching so many prisoners, soon gave up the task and concentrated on endeavouring to get them into columns which were moved off as quickly as possible. It seemed as if there were more guards than prisoners, as besides German infantry, tanks of all descriptions moved up and down the columns.

At first, the Kensingtons endeavoured to keep together in one block, and although the Germans eventually separated the officers from the men, as the former were feared to be a bad example to the latter, the men also found it impossible to remain together. The day's march was the first of many such nightmares: it was boiling hot, and most people carried a heavy pack containing their worldly possessions, which made things worse. It must be remembered that no one had any sleep for some days and not much food, and the enemy permitted a halt of only ten minutes every three hours. The crying need was for water, and water fit to drink was not easy to find in France—not that that mattered now, as any water, however green, stagnant, or evil-smelling, was like nectar to the tired and weary men. After marching from 10.00 hrs. to 20.00 hrs. a halt for the night was made at last, but no food was issued and aching bodies lay down in the fields. Any hope that anyone had of slipping off during the night was speedily dispelled as the German guards formed a perimeter around the various batches of prisoners and almost touched hands.

At 05.00 hrs. the next morning the long columns, still foodless, were on the march again, and so it was to happen every day for more than fourteen days until the distance of 220 miles to the River Scheldt in Holland had been covered. How anyone managed to survive the forced marches on such empty stomachs will always be a source of wonderment to those who took part. After the first two days, rations of a sort were issued, but they were extremely meagre: a cupful of *ersatz* coffee and three small biscuits in the morning, and at the end of the day's march a hunk of stale bread and possibly a piece of horse-meat or a cupful of weak soup, supplemented by anything the prisoners could scrounge on the way such as raw mangels, turnips, and carrots. French, Belgian, and Dutch civilians, whenever the opportunity offered, pressed small packets of food into the eager hands of the unfortunates, and no P.O.W. will ever be able to forget the kindness and courage of these people. An example was seen at Doullens of the "New Order" which Germany was bringing into the conquered countries: a young girl with a baby in her arms attempted to give a packet of cigarettes to a prisoner; she was seized by two guards, thrown into the gutter, and the baby rolled screaming from her arms on to the cobbled road, and but for the raised guns of the other guards there is no doubt there would have been two fewer of the so-called "Master Race".

After the Franco–Belgian frontier had been passed the attitude of the civilians was very hostile to the British prisoners in particular, and not even the much-desired water was provided. However, after the first day's march in Belgium the attitude changed, and the Belgians acted in much the same manner as did the French, and as the Dutch were to do when Holland was reached. Eventually the River Scheldt was sighted and the prisoners were loaded, like cattle, on barges to be transported into Germany. Cattle, however, were given enough space to lie down; prisoners-of-war were not.

At Wesel, the German frontier town on the Rhine, the P.O.W. disembarked, and the civilians showed little interest and, despite the flags flying from all buildings to celebrate the victory over France, seemed very apathetic.

It was noticed that the majority of shop windows were empty except for a portrait of the Führer, but the populace certainly did not look starved, although many children ran about barefooted. After staying in the local park all day, fortified by a meal of watery soup, the prisoners entrained in cattle-trucks, in the early evening, for various transit camps. At these camps all ranks realised for the first time the utter boredom which is ever the lot of a P.O.W. The exercise space was limited, there were no books to read, no writing-materials, and the German rations, consisting of two scanty meals per day, could not be supplemented by the gifts of civilians. In between meals a P.O.W. could only think, and his first thoughts were of his next meal, which made him even hungrier.

Generally, a week was spent in the transit camp and the prisoners were then moved to permanent camps where, although living conditions were a shade better than the dreadful conditions in the transit camps, the food was neither better nor more plentiful. The troops were dispatched in the main to various old Army camps in Poland, and the officers to an incredibly ancient *Schloss* in Southern Germany.

Overcrowding was probably the worst of all the evils of German prison camps, and for five long and weary years no P.O.W. was to know the meaning of the words "privacy" and "quiet" unless he was fortunate enough to obtain a sentence of solitary confinement. Then, being alone more than compensated the even smaller rations.

The main worry of the prisoners in the early days was the knowledge that the next-of-kin were still without any information of their whereabouts as, owing to the complete disruption of communications in Europe, the two letters and two cards which each prisoner was allowed to write were not leaving Germany and no mail was, of course, received in Germany from home. The International Red Cross endeavoured to ascertain the names of prisoners from the various camps, but this took a long time due to the gross inefficiency and callousness of the German camp staff. It was not until October 1940, four months after St. Valéry, that the majority of the next-of-kin had definite news of those posted "missing".

In the early months all prisoners suffered considerably from enteritis due to the very liquid diet, and these months were the most trying in all the five years. No books, no letters, no cigarettes, only the clothes one was wearing, despite the fact that the detaining Power was bound according to the Geneva Convention to adequately clothe and feed prisoners. It was soon realised that the enemy paid scant attention to the Geneva Convention and copies of it were unobtainable at some camps.

During the day the monotony was relieved, at least for the other ranks, by going out on working parties, but the evenings in both *Oflags* and *Stalags* were always difficult to fill. Thanks, however, to various organisations in Switzerland and Sweden, all camps were soon provided with musical instruments, so that bands and orchestras were rapidly formed. In addition, excellent plays and shows were evolved, and in various camps in which he was interned Sgt. Greenhill produced, at times out of almost nothing, wonderful scenery and stage "props" which gave the shows a most professional air.

Towards Christmas 1940 clothes-parcels (one a quarter could be sent) began to arrive from England; by this time prisoners had reached a very weak state, due to insufficient food and clothing in the bitter German and Polish winter. However, Red Cross food parcels in quantities also arrived, and, although the issue should have been one per week a head, owing to frequent long hold-ups in supplies due generally to various military and air operations but often to lack of foresight at home, the average of parcels received was just over one-half per week over the five years. Nevertheless, the P.O.W. was extremely thankful for anything extra he received in the way of food, and there is no doubt that but for these parcels a large number of prisoners would not have endured the rigours of life in a Nazi prison camp.

As well as providing material comfort for the prisoners, the food, clothing, and cigarettes parcels were of immense propaganda value: the Germans were being constantly told by radio and newspapers that owing to the total blockade of England nothing was reaching that country and the inhabitants were starving and ill-clad. Yet this "blockaded" country was able to send to its prisoners (which the Germans could not do for theirs even if there had been need for it) vast quantities of food, chocolate (unseen in Germany throughout the war), clothing, shoes, and unlimited cigarettes. There was much shaking of German square-heads over this, and the P.O.W. themselves seized every chance to ram it into the shaven heads of their captors.

To relieve boredom and to endeavour to keep mentally and physically fit as far as possible, prisoners took up all kinds of sports and hobbies, though the former depended on the rations available. Sports gear of all kinds arrived from England and Switzerland, and when games were not possible there was always the old sport of "Baiting the Hun", which inevitably led to the Hun winning in the end by withdrawal of such "privileges" as had been granted, i.e. camp-theatre shows, and the closing of canteens. As there was never anything to buy in the canteens anyway, this was never a hardship. Many prisoners took up wood-carving (there was certainly no shortage of wood in Germany except, of course, when prisoners wanted it for fires in the harsh winters), and some examples of C.Q.M.S. Minski's work were seen at the exhibition which the *Daily Telegraph* organised, and also at H.Q.

Others took up or continued civilian studies, and by an arrangement between the British Red Cross and various examining bodies it was possible to take nearly every commercial and professional examination in the prison camps. Great credit is due to all who managed to study and pass examinations in such overcrowded conditions and amidst so much noise.

As the war progressed shortages of all kinds increased in Germany, and particularly so in cigarettes. In the last two years of the war the ration of cigarettes for Army base personnel was three per day and for civilians (men only) one per day. This, combined with the inferior type of guard now on duty at most camps, led to the organisation of a very successful "Black Market", which not only helped the prisoners but also helped to destroy the morale of the enemy and provided a good method of "blackmail" over the guards. A loaf of bread or a pound of flour could be obtained for between two and five cigarettes, and every conceivable object from a lighter to a camera had its value in cigarettes. Much equipment essential for escaping-purposes was also obtained in this way.

A feature of prison-camp life and the most annoying were the regular searches conducted by the camp security officer (always a hardened Nazi of the worst type) assisted by the Guard Company, S.S. Forces, and Gestapo. Whatever the weather, even in blinding snow, everyone was turned out of barracks or huts for hours on end and hordes of Huns poured into the camp to try to discover contraband articles such as civilian clothing, maps, tools, etc. Despite the skilled Gestapo men employed, very little was ever found, as P.O.W. with not much else to do had plenty of time to make impregnable hiding-places for their ill-gotten gains. If anything was lost, it was generally overcoats and hats belonging to the Gestapo and civilian police and this, of course, led to further searches to try to regain the missing articles. After the searches, which often lasted all day, the barracks looked as if a cyclone had hit them—everything was turned out of lockers on to the floors, straw pulled out of palliasses, and the small amount of barrack furniture thrown out of the windows.

Numerous attempts to escape were made from all camps, but no Kensington was fortunate enough to get back to England and continue the fight against the enemy in a more active rôle. It would be invidious to mention any Kensington in particular, but perhaps Major Dodge was the most spectacular. In 1940 he managed during the night to slip away from one of the barges in the River Scheldt and was at large in Holland for some weeks before being recaptured. Thereafter, he made numerous further escapes, culminating in the tunnel "break" from the R.A.F. Camp at Sagan in 1943, and he was one of the few officers who was not murdered in cold blood by the enemy on recapture. Mention should also be made of L/Cpl. Bailey and Pte. Ford, who in common with several other Kensingtons managed, despite the large number of guards, to escape from the march in France and Belgium in 1940 and arrived back in England. They were more fortunate than some of their comrades, who if not recaptured by the enemy were handed over by French and Belgian collaborators.

Escaping was far more difficult in this war than in the last owing to the almost complete subjugation of Europe by the Germans, and the would-be escaper found the dice loaded heavily against him. There were three ways out of any camp: over the wire, through the wire (which included getting out of the main gate), and under the wire, and all were tried at various and frequent times; the last method, although the most popular, was also the most fatiguing. To dig a well-shored-up tunnel with a proper chamber took about six months, and whilst burrowing one was liable to use all one's reserves of energy, which were never very great due to the inadequate diet. Thus when the day (or rather night) came to break out one was in a poor physical condition, particularly if it had been decided to go on foot. Tunnelling could also be the most disappointing method of escape, as it might be discovered half finished or the camp might be moved before the tunnel could be "broken". Many attempted after escaping from a camp to cross Germany by train, but this necessitated identity cards, travel permits, etc., and although these were expertly forged in the camp there was always the risk of detection. In addition, civilian clothes made in the camp would not in daylight bear too close a scrutiny, and the German "war effort" was so complete that nearly every male from ten to seventy was in some uniform or other, so that any male seen travelling in civilian clothes was bound to invite attention. Even if the escaper crossed Germany successfully there was still the enemy in the occupied countries with which to contend. Switzerland, a part of which jutted over the River Rhine at Schaffhausen, was, naturally, a popular Mecca for escapers, but the frontier was extremely closely guarded.

During the five years, the Hun displayed many times his flair for so-called "reprisals". The first was visited upon the officers; in March 1941 Major-General Fortune and over two hundred officers, including five Kensingtons, Capt.

Mountford, Lieuts. Meikle, Wood, Hammond, and Lavington, were sent to a *Strafe Lager* at Posen in Poland. This was an underground fort unused since the 1914–18 War, and abounded with fleas, lice, and other choice bugs. All rooms were below ground-level, surrounded by an evil-smelling moat, and the living and sanitary arrangements were appalling. Although it was with no regret that the officers left the fort just prior to the German invasion of Russia in June 1941, the sojourn there had one gratifying result: it enabled the officers to meet several of their men who were at a *Stalag* in the town and who gained admittance to the fort on various pretexts.

Perhaps the most annoying reprisal was the chaining of large numbers of officers and other ranks following the Dieppe raid in 1942, when the British and Canadians bound the hands of German prisoners to prevent them from destroying identity cards, documents, etc., before they could be searched back in England. No German was probably bound for more than two or three hours, but as a reprisal and until the British apologised the Germans ordered the chaining of all prisoners captured at Dieppe, and this was eventually extended to many more prisoners. The other ranks were, however, desperately required on working parties, and after a short time they were released from their chains and an equivalent number of officers and non-working N.C.O.s shackled. It did not take long for the prisoners to discover ways and means of undoing the handcuffs, which was just as well, as the shackling continued for over a year.

Other examples of reprisals inflicted, in defiance of the Geneva Convention, on defenceless prisoners by a small-minded race were: the confiscation for a fortnight of all washing and shaving materials, the holding-up of mail for four months (the most unkind and dispiriting act of all), and the confiscation of all bedding and most barrack furniture.

Despite the many hardships the morale of all ranks in Germany was amazing. Even in the darkest days of the war no opportunity was ever lost of telling enemy officers and guards that Britain would win in the end. Perhaps the greatest factor in maintaining morale was the really large-scale bombing of Germany (which began with the raid on Cologne in May 1942), and the results of which prisoners could see from time to time and hear almost every night. P.O.W. camps were bombed in error on occasions, but fortunately few casualties were received by the prisoners.

Following D-Day the enthusiasm of the P.O.W. knew no bounds and all began "counting the days", but the last months of the war were to be the hardest. Nearly five years of the unnatural life of a prison camp, coupled with insufficient food, were beginning to tell on all prisoners, and during the fifth winter, in addition to mental strain, they suffered severely from the cold due to the fuel shortage and even scantier rations, while to make matters worse very few Red Cross parcels arrived at any of the camps.

In March 1945, as the American, British, and Russian Armies approached the various camps, the Germans, to prevent the release of the prisoners, marched them out, and in Poland and North-east Germany the Kensington other ranks endured long forced marches through the bitter winter snows, suffering frost-bite and hunger. They were also subject to air attacks from their own and Allied airmen, who were apparently unable to distinguish the columns of prisoners from enemy troops, and several Kensingtons were thus wounded.

In the south of Germany the officers' camps were also moved, and one column was heavily machine-gunned by American aircraft, sustaining many killed and wounded, but fortunately the Kensington officers in the column escaped unscathed. It should be recorded that Himmler, who was in charge of the internal security of the Third Reich, had issued orders that all P.O.W. were to be massacred if there should be any danger of their being liberated, but due to the chaos of communications in Germany at this time the order did not reach Camp Commandants, and if it did was wisely not put into effect.

One by one the various camps and marching columns were liberated, and within a short space of time all ex-P.O.W. were flown out of Germany and back to England by the British and American Air Forces. A large number of Kensingtons arrived back in England on the two V.E. days, only to find that all the "pubs" had run out of beer! None the less the welcome extended was wonderful, and thanks to amazing Army efficiency all ranks were in their own homes within a few hours of landing in England.

On May 24th, Empire Day, Lieut. B. R. Wood, as the representative of the Kensingtons' P.O.W., had the honour of attending a Garden Party at Buckingham Palace, at which Their Majesties The King and Queen and T.R.H. the Princess Elizabeth and Princess Margaret were present.

Finally, on Tuesday, July 31st, the Old Comrades' Association gave a wonderful Reunion Dinner to all the repatriated prisoners, many of whom had not seen each other since that dark day in June 1940.

THE 2ND BATTALION
By
MAJOR S. JACOBSON, M.C.
AND
MAJOR R. J. CANNON, M.C.
(1939—May, 1944)

FOREWORD

THE history of this Battalion in the Second World War is founded upon a single purpose and one supreme task. In the spring of 1939, when the sands of peace were already running out fast, the Battalion was re-created to prepare for the conflict with Nazi Germany. By September 1st, before it was six months old, its citizen spare-time soldiers found themselves embodied "for the duration". Two days later, the war began.

What followed is the story of many other units in this strange conflict. With one interlude in Iceland, the Battalion prepared in Britain, first to repel a German attack, then for the final, decisive struggle—the assault on Hitler's Fortress of Europe, the liberation of Allied peoples and the invasion of Germany. These were long years, sometimes frustrating. The Battalion lost many valued comrades, suffered some disappointments, earned some praise. But throughout, the purpose remained, and the tremendous task came closer. It was this sense of purpose, felt perhaps rather than stated in word or writing, which gave the Battalion its unmistakable and unshakable spirit. Few, indeed, who served with the Battalion failed to sense this spirit, to share it, and to remember it afterwards with deep affection and respect.

The Second Battalion's war history, therefore, falls naturally into two main parts. The first, covering the period from the re-creation of the Battalion to its departure for Normandy, has been contributed by Major R. J. Cannon, M.C.; the second, from Normandy to the disbanding of the Battalion in Germany after the end of the war, by Major S. Jacobson, M.C.

PART I—DEFENCE AND PREPARATION

September 1st, 1939–October 14th, 1941 : HOME SERVICE.
October 14th, 1941–September 8th, 1942 : ICELAND.
September 8th, 1942–June 6th, 1944 : TRAINING FOR INVASION.

REBIRTH OF THE BATTALION

THE life of the 2nd Bn. in World War II was divided into four phases—the building together of a team of Territorial civilians; a period of winter warfare training on the borders of the Arctic circle; chaos and confusion in the continuous reorganisation of personnel, arms, and transport; and finally the invasion of Normandy and the pursuit through France and the Low Countries.

The Bn. came into life again in the early spring of 1939, when the urgent call was announced for the formation of second-line T.A. Bns. The response was immediate, and the continual flow of keen, excited, and very loyal Londoners could be seen filtering through the busy highways of Hammersmith with one goal in mind—the new and proud Regimental Headquarters, which welcomed with open arms the enthusiastic volunteers who flooded the Drill Hall and offices in their efforts to sign up and become "Terriers", bearing the badge of a Regiment whose name was so well known.

The first introduction to Army life was through the medium of a handful of P.S.I.s who did so much to imbue the Bn. with a fine spirit of loyalty and comradeship, which ever grew as the years went by. So rapid was the recruitment that on any night of the week one could witness the unusual sight of men being sworn in by P.S.I.s, such as Sgts. McCormick, Taylor, Corbett, Parsons, etc., in the hastily improvised surroundings of the ablution rooms and any other square inch available. The onerous duty of forming this Bn. fell to the lot of Lieut.-Col. G. C. Pim, a C.O. who from the very first commanded the utmost respect and admiration from all who had the fortune to serve with him. The task must have seemed formidable in the extreme, but under the experienced hand and skilful judgment of Lieut.-Col. Pim, the unwieldy body of four or five hundred civilians quickly found itself moulded into platoons, companies, and, to the admiration of all, into a keen Battalion.

The success of the early days was largely due to a figure whose very presence made those on parade wonder how they could breathe without making a movement. R.S.M. Trott, by his tireless efforts and unswerving loyalty, set an example which all were proud to follow, and the initial awe inspired by his presence soon developed into a deep affection for a W.O. whose every thought and deed were for the future of the 2nd Bn.

Many remarkable scenes took place in the playground of a school immediately opposite Regimental Headquarters—quite a trying time for the newly-appointed officers and P.S.I.s, but thanks to their patience, a high standard of drill and discipline was very soon achieved. The promotion and appointment of W.O.s and N.C.O.s from the ranks of the brown denim, the only uniform then available, was an extraordinary achievement which spoke highly for the foresight and judgment of the officers, many of whom had had little or no experience themselves.

The Bn. Headquarters for the first few months was located in a small shop only a stone's throw across the road from R.H.Q. This important centre was very fortunate in having such a wealth of experience from Capt. R. M. Watson, whose appointment as Adjutant was one of the first made. Working closely with Capt. Watson in another room of the shop could be found a figure whose name for generations to come will be legendary in the history of the Kensingtons. Lieut. and Quartermaster W. A. Blakeley was one of the first personalities any new recruit encountered, and the Bn. was indeed fortunate in retaining his services as Quartermaster until just before its disbandment in 1945.

The rôle of a Machine-gun Bn. commenced in Knightsbridge Barracks, which became a nightly parade-ground. Capt. S. J. Wills undertook a series of cadres on elementary gun drill, and very soon trained the N.C.O.s up to a standard whence they themselves could undertake the instruction under his tutorship.

The first memorable Bn. parade was held in these Barracks by Lieut.-Col. Pim, ably and vociferously assisted by R.S.M. Trott. Few will forget the anxious murmurs from Platoon Commanders as they sought guidance from P.S.I.s as to the next command they should give to their platoons. It was a remarkable achievement in the rather confined area of the barracks, terminating in a march through Hyde Park and a surprisingly orderly re-formation in the Barrack square.

The Bn. having overcome its initial teething troubles was then ready to proceed in August to the annual camp at Beaulieu, in the New Forest, where a very waterlogged site was taken over from the 1st Bn. Fortunately the weather was kind and an enjoyable and instructive period of training was carried out. This camp completely made the Bn., and a comradeship was struck up in every quarter which played a great part in the trying weeks of soldiering that were to come so soon after. The last days of camp became rather confused as the international situation worsened, and they found the unit confined to camp, spending most of the days digging trenches in readiness for the unknown future.

A small group of key Embodiment Personnel was actually embodied at camp and when the remainder of the Bn. returned home, this vital handful of N.C.O.s and men, under the command of Lieut. A. Wray, was stationed in Hammersmith Town Hall to prepare for the reception and embodiment of the Unit. The Town Hall thus became Bn. Headquarters, and on September 1st, 1939, the general mobilisation order was issued and a frenzied scene of activity took place inside the dignified walls of the Mayor's inner sanctum.

Thus was the 2nd Bn. formed in readiness for many years of trial and tribulation.

CHAPTER XX

HOME SERVICE

September 1st, 1939–October 14th, 1941

THE momentous news came through at 11.0 a.m. on September 3rd: WAR. Thirty minutes later there was a controlled scramble into the Town Hall vaults, with everyone endeavouring to secure his newly acquired respirator. The Bn. H.Q. during these strange air-raid warnings were transferred hastily into the Mayor's safe, well protected by anti-gas blanket screens improvised from the Q.M. stores.

The first rôle undertaken by the companies was the guarding of various vulnerable points in Stanmore, Shepherd's Bush, and last, but by no means least, the Tower of London. F Coy. bore the honour of being the first T.A. unit ever to take over guard duties at the Tower, complete with the ceremony of the Keys at guard-mounting each afternoon. During the coming two months very little time could be given to training, as guard commitments were very heavy. Quite a variety of V.P.s, ranging from R.A.F. Headquarters, ammunition dumps, and mobilisation stores, were protected against all comers.

The month of October saw the promotion of Capt. R. M. Watson to 2/i/C. of the Bn., and Lieut. the Lord Brougham of Vaux to Adjutant. Shortly after, on October 21st, Lt.-Col. Pim took over command of the London Dock Sub-Area, and the Bn. moved into the docks north and south of the Thames. This period proved to be a very trying experience of arduous guard duties in far from pleasant surroundings; the condition of guard-rooms was by necessity undesirable, and chiefly consisted of disused warehouses and decrepit watchman's shelters. Many long nights were spent patrolling quaysides, lock-gates, and warehouses in the dark, foggy, and unsavoury atmosphere which prevails over the London Docks in the winter. The gloomy buildings and wharves were made even more unfriendly by the infiltration of a strong element of I.R.A. sympathisers, who lurked in and around dockland. These gentlemen were the cause of more than one sentry being unceremoniously decanted into the slime of the Thames. So serious became the menace that no person was allowed to walk unaccompanied by day or night.

Machine-gun training during this period suffered heavily through continual guard commitments. But rifle practice during hours of darkness became the vogue, and an extraordinary number of rats who had not taken the elementary precaution of learning the password for the day suffered the extreme penalty. The thought of a "2 on, 4 off" Christmas in semi-nautical surroundings was viewed with grave foreboding, but the authorities came to the rescue on December 10th and the Bn. moved to a concentration area in the Northwood district. The comfort of suburban dwellings after the assortment of billets in the East End, including the old paddle-steamers the *Golden Eagle* and *Crested Eagle*, provided a wonderful tonic in spite of the half-filled palliasses and wooden floors.

The inhabitants of Northwood saw little of the Kensingtons, as on January 18th a convoy of buses, furniture vans, and every other type of impressed vehicle available, transported the Companies across London to complete concentration under the one roof of the Royal Wanstead School near Epping Forest. For the first time since camp, all ranks, including the junior officers, began to experience barrack life and regimental discipline under the firm control of the R.S.M. Deep regret was felt when R.S.M. Trott, who had done so much in building up the Bn., was posted from the unit through ill-health. His successor, C.S.M. McCormick, carried on the tradition very ably, strengthened with his infinite sense of Irish humour. Wanstead School, for those who knew it, brings back memories of an existence of frozen pipes, deep snow, and a particularly virulent epidemic of influenza that raged through the entire Bn. in a few weeks. This, however, in no way interfered with a course of drill and map-reading which was attended by approximately eighty N.C.O.s. In between periods of 'flu and drill parades a very fine task was carried out in wiring a defensive belt round the small-arms factory at Enfield. The success of this tedious operation in most adverse conditions can be seen in the following special Order of the Day issued on April 9th by the Commander, Brigadier T. Rose-Price, D.S.O., M.C.:

> On conclusion of your long wiring operations, I wish to express my full appreciation to all ranks concerned of the fine work put in during the past two months or more. The results are excellent!

Then back to dockland again, to the excitement of a conflagration in McDougall's warehouse which destroyed the entire Headquarters of F Coy., and all arms, kit, and equipment. A sigh of relief from the C.Q.M.S. and other members of F Coy., who to that day may have suffered from various kit deficiencies, and a groan of despair from the Q.M. After a complete reissue of stores, etc., the incident was assumed closed, that is, to all but the H.Q. of London Dock Sub-Area. In 1942, just prior to embarkation for Iceland, Lieut. W. A. Blakeley received a curt note suggesting that he might like to dispose of 120 burnt-out rifles, 100-odd sets of charred equipment, and numerous other articles. The Q.M. was heard to murmur that the Germans might at least have had the decency to drop a bomb on that one particular warehouse during the air bombardments of previous years.

During a few weeks stationed in the area of Hampstead, Private Harris and Private Farthing had the honour of receiving congratulatory letters from the Brigade Commander of North London Sub-Area and the Commander of the 3 London Infantry Brigade. In the course of their duties they had been instrumental in the arrest of civilians obtaining vital information of a secret military nature.

In July 1940 the 2nd Bn. was considered fully trained in the rôle of a machine-gun Bn., and ready to join a field-force formation. Accordingly the 55 Infantry Divisional sign was affixed to battle-dress, and the east coast of Norfolk and Suffolk was strengthened by the machine-gun support provided by platoons who had for many months wondered when they would have the chance of proving themselves. Although not in actual battle, it was at least a task they could tackle and be proud of. Headquarters were established in a workhouse at Claydon, near Ipswich, and the Coys. were dispersed some fifty to sixty miles away, covering a stretch of coast from Lowestoft to Felixstowe. Many weeks of strenuous work went into the preparation of gun positions on a very wide front, platoons covering a section of six to seven miles in some cases. This, with the still very varied assortment of civilian vehicles, was no mean achievement, but one which all ranks took great pleasure in, added to by the excitement of numerous sneak raiders swooping in from the sea at low level. They provided excellent anti-aircraft practice and a chance of occasional patrols in the marshes to round up battered and wandering German airmen, who seemed only too glad to find captors in the lonely wastes in which they had been shot down.

Associations with the 55 Division were to last for over a year, and it was a great delight to serve under a Divisional Commander with such a fine reputation as Major-Gen. V. H. B. Majendie. The Cockneys very soon made friends with their northern infanteers from Yorkshire and Lancashire, and lost no time in obtaining their complete confidence through the close support afforded in training on field-firing ranges by machine-guns which so many infantrymen had hitherto viewed with distrust. Considerable relief, nevertheless, was experienced when the thin red line of 55 Division was withdrawn to winter quarters in Oxfordshire. However well prepared to meet any invaders from over the Channel, the glaring fact of only a few belts of ammunition per gun being available at that time did not encourage complacency towards an invasion. Fortunately, Hitler did not think fit to follow up the Dunkirk rout, and the Bn. was thus left intact to proceed with the Division on November 15th, having handed over the numerous gun positions and defensive areas to the 4th Bn. the Cheshire Regiment. Winter quarters covered a widely dispersed area and the companies were located within Brigade boundaries to facilitate field training on a Brigade level. These formation exercises, incorporating all supporting arms, were the first to be experienced by the Bn., and after a short while the

M.G. Coys. settled down and fitted into the intricate machinery of a Brigade in attack, defence, etc., with the utmost ease. The Commanding Officer took the opportunity of holding a number of T.E.W.T.s for officers and N.C.O.s, and finally exercises in the area of Stow-on-the-Wold in which all companies took part.

On December 12th the Bn. was granted the honour of supplying a Machine-Gun Coy. for the 24 Independent Guards Brigade. It was indeed a sad blow to lose a complete Coy. now fully trained to operate in field formation, but thus it was, and G Coy. reluctantly said farewell, never again to return, to the 2nd Bn. It was, however, a comforting thought that the Kensingtons' badge would serve with such a fine body as the Guards Brigade. The strenuous task of forming a new G Coy. was allotted to Capt. W. A. Ballard, who received a complete draft of N.C.O.s and men from the 1st Holding Bn. of the Middlesex Regt. This remoulding of regimental customs and traditions entailed the utmost patience for all concerned, and great credit is due to the men who suffered the wrench of removing their old badges and donning those of another regiment overnight. In this replenishment of numbers gratitude must be recorded to the Colonel of the Middlesex Regt., Col. M. Browne, who with his fine spirit of military tradition took such a very real interest in the well-being of the 2 Kensingtons throughout its war-time career. It was always a great pleasure and honour to welcome this fine figure on his visits to the companies.

Great preparations were made and a certain amount of trepidation felt early in 1941, when Bn. H.Q. and H Coy. were inspected by the Commander-in-Chief, Gen. Sir Alan Brooke. This ordeal, however, was surmounted with great credit, and the Bn., still under command of 55 Division, prepared to move south to take over a wide front on the south coast. The move to Sussex was achieved with ease, largely due to the excellent staff work of Captain Alastair Wray, who in this, as in all other operations, saved endless worry and confusion through his capable brain and invaluable knowledge of orderly room procedure. Life in this new area turned out to be one of comparative comfort and pleasure. The summer was delightful, and although swimming was somewhat restricted, most other amenities of a seaside vacation could be enjoyed. This, of course, does not mean that the defence work and training were in any way forfeited, but the surroundings alleviated greatly the inevitable hardships. Again the Bn. was widely dispersed into Brigade groups embracing such pleasant resorts as Newhaven, Eastbourne, Hastings, Winchelsea, and Rye. It was in 199 Infantry Brigade Area in and around Rye that H Coy., under the command of Major R. E. N. D'Abo, with its H.Q. comfortably situated in Peasmarsh, came first into contact with Brigadier "Babe" MacMillan, whose distinguished military career led him to control the Bn. again when he assumed command of 49 (West Riding) Div. several years later during the advance through Holland.

This phase of the war in Sussex proved to be the only occasion when the two Kensington Bns. were located as neighbours. Commitments were such, however, that, apart from occasional visits by the respective C.O.s, the only meeting that could be arranged was an Inter-Bn. Cricket Match, in which the 2nd Bn. proved their strength by defeating their left-flanking neighbours. Apart from invaluable exercises on the South Downs, in which all platoons of infantry advanced under live machine-gun and mortar-fire, the Bn. was given a new rôle to master. The problem of moving a Division over long distances was always an operation involving subsequent post-mortems, as to why certain units took the wrong route and why convoys of A.F.V.s and 3-tonners careered through towns at breakneck speeds of fifty miles an hour. The Divisional Commander decided that a Machine-Gun Bn., being fully mobile and self-contained in small units, was the ideal organisation to undertake the control of traffic in addition to its prime rôle as a supporting arm. A series of discussions and trials was held until a well-conceived drill was devised to meet all contingencies. The weeks of study in policing roads were put to the test on July 4th, when the Division was relieved by the 2 Canadian Infantry Division and a move to concentration in Aldershot was completed with ease and excellent transport discipline. The work put in by all ranks of the

HOME SERVICE

Bn. was gratefully acknowledged by the Division, and resulted in an Order of the Day being issued to 2 Kensingtons by the Divisional Commander:

> I would like to congratulate the 2nd Kensingtons on their performance. The success of the move and the good chit we got from higher authority was largely due to the help they gave to their units.

This concentration in Warburg Barracks enabled the Bn. to train as a single fighting unit under command of Bn. H.Q. for only the third time in over nine months. The benefits of being stationed in barracks could be enjoyed for only a bare five weeks; but in this time great strides were made, and a corps of drums was even formed under the able tutorship of C.S.M. Reg. Taylor, who achieved wonders in such a short time. For the first time, too, opportunities were granted for a number of Bn. functions, including a most successful inter-company sports meeting, which was deservedly won by E Coy., with the exception of the tug-of-war, when H.Q. Coy. literally walked away with their opponents. This was due almost entirely to their coach, Lt. Q.M. W. A. Blakeley—a sight that none who saw will ever forget—this tall, dignified figure, with moustache bristling, urging his team on with an occasional calm, almost imperceptible flick of the wrists. The other meeting on the field of sport, however, ended in a grave mishap. During the cricket match between the officers and sergeants, Lt.-Col. G. C. Pim collapsed whilst running between the wickets with an injury which was later found to be a torn Achilles tendon. This accident, although apparently trivial, proved to be the turning-point of Col. Pim's brilliant military career and caused the irreplaceable loss of a Commander who had done more than seemed possible to create a fine unit of soldiers out of a body of civilians in such a short time. It was a cruel blow that Col. Pim was denied the honour of leading his men into battle after so many months of preparation.

Shortly after this misfortune at Aldershot, the Bn. again obtained distinction in its proficiency as a Traffic Control formation; steps were retraced and the old gun positions were re-manned for a little under two months. Towards the end of September the Bn. was in the incongruous position of having neither a C.O. nor 2nd in Command, Major R. M. Watson having been posted to assume an important rôle in the Spears Military Mission. Mention has already been made of the fine work Captain Alastair Wray had contributed as Adjutant, but his powers of organisation and control in the last two weeks of September, with no C.O. or 2nd in Command, were unequalled in the history of the Bn. On September 24th, Major A. H. M. Field, who had assumed temporary command of the Bn., and Captain A. Wray were summoned to the War Office, where an order was received to mobilise the Bn. on special Arctic scales of kit and equipment in readiness for embarkation to Iceland. Rumours had, of course, been rife for some time, but no one had entertained the idea of this desolate and deserted field of Active Service. Urgent and tense activity followed the news, and an advance party under the command of Lt. D. A. Thomas parted from the homely atmosphere of Sussex on October 1st to what seemed a chilly future.

After all preparations had been carefully conceived and carried out, the new Commanding Officer, Lt.-Col. C. C. Musselwhite, was greeted by the Bn. He arrived after the other new appointment of Major John Worton as 2/i/C. Having laid all the foundations for a successful mobilisation, Captain A. Wray took over command of E Company with the rank of Major, handing over the unenviable duties of Adjutant at this trying time to Captain Mark Palmer. Guns having been tested, transport handed in, and A.F.G.1098 stores completed, the Bn. was now ready to move off with its weird collection of clothing and specialised Arctic accessories. Farewell was said to Sussex with a number of severe heart wrenches, and the years of training in the U.K. were rewarded at long last by embarkation to an Overseas station.

CHAPTER XXI

ICELAND

October 14th, 1941–September 8th, 1942

THE last glimpses of Great Britain were caught from the crowded decks of the troopship H.M.T. *Bergensfiord* as she steamed slowly westward down the Clyde from Greenock, where a very orderly embarkation had taken place on October 15th. The comforting grandeur of the high ground overlooking this bustling estuary caused a nostalgic impression which was ever present during the days to come as the voyage progressed westward along the coast of Scotland.

The *Bergensfiord*, in common with most troopships, seemed designed to take a far smaller consignment of passengers than she had embarked. As a result, conditions below decks were extremely cramped and the landlubbers' handling of hammocks and mess decks left a certain amount to be desired for the first day or so. All ranks were in fine spirits when retiring for the first night, but little was it realised how conditions were to change. The North Atlantic received the little convoy of the troopship, one destroyer, and a Coastal Command aircraft, with open arms and open seas. The cold, grey, and unfriendly morning of October 16th found a very sad and sorry Bn. prostrate and groaning in their bunks, hammocks, and cabins, while the heaviest of seas buffeted the 13,000-ton ship until life had little meaning for anyone on deck, and still less below decks. Fortunately conditions improved slightly the following day.

Without further incident, land was first sighted at 08.30 hrs. on the morning of October 18th. Iceland: and what then? A tumult of speculation and conjecture whirled in the minds of those who peered across the ocean at the rugged eruption of snow-covered mountains thrust upwards in the cold morning light. Having crossed west, parallel to the south coast for approximately three hours, the first signs of civilisation were sighted as the capital and main port Reykjavik came into view. Rounding the peninsula, anchor was dropped at midday. Disembarkation began on the morning of October 19th, and ashore the Bn. was greeted by the advance party, who had done sterling work in preparing for a simple and comfortable hand-over from the 1/9th Bn. of the Manchester Regiment, whose generous hospitality did much to assist the new-comers in settling in to their semi-Arctic surroundings. It was learnt that the arrival of the 2 Kensington advance party had

caused many eyebrows to be raised as the small body reported to Iceland (C) Force H.Q., headed by a mere Lieutenant. But the occupants of Iceland soon learned that Lieut. D. A. Thomas was no officer to be trifled with, and his capabilities were held in high esteem by the time the main body arrived.

Before relating the type of life led on this lonely island, a brief picture of Iceland should be presented. To say that Iceland was perhaps one of the safest countries in the world during World War II is perfectly true, but that it was one of the most unpleasant and vital of occupied countries to the Allies is equally correct. The defence of

Iceland proved to be one of the major geographical factors in determining the degree of assistance that could be given by Canada and the U.S.A. This desolate spot provided a naval and air base in the North Atlantic which alone could safeguard the continual stream of convoys back and forth between the two great continents. Had the Germans forestalled the British occupying forces, a very different story might have been unfolded.

Iceland is an island of volcanic origin, with a population of some 126,000 inhabitants scattered round the west, north, and east coast-line. Approximately two-thirds of the island is covered by a gigantic glacier named the Vatna Jökull, and other smaller glacial mountains. The very small sections of lowland consist of mile upon mile of lava-strewn beds devoid of any trees or undergrowth. Amidst the jagged boulders a very poor type of browny-green grass strives to flourish and provides facilities for one of Iceland's two industries—sheep-rearing and fishing. Communications round the island are primitive in the extreme. In the winter months it is impossible to travel on any road for more than thirty to forty miles, and even in the short summer one can proceed only round the west, north, and east coasts. All other travelling is carried out in small coastal steamers, which ply to and fro in turbulent and angry seas, calling at the little fishing-villages scattered round the rugged coast-line.

Any hopes of the Bn. operating under a unified command vanished immediately Lt. Thomas handed over his information. Bn. H.Q. and F Coy. (under the command of Capt. G. D. Paterson) were located in Reykjavik; G Coy., under the command of Capt. W. A. Ballard, in Hafnafjördur, six miles away; H Coy., approximately 500 miles north in Akureyri; and E Coy. was tucked away on the extreme east coast in Budareyri, approximately 550 miles round the coast. Both E and H Coys. could be reached only by a two-day sea trip, and the communications were so poor that the powers of Detachment Commander were granted to Major A. Wray and Major R. E. N. D'Abo, respective Commanders of E and H Coys. What should have been a comparatively simple process, telephoning to these two Coys., turned out to be a major operation. Calls would take anything up to twenty-four hours before contact could be established.

Climatic conditions on the borders of the Arctic Circle were totally different from anything envisaged. One would normally expect a clean, pure atmosphere of continual frost in these latitudes, but instead, most undesirable varied conditions prevailed. Torrential rainstorms, 80–90-mile-an-hour gales, raging blizzards, and 40-odd degrees of frost —all these violent expressions of nature were experienced in a matter of weeks, changing suddenly overnight into two or three feet of snow. It can be seen that a winter spent in this barren land is not a life one would choose, particularly when machine-guns had to be manned by sentries throughout the day and night.

On landing at Reykjavik Bn. H.Q. and F and G Coys. went straight to their respective camps and took over the static beach defences from 1/9th Bn., Manchester Regt. Accommodation was occupied and Bn. H.Q. was particularly lucky in being allocated Bytown Camp, reputed to be the most comfortable and luxurious camp on the island, civilised to the extent of the Officers' Mess having electric light and running hot and cold water installed. This modern plumbing soon broke down, however, and the local Icelandic engineers were so proficient in their repairs that Lieut.-Col. Musselwhite immediately took advantage of a shower-bath only to receive a violent electric shock when turning on the cold-water tap, followed by a rush of steam when pulling the chain of a revolutionary latrine.

The two other Coys., who had yet another sea voyage before them, resided for two nights in the transit camp, whence they embarked on the S.S. *Leinster* and set off round the south coast to deposit first E Coy. at Budareyri on October 22nd, and finally H Coy. at Akureyri two days later. Major Wray took over a well-established camp on the east coast, and the Londoners soon acclimatised themselves to their new surroundings. October 28th, however, upset their equilibrium somewhat, when a particularly vicious gale sprang up overnight and completely destroyed the workshop and drying hut, to the extreme discomfort of E Coy.'s two mechanics, who were hard at work with their heads buried inside a rather decrepit engine of a 15-cwt. truck. Lce/Cpl. Wynne escaped with a severe bruising, but Cpl. Clifford was not so fortunate and received a broken collar-bone as his workshop crashed round him.

H Coy. were not so fortunate in their encampment, and arrived in a three-week-old camp of Nissen huts with neither light nor water. Major R. E. N. D'Abo soon set to work, and persuaded the local sappers to spare no effort. As a result a magnificent parade ground was very soon laid for the appeasement of C.S.M. Robertson, and the other minor essentials soon followed. This camp became almost unrecognisable in a few days, and permission was obtained from the G.O.C., Major-General H. O. Curtis, C.B., D.S.O., M.C., to rename the H.Q. "Knightsbridge Camp" —a fitting title for the home of a Coy. whose drill on the barrack square equalled that of any Guards Bn.

Manning exercises were held by all machine-gun posts soon after arrival, and great satisfaction was achieved in being able to observe strike on the beaches as D.F. tasks were fired on their fixed lines. All guns behaved magnificently, and with the assistance of anti-freeze mixtures and barrel covers no trouble was experienced even in the most severe temperatures. The early days of November were spent in further improvement of camps and gun emplacements until life was made as civilised and comfortable as conditions would permit. One of the most disconcerting peculiarities of winter in this latitude were the long nights, which left only about four hours of daylight in which to carry out training and take essential physical exercises. The physical fitness of the Bn. in most gruelling marches and mountain climbs with full gun kit and ammunition proved to be of a remarkably high standard, and H Coy.'s boxers, coached by Lieut. P. Greville, soon achieved fame in winning the North-West Sector Boxing Championship. In their struggle to the top of the ladder this team of worthy pugilists, drawn from a strength of only 150 men, proceeded to rout two infantry Bns., one battery of 69 Field Regt., and the 18th Heavy (A.A.) Battery. This fine performance inspired aspirants to boxing fame in other Coys. to commence earnest training for a Bn. Boxing Meeting, which was held at Reykjavik in late February. From this meeting a Bn. team was concentrated in Bytown Camp in preparation for the Iceland Inter-Unit Boxing Championship. Thanks to the fine coaching of Lt. Q.M. W. A. Blakeley and Sgt. Donegar, a formidable team was formed to give added distinction to the 2 Kensingtons by conquering the 1/6th Bn. The Duke of Wellington's Regt. and the 1/7th Bn. The Duke of Wellington's Regt., and only just failing to walk off with the Championship by losing in the final to 294 Field Coy. R.E., after a thrilling evening of well-fought bouts, the final score being 18 points against 13.

On November 18th news came through that the Bn. was to commence training in the rôle of a mountain force equipped to wage war with the aid of mules and man-drawn sleds. This was a completely new departure, and one which promoted great interest and enthusiasm amongst the companies. The two far-flung detachments were best suited to commence this training, as the Reykjavik area had as yet seen little snow in the low-lying coastal belt. Major Wray felt particularly smug in Budareyri with a good foot of solid snow, but not for long. On November 19th the skies opened and the temperature rose, causing the river to break its banks and find a new bed straight through the Nissen huts in which E Coy. thought themselves so comfortable and secure. All hands were mustered, and four hours of toil, waist-deep amid floating ice, staunched the flow with a hastily constructed dam. H Coy. were more fortunate, and carried out extensive experiments in mounting guns on sleds and distributing loads for long mountain carries. Great strides were made, and having performed a long carry with seven belts per gun for eight miles, the Coy. finally climbed the 3000-foot mountain Storihujuker and got into action with seven belts per gun in 2 hrs. 20 mins.—a truly remarkable feat of endurance and stamina.

F and G Coys. could not participate in these trials owing to the lack of snow and heavy commitments in manning static gun positions; but every facility was taken in route-marches and mountaineering activities. A number of officers attended the Winter Warfare School in the north, and others, with selected N.C.O.s, returned to the United Kingdom to learn the intricacies of mule management in South Wales. The introduction of skis and snow-shoes in the early part of December caused much interest, and under the guidance of a Canadian instructor, Lieut. ("Snow-Shoe Pete") Green, whose skill with the dice equalled that of his ski-ing, most ranks could manœuvre nursery slopes on their skis with some nonchalance. Unfortunately the snow in the south was still very thin, and protruding lava rocks accounted for more than one pair of battle-dress trousers.

With the aid of recently issued equipment E Coy. set out before the New Year on their most ambitious route-march, from Reydarfjord, to Eskifjord. All possible ranks were mustered, and the stalwarts, 135 strong, set out on their sixteen-mile trek. The route selected entailed the most gruelling test of endurance: climbing through deep snow and areas of treacherous ice to a height of 3000 feet, the going was severe, and, as in all similar route-marches, great attention had to be given to that most deadly enemy, frost-bite. Each man was held responsible for keeping a continual watch on the ears, the most vulnerable part, of the man in front, and many halts were called to administer the elementary first-aid of rubbing circulation back into the extremities. Only one or two minor casualties were sustained, and the Coy. embarked at Eskifjord to return by sea, weary but satisfied, to their warm and welcome camp. This expedition, as with many others, wrung deep admiration from the local infanteers, who had previously attempted no such feats of stamina. It cannot be realised by those who have not experienced the extreme will-power required to battle on over thick snow in the face of driving blizzards, how marching becomes purely automatic, and the very struggle for existence at times tortures the mind into the danger of submission. The Kensingtons may have been born and bred in London, but when called on they produced a quality of strength and fortitude which won respect from all who knew them. Some idea of the esteem in which they were held can be gained from this brief extract of a letter written by the G.O.C., Major-Gen. H. O. Curtis, C.B., D.S.O., M.C.:

Your men are fit and of particularly fine physique; their clothing and equipment is in good order, and proper attention is paid to administration. Drill and discipline is of a high standard. I congratulate the Officers, N.C.O.s, and all ranks on the smartness and readiness for war of your distinguished Regt.

Christmas fare provided by the supply branch of the R.A.S.C. quite exceeded all expectations, and an enjoyable day was spent consuming a sumptuous meal of goose, beef, Christmas pudding, etc., trimmed with all the essentials of beer, fruit, nuts and cigars to complete a memorable dinner. Local talent provided concerts in the evening with two notable high-lights. Cpl. Wasner, at Knightsbridge Camp, discarded his stripes and assumed command of H Coy. in an uncanny likeness of Major R. E. N. D'Abo's individual style of running a Coy., with the able assistance of "Robbo". This gift of mimicry had already gained him utmost respect in the hours of darkness with a few curt orders *à la* D'Abo. The other festive incident was witnessed in Hafnafjördur, when Sgt. "Dominic" Curtin was giving his realistic impersonation of Adolf Hitler addressing the Reichstag to a mixed audience of Kensingtons and American G.I.s. So freely had the wine flown in American camps that the worthy Allies thought for the moment that Hitler really had descended into their midst. Sgt. Curtin was hastily dragged to safety from the stage as a rain of beer-bottles, oranges, and chairs sped through the air to destroy this symbol of Nazism.

The New Year of 1942 burst upon Iceland with one of the most severe gales experienced. All Nissen huts had for many months been banked high with boulder walls, but this proved quite inadequate and in many cases complete huts could be seen sailing through the air, leaving the occupants exposed but unhurt in a pile of débris. The most fortunate man of all was R.S.M. McCormick, who avoided a fate worse than death by inches as the latrines rose gracefully in the air en route to their new location. These gales were so powerful that road transport became at times impossible, and even in the camp progress could be made only by crawling on all fours. Following these devastating storms, temperatures fell, and the Reykjavik sector could at least settle down to winter warfare training in earnest. Capt. G. D. Paterson, who had recently attended the rigorous hardships of the Winter Warfare School in the north, carried out a series of experiments with F Coy. in the use of new Arctic sleds and equipment. Two-man tents were issued, and during February and March 100 per cent of the battalion strength slept at least two nights in these minute tents pegged down in deep snow with a temperature of anything from 0–20 degrees of frost. The art of living under these conditions entailed endless practice and a very strict drill and discipline by those concerned. Teamwork was the secret of all success in this unusual form of soldiering. Progress in these rugged mountains could be made only on foot without even the assistance of sleds, and all food, bedding, and tents had to be carried in rucksacks with an average load of 60–70 lb. per man.

Before embarking on any expedition a scientifically balanced diet of food was weighed and prepared, consisting mainly of oatmeal, chocolate, cocoa, sugar, biscuits, fats, cheese, and smoked bacon, with an emergency reserve of concentrated food extract sealed in a small tin. Climatic conditions were so variable and dangerous that two weeks' rations were always taken, in the event of unforeseen blizzards and storms. Equipment was shared between the two partners, and rucksacks were packed with a basic load of food, sleeping-bag, two-man tent, Primus stove, change of clothing, rope, and one or two other minor accessories. Ski-suits were worn, and complete with rifle and ice-pick the laden warrior was then ready to set off into the unhospitable wastes. Living conditions in a two-man tent were far from spacious. The tent was approximately $2\frac{1}{2}$ feet high with a floor space of 6 feet 3 inches by 5 feet 6 inches. In this confine all equipment had to be stacked and sleeping-bags laid before the two occupants could commence preparing their frugal repast on the Primus stove or solid-fuel burners. Few who have not experienced it can conceive the delicacy of a breakfast of sweet cocoa, half-cooked oatmeal, biscuits, and raw smoked bacon. For once in the history of the 2 Kensingtons, the monotonous query of "any complaints" could not be made and no meals could have been more eagerly consumed.

Prior to sleeping-out exercises, as they became known, a period of reconnaissance was carried out to explore suitable sites for setting up camp. E and H Coys. were fortunate in having snow-covered mountains rising literally from their doorsteps, but for Bn. H.Q. and the three southern companies the problem was rather more acute, as Reykjavik and Hafnafjördur lay within a wide belt of lava-strewn plains stretching for many miles to the mountain ranges.

On March 7th an organised party, composed of Capt. G. D. Paterson, Lieut. R. J. Cannon, and Sgts. Dale and Godfrey, set off by truck north-east to a point some forty to fifty miles from the nearest sign of civilisation. From this base the party marched for a period of four days to climb an extinct volcano, Skaldbreider, in the search of a desirable camping-site. From the summit of this mountain, within which lay a glacier-filled crater, could be seen the interminable expanse of Iceland's greatest glacier, Vatna Jökull, stretching away to the east in a vast monotony of ice and snow. This area was thought to be too untenable in the event of prolonged storms, and another site was selected closer in to the 147 Bde. area south-east of Lake Pingvetler.

It was during this vital period of training that H Coy. suffered one of the not-infrequent blows experienced whilst British Forces were stationed in Iceland. On March 30th, a party of one officer and twenty-one other ranks set off and pitched camp on the northern approaches of the Vindheima-jökull, one of the massive glaciers in the north-west area, while a base camp was established some forty-five minutes' march down the mountain-side. At 19.00 hrs. on March 31st, a corporal from the base camp contacted Coy. H.Q. with the news that a particularly vicious blizzard had blown up on the Jökull, destroying some of the base-camp tents. The Coy. Comdr., Capt. T. A. Lovibond, immediately set off with a relief party bearing additional tents; on arriving at the lower camp all seemed well and the party bivouacked for the night. Meanwhile, however, four men from the top camp fought their way down to Coy. H.Q. with a request from the officer in charge that they be relieved at the earliest possible opportunity, as conditions on the glacier were extremely bad and showed every sign of worsening. A further relief party set off on April 1st, and after considerable difficulty linked up with Capt. Lovibond at the base camp. This reinforced body battled their way up the Jokull until at last, through driving ice and snow, they came upon the main camp. Here a scene of grim destruction met their eyes. Many tents had collapsed, but most of the occupants had built snow-holes and were comparatively safe, but suffering from exposure and minor frost-bite. During the previous night the blizzard had reached its peak and raged mercilessly round this small body of men, and driving snow had continually piled high against tents and snow-holes. This heavy drifting completely obliterated the shelter of Pte. H. McCormick and Pte. M. Wilson, and their bodies were eventually found in the early morning. These fatal casualties were not all, however; two more men were missing, and it was not until the morning of April 2nd that L/Cpl. Worrall and Pte. Dillon were found buried under three feet of snow. Pte. Dillon was dead, but by some miracle L/Cpl. Worrall still showed signs of life. His evacuation was immediate, and after being a considerable time on the danger-list he recovered rapidly, to rejoin the Coy. on April 21st.

This disaster was a cruel and vicious blow which, but for the cool courage and utmost fortitude of all, could have been so very much more serious. Typical of the fine spirit was Pte. Best, who later received an award of the B.E.M. for his gallant conduct in those three days of stress. As his snow-hole became submerged under an ever-growing pile of snow, Pte. Best saved the lives of his companion and himself by unceasingly forcing his hand through the snow to keep clear a channel for ventilation. He suffered severe agonies of frost-bite and ultimately lost four fingers of his right hand; but his courage and cheerfulness were unshakable.

The rigours of winter warfare proved too great for the normal medical category of A.1 fitness, and a severe medical examination was carried out to grade all troops in Iceland to an A.1 plus standard of physique. As a result of these tests the Bn. regretfully saw the parting of thirty

N.C.O.s and men to the U.K. for posting to normal field-force formations.

Since December an ever-increasing flow of American troops had filtered on to the island, and by April 1942 the southern sector was ready to hand over to the Allies who had now entered into the war. On April 2nd the welcome order was received for embarkation to U.K., and with a sigh of relief preparations commenced with great enthusiasm. Unfortunately this rejoicing was not shared by E and H Coys., who were to continue their stay until the end of August and the early days of September. Life for these two Coys. continued on very similar lines to the previous months, with a gradual improvement of climatic conditions and lengthening hours of daylight. The main body of Bn. H.Q., F and G Coys. embarked, after two postponements due to gales, on to H.M.T. *Orduna,* and sailed at 20.00 hrs. on April 8th. This voyage, in contrast to the outward journey, was made in brilliant sunshine on a dead-calm sea, and it was almost with regret that Greenock was sighted on April 11th.

Home to Great Britain again, after a winter full of memories, both pleasant and grim! Life had been essentially hard, but a brief reflection quickly showed what great value this experience had been in testing the Bn. and knitting an even closer bond of comradeship and loyalty.

CHAPTER XXII

TRAINING FOR INVASION

September 8th, 1942–June 6th, 1944

THE warm, sunny spring-time of South Wales provided a glorious welcome after the frozen wastes of Iceland, and the district around Velindre in Carmarthenshire held some of the most beautiful countryside one could wish to see. Cilwendig Camp was occupied in the early hours of April 13th, and arrangements had previously been made for the immediate departure of 85 per cent. of the Bn. on disembarkation leave. The other two Coys. were unfortunately still showing the flag overseas, in patient expectation of their American relieving formation. Their reward of leave was to come later in the year, and it was not until September that the Bn. as a whole began serious training.

Within forty-eight hours of the main bodies' return from a taste of civilian freedom, an advance party was whisked up to Huntly with the object of continuing mountain warfare training in the Highlands of Scotland. This plan was short-lived, however; within four days steps were retraced, as it was learnt that the previous months of grim training were of no value; the formation was to assume the rôle of normal infantry division. This was only the first of many changes to be suffered by the Bn. during the next eighteen months.

On May 28th, a sincere welcome was extended to Lt.-Col. D. V. G. Brock, who was posted from the 2/7th Bn., The Middlesex Regt., to assume command of the Bn. His first training directions were gladly received when daily bathing parades were dispatched to Aberforth in order that the more kindly atmosphere of the British climate could be enjoyed to the full. This form of relaxation was of great assistance in settling down to more normal soldiering, and on June 9th a move was made to the summer camp in the mountains of Radnorshire and Herefordshire. Contrary to normal practice in moving by transport from one H.Q. to another, G Coy. decided to embark on a cross-country march from Velindre to Penybont, a distance of some sixty to seventy miles. The route chosen passed over some of the remotest districts of Wales, and many natives were encountered who could speak no single word of English. The march, a great success, was completed on June 17th without undue incident.

The formation, prior to leaving Iceland (C) Force, was reinstated as 49 (W.R.) Division, the title it held earlier on in the war when it gallantly took part in the forlorn defence of Norway. As can be seen, any hope of Divisional training during the years of soldiering in Iceland was quite out of the question, and this period of immobility had a severe effect when formation exercises were commenced from the summer camps. An intense period of training soon rectified this set-back, and a well co-ordinated force of infantry, supporting arms and ancillary troops quickly began to develop.

E and H Coys. rejoined the Bn. by September 9th at Pencerrig, near Builth Wells, where the summer camp was still struggling on against a very doubtful September of mud and rain—a bitter disappointment to those troops who were entitled to expect comparative comfort on their return to Great Britain. Fortunately, however, these conditions were not to last long, as a move to winter quarters took place on October 15th to the south coast of Wales in the area of Llantwit Major and St. Athans, overlooking the Bristol Channel. Prior to the move from Pencerrig, instructions were received for a complete reorganisation of the Bn. into an Infantry Divisional Support Bn. No War Establishment had been prepared when the order was received on September 21st, but a broad outline was issued for immediate action. The new unit was to consist of one Divisional Support Coy., to be equipped with Oerlikons and Hispanos for the A.A. Defence of Divisional H.Q., and three Infantry Brigade Support Coys. equipped with machine-guns. This was acted upon with some mistrust until the War Establishment was finally issued on November 11th, when it was learnt that a Divisional Support Bn. was to dispense with the services of a number of vital personnel, including the 2nd in Command, Q.M., R.S.M., R.Q.M.S., the Orderly Room Sgt., and the complete disbandment of H.Q. Coy. This was a disastrous piece of news, and one which caused great consternation. The object of this new organisation was to form a small skeleton of Bn. H.Q., consisting of three officers and about eighteen other ranks, with four completely independent Coys. organised to operate apart under command of Div. and Bde. H.Q.s.

Fortunately the Commanding Officer used a considerable amount of initiative and resource in imposing this new War Establishment, and after repeated representations on the impracticability of this organisation a new War Establishment was issued on February 1st, 1943. Bn. H.Q. was re-established, with three Infantry Brigade Support Groups. These were formed from E, F, and H Coys., each Group consisting of Transport and Signal Platoons with a Machine-gun Coy., 4·2-in. Heavy Mortar Coy., and an A.A. Coy.—a large force of 22 officers and 400-odd other ranks, with a unified command operating under direct control of the Brigade Commander concerned.

This period of continual re-shuffle proved to be a very trying time for all concerned, and Lt.-Col. D. V. G. Brock, with his Adjutant, Capt. R. J. Cannon, was sorely tried in the initial stages sifting and sorting out the Bn. into new formations to everyone's satisfaction. In connection with this a word of praise must be given to the Orderly Room staff under the leadership of O.R.Q.M.S. Reay, and later Sgt. J. Norton, with the able assistance of Cpl. R. Field, who gave the finest service any Commander could possibly wish to expect. The one big consolation of Bn. H.Q. in those frustrating weeks of labour was found in the delightful surroundings of St. Donats Castle, within whose walls the many decisions of policy had to be made.

Whilst stationed in South Wales, the programme of training was anything but monotonous : there were the new arts of 4·2-in. mortars to be mastered, A.A. guns to fire, machine-guns to exercise, and last, but by no means least, the modern vogue of battle training. This last departure was greeted with much foreboding, and a Bn. Battle Course was started in October under the gruelling leadership of Capt. D. A. Thomas. The Battle School was housed in its own headquarters, and all ranks of the Bn. were put through tests of endurance and battle inoculation with a severity equal to anything experienced in the past year's hardship of Iceland. Few fell by the wayside, and a fine quality of pugnacious determination developed in the most gentle individuals. Battle training appeared to suit the Londoners admirably, as, amongst other notable successes, Lieut. S. R. Pinks obtained a Distinguished report from the Divisional Battle School at Presteign and was immediately attached as a Permanent Staff Instructor.

This new form of training was unfortunately not completed without disaster. Whilst attending a demonstration given by the Divisional Permanent Staff at Presteign, Major Alastair Wray was the victim of a fatal accident caused by a 2-in. mortar bomb. It was one of the major tragedies yet experienced in the history of the Bn., and his loss was sadly felt. No officer had done more for the unit, and a fine and stalwart soldier was honoured in a Memorial Service conducted by the Rev. A. A. Chapman, C.F., and attended at Llantwit Major on February 3rd by Major-General H. O. Curtis, C.B., D.S.O., M.C.

Since leaving Sussex in 1941, the Bn. seemed doomed never to be stationed again in England. On April 15th the Division commenced a four-day move from South Wales to the Lowlands of Scotland, harbouring *en route* at Warrington, Preston, and Carlisle, ultimately arriving at Doune and Callender on April 18th. The new quarters were found to be very comfortable and spacious and seemed too good to last, as it transpired they were. On the afternoon of April 28th the Adjutant was summoned to Headquarters, when it was learnt that hasty plans had been issued to return back immediately to the old camps in South Wales. With a mad flurry the advance parties left the following morning, and the main body left by road within thirty-six hours of the order being received. During this brief stay a severe loss was sustained by the Bn. when a large party of N.C.O.s and men were posted for overseas duty with 1 Kensingtons and 2/7 Middlesex. Among the party were such stalwarts as C.S.M. Robertson, now to become R.S.M., C.S.M. Smith, and Sgt. Waymark.

On returning to St. Donats an immediate drive was made to promote training cadres embracing all branches of signals, transport, machine-gun, and 4·2-in. mortars. Great strides were made in this concentrated instruction, and a field-firing range was opened at Ystradfeldte, where Coys. spent four days at a time under canvas. This was the first time that 4·2-in. mortars had been fired by the Mortar Coys., but after one or two alarming experiences in handling this new weapon a degree of accuracy was obtained and the value of this heavy bomb was soon appreciated. On July 10th heavy mortars were introduced to the Division for the first time at a demonstration in the use of smoke on the Sennybridge field-firing range. Infantry Bns. felt a little unhappy at first with the thought of advancing under close support of a mortar barrage, but the skill and accuracy of handling set their minds at rest in realising what a valuable addition this was to a supporting fire-plan. This demonstration had been preceded in June by a thorough inspection of the Bn. by the recently appointed G.O.C., Major-Gen. E. H. Barker. Once again a searching ordeal was passed with flying colours.

In July, emphasis was placed on the initial training for combined operations, and on the 22nd a party of seventy-eight drivers set off for the No. 3 Combined Operating Centre to be introduced to the peculiarities of waterproofing vehicles. The Bn. again moved north on July 28th to join in this training from the same location as vacated in the spring. This time, however, the original nomenclatures of Companies E, F, and H were dropped, and the prefix of "A", "B", and "C" Groups adopted. The natural training areas of Scotland provided ideal conditions for deployment and field-firing practice, in which all arms could participate with the greatest latitude. Apart from these daily exercises all interest and attention were paid to the new drill of combined assault on enemy-held coast-lines. Exercise "Bridgehead", in which all units and corps took part, showed clearly the complications to be overcome on landing in a strange terrain. The exercise commenced in mock-up boats on the beaches of Troon and advanced inland through three days of the worst weather possible. Conditions were far from being ideal, but the high standard of morale spurred the Groups on to a successful completion.

Following this full-scale exercise on dry land, "A" Group set off with 146 Inf. Bde. to the Combined Training Centre at Inverary, where a strenuous month of combined training with the co-operation of the Royal Navy was experienced. A great strain was imposed on all ranks in this strenuous training, incorporating the wading of vehicles, loading and unloading of carriers, jeeps, into L.C.T.s, and realistic battle assaults in the early hours from the lochs on to field-firing areas. No detail was allowed to pass, and the final day of a weary but satisfying month came when all ranks, regardless of their ability to swim, were taken thirty yards out into the loch and, with the assistance of Mae West life-belts, ordered to jump from the L.C.M. into the icy depths and make their way ashore as best they could. While "A" Group were being put through their paces at Inverary, "C" Group were having similar trials at the C.T.C. at Rothesay, and after "B" Group, now under the command of Major S. Jacobson, had followed on with 147 Bde. at Inverary, the entire Bn. had received their first taste of battle training with the Royal Navy. During these weeks of combined operations the long-awaited order for mobilisation was issued on October 10th, and it seemed at long last that final preparations were in the process of being made. The Q.M. and his staff were now hard at work absorbing and reissuing an unending flow of new equipment which started to pour in. A trying task under normal conditions, but with two moves of location, in October and December, 1943, the job was made doubly hard.

After a stay of only a few weeks at Johnstone, near Glasgow, the Bn., less "B" Group, moved south after three nightly stages to its final concentration on the east coast. "B" Group remained over Christmas at Johnstone to assist in the completion of combined-operation training of Inf. Bn. Groups at Tignabruaich, a peninsula off the west coast of Scotland near Rothesay, the remaining Groups having already completed these final exercises. Suffolk was well known to many of the older members of the Bn., and it was a happy coincidence that the 2 Kensingtons were able to proceed into battle from the same district in which it first joined a field-force formation in the summer of 1940. On arrival the Groups were placed in direct command of their Bdes., in the following order:

"A" Group with 146 Inf. Bde. at Corton.
"B" Group with 147 Inf. Bde. at Caister.
"C" Group with 70 Inf. Bde. at Benacre.

This new distribution of command placed the C.O. in the frustrating position of being able to control training only to a platoon level, and being held responsible for matters of discipline and administration. However, the life of this organisation was brief, and yet another major re-shuffle of personnel and equipment was to take place. On January 14th, Lt.-Col. Brock was summoned to H.Q. 21 Army Group, where he learnt that the months of rigorous training as Bde. Support Groups had been all to no avail. The old M.G. Bn. had been reintroduced, with three M.G. Coys. and one 4·2-in. Mortar Coy. Once again conferences were held to decide the best means of distributing personnel and reducing the Bn. to its new proposed War Establishment. It was a sad blow to the scores of officers and other ranks who had formed such efficient Mortar and A.A. Coys., and with great reluctance a Holding Coy. was formed to absorb the 24 officers and 247 other ranks who had now become redundant through this last irrevocable order for reorganisation. New Coys. were superimposed on the M.G. Coys. of the old Support Groups, and the mortar-trained personnel were centralised to form a new "D" Coy.

A change of locations was made, and finally the Bn. was distributed as follows:

Bn. H.Q. and H.Q. Coy., Rollesley Hall.
A Coy. (Major R. J. Cannon), Corton Camp.
B Coy. (Major S. Jacobson), Caister.
C Coy. (Major S. R. Pinks), Corton.
D Coy. (Major R. Bare), Caister.

The new War Establishment was ultimately received on February 17th, 1944, but it was not until March 4th that the Bn. was ordered to re-mobilise. During this time, amidst the chaotic changes, great advantage was taken, both day and night, of the numerous field-firing ranges in the Suffolk marshes. This, together with the utmost practice of wireless procedure, soon built the new Coys. into efficient fighting units. Having sorted out transport and equipment into the new lay-out, the question of reducing the full establishment to "light scales" became the next problem to face. It was learnt that the formation would land shortly after "D-Day" as a "follow-up" Division, and only a limited amount of transport could be taken over in the initial stages. As this transport would most probably have to wade ashore in unknown depths of water, priority was given to the task of waterproofing vehicles to withstand this expected submersion. Drivers and mechanics were trained, and on the first try-out at Great Yarmouth approximately 80 per cent. of all A and B vehicles waded half-way through the trial tank of sea-water and drowned with an ugly splutter. This caused great consternation and redoubled efforts until all types of transport were satisfactorily proofed; so well was this done that jeeps were driven through the water with nothing visible but the windscreen and a projecting exhaust-pipe.

The month of April saw a five-day exercise "Bump", held in the Dunwich training area, to try out the fighting efficiency of the new light scale, and a very hectic month was completed on April 27th by an inspection of 49 (W.R.) Inf. Div. by His Majesty the King. In May it was obvious that the day was drawing very near. Final preparations for the coming assault were made, and a full-scale Divisional dress rehearsal was held between the 12th and 17th to practise the movement of troops to and fro through assembly and concentration areas in a newly acquired bridge-head. Final instructions were received that all transport was to be taken off the road on May 23rd and waterproofing completed by May 30th. All Coys. remained in their existing locations with the exception of D Coy., who moved to Bury Church Camp prior to waterproofing their Lloyd carriers, as the maximum distance these "A" vehicles could travel, having once been waterproofed, was only seventy-five miles.

The atmosphere in all camps became very tense, mingled with an indescribable feeling of relief that the climax of weary years of training was soon to come. Days went by rapidly as the flurry of last-minute problems reared their heads, and on May 26th all ranks were confined to camp with nothing further to do but eat, sleep, and enjoy the luxuries of an East Coast seaside resort, in readiness for the final blow against Nazi-held Europe.

The last warning order issued prior to the actual move to marshalling areas, came on May 31st, when the 2 Kensingtons were instructed by Movement Control to stand by in readiness to move at six hours' notice. The ultimate destination was unknown to all but the C.O., and all ranks waited patiently for the final word to go. A future of grim fighting lay ahead, but what actual form it would take no one could tell. What was realised, however, was the fact that this next stage in the history of the 2nd Bn. must be a decisive one, and whatever else happened, it would be the last step in ending these fruitless years of war.

PART II—INVASION AND VICTORY

June–December, 1944: NORMANDY TO NIJMEGEN
January 1945–February 1946: VICTORY AND
                                OCCUPATION

FROM this point, it becomes difficult to continue the story of the 2nd Battalion as a single consecutive record. During long spells of fighting, the Machine-Gun Companies were under command of their respective Brigades, while the platoons of the Mortar Company were often spread over the whole of the Divisional Front. Meanwhile, Bn. H.Q. and H.Q. Company carried out the vital functions of administration and supply of stores, transport, and reinforcements, and the Commanding Officer and others were tireless in their visits forward and help to company officers. Nevertheless, the companies' activities were mainly bound up with their Brigades rather than with the Battalion as a whole, and often resolved into the actions of widely-separated platoons. It was rare, until the end of 1944, for the Battalion to operate as a single fighting unit. For this reason, the period from the invasion of Normandy to the end of December 1944 has been covered by separate chapters on each company and on Bn. H.Q. and H.Q. Company. The writer has tried to give a general impression of these crowded months, and to pick out incidents that were typical of the life and operations of the companies, rather than to present a detailed record of all that took place. There are omissions and some overlapping, but it is hoped that these will be forgiven as unavoidable in this form of war history.

From January 1945 to the disbanding of the Battalion in Germany in February 1946 it has been possible again to follow the activities of the Battalion as a whole.

CHAPTER XXIII

BATTALION H.Q. AND H.Q. COY.

June–December, 1944

THROUGHOUT May it had been clear that invasion of Europe was imminent, and the Battalion's activities were centred on the final preparations. A steady deluge of orders, passed down from 49 Div., had to be assimilated and put into effect, and all ranks were tremendously busy, a particularly heavy strain falling on administrative staff and Coy. Comds. The Commanding Officer, early in May, had attended a briefing at Div. H.Q. on maps of the actual invasion area from which all names were omitted, and on May 27th he was present at the Commander-in-Chief's conference at Lower Hare Park. The chief task during this month was the waterproofing of vehicles, but there was also a host of other arrangements to be made, ranging from instructions on pay to the issue of sealed Operation Orders to Coy Comds. On May 26th all ranks were confined to barracks, and on May 31st the entire Bn. was put on six hours' notice by Movement Control. The stage was now set, and so far as was humanly possible the Bn. was ready down to the last detail. But before the curtain went up, there were to be a few welcome days for rest and catching up on lost sleep.

At this point, the composition of Bn. H.Q. was:

C.O., Lt.-Col. D. V. G. Brock, 2/i/C., Major R. E. N. d'Abo. Adjt., Capt. I. A. Strawson. Asst. Adjt., Lieut. G. A. Hunt. Intelligence Officer, Capt. M. Palmer. Signals Officer, Capt. E. J. Braybrook. Medical Officer, Capt. D. Beddard, R.A.M.C. Chaplain, Rev. R. J. Blofeld, C.F. Reinforcement Officer, Lieut. P. Lawrie. R.S.M. R. Watts. Orderly Room Sgts. Norton, Field.

H.Q. Coy. was composed as follows:

O.C., Capt. E. Dudley. Transport Officer, Capt. T. Sheppard. Q.M., Capt. W. A. Blakeley. R.Q.M.S. Young.

On June 5th came the long-awaited order to move, and that night Bn. H.Q., H.Q. Coy., and B Coy. drove in convoy from Rollesby to the marshalling area at Purfleet Ranges. Just before arriving in London on the morning of June 6th the news of the Allied landings in Normandy was heard on the wireless. The Bn. Transport left the marshalling area for the Docks soon after midnight on June 6th/7th, and T.C.V.s took personnel down to West India Docks the same evening, but embarkation did not take place until the next morning. The intervening night was spent in a warehouse on the quayside, and it was a queer coincidence that many members of the Bn. should have remembered it from their service in the same area in 1939 and 1940.

The crossing to the Normandy coast took from June 8th to June 11th; early that morning the *Fort Poplar* anchored off the beach-head amidst an immense fleet of Royal Navy and Merchant Navy shipping, marking the greatest amphibious operation in history. As the *Fort Poplar* came inshore, an officer on deck noticed a corvette opproaching in a fast and purposeful manner, and braced himself for an order to disembark at once. But from the corvette's loud hailer a cheerful voice sang out "Good morning" as she passed by. It was, he said, an anti-climax—but very reassuring. Lack of landing-craft, in fact, delayed disembarkation that day, but by June 12th the greater part of Bn. H.Q. and H.Q. Coy. were ashore and concentrated at the village of St. Gabriel. The last day on the *Fort Poplar* was marked by an enemy air attack, a stick of six bombs straddling the ship.

The next two days were spent at St. Gabriel in conferences and preparations for the move forward, which took place on June 15th. Bn. H.Q. and H.Q. Coy. were now sited at Cancagny, near Main Div. H.Q., while the M.G. Coys. moved on to forward areas with their respective Bdes. Since Cancagny was to remain the location of Bn. H.Q. for over a month, it will be appropriate at this point to give an impression of its daily routine and lay-out. H.Q. was sited in a small triangular field on the edge of the village, with Div. H.Q. fifty yards down the road. It was flanked on one side by an Air O.P. Auster Flight, on the

BATTALION H.Q. AND H.Q. COY.

other by 40-mm. Bofors guns. There were a few tents, and the rest of H.Q. lived in their vehicles or in bivouacs under tarpaulins, with slit-trenches handily adjacent. Reveille was at 6.30, breakfast for all ranks at 7.15, and the R.S.M. held a parade for all other ranks immediately afterwards. The Commanding Officer set off early for visits to forward Coys. and platoons, keeping in touch with H.Q. by wireless.

The centre of H.Q. life at this period was the Bn. Office Truck, which seemed to be always full, noisy, and cheerful; apart from pouring out a flow of daily orders and instructions, it was the main purveyor of gossip, news, and advance information. Alongside the office truck was the "Intelligence" Tent, where, on large maps, all available information was decoratively presented by the I.O. and Sgt. Trew. Here, too, was a powerful receiving set which could be tuned in to whatever net in the Div. was the most interesting at the time. Thus, when a battle was on, the "I" tent, on the Div. Comd.'s net, was extremely well informed. In addition to these sources of information, all ranks at Bn. H.Q. were able to attend daily briefings by the Div. I.O. The daily round and common task were occasionally enlivened by low-flying German fighters; a Bren was kept handy for these occasions for use by whoever was nearest to it at the crucial moment, but no kills were ever claimed.

The Signals were among the liveliest sections at Bn H.Q. Their adventures began soon after landing, when an R.T. truck with Capt. Braybrook, Cpl. Penford, and Pte. Sturmey tried to locate a forward Coy. at night, and found themselves in close contact with the German F.D.L.s. There were heavy demands for replacements and batteries from the Coys., and Sgt. Butterworth did well in keeping pace with them.

H.Q. Coy., too, were kept busy with supplies and services for the Coys., particularly on such occasions as when one M.G. Coy. fired nearly half a million rounds and used thirty-four barrels in twenty-four hours, and the Q.M., Capt. Blakeley, had to commandeer all available transport to keep them supplied. Indeed, one Bn. on this occasion used every M.M.G. spare possessed by B.L.A., and a Dakota flew out replacements from Britain especially for the job. Battle casualties in vehicles were heavy, and the Transport Officer, Capt. Sheppard, had to be one of the most mobile officers in the Bn. (From landing in Normandy to his departure on release in October 1945 he covered 28,000 miles in his jeep.) His total turnover in vehicles for the campaign may perhaps be given here : 90 motor-cycles, 25 cars, 62 15-cwt. trucks, 36 3-ton lorries, 224 carriers, and 54 trailers.

Before returning to the record of the campaign in Normandy it must be said that, since the duties of H.Q. Coy. remained much the same from day to day and sector to sector, they will not be frequently mentioned. This does not mean that they were either unimportant, or unappreciated by the rest of the Bn. Throughout, H.Q. Coy. did a fine job, and Coys. in action had nothing but praise for the way in which their calls were met.

On landing in Normandy, 49 Div. came under Comd. of XXX (British) Corps, then commanded by General Sir Brian Horrocks (late Mx. Regt.). Its task was, first to enlarge the beach-head, then to hold it until the Allied build-up was far enough ahead to enable a break-through to be tried. After the initial assault had reached Villers Bocage and the outskirts of Caen, counter-attacks had forced some withdrawals, while heavy storms badly delayed the build-up. The first battles fought by 49 Div. were therefore advances through the murderously close Bocage country, then defensive actions to check German counter-attacks. Details of the fighting, as it affected the Battalion, will be found in the separate chapters on the Coys. For them, as for the bulk of the Div., it was a tough introduction to battle, and although casualties were not heavy by comparison with the infantry, they took a heavy toll of N.C.O.s and key tradesmen such as driver-operators. Bn. H.Q. found that the reinforcement situation was unsatisfactory—they were few in number, the routine for sending them up seemed defective, and only personal visits by the Adjutant to Reinforcement Holding Units bore any fruit.

After some small-scale actions, the first big break in the German defences was made by 49 Div. in attacks on June 25th and 26th. All Coys. were heavily engaged, and the

The Rauray Battle: 2nd Battalion M.M.G. Carriers halt beside a Shattered German Tank in the much-fought-over Village of Rauray in Normandy. (See Chapter XXV.)
(Photo by courtesy of Imperial War Museum. Copyright reserved.)

Sergeant Durbin indicates a Target to Men of his Section during the Operations in Normandy.
(See Chapter XXVI.)
(Photo by courtesy of Imperial War Museum. Copyright reserved.)

BATTALION H.Q. AND H.Q. COY.

crack German 12 S.S. Panzer Div. fought back savagely. But the battle ended in complete success for 49 Div., and in a Special Order of the Day, Maj.-Gen. Barker, the Div. Comd., paid a tribute to the "magnificent spirit, efficiency, and fighting qualities of the commanders and troops that took part . . . the 49 Div. has now proved itself in battle." A furious German counter-attack with armour, at the beginning of July, was pulled up short, C Coy. taking a notable part in the fighting at Rauray, before the Div. settled in to a spell of static warfare, broken only by aggressive patrolling. During this period there was an acute shortage of ammunition, particularly for 4·2-in. mortars.

The Bn.'s part in the fighting since the landing was acknowledged on July 4th in the following message received from Maj.-Gen. Barker:

Will you please convey my congratulations to your Bn. on the excellent co-operation they have given to the Bdes. and their individual Bns. during the fighting since the Div. has been engaged. I have had more than one message of appreciation from Bde. Comds., which shows a most satisfactory state of affairs. I should like to make special mention of the gallant teams who remained fighting in the Parc de Boislondes on 18 June and on the 110 Feature on 1 July. These actions have given the infantry the greatest confidence in your unit and I must congratulate you personally on the results obtained, and on the splendid way your chaps have kept up the good name of your Regiment and the Div. The best of luck for the future!

During July it became possible to withdraw Coys. in turn for brief spells of rest, and for overhaul of transport and equipment in the Bn. H.Q. area. An important rôle was assumed by the Bn. when the Div. Comd. made the Commanding Officer responsible for co-ordinating all counter-mortar activities in the Div. The Germans were well supplied with mortars, which had been a major cause of casualties. A Counter-Mortar Office, manned by Lieut. G. A. Hunt (Assistant Adjutant), was set up at H.Q. R.A.; the Counter-Mortar Officer had a call on fire from Corps and Div. Artillery, 4·2-in. mortars and 3-in. mortars. He had a line link with Bn. H.Q., and all Mortar and M.G.

Plns., spread over the Div. front, passed on messages of enemy mortaring. The code word was "Poppycock" followed by the bearing of the suspected mortar position. A number of reports enabled cross-bearings to be made, and the offending German mortar line to be engaged and heavily plastered. This system was quickly successful, and great pleasure was derived soon afterwards from a captured German Intelligence report which complained of a new British counter-mortar weapon which was punishing their mortars, however quickly they moved.

A change in the Bn.'s communication system was also made at about the same time. All M.G. Coys. and Pls. were put on one net, and the Coy. rear link set were put into use as Coy. Comds. rovers, to be used on a flick between Coy. and Bde. H.Q. This gave Coy. Comds. greater opportunity to get away from Bde. H.Q. without losing touch, and although the plan had many critics to begin with, it worked well in practice.

Meanwhile 49 Div. had been transferred from XXX Corps to I Corps, then in the sector S.E. of Caen. It was interesting to find that, as a result, the Bn. was now in the same Corps as 2 Middlesex (3 Div.) and 1/7 Middlesex (51 Div.), and there were several opportunities for visits and exchange of experiences. All Coys. and Bn. H.Q. moved to the new area between July 24th and 26th, H.Q. being sited at St. Honorine. Here it was occasionally shelled, but a far greater plague than the German artillery were the mosquitoes, which descended in hordes at dusk. They made life miserable for everyone, particularly for the signallers on night duty in their dug-out. One signaller set himself on fire in an over-zealous attempt to smoke them out.

I Corps was on the left of the Allied flank, and the Div.'s task was to hold the line, overlooked by the enemy, on which the eventual break-through would hinge. Before the break-through, however, the Bn. underwent some three weeks of static fighting in hot weather, harassed by dust, mosquitoes, and frequent shelling and mortaring. There was a steady drain of casualties among the Coys. It was a relief, therefore, when on August 15th the Div. began a general advance towards the Seine by way of Vimont. The

Bn.'s first taste of mobile warfare brought it to higher, greener country, where undamaged farms and villages were at last to be seen. The German rearguards fought with determination on natural obstacles, but elsewhere the retreat quickly became a rout, and large numbers of prisoners and vast quantities of enemy equipment were captured. The Machine-gun Coys. moved with their Bdes., usually with a platoon in the advance guard, and were in action at a number of river crossings, forest clearances, and engagements for commanding hills; in the case of the Mortar (D) Coy., it was found difficult, with some exceptions, to deploy in time to keep within range of the retreating enemy. Mortar positions had to be looked for well forward, and it was partly this which caused the Bn. to sustain a grievous loss in the wounding of Maj. R. Bare, D. Coy. Comd., on August 18th. D Coy. had supported the successful attack on Mezidon on the night of August 17th/18th, and the following afternoon Major Bare, accompanied by the Commanding Officer, Lt.-Col. Brock, was reconnoitring towards Lisieux in preparation for a further advance. While they were at the approach to a blown bridge across the River Touques, Maj. Bare was fired on by a sniper at 200 yards' range, and severely wounded in the side, back, and left arm. He had to crawl back to a hedge under fire and then walked half a mile to his jeep. Maj. Bare was later evacuated to the U.K. (where he spent fourteen months in hospital), and the Bn. thus lost the services of this fine officer.

The end of August saw the Bn. pulled up by a bridgeless Seine. It was known that, while the rest of the Allied forces were speeding to Brussels and Antwerp, 49 Div. would be swung west after crossing the Seine to capture Le Havre, an essential port. The question of the moment was, "How do we get across?" The Reconnaissance Regiment and Sappers tried rafting and ferrying; but as more craft capsized than got across, some relief was felt when the attempt was abandoned and the Div. eventually crossed, by less adventurous means, at Rouen and Elbeuf. It then concentrated for the attack on Le Havre, Bn. H.Q. being sited at Étainhus.

Le Havre was defended by a strong garrison, with a perimeter of field-works and concrete pill-boxes. It was well stocked with supplies, and the German Commander had been ordered by Hitler himself to defend the port to the last man. 49 Div., for the assault, had under comd. considerable armour, and the defences were softened-up by massive air attacks. The attack, in which 51 Div. participated on the right, was very carefully planned and was carried through like a perfect exercise. Within forty-eight hours Le Havre was in Allied hands, with amazingly low casualties on our side, and a huge haul of prisoners. All Coys. were deployed on the flanks, and were able to put down enfilading fire in front of the Advance.

On September 12th the G.O.C. issued this message :

> Today has been a memorable day for 49 Div. After an attack against very strong defences, in a matter of hours the Div., supported by the armour, has broken through and relieved the port of Le Havre, which is most essential for the maintenance of the American Army. I should like to congratulate all ranks for this magnificent performance, and to thank them for the effort which has been made by everyone in their own spheres to produce this remarkable success with such relatively light casualties.

After the fall of the port the whole Bn., for the first time since landing, was concentrated in one area, with no front and no enemy, and enjoyed a few days' rest and overhaul. Meanwhile, the Allied Armies had liberated Brussels and Antwerp, and on September 21st the Bn. set out on a two-day convoy march to catch up with them, along a route that rang like an echo of the Battle Honours of 1914–18 : Lille–Menin–Courtrai–Termonde–Malines–Morkhoven. This was a severe test for any tracked vehicle, and while the Universal carriers came out of it well, the Lloyds were spread out in a sorry procession covering several days in time and hundreds of miles in space, once more demonstrating their menace to any mobile operation covering more than thirty miles at a stretch.

On September 25th the whole Bn. moved into Vorselaar, where it was given a rapturous welcome, these being the first British troops in the town. Unfortunately, B and D Coys. did not have time to enjoy the subsequent festivities, being called into action by 147 Inf. Bde. the same day. The other Coys. followed within a day or two, and the month ended with some hard fighting along the Antwerp–Turnhout Canal. This obstacle was crossed at the beginning of October, and the Div. then found itself holding a very long line. While the left and centre moved up to capture Wustwezel and Loenhout, the right flank was held by a Group, Bob Force, consisting of Light A./A. acting as infantry, with A and C Coys. (less one Pl.) and one Pl. of D Coy. under Comd. The subsequent fighting provided an interesting test of the Bn.'s flexibility, since the M.G. Coys. and Mortar Pl. operated in turn with the Reconnaissance Regt. and Polish and Canadian formations as well as with their normal Bdes. At times, Bob Force line was so thinly held that at least one M.G. Coy. H.Q. had to find protective patrols. It speaks well for the adaptability of the Bn. that there were no administrative hitches, although communications were at times very difficult.

While Bob Force first held its ground and then advanced to maintain contact, the rest of the Div., with Bn. H.Q., H.Q. Coy., B Coy., D Coy. less one Pl., and one Pl. C Coy., captured Wustwezel. German artillery, particularly self-propelled guns, was active in this sector, and Bn. H.Q. arrived at Wustwezel in the midst of severe shelling. Reports that the Q.M. had been seen determinedly digging a slit-trench raised spirits throughout the Bn., as did a subsequent incident when the Intelligence Officer, driving along a road in search of a site for Bn. H.Q., found himself passing our infantry vanguard crawling along ditches. (It was, perhaps, the fate of all M.G. Bn. H.Q.s to have their sporadic excitements treated with levity by the rest of the Bn.).

After the capture of Wustwezel, 49 Div. were relieved by 104 U.S. Div. and swung left into Holland, to clear the northern approaches to the Scheldt estuary and capture Roosendaal, the first Dutch town of any size to be liberated. These operations were carried out in steadily deteriorating weather over flat, wet country, and against determined German rearguards covering the withdrawal of the main enemy forces into Western Holland; Roosendaal was taken at the end of October, and by November 6th the line of the Maas had been reached. All these operations were carried out

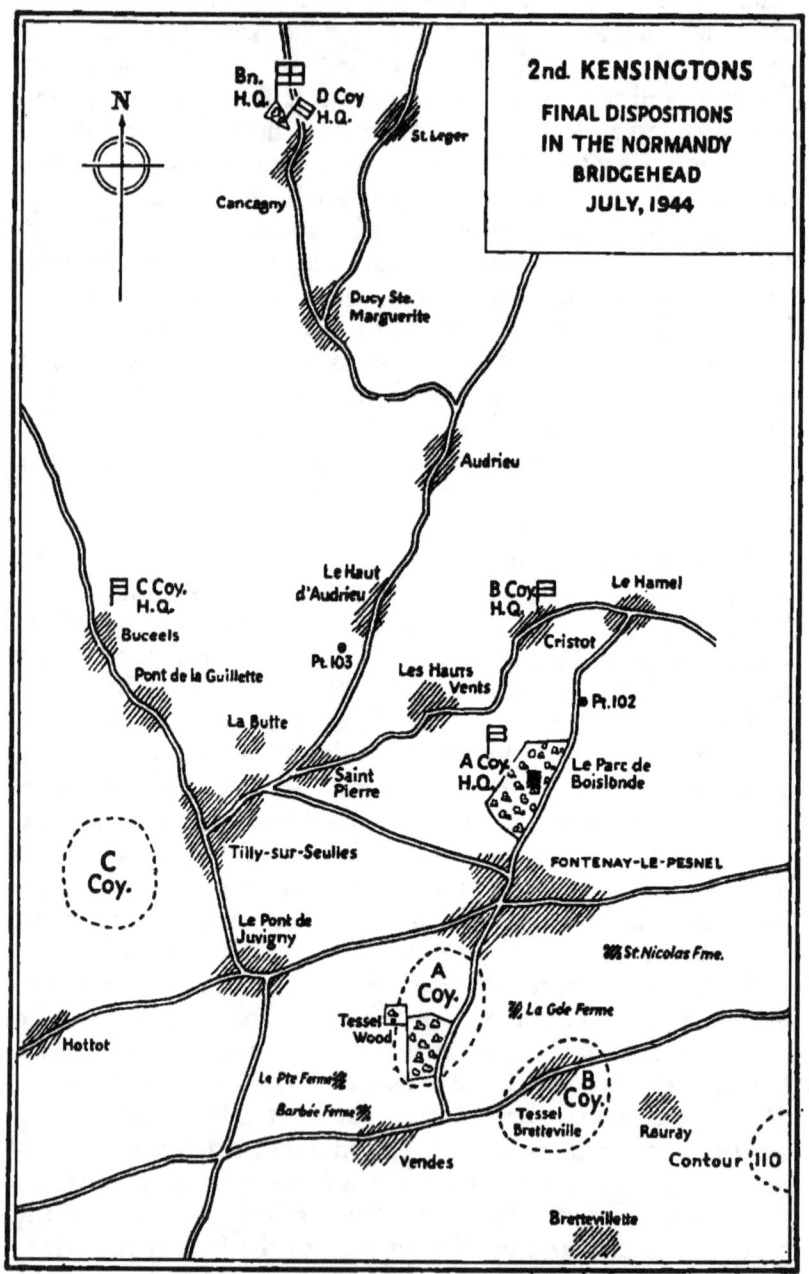

under comd. of the Canadian Army, but on November 9th the Div. moved back into Belgium to join XII Corps, Second British Army, which was directed on Venlo; and after a bitterly-cold day-long drive from Roosendaal, the Bn. concentrated at Hamont. During October there had been a number of changes among senior officers: Maj. R. E. N. d'Abo, the 2/i/C., had left the Bn. to return to U.K. prior to release on business grounds, and had been succeeded by Maj. S. Jacobson. Maj. E. Dudley took over B Coy. and Capt. H. Fenwick became the new O.C. H.Q. Coy.

The Bn.'s first tasks in the new sector were to take part in advances by 53 and 51 Divs. towards Venlo. These attacks are described in the separate Coy. chapters, as all M.G. Coys. and the Mortar Coy. came under comd. 1 Manchesters (53 Div.) and 1/7 Middlesex (51 Div.). From Bn. H.Q.'s point of view, these operations gave a valuable opportunity to compare methods. In both these Divs., particularly 53 Div., the grouping of Mortar Pls. in pairs and the centralising of M.G. Coys. had been carried much further than in 49 Div. On the other hand, neither Bn. had experimented to the same extent with R.T. communications, and the Kensington's single net for M.G. Coys. aroused great interest.

After the initial attacks, 49 Div. continued the advance towards Venlo. Wretched weather, deep mud, bad roads, and mine-fields provided greater opposition than the Germans, as did the numerous canals which had to be bridged. For the first time it became essential to site all H.Q. and rest areas in houses or barns, while break-downs among vehicles, particularly Lloyds, threw a heavy strain on M.T. personnel. Among the worst sufferers were the dispatch riders, who frequently found their machines entirely sinking in mud, and despite noble work by the men concerned, notably Pte. Carver of Bn. H.Q., who had for nearly five years been a pillar of the D.R. section in the Signals Platoon, it was found that dispatches had in most cases to be carried by jeep or trucks. By November 25th the Div. had reached positions overlooking Venlo, and planning had begun for the assault. At this point, however, it was learned with regret that the Div.'s stay with XII Corps was to be cut short, and that it was to rejoin the Canadian Army (II Canadian Corps) in the Nijmegen–Arnhem sector. The move to this area took place between November 28th and 30th, Bn. H.Q. first being sited at Oosterhout, on the far side of the Waal.

The gallant failure of the Airborne attack on Arnhem had left an Allied bridge-head between the Rivers Waal and Rhine. Nijmegen, on the south bank of the Waal, was a major base, and three bridges spanned the Waal into the bridge-head—a damaged railway bridge, the famous road bridge, and a pontoon bridge. All these were within observed artillery fire from the German positions overlooking Arnhem on the far side of the Rhine, where the bridges had been blown. The bridge-head thrust out towards the Rhine, with strong enemy positions on either flank and on the approaches to the Rhine. The country was low-lying and could be easily flooded in parts by blowing breaches in the river dykes, and soon after the Div.'s arrival the enemy did this. All civilians had been evacuated from the island, and the Div.'s task was defined as aggressive defence on a wide front which was thinly held, particularly after 51 Div. were withdrawn.

The "island" and the Nijmegen bridges were to be the Bn.'s sphere of operations for four months. Bn. H.Q., which had been pulled back into Nijmegen, was given the task of operating and administering Brock Force, a Group (commanded by Lt.-Col. Brock) formed to defend the bridges. The Coys., with intervals in Nijmegen, were in action on the "island" throughout the winter, and although casualties were fortunately light there were heavy calls on all Pls. During December, however, the Div. Comd. decided that M.G. Coys. and Mortars would normally remain under Bn. Comd., so that H.Q. again took on an active part in the tactical handling of all Coys. and it was possible to carry out a satisfactory programme of reliefs and overhauls. [A fuller account of the activities of Brock Force and the Bn. will be found in a subsequent chapter ("Victory and Occupation").] December passed with the Bn. settling down for a prolonged stay, with floods followed by hard frost, and with threats of German paratroop attacks, reinforced by promises of annihilation for the Div. broadcast by Lord Haw-Haw and the notorious "Mary of Arnhem". It was, perhaps, an uneasy Christmas; but it was nevertheless possible to hold festivities in turn for every part of the Bn., and the momentous year of 1944 ended with the Kensingtons in Holland, well dug in and in good heart.

CHAPTER XXIV

A COY.

June 8th–December 31st, 1944

THE first definite sign that action was now very close came on May 31st, when the Coy. Commander, Major R. Cannon, with C.S.M. Wakeford and Sgt. Smith, left camp in Suffolk to join 146 Inf. Bde. advance party for an unknown destination. The composition of the Coy. at that time was:

>Coy. H.Q., Maj. R. Cannon, Capt. D. A. Thomas, C.S.M. Wakeford.
>3 Platoon, Lieut. C. E. Banyard.
>4 Platoon, Lieut. C. P. Douet.
>5 Platoon, Lieut. K. Attrill.

The task of moving the company to its assembly area therefore fell upon Capt. D. A. Thomas. All vehicles had been waterproofed up to the final stages and were heavily over-loaded, but the long drive was accomplished without mishap. The move took place at last light on June 3rd, and the convoy moved out of camp among the cheers and good wishes of the small rear party. From that moment it passed into the complex machinery of administration, which already gave evidence of the careful planning, down to the last detail, that enabled an unending stream of men and material to move without delay towards the shipping that was awaiting them.

The Coy. arrived at Wanstead flats on the morning of June 4th. This huge area, near the docks and set among one of London's worst-blitzed centres, seemed appropriate to the task ahead. At this stage all ranks were confined to camp, and the air was heavy with rumours and expectation.

Early on June 6th, the great news broke: the invasion of Normandy had been launched that morning, and for the first time, the Coy. knew its destination. This was an unforgettable day. Then came an unexpected stroke of luck, particularly for those with homes in London. The need for security now being relaxed, six hours' walking-out was allowed and eagerly seized upon. The next day, June 7th, the work of embarkation on a Liberty ship began, but was held up by an unfortunate incident, the dockers stopping work in the evening over a wages dispute. This delayed embarkation until the following morning.

Except for the Liberty ship's narrowly escaping a collision on its way down the Thames, the voyage was uneventful. As the vessel approached the coast of France there was increasing evidence of the weight and complexity of the Invasion—a stream of shipping, the grey hulks of battleships, and, farther out at sea, portions of the Mulberry harbour in tow. Off the coast, the volume and movement of traffic was like Piccadilly Circus on a Saturday night. Mention must be made here of the noble work done by Lieut. Banyard and the Coy. cooks during the voyage in organising meals from the tiny ship's galley, and of the friendliness and hospitality of the Merchant Navy hosts during the crossing.

The Coy. disembarked by rhino ferry on June 11th and passed to their first concentration area, near a village southeast of Bayeux. The first surprise came when it was found that two out of the three in the advance party had not yet landed. Two days were then profitably spent in overhauling transport and other equipment, and in conferences at Bde. H.Q. and Bn. H.Q.

On June 13th came the first, long-awaited, operational task for the Company. It went into the line, overlooking the much-battered village of Tilly-sur-Seulles, to relieve C Coy., 5 Cheshires. As part of the famous 50 Division, the Cheshires had been in action since D-Day, and this was a welcome, although unfortunately brief, respite for them. This was, at that time, a quiet sector, and the first few days in action were comparatively peaceful, giving the Coy. a chance to find its way around and accustom itself to the close, wooded Bocage country, so ill-adapted to conventional machine-gun shoots. During this period, 6 Pl. of B Coy. came under command, in support of the 1/4 K.O.Y.L.I., and B Coy. Comd. moved his Tactical H.Q. into the Coy. area.

The Coy.'s first serious action came on June 16th, when the 1/4 K.O.Y.L.I. were ordered to attack Cristot. 4 Pl. were given a consolidation rôle, with the rest of the Coy. in close support, and the heavy mortars of D Coy. were also called upon. The K.O.Y.L.I. attack was launched after the heaviest artillery barrage ever put down for one battalion, heavy Naval guns supporting the Divisional and Corps artillery. The resultant score, however, was disappointing, since the enemy had previously withdrawn. Six Germans and five civilians were killed in the barrage, the other casualties being a large number of cows, who took a posthumous and pestiferous revenge until disposed of by various means, orthodox and otherwise. Cristot was soon taken, and its shattered houses around the large stone cross in the centre of the village became a familiar sight. Much elated by the success of their action, 4 Pl. moved to the eastern edge of the village, and quickly dug in.

Shortly after this, however, the Coy. sustained its first casualty, when Pte. Wasley, a Coy. H.Q. driver-operator, was wounded in the arm by a shell splinter. Pte. Wasley's W.T. truck subsequently acquired an unhealthy reputation, since within the next six weeks its two other drivers, Cpl. Raworth and Pte. Fielding, were also wounded. During the next few days, Coy. H.Q. and Pls. were intermittently shelled and mortared, and the value of head cover in slit-trenches was quickly learned; there were fortunately no further casualties during this period, when preparations were afoot for the first full-scale Divisional attack.

The line held by 146 Inf. Bde. at this point was St. Pierre–Les Hauts Vents–Cristot. The Bde. task was to advance and capture the village of Fontenay at the first bound, with the high, wooded ground south of the village as the final objective, and H-hour was set for 02.50 hrs. on June 25th. In the opening phase of the battle, all Pls. occupied indirect fire positions N.E. of St. Pierre, engaging enemy positions west of Tessel Wood. At daylight, 3 Pl. (Lieut. Banyard) and 4 Pl. (Lieut. Douet) supported the attack from direct fire positions. When the first objective had been reached, 5 Pl. (Lieut. Attrill) came under comd. of 1/4 K.O.Y.L.I. for consolidation of the second objective, while the other Pls. continued to engage enemy targets by observation. At about 12.00 hrs., 4 Pl. came under comd. of the Hallams for consolidation of the south edge of Tessel Wood.

During this phase of the attack the Coy. was under mortar- and shell-fire, and was harassed by snipers from the trees and hedgerows of this close, difficult country. Four men—Ptes. Cowlard, Thomas, and Woodward and Corporal Murphy—were wounded, and Pte. Cohen (4 Pl.) drew blood from snipers infesting a gully by shooting one with his rifle. Pte. Long (5 Pl.) also killed a sniper. While attempting to help a wounded German, Pte. Woodworth—wounded later the same day—was sniped and had a narrow escape, the bullet glancing off his steel helmet. A shell that later wounded this Private also blew the tracks off a carrier, and it was put on the road again under fire. 3 Pl. came repeatedly under mortar-fire, and had twice to change their positions, fortunately without casualties. The day ended with 4 and 5 Pls. dug in side by side, and with K.O.Y.L.I. patrols in Tessel Wood.

The next day (June 26th), the Hallams completed the capture of Tessel Wood, with 4 Pl. under comd. for consolidation. Defensive positions were prepared and the guns dug in for what was to prove a fairly long and very uncomfortable stay.

Tessel Wood soon became a name of evil repute in the Coy. An exposed landmark, it drew prolonged attention from the enemy in the shape of shelling and mortaring. On June 27th, Pte. Pritchard was killed and Pte. Barter wounded when their carrier was hit by an 88-mm. shell. During the next two days further casualties were sustained: Pte. Ford (5 Pl.) was killed, and Cpl. Dunan (3 Pl.) severely wounded. 3 Pl. H.Q. had been set up on the edge of the wood and the Pl. had just moved into position when heavy and accurate mortaring from *Nebelwerfer* (6-barrelled mortars) broke out. Mortar shells fell among Pl. H.Q., and one section and a carrier, loaded with ammunition and grenades, was hit and burst into flames. Cpl.

Dunan was struck by a large fragment, which cut off both feet, as well as by splinters. Prompt action by his comrades enabled him to be evacuated almost at once, while the carrier burned fiercely and ammunition was exploding all round. It was here that Sgt. Carter, the platoon sergeant, distinguished himself by his courage and presence of mind, taking charge while the Platoon Commander was forward with an outlying section. Sgt. Carter was subsequently awarded the M.M. Many weeks later, the whole Bn. heard with pleasure that Cpl. Dunan was out of danger and making a gallant recovery.

Excitement in this area was not confined to Tessel Wood. Coy. H.Q. was in a field at the side of the much-fought-over Parc de Boislonde, then a spot of comparative peace until a Corps Deception Unit set up a dummy Armoured Division in the area overnight. The deception was brilliantly effective, for the following night the *Luftwaffe* paid a steady stream of calls, with bombs for visiting-cards. Coy. H.Q. were lucky to escape with only one casualty, Cpl. Raworth, who was wounded in the arm. These days after the first Divisional attack were unspectacular but tiring. Bad weather and news of the storms that held up the landing of so much vital equipment added to the trials, and it was a welcome relief when, on July 19th, the Coy. were pulled out for a few days' rest and overhaul in the Battalion H.Q. area at Cancagny. They had then been thirty-six days in the line, and, in addition to the casualties already mentioned, a number of men had been evacuated suffering from shell-shock.

Good use was made of this rest period, both for overhaul of transport and weapons and for recreation. A number of officers and men visited the sparse amenities of Bayeux, and some football matches were played. This interlude came to an end when 49 Div. was ordered to a new sector S.E. of Caen.

On July 25th, 3 Pl. was put under comd. B Coy., where it remained for several weeks, carrying out tasks in the unpleasant area of Cagny. The following day the rest of the Coy. rejoined 146 Inf. Bde. and moved to the other flank of the bridge-head, S.E. of Caen, with 6 Airborne Div. on the left opposite Troarn. This proved a fairly uneventful, but extremely uncomfortable, sector. There was intermittent shelling and mortaring, and occasional attacks from the *Luftwaffe*. But dust, dysentery, and, above all, the mosquitoes proved even greater plagues. Against the latter every sort of counter-attack was tried, from anti-gas ointment to an official mosquito spread, but with little success. There was little rest for anybody, and this protracted spell of positional warfare was a disappointment to those who had expected, after the capture of Caen, a rapid advance. Nevertheless, behind the line the big build-up was going on, and at last the great break-out took place at Falaise. Shortly before then the Coy. had moved with 146 Inf. Bde. to the area of St. Silvain, taking over from 51 (Highland) Div.

On August 15th, the starter's flag went up for the advance to the Seine, and from then, for the next two weeks, the Coy. was on the move. There was little serious fighting, since the Germans put up, at most, scattered rearguard resistance which was often overcome before the M.G. Pls. came into action. Nevertheless, Pls. were kept busy and there was little rest. But spirits were high, since the Coy. was advancing, the mosquitoes had been left behind, and the troops were now passing through less ravaged country. Two minor incidents in this phase are perhaps worth mentioning. While covering an infantry crossing of a river, 5 Pl. occupied a direct fire position in the finest tradition of Netheravon, giving observation of enemy positions in Breuil, including a cook-house. That day the Germans went hungry. Clearing the Forêt de Bretonne was another notable action, distinguished by the leading carrier of one section fighting a successful duel at 150 yards with a Spandau, and by the triumphant appearance of 4 Pl. at Coy. H.Q. It was led by Lieut. Douet and pipe seated in an enormous twelve-seater staff car, followed by a lesser, but still desirable, saloon, a motor-cycle, a truck, and an ambulance—all German. There was great indignation when all (except Lieut. Douet) had to be left at a dump for captured enemy vehicles.

The Coy. crossed the Seine at Rouen and proceeded to take part in the capture of the vital port of Le Havre. Here it had a straightforward task, firing from the high ground east of the port. Cpl. Gibbs was unfortunately wounded by a fragment from one of our own shells which fell short. It was during the assault on Le Havre that Lieut. Douet won a Mention in Dispatches by crawling over bullet-swept ground to bring in a badly-wounded infantry officer. The capture of Le Havre was followed by a few days in a Battalion area, before, on September 21st, the Battalion moved off for a long drive through France and Belgium to catch up with the rest of B.L.A. Before the Coy. left, however, it was unfortunate enough to lose Lieut. Ken Attrill, through illness. 5 Pl. was taken over, and subsequently led most ably for many weeks, by Sgt. Morgan, whose work was later rewarded by a Mention in Dispatches.

The Coy. next went into action in Belgium, when it occupied positions near Poppel, north of the Turnhout Canal, where the enemy was fighting a delaying action. The same day 3 Pl. had an unhappy experience. The movement of the Reconnaissance Regiment through the platoon position drew enemy shelling, in which Pte. Cox, a carrier-driver of outstanding ability and spirit, was killed, Pte. Willard seriously wounded, and Ptes. Kent and Dix slightly wounded. Another old member of the Coy., Pte. Parrott, was also killed subsequently near Poppel.

During the next few days, 146 Inf. Bde. edged forward towards Tilburg, and on October 6th and 7th there was lively fighting in the wooded area of the Dutch–Belgian frontier. A section of 3 Pl. fired on fixed lines after a counter-attack against the forward Coy. of the 4 Lincs. had overrun its two forward Pls. On its flank there was a small enemy penetration of the forward Coy. of the Hallams, in Aerle. 4 Pl. was in this area, and at first light on October 7th, it was "stonked", two shells making direct hits on the barn where part of the Pl. and some carriers had just moved in. The loft of the barn burst into flames and rapidly burnt out, but fortunately there were no serious casualties, among either men or transport. Later the same day, however, Pte. Flenley was killed by a shell.

Shortly afterwards, A Coy. relieved B Coy. in Bob Force. This was a force built up on 89 Light A./A. Regt. turned into infantrymen, with supporting arms, with the task of holding the right flank of the Division on a very wide front,

4·2-IN. MORTARS IN ACTION IN TYPICAL SCENERY ON THE FRONTIER BETWEEN BELGIUM AND HOLLAND.
(See Chapter XXVII.)
(Photo by courtesy of Imperial War Museum. Copyright reserved.)

The Island between Arnhem and Nijmegen. A Typical Scene after the Enemy had breached the Dykes and flooded much of the Area. (See Chapter XXVIII.)
(Photo by courtesy of Imperial War Museum. Copyright reserved.)

with no depth whatever. The Force burned with martial ardour, but the enemy in this sector was inactive and equally thin on the ground. Nevertheless, Bob Force provided a novel and sometimes alarming experience. Coy. H.Q. found themselves in the F.D.L.s, ahead of Pls., and Pl. Sgts. suffered the indignity of having to go *forward* to collect rations. On one occasion, Coy. H.Q. sentries fought an exuberant, and fortunately bloodless, night battle with 5 Pl. entrenched in a near-by farm. After the main Divisional advance had begun on the left, Bob Force, too, advanced to contact, and during this phase the Coy. 2/i/C., Capt. Thomas, and Pte. Williams had the alarming experience of being blown up by a necklace of Teller mines. Capt. Thomas, who was standing in the back of the truck, was unhurt, but Pte. Williams was blown from the driving-seat into a field, alongside the shattered vehicle. He was not, however, seriously injured. A few days later Bob Force was disbanded and the Coy. rejoined the rest of the Battalion in the Division, which had in the meantime liberated the first big Dutch town, Rosendaal, and was now moving towards the Maas to complete the clearing of the northern approaches of the Scheldt estuary. It was now the end of October and, over these flat lands, winter was beginning to set in. Cold, rain, and mud were to be features of the next months of the campaign which, it was already clear, would not now end in 1944. The high hopes aroused by the dash across Belgium and France had been disappointed.

Three useful days were spent in billets in Rosendaal before the Coy. went into action again with 146 Inf. Bde. On the morning of November 4th the C.O. of the Hallams made an urgent request at 04.15 hrs. for an M.M.G. Pl. which he wanted to put on the ground before first light. A skeleton platoon (3 Pl.) carried out this operation, leaving behind one range-taker, batman, Pl. Sgt., and all No. 3's. At the same time 4 Pl., similarly stripped down to essentials, moved up to support 1/4 K.O.Y.L.I. When daylight came, it was found that 3 Pl. were in an unhealthy position under enemy observation, and the Pl. area was shelled and mortared throughout the day. Digging-in was difficult because of the wet ground, and no movement above ground was possible during the day. There was one fatal casualty, Pte. Sherwood, who was killed by a mortar bomb. For the rest of the Coy. it was a quiet day, 5 Pl. remaining in reserve. This Pl. and Coy. H.Q. attended a service held by the Bn. Chaplain in the Protestant Church at Rosendaal, this being the Coy.'s first service in a church since landing in Normandy.

Enemy resistance in this area was now centred on Klundert, which was heavily attacked by rocket-firing Typhoons, and left blazing. The Germans withdrew towards Willemstadt, on the south bank of the Maas, across which they were ferrying men and supplies. 4 Pl., in support of 1/4 K.O.Y.L.I., moved through Klundert and occupied positions north of the town, while 5 Pl. moved up with 4 Lincs., who were to attack Willemstadt. At 18.00 hrs. on November 6th there was a four-hour cease-fire to allow the evacuation of civilians from this town, and 5 Pl. were able to carry out a comfortable daylight reconnaissance for night occupation. The shoot took place that night, with excellent results, reported by the 2/i/C. of 4 Lincs., who subsequently visited the target area and found a considerable number of enemy dead.

With the capture of Willemstadt, the northern approaches to Antwerp were cleared of the enemy, and the Division was freed for further tasks. On November 7th orders came that the Division was to pass under comd. of XII Corps, Second British Army. This called for a long convoy drive to Hamont, which was carried out on November 9th in the worst conditions yet experienced—snow, hail, and driving wind. At Hamont it was learned that the Coy. was to pass under command of 51 Division which, with 53 Division, was directed towards the Maas. A Coy. was put under comd. of its old friends, 1/7 Middlesex, last encountered in Normandy. The first task of 51 Div. was to cross the Zig Canal, and the operation began on November 14th, when all Pls. carried out a fire programme from H to H+100, and again at 19.30 hrs. on a large wood known to contain enemy. There was heavy enemy shelling of the area, but the Coy. suffered only one casualty, Pte. Southwell, who was wounded by a stray bullet. The Coy. received the congratulations of the Bde. Comd. on the success of its fire programme and, much elated despite the foul weather, reverted to comd. of the Bn. on November 15th.

49 Div. were now given the task of clearing up to the line of the Maas. There was heavy rain, and roads were a morass of mud, with many mine-fields, and this, rather than determined enemy action, delayed the advance. It was already very cold, and Pls. were now using farms and barns as H.Q. A great strain was put upon all M.T. personnel, especially carrier-drivers and D.R.s, whose motor-cycles sometimes disappeared in mud. Teller mines abounded, and on one occasion Sgt. Baldwin stubbed his toe against one. It was then found that the two Sec. positions of his Pl. were separated by a substantial mine-field, which was cleared with the help of the Royal Engineers. Four days of this slogging advance, with Pls. occasionally in action against small enemy rearguards, brought the leading Bdes. of the Div. to the banks of the Maas, overlooking Venlo, with its demolished bridges. Planning had begun for the assault on Venlo when the Div. was ordered to be relieved by 15 (Scottish) Div., and to proceed to the Nijmegen sector, under comd. of II Canadian Corps.

On the first day of December the Coy. moved into their new zone of operations, where they were to spend so many months. The outstanding features of the country between Nijmegen and Arnhem, and the rôle of 49 Div., have already been described in the chapter on Bn. H.Q. and H.Q. Coy. The "island", reached by the Nijmegen bridge across the Waal, or a subsidiary pontoon bridge, became as familiar to the Coy. as had the orchards and sunken roads of Normandy in the summer. On a clear day, the higher parts of Arnhem and the hills on the other side of the Rhine could be seen clearly; and so, from enemy-held Arnhem, could the British positions on much of the low-lying "island." The bridge itself must have been under steady enemy observation, and in the early days was subject to much shelling, as well as other forms of attack described elsewhere.

A Coy. took over positions from 2 Cheshires on December 1st; their previous meeting with this M.G. Bn. of 50 Div. had been in the Normandy beach-head. Two quiet days followed, but on December 3rd, the enemy blew breaches in the dykes, and water from the Lek, which joins the Rhine to the Waal to the east of Nijmegen, began to flood the low-lying portions of the "island". 3 and 4 Pls. were the first to become swamped, and 4 Pl. hastily moved into a row of houses near Elst. Conditions quickly became worse, and improvised rafts were built for use in emergency. Fortunately, it never came to that, although Pl. positions were entirely surrounded by water and could be approached only by carrier or jeep. Pl. transport was thinned out to the utmost to reduce the flow of traffic over the bridge and the few usable roads. Although the withdrawal of 51 Div. to take part in the Ardennes operations gave 49 Div. a very wide front, there was comparatively light activity so far as supporting arms were concerned. Each Pl. had a programme of harassing and defensive fire, and except for occasional flare-ups or shoots in support of Inf. patrols, they were able quickly to settle down into a routine, relieved by regular spells of rest in Nijmegen. Most of the firing was done at night, so that while on the "island" sleep was limited. It was during this period that Lieut. Telfer joined the Coy., taking over from Lieut. Green, who had been in comd. 5 Pl. since the Venlo operations. C.S.M. Wakeford, an old stalwart of the Coy., left to take a direct commission, fortunately remaining with the Bn. His place was taken by C.S.M. Bund, who had rendered most valuable services as a Pl. Sgt. in B Coy.

The only other incident of note in the early days on the "island" was that A Coy. took their turn in the seemingly ineluctable burning-down of Coy. H.Q., with the loss of a vehicle and other equipment. More important were the formation of Brock Force, to defend the Nijmegen bridges, in which the Coy. took its turn, and the reversion of all Coys. to Bn. comd. This was the result of a decision by the Div. Comd. that M.G. Coys. and the Mortar Coy. would in future normally be in support of Bdes. and placed under comd. only for special occasions. From this point, Bn. H.Q. resumed an active part in the tactical handling of M.G. Coys., and the remaining portion of A Coy.'s war history can therefore be blended with that of the rest of the Bn.

CHAPTER XXV

B COY.

June 5th, 1944–December 31st, 1944

WHEN the long-awaited order to move came on the evening of June 5th, 1944, B Coy. was well prepared for it. Transport was loaded, except for personal kits, all equipment had been checked and rechecked many times, and the last few days had been spent on cricket and, in the case of Coy. H.Q., catching up on arrears of sleep. The composition of the Coy. at that time was:

Coy. H.Q., Major S. Jacobson, Capt. J. Wilmot, C.S.M. M. Rosen.
6 Pl., Lieut. D. Kennedy.
7 Pl., Lieut. F. Mowbray.
8 Pl., Lieut. L. Jones.

The Coy. left the hutted holiday camp at Caister-on-Sea the same night, under the command of Capt. Wilmot, the Coy. Comd. having left two days earlier with a small advance party. It travelled throughout the night in convoy with Bn. H.Q. and H.Q. Coy., and at daylight on June 6th drew into London. As the convoy moved towards its marshalling area near London Docks, the news was heard of that morning's landings in Normandy, and spirits rose. At last, it was known where the Bn. was bound for, and it was clear that action was near. The camp proved to be at Purfleet Ranges, and here the Coy. spent June 6th and the morning of June 7th. In the afternoon of June 7th, its own transport having gone ahead, the Coy. was moved in T.C.V.s to the West India Docks—an area familiar to those who had served there with the Bn. in 1939 and 1940. Embarkation began the next morning, the Coy. spending the night in warehouses, and at 14.00 hrs. the S.S. *Fort Poplar* sailed down the Thames.

Three days later, the *Fort Poplar* anchored off the coast

of Normandy, where the immense array of shipping lying at anchor was an impressive demonstration of the weight of the invasion and Allied air superiority. A slight corrective was applied the next day when six enemy aircraft flew low over the anchorage and straddled the *Fort Poplar*, fortunately without damage. Disembarkation, which had been delayed by a shortage of landing-craft, was completed on June 12th and was notable only for the fact that, having been scrupulously waterproofed for $3\frac{1}{2}$ feet, all vehicles but one were landed in one or two feet of water. The unfortunate exception was the M.T. Truck. The landing-craft dropped anchor too soon, and Cpl. Turnock and his crew drove down the ramp into 12 feet. It was a tribute to their previous work that the engine kept running, although the vehicle was so badly damaged as to become the Bn.'s first transport casualty. The Coy. drove off the beach, through their first French village, and to its allotted concentration area, some fields near St. Gabriel. The only hitch at this point of the proceedings was the non-appearance of the Coy. Comd. at the R.V. However, he arrived at dusk (having, like so many other advance parties, been landed after the main party). The Coy. then turned in, for their first night on French soil, to the sounds of gun-fire and a pyrotechnic display of A.A. tracer over the beaches.

The next few days were spent on conferences at Bn. H.Q. and 147 Inf. Bde. H.Q. The first to go into action were 6 Pl. (Lieut. Kennedy), who were put under comd. A Coy. Relieving a pl. of the Cheshires, they took over a counter-penetration task at the edge of a wood near Cristot. This was a quiet sector, except for occasional sniping and mortaring; however, the Coy. Comd., Lieut. Kennedy, and Sgt. Bass claimed to be the first in the Bn. to come under small-arms fire, being fired at by snipers while on a reconnaissance of the area. After two days, 6 Pl. were relieved and returned to the Coy., who were now concentrated in 147 Inf. Bde. area. Preparations were then in hand for the first major operation by the Bde. This was to advance through Cristot, captured two days earlier by 146 Inf. Bde., and capture Point 102 and a dense wood, the Parc de Boislonde, adjoining it. Point 102 was a key feature in this area, overlooking the wood and the approaches to Fontenay-le-Pesnel. The attack on Point 102 was to be carried out by the 7 D.W.R., and the assault on the wood by 6 D.W.R. B Coy.'s rôle was to cover the attack on the Parc de Boislondes by a direct shoot on the flank against enemy positions in Tessel Wood, and to provide a Pl. for consolidation after the capture of the wood.

The Coy.'s shoot was successfully carried out from high ground near St. Pierre. It was believed that the 6 D.W.R. would meet only light opposition in the Parc de Boislonde, but, in fact, the wood was strongly held and savagely defended. They had to fight their way through yard by yard, and in this, their first major battle, they suffered heavy casualties, particularly among officers and N.C.O.s. However, by the evening of June 17th the wood was cleared, except for some fanatical snipers, and 8 Pl. (Lieut. Jones) had gone in to consolidate at the far edge of the wood. All four guns were sited in the infantry F.D.L.s, and were mounted on the banks of hedgerows. None of them had a range of more than 150 yards, and in some cases high cornfields and the slope of the ground reduced the range even more. It was not an orthodox M.G. position, but the presence of the widely-separated sections was welcomed by the infantry Coys., who had suffered such a rough handling in their bloody passage through the wood, where British and enemy dead lay twisted under trees, or in the clearings where they had been caught by small-arms fire. It was a grim setting for the further struggle that was to come.

During the night there was some enemy mortaring, and 8 Pl. had one N.C.O. wounded, Cpl. Clarke. Some enemy snipers who had remained behind, or slipped back during the night, became active at first light, firing at single men or small parties moving around the wood. There were also reports of enemy tanks moving up towards the wood from Fontenay. Later that morning enemy activity died down, and when the Coy. Comd. visited the Pl. he found them alert and in good spirits. In the afternoon, however, heavy mortaring began again, and during this the Pl. Comd, Lieut. Jones, and his driver-operator, Pte. Alexander, were killed. Hard on the heels of the mortar barrage came a determined counter-attack by S.S. troops, who overran the infantry positions and burst into the wood.

All gun-teams of 8 Pl. opened fire, and, although under fire from small-arms and grenades and harassed by snipers, they inflicted very heavy casualties. One gun at least fired a swinging traverse into the advancing enemy, and the Gun Corporal, who was wounded, later sent a striking account of the action, of which part may be quoted here. His gun was covering a cornfield less than 100 yards away :

> As soon as the mortaring stopped we could hear shouts and see movement in the field, and then they came on, some yelling, some weaving quietly like Indians through the corn. I fired through battle sights, swinging traverse, and saw them fall, and it was a queer feeling because this was the first time I had seen Germans, and it all seemed unreal. We pulled them up in front of us, but they got by on either side, and the infantry were running back. Grenades were bursting all round us, and bullets whistling through the branches, and the Sec. Comd. told us to take out the locks and fall back. We made our way back through the wood.

Other gun-teams fought similar actions. Sgt. Bund, the Pl. Sgt., tried to collect groups of retiring infantrymen and M.G. teams to hold a line of hedgerows, but by then the Germans had got deep into the wood, and our own gunners were beginning to shell the edge of the area. The Pl. was split up and small groups of men under N.C.O.s, carrying their wounded with them, made their own way back to the H.Q. of the Inf. Bn. and later to Coy. H.Q., wireless contact having been lost. It was not until later that evening, when another infantry Bn. had recaptured the wood, that a tally could be made of casualties. In addition to those already reported, Pte. Feltham had been killed and eight others wounded, four of them N.C.O.s. Much equipment had been lost or destroyed, although a party from Coy. H.Q. later recovered all carriers except one. It was a heavy loss for the Coy in its first major engagement, but the Pl. had acquitted itself well, a tribute to the training and spirit inculcated by Lieut. Jones. Some days later a burial party found nearly forty dead Germans in the field opposite one Sec. position. Cpl. Calland, who had handled his section with great presence of mind and courage, and inflicted casualties on the enemy in hand-to-hand fighting, was subsequently awarded the M.M.

After the recapture of the Parc de Boislonde, 8 Pl. were withdrawn into the Bn. H.Q. area to refit. Here Lieut. H. Brake took over comd. of the Pl. During this period, 6 and 7 Pls. had been in turn occupying forward positions under comd. of 7 D.W.R. and 11 R.S.F., with H.F. tasks and shoots in support of fighting patrols. They were spasmodically mortared and fired on by Spandaus from enemy positions some 400 yards away, but sustained no casualties. Dummy M.G. positions set up on the edge of a crater were successful in attracting considerable attention from the enemy. As the Bde. at this stage was thin on the ground and enemy patrols were active, Coy. H.Q. found a standing patrol nightly to cover Bde. H.Q. area. On June 23rd, the Pl. not in action and Coy H.Q. were able to visit the mobile baths at Bronay, but the satisfaction over this was offset by a carrier of 6 Pl. being blown up by a mine on its way back to Coy. H.Q. Three men were wounded. Since this road had been in heavy use by Bde. vehicles for some days, it was believed that the mine had been placed by an enemy patrol at night, or by a German agent.

On the night of June 24th the Coy. prepared to take part in the first full-scale Divisional attack, the Bde. objectives being Fontenay-le-Pesnel and Rauray. H-hour was set for 02.50 on June 25th, and during the night, gun positions were dug outside the F.D.L.s on the forward slope of Point 102 and the edge of the Parc de Boislonde. 8 Pl., who were to occupy Point 102, had a particularly difficult task, as they had to dig lying, and were under enemy M.G. fire, while enemy patrols could be heard moving near by. At H-hour, the attack of 11 R.S.F. towards Fontenay-le-Pesnel was supported by an indirect shoot by these Pls., and at first light the direct fire positions dug during the night were occupied. Tac. Coy. H.Q. was also established in this area, and the Coy. Comd. was able to direct the fire from both Pls. Pre-arranged targets were engaged throughout the day, and also observed enemy positions. 6 Pl. spotted a number of Germans moving across open country and engaged them, with satisfactory results. The area was under intermittent mortar and Spandau fire and three men were wounded.

Meanwhile, 7 Pl. had remained under comd. 7 D.W.R. for a consolidation in Fontenay-le-Pesnel, where there had been heavy house-to-house fighting by 11 R.S.F. The village was finally cleared and the 7 D.W.R. moved through towards Rauray, but at this stage the enemy put in a counter-attack as 7 Pl. were moving through the village. There was heavy mortaring and some confused fighting in the streets, in course of which a gun-carrier commanded by Cpl. Pharaoh found itself confronted by a Tiger tank. Both sides in this unequal combat opened fire, and Cpl. Pharaoh's carrier was hit. Fortunately, the German tank did not press home its attack. The Pl. Sgt., a Sec. Comd., and three others became casualties during this action, but by nightfall the position had been restored and 7 Pl. were put back into reserve at Coy. H.Q.

The Divisional objective having been reached with the capture of Rauray, a period of comparative quiet followed while supplies and provisions—delayed by the storms at the beginning of July—were being built up. A few local advances were made, and the Coy. took part in the repulse of German counter-attacks all along the Div. front on July 1st; but the main outline remained unchanged. The Coy. enjoyed three days' rest in Bn. H.Q. area from July 8th to July 11th, and returned into the line on July 12th in time to take over in the relief by 147 Inf. Bde. of 158 Bde., the Coy. taking over Pl. positions from B Coy., 1 Manchesters, in the Bretteville area. Here there was a good deal of enemy mortaring, and a number of casualties were sustained; but by now, the value of head cover to slit-trenches having been appreciated by all, short of a direct hit or being caught in the open, the risks had been greatly reduced. Perhaps the most lively incident of this period was the arrival at Coy. H.Q., in the course of an enemy air-raid, of the rear party from U.K., which included one private who had long and loudly proclaimed that the Second Front was all a gigantic bluff, and would never take place. On July 20th the Coy. moved back to the Bn. H.Q. area at Cancagny, to prepare for its move to a new sector, S.E. of Caen, where 49 Div. was to relieve 51 (Highland) Div. in I Corps.

The move to this area took place on the night of July 24th, 3 Pl. of A Coy. (Lieut Banyard) coming under comd. of B Coy., who were to take over Pl. positions on a wide front from B Coy. 1/7 Middlesex. 147 Inf. Bde. was in the area Frénouville–Cagny, which formed a salient, most of it under enemy observation from high ground to the south-east, and at places in close contact with the enemy positions. Roads leading to forward positions were thick in dust and under frequent mortar and 88-mm. fire, and supplies had to be brought up at night. The disposition of the Pls. was : 6 Pl. in support 11 R.S.F. forward of Cagny, on the embankment of the railway line running from Caen to Mezidon; 7 Pl. in support 7 D.W.R., with one Sec. in a cemetery covering the east of the village, and the other in a field south-east of the village; 8 Pl. in support 1 Leics. (who had replaced 6 D.W.R. in the Bde.) in the village of Frénouville, on the right flank of the Bde. front, with a good direct arc of fire from high ground; 3 Pl. (A Coy.) in a counter-penetration rôle north-west of Cagny. Tac. Coy. H.Q. was established with Bde. Tac. H.Q. in fields north of Cagny where the *Luftwaffe* made frequent low-flying raids and 88's, with typical German punctuality, shelled the area at dusk. All vehicles were deeply dug in, movement by day was severely restricted, and even a single vehicle often attracted unwelcome attention. A round of the Pl. positions by day took up to three hours, and was punctuated by frequent dives for the nearest ditch. As great a plague as the enemy gunners were the mosquitoes, which attacked ferociously in huge numbers at sundown, and made sleep difficult.

In these unpleasant conditions, the Pls. carried out a heavy programme of H.F. and D.F. tasks, with occasional direct shoots in support of local attacks. There was a steady trickle of casualties, only one, however, being fatal, when Pte. Morris of 6 Pl. was killed by a shell. Pl. positions were steadily improved with sandbags and thick head-cover, it being impressed on all that the forthcoming attack would hinge on this sector. At Main Coy. H.Q. in the Démouville area, Sgts. Cardew and Reeves put in good work on transport and W.T. sets respectively, which paid dividends when the advance began. On the Coy.'s last night in the Cagny area the Coy. Comd. had a fortunate escape when, returning from a visit to a Pl., he found his slit-trench had had a direct hit from a shell.

The long and trying wait in static positions at last ended on August 10th, when the Bde. advanced without major opposition. During the next few days the Coy. supported an attack by 11 R.S.F. on Vimont, astride the main road, in the course of which the B.B.C. was overhead, while the attack was in full swing, announcing the capture of the town, and on St. Crespin, where the 11 R.S.F. took fifty prisoners at the cost of one casualty.

The advance then became general, and during the rest of this month the Coy. was mostly on the move, with only occasional Pl. actions against enemy rearguards. The dust and mosquitoes had been left behind, the country was largely undestroyed, there was fruit in abundance, and spirits rose as the Coy. approached the River Seine and waited its turn to cross. This did not come until September 3rd, at Elbeuf, the bridge at Rouen having been put out of action. It then became known that the Div.'s next task was the capture of the strongly-held and important port of Le Havre, and by September 6th the Coy. was concentrated on the approaches to the town, and reconnaissance and conferences were in full swing.

The assault on Le Havre began on September 10th, the initial task of 147 Inf. Bde. being the capture of Harfleur Hill, a flat-topped feature dominating the town, and known to be studded with German pill-boxes and other defensive positions. 7 Pl. moved up under comd. 7 D.W.R. for consolidation, while 6 and 8 Pls., under Coy. comd., first carried out an indirect shoot on the approaches to Harfleur Hill, and then moved to direct positions from which flanking support would be given to both 56 Bde. in the initial assault, and 147 Bde. later. 6 Pl. put their guns on the first floor of a building overlooking a ravine, from which a wide arc of enemy positions could be engaged, and 8 Pl. positions were in a hedgerow a little to the right. Both

B COY.

Pls. were in action throughout September 10th and the morning of September 11th, when Harfleur Hill was occupied, without a single shell, bullet, or mortar bomb being fired at them. When, however, the leading tanks and Inf. troops reached the ground on the other side of the ravine, they were amazed and a little staggered to see German troops, only a few hundred yards from the gun lines, running out of bunkers and trenches to surrender. Had these troops been more aggressive, they could have inflicted heavy casualties on the M.G. Pls., and that they did not do so is an indication of the extent to which they had been shaken by previous bombing and shelling.

Following Le Havre came nearly a week of rest and overhaul in Bn. concentration area, the first time since landing that B Coy. had found itself in the same area as all the other Coys. of the Bn.; and on September 21st began the long move across France and Belgium to catch up with the rest of B.L.A., who were now on the frontiers of Belgium and Holland. Four days later the Bn., still concentrated, moved into the little town of Vorselaar, N.E. of Antwerp. Although there were no enemy within miles, the Kensingtons were the first Allied troops in the town, and were given a wonderful welcome as, vehicles piled high with flowers and fruit, they drove past the Commanding Officer and Civic dignitaries in the town square. Much elated, B Coy. settled themselves in a school, and, word having been received that a stay of some days might be expected, prepared to enjoy the military and other amenities of Vorselaar. On the one hand, all transport was unloaded, and the M.T. Sgt. began an overhaul of carrier tracks, the sergeant-major surveyed the playground and dreamed of a drill parade on solid ground, and the 2/i/C. saw a chance of catching up on paper work. On the other, dates began to be made, the officers arranged to dine with A Coy. officers in a local hotel, and football was discussed. In the midst of all this, a message came from the Coy. Comd., who had strolled round to Bn. H.Q. The Coy. was to stand by to move immediately. The same night, two Pls. were in action along the Antwerp-Turnhout Canal.

The position there was that 147 Inf. Bde. had captured

the town of Turnhout and the enemy retired across the canal. German patrols were active all along the canal, and the crossing was being hotly opposed. On the flanks of 11 R.S.F., who were occupying Turnhout, German patrols had recrossed the canal, and a counter-attack from that direction seemed possible. Lieut.-Col. Eykin, commanding 11 R.S.F., had been given B Coy. and the Reconnaissance Regt. to strengthen his flanks and help in the crossing of the canal. On the evening of September 25th, 6 and 7 Pls. occupied positions along the canal, while 8 Pl. was kept mobile under comd. 49 Reconnaissance Regt. The next day, 4 Pl. A Coy. (Lieut. Douet) came under comd. B Coy., and went into positions N.E. of Turnhout, and a Pl. of C Coy. relieved 8 Pl. with the Reconnaissance Regt. The following day, a Section of 8 Pl. occupied a novel position in the tower of a medieval fort in Turnhout, from which they had an excellent arc of fire on German positions on the other side of the canal. Unfortunately, while making a reconnaissance, Lieut. H. Brake, the Pl. Comd., was wounded in the arm by a sniper, and the Coy. lost the services of an imperturbable and gallant officer. He had joined the Pl. after its heavy losses in the Parc de Boislonde, and had commanded it with great dash. Sgt. Bund now took over comd., and the Pl. carried out some effective shoots from the fort, the Germans replying with Spandaus. At the suggestion of Belgian Resistance officers, a number of suspected collaborators under arrest in the fort were put to extra fatigues, on behalf of the Pl., as ammunition carriers and general hewers of wood and drawers of water.

In the meantime 7 Pl. (Lieut. Mowbray) carried out a most successful shoot in covering the withdrawal of an R.S.F. bridge-head across the canal. Spandau fire was silenced and the infantry reported eight enemy killed by 7 Pl. fire. The next few days passed without noteworthy incident, all Pls. being occupied with D.F. tasks and harassing shoots. On October 1st, however, the 11 R.S.F. crossed the canal and all pls. took up positions on the northern bank, except the C Coy. Pl., which now returned to its parent Coy. The next day, the entire Coy. moved to the area Dépôt de Mendicité, and came under comd. 49 Reconnaissance Regt., to hold a wide front with very few troops on the ground. The Depôt, where Coy. H.Q. was located, had been a criminal lunatic asylum, but by this time the majority of the inmates had fortunately been evacuated. It had been fiercely defended by the Germans, and in the assault on it Cpl. Harpur of the Hallams had won a posthumous V.C. On either side of the grounds of the Depôt was a wide stretch of country, not held by our troops and open to enemy penetration, and Coy. H.Q. and reserve Pls. manned standing patrols to cover it. Meanwhile, on October 3rd, 6 Pl. (Lieut. Kennedy), with C Squadron of 49 Reconnaissance Regt., was involved in a brisk action on the Dutch frontier near Polderheide. The Pl. moved forward with the leading Reconnaissance troop and came under heavy mortar and small-arms fire. The Reconaissance troop Comd. was killed, and after some confused fighting our troops withdrew to Bolk, where the Pl. formed a firm base and spent the night exchanging shots with enemy patrols. Coy. Tac. H.Q. also moved to Bolk, where 8 Pl., with B Squadron of the Reconnaissance Regt., formed a firm base at Papenvoortbrug. On the same day, 7 Pl. supported an attack by 2 S.W.B. of 56 Bde. on Rueleinde and Achtel, covering their right flank during the advance

The next few days the Coy. was static in this area, carrying out H.F. and D.F. tasks in turn for the Reconnaissance Regt., 2 S.W.B., and Bob Force, which was later formed to hold this exposed right flank of the Div. With some relief, B Coy. handed over this rôle to A Coy. on October 11th and rejoined 147 Inf. Bde. for the main advance into Holland, which began on October 20th with an attack on Wustwezel and Loenhout.

During this operation, 8 Pl. were under comd. 1 Leics. on the right flank of the Bde., and one Sec. was moving with the leading Inf. Coy., which had passed over a small river at Stonebridge, crossed the metalled road east of Wustwezel, and occupied some fields and orchards on the far side of the road on the morning of October 21st. A sudden and determined German counter-attack was launched on this Coy., supported by tanks and S.P. guns. The leading infantry were temporarily overrun, with heavy casualties and the loss of their six-pounder guns, and the M.G. Sec., under Sgt. Calland, came under fire at very close range from S.P. guns. Cpl. Elliot's carrier was hit, but the driver, Pte. Morris, continued driving although wounded, until a second hit set the carrier in flames and it had to be abandoned, the crew leaping into a ditch. A second gun-carrier, commanded by Cpl. Fletcher, was also hit and put out of action, and Pte. Bolton wounded. The carrier crew, under fire, took shelter in a cellar of a near-by house, where they were pinned down all night with German S.P. guns and infantry round them, but managed to rejoin the Pl. the next morning. The remainder of the section were scattered and for a time it was feared they had become casualties, but all later rejoined the Pl.

Meanwhile, the remaining Sec. and Pl. H.Q., under Sgt. Bund, took up positions with the rest of the Inf. Coy. near some houses just off the road, along which enemy tanks and S.P. guns were moving. These houses, and the bridge about 150 yards away, were under heavy fire, and the bridge was jammed with a blazing Sherman tank and other abandoned vehicles. Enemy infantry could be heard, forming up for an attack, in some woods to the right. Bn. H.Q. of the 1 Leics., in a farm some 200 yards to the rear, was also under fire, and any movement was difficult. At this point, Coy. Comd., with Major Dudley,[1] arrived on foot, having left their jeep near the bridge. He ordered the remaining Sec. to take up positions in a ditch on the right, to be able to fire across the Inf. front, but before this could be done another gun-carrier was hit and put on fire. The Pl. now had only one M.G. in action. Some enemy were seen moving across open ground, and the Coy. Comd. and Major Dudley opened fire on them with Brens, but the main counter-attack was broken up by heavy D.F. from the gunners, some shells falling very close to the Pl. This, however, gave time for the Pl. to sort itself out, and the rest of the afternoon and the following night it occupied rifle and Bren positions with the Infantry Pls. During the night, Sgt.

[1] Major Dudley was understudying Major Jacobson before taking over comd. of the Coy., Major Jacobson having been appointed 2/i/C of the Bn. The change-over took place a few days later.

B COY.

Bund and a small party recovered two guns from the damaged carriers, and by daylight 8 Pl. was able to resume its normal rôle. The courage and coolness of Sgt. Bund in this confused fighting cannot be praised too highly, and it was largely due to him that casualties were not more serious.

On October 23rd, the Coy. handed over its positions in this area to units from the 104 (Timberwolf) U.S. Division, meeting its American Allies for the first time in this campaign. The Division was now directed towards the Dutch town of Roosendaal in the operations, over bleak, wet, and mostly coverless country, designed to clear the northern approaches of the Scheldt estuary up to the Maas. This was a slow, slogging advance in atrocious weather, held up by a formidable anti-tank ditch on the approaches to the town. This was assaulted by 1 Leics., 6 and 7 Pls. shooting them across the open approaches from excellent direct positions, while one Sec. of 8 Pl., now commanded by Lieut. Edgcumbe, followed the leading Inf. Coy. with a very long carry, culminating in the 15-foot ditch and through 4 feet of water. They came under heavy fire on the former side, and Pte. Archer was buried for nearly ten minutes by a near miss on his slit-trench, but dug out unhurt. Later, however, severe shelling killed Pte. J. Jones, a driver-operator, and slightly wounded Sgt. Calland and Pte. C. Wilson. This was the enemy's last effort before Roosendaal, and early next morning 7 Pl. were in the outskirts of the town, which was cleared the same day. The Coy. then enjoyed a short rest in Roosendaal before taking part in the final stage of the operations, which took the Div. up to the Maas.

Early in November the Div. was ordered to the east sector of the Front, B Coy., with 12 Pl., D Coy., moving on November 7th with 147 Inf. Bde. The Coy. was put under comd. 53 Div. in XII Corps for operation "Mallard". This attack was launched on November 14th and objectives were quickly reached, all Pls. firing an extensive programme without casualties. The Coy. then reverted to Bn. command and took part in the slow advance through mud and rain to the line of the Maas, preparatory to the attack on Venlo by 49 Div.; but, when it was able to see this much-shelled town on the other side of the river, orders came for the Div. to be relieved by 15 Div. and move to the Nijmegen–Arnhem sector.

On November 28th, the Coy., with 147 Inf. Bde., moved to this new area, and the following day took over positions on the "island" between Waal and Rhine from old Normandy friends, the 2 Cheshires. Almost immediately, the breaching of dykes by the enemy flooded some Pl. positions, and transport had to be thinned out, while all ranks became adept at the minor arts of navigation. The first major action on the "island" came on the morning of December 4th, when, in a last desperate attempt to reach the vital Nijmegen bridge, the enemy made a heavy attack on 7 D.W.R. in the Bemmel area. 6 and 7 Pls. were in action of D.F. tasks, and had the satisfaction of seeing the attack smashed, with heavy losses and a large haul of German prisoners.

That over, the Coy. settled down to a period of static operations which lasted longer than anyone expected, broken only by occasional moves as the floods advanced or receded. It was possible to relieve Pls. in turn at regular intervals, and give them periods of relaxation in Nijmegen. On the "island", although the enemy was comparatively inactive, conditions were not so pleasant; rain, snow, and biting winds sweeping over the flat Dutch landscape were normal conditions for many weeks at a time, and all Pls., when in the line, had heavy programmes of D.F. and H.F. tasks, often at night. During the floods, 8 Pl. were cut off from land and were supplied by C.S.M. Rosen in a daily sail by Weasel.[1] Eventually, relieved by pontoon ferry, they went phlegmatically back a few days later by Buffalo.[1] During this stage of the Coy.'s stay on the "island", it lost with great regret the services of Sgt. Bund, who was promoted C.S.M. and posted to A Coy. Sgt. Bund's notable part in the Coy.'s fighting in Normandy and elsewhere have been briefly described; for long periods, after his first Pl. Commander had been killed and second wounded, he commanded 8 Pl. with great success. His services were recognised by the award of a Croix de Guerre and a Mention in Dispatches, and the whole Coy. was sorry to see him go.

[1] Amphibious Vehicles.

B COY.

At the end of December B Coy., with other Coys., came under tactical command of the Battalion, and its further operations will be described in another part of this book. Mention may perhaps be made here of Christmas 1944, spent in part on the icy "island", in part in billets among the warm hospitality of the people of Nijmegen. Each Pl. came out of the line in turn to enjoy the festivities, heightened by the feeling that this would be the last Christmas of the war. For Coy. H.Q., preparing and participating each time, it was a period of severe but enjoyable strain in the most literal sense of the word.

CHAPTER XXVI

C COY.

June–December 31st, 1944

C Coy. reached the Normandy beaches on June 12th and 13th, with 70 Inf. Bde. Group. Its journey there had been much on the lines of the other Coys., and calls for little comment, except, perhaps, to record the surprise felt when vehicles prepared over many wearied weeks for a landing in $3\frac{1}{2}$ feet of water splashed to the beaches through 6 inches. The Coy. concentrated near the village of St. Gabriel without incident. Its composition at that time was:

Coy. H.Q., Major S. R. Pinks, Capt. J. T. Stanyer, C.S.M. A. Rampton.
9 Pl., Lieut. J. T. Griffiths.
10 Pl., Lieut. V. de P. C. Johnson.
11 Pl., Lieut. J. G. Vaughan.

First to be deployed was 10 Pl. (Lieut. Johnson), but the Coy.'s first serious action took place on June 17th, when the 10 D.L.I. advanced to attack the village of St. Pierre. 11 Pl. had a consolidation task, and moved off from the startline under shelling and mortaring. Here it sustained its first casualty, when Cpl. Wilcox was wounded; the following day another N.C.O., L/Sgt. Clark, was also wounded. 11 Pl. were so sited, S. of St. Pierre, as to be able to redeploy swiftly in another sector of the line for harassing shoots and other tasks in support of the very aggressive patrolling being carried out by 10 D.L.I. It was after one of these shoots than an incident occurred, slight in itself but perhaps worth recording as an example of the high spirits of the Coy. Pte. Panter of 11 Pl. celebrated his twenty-first birthday by taking part in a harassing shoot. On returning to the Pl. area, he found that the Pl. cook had prepared a special tea in honour of the event, with a neatly-laid table in a barn. Proceedings were interrupted, but not unduly spoiled, by a nasty spell of enemy mortaring. Meanwhile, Coy. H.Q. and 9 and 10 Pls. were at St. Leger, where the Coy. area suffered some slight attentions from the *Luftwaffe*.

The capture of St. Pierre gave 70 Inf. Bde. Gp. a salient in the line held by 49 Div. 147 Inf. Bde. and 146 Inf. Bde. Gps. straightened the line by clearing, after some very hard fighting, Fontenay-le-Pesnel and Tessel Wood respectively. 70 Bde. were then switched over to the left of the Div. front to attack Brettevillette and Rauray. The attack went in on June 28th, and led to a battle in which 9 Pl. took a notable part and suffered serious losses. The action began by an attack on Brettevillette by 1 Tyneside Scottish, while 9 Pl. fired on the village. The infantry passed through the village, and 9 Pl. moved forward in carriers to consolidate. At this point the enemy counter-attacked strongly with tanks, and succeeded in forcing back the infantry at some points. Lieut. Griffiths, commanding 9 Pl., at once deployed one Sec. on carriers to fire on the outskirts of the village and a wood beyond, to enable the infantry to fall back around him.

The situation became very confused and Lieut. Griffiths went forward into the village to reconnoitre. He was still within sight of the Sec. when enemy infantry, supported by a Tiger tank, burst through on his right. The Section gallantly fired on the enemy troops, inflicting casualties, but came under fire from the tank, which quickly ended this unequal battle by destroying both gun-carriers. One complete crew, Cpl. F. S. Bushnell, L/Cpl. J. P. Wallace, and Pte. R. F. W. Perry, were killed, and the Sec. Comd., Sgt. Bone, was wounded. The surviving men of the Sec., after trying unsuccessfully to get away their dead, had to fall back. Fortunately, the German tank also withdrew, and Lieut. Griffiths was able to rally the rest of the Sec. and deploy the other Sec., which became a rallying-point for the infantry. The Coy. Comd., Major Pinks, had in the meantime arrived on the scene and, in view of the grave danger of further counter-attacks, he ordered a Sec. of 11 Pl. forward to reinforce 9 Pl., and had Coy. H.Q. stand to. No serious attacks developed, however, at this stage. 9 Pl. had conducted itself gallantly in its first serious clash, although at heavy cost. The bravery and presence of mind of Lieut. J. Griffiths was recognised by the award of the Military Cross.

Heavy fighting continued during the next few days, when the Bde. attack on Rauray developed. The assault was made by 11 D.L.I., with 10 Pl. in support for consolidation. Our infantry lost heavily in the operation, which, however, ended in the capture of Rauray. 10 Pl. were deployed in the F.D.L.s to cover the Bn. front with cross-fire; but so close was the ground that all firing had to be done on fixed lines. The Pl. was in action much of the night, the enemy still being in an aggressive mood. Moreover, Rauray village had not been cleared of snipers, and parties travelling to and from the Pl. had some uneasy moments. Members of the Pl. helped to flush snipers from the houses; and these little isolated actions produced some odd attendant risks, as when an enthusiastic rifleman, trying to lob a 36 grenade through the upper window of a house, managed to land it into one of the Pl.'s carriers. Fortunately, the carrier was unoccupied, but the vehicle was badly damaged.

The next day "Ringed Contour 110", a dominating feature about 1000 yards beyond Rauray, was attacked and captured. 10 Pl. moved forward to consolidate, and were able to occupy excellent positions overlooking Brettevillette to Quadeville. The whole Bde. front was heavily shelled that day, mobile 88-mm. guns being especially troublesome. During this action, Ptes. F. Edwards and W. Gilbert were killed and Sgt. Greenland wounded. The other two Pls. were engaged in map shoots on Brettevillette and Quadeville, with first-class results proved later by enemy dead found lying in these areas.

The night of June 30th and early morning of July 1st brought bitter fighting. During the night 10 Pl., forward of Rauray, were relieved by 9 Pl. and brought back to Coy. H.Q., which was heavily shelled throughout the night. Deep slit-trenches and head cover saved the Coy. many casualties, but C.Q.M.S. Breckill was badly wounded in the legs. At first light on July 1st it became clear that this shelling of the Bde. area was the preliminary to a heavy German counter-attack, part of the last desperate attempt by the enemy in Normandy to drive the British back into the sea. On 70 Bde. front, the attack came on that scarred key feature, "Ringed Contour 110". German infantry, well supported by tanks, advanced in strength. 9 Pl. engaged the infantry over battle sights, killing and wounding many, and shooting down German crews as they leaped from their damaged tanks; a stubborn battle was temporarily broken off when new waves of Germans eventually fought their way to the top of the hill. During this fighting, one Sec. of 9 Pl. were put out of action, but its guns were quickly replaced and the whole Pl. was soon in the fighting once more, Pl. H.Q. joining in with Bren and rifles. 70 Bde. now counter-attacked, and by late afternoon Contour 110 had been recaptured and the only gain made by the enemy on this front had been wiped out after savage fighting. 9 Pl. had one fatal casualty, Pte. H. McNulty, but by nightfall many of the Pl. were near exhaustion. It was found possible to relieve them by 11 Pl. during the night, and bring them back to Coy. H.Q. area.

Thus ended the second battle of Rauray. The Coy. was later congratulated by the G.O.C. for its part in the fighting, and, like the rest of the formation, took intense pleasure in hearing that Lord Haw-Haw had referred to 49 Div. as the "Polar Bear Butchers." It was a striking sign of the Nazis' rage and disappointment over the outcome of the battle.

Two days later the whole Bde. came out of the line for a few days, and the Coy. enjoyed a badly-needed rest in the Bn. H.Q. area near Cancagny. The next spell in the line was in the area of Tilly-sur-Seules, which was a haven of rest compared to Rauray, but nevertheless provided its diversions. One of these came on July 11th, when the Coy. carried out a marathon map shoot in support of an attack by 50 Div. on the Hottot area. In this single day the Coy. fired 465,000 rounds. What its effect was on the enemy was never discovered, but it had widespread repercussions on our side. The Bde. infantry were exasperated by the chatter of the guns, and years were added to the life of the Q.M., Capt. Blakeley, in supplying astronomical replacements of barrels, firing-pins, etc. In fact, a shortage of

Mark VIII.Z was caused, and it later became known that the War Office was seriously perturbed.

This was followed by a few days of manœuvre along the Div. front, including a successful shoot, with A Coy., in support of a raid on Barbée Farm. On July 21st the Coy. was relieved by the Royal Northumberland Fusiliers and moved into a harbouring area before switching over to a new sector, S.E. of Caen. A few days of rest and reconnaissance were followed on July 24th by the move to this area. During the move, which took place at night, Lieut. Griffiths's carrier ran over a Teller mine and was overturned and completely wrecked, fortunately without fatal casualties, but wounding two of the crew. The Coy. also lost its 2/i/C., Capt. Stanyer, who was badly hurt in a motor-cycle accident and evacuated to U.K. His post was filled by Capt. Vaughan, while 11 Pl. was taken over by Lieut. Halstead. The next day the Coy. went into positions on the left of the Div. flank, where, with minor changes, it was to remain for about three weeks. For C Coy. it was a comparatively quiet period marred by mosquitoes, dust, spasmodic mortaring and shelling, and attacks from the air. The main task of the Pls. was H.F. and D.F., and, although some vehicles and equipment were destroyed, it suffered only one casualty, Pte. King, who was wounded in the leg, but later rejoined the Coy.

By mid-August the great break-through had succeeded, and the enemy was in full retreat. On August 17th, to everyone's joy, the Coy. was mobile again, and supported 70 Bde. in establishing a bridge-head over the River Dives. Before the chase to the Seine developed, however, the Coy. suffered a severe blow. 70 Inf. Bde., with which it had trained so long and hard in Britain and shared so many bitter encounters in Normandy, left the Division at Mezidon. This was a sad disappointment, not only because the Coy. had enjoyed such pleasant and efficient relations with the Bde. Staff, but also because many friendships had been formed with the battalions in the Bde., 10 and 11 D.L.I. and 1 Tyneside Scots. Their place in the Div. was taken by 56 Inf. Bde., comprising 2 S.W.B., 2 Gloucesters, and 2 Essex. With them C Coy. soon formed equally satisfactory links, and this association was to continue happily until the end of the campaign.

Mosquitoes and static positions were now joyfully left behind, as the Coy., with 56 Inf. Bde., continued the pursuit. Undamaged farmhouses and rubble-free villages came pleasantly to the eye, and enemy opposition was scattered. The Pls. moved in turn with Bn. Advance Guards, and occasionally went into action against German rearguards; during these halcyon days, 11 Pl. carried out a classical shoot at Pont Audemer, where the field of fire was in the best traditions of the training landscape targets. A great cheer went up when a Sec. Comd. gave the order to engage "inverted T-shape junction of hedgerows". The Coy. reached the Seine through the Forêt de Bretonne, where many prisoners were rounded up and a good deal of enemy equipment found. There was a two-day wait before the Seine could be crossed, which gave the M.T. Sgt., fitters, and drivers a chance to overhaul transport. In this interval, the rest of the Coy. took to bareback riding, the country being littered with loose German horses, and some notable and unorthodox equestrian feats took place.

The Seine crossed, it was learned that the Div.'s next serious task was to capture Le Havre, which was held in force and had a heavily fortified perimeter. 56 Inf. Bde. deployed north of the approaches to Le Havre, and during the preliminary phases of the attack C Coy. enjoyed some excellent shooting from carriers in "hull down" positions from a long ridge in front of the infantry. A section at a time crept up the ridge in carriers until the Gun Corporals could see the mass of barbed wire, earthworks, and concrete emplacements of the enemy. A couple of belts were fired, and the section withdrew behind the ridge, only to bob up again in another area. This alarmed and infuriated the enemy, who invariably replied with mortar and shell-fire, but always too late. For the main attack, the Coy. was deployed on the flank of the Bde. and was able to give excellent support to the Inf. Bns. Within thirty-six hours the port was in British hands, with a huge haul of prisoners. During the whole of the Le Havre battle, C Coy. suffered one fatal casualty, Sgt. M. R. Hilburn, and one N.C.O.

wounded, L/Cpl. Sharp. The operation was followed by a few days' rest and overhaul in the Bn. area, before the long drive into Belgium began on September 21st. By this time 21 Army Group had liberated Brussels and Antwerp, and were poised on the Antwerp–Turnhout Canal.

The Coy. transport stood up well to the four-day convoy, and on September 25th, with the rest of the Bn., drove amidst cheers, flowers, and a shower of fruit into newly-liberated Vorselaar. Here the Coy. hoped to settle down to enjoy the general celebrations, but these were cut short the next day when it was called forward to the Antwerp–Turnhout Canal, and soon found itself deployed in the Oostmalle area. Here, all Pls. carried out D.F. and H.F. tasks, and Lieut. Halstead, 11 Pl., in one action controlled fire by wireless from an O.P. At the end of the month a crossing of the canal was forced by the Div., and its front, already wide, was stretched even further. To hold the right flank of the front, while the rest of the Div. pushed into Holland, a group known as Bob Force was formed. It consisted of the A./A. Regiment, acting as infantry, A and C Coys., 2 Kensingtons, and some A/Tank and Artillery support. While 11 Pl. went off with 56 Inf. Bde. to take part in the capture of Roosendaal, Coy. H.Q. and the remaining Pls. joined Bob Force for what turned out to be a novel and somewhat hazardous operation.

The task set Bob Force was to hold the right flank and maintain contact with the enemy, and for two weeks the sector was static in the Rijkevorsel area, with only spirited patrolling and harassing fire. Then the enemy, left in a salient by the advance of the main Div. attack on our left, withdrew, and Bob Force advanced to contact, now supported by Canadian armour. Control of this very mixed force was not easy, there were a number of mine-fields, and German rearguards and shelling were encountered. On October 26th the Coy. suffered a severe loss when Sgt. A. D. Monks, a Sec. Comd., was killed during shelling of 9 Pl. area. Three days later the Coy. experienced yet another change, coming under command 1 Polish Armoured Div. In one month, therefore, it had operated with British, Canadian, and Polish troops. However, its stay under Polish command was brief, since shortly afterwards 104 U.S. (Timberwolf) Div. came in on 49 Div. right, pinching out Bob Force, which was disbanded, leaving C Coy. free to rejoin 56 Inf. Bde. at Roosendaal, and join in the advance to the Maas north of the Scheldt estuary. It was now becoming cold, and mud, rain, and biting winds added to the troubles of advancing over flat country.

The Coy. was quickly deployed in the village of Oude Castel, north of Roosendaal. The subsequent advance to Willemstadt was supported by all Pls., who were fortunate enough to escape serious casualties despite frequent enemy shelling and mortaring of their gun-lines. Good evidence of the value of indirect fire programmes was found in a factory at Stampersgat, where lay the bodies of many Germans caught by M.G. fire. During this advance the entire Coy. was grieved at the death in action of 56 Inf. Bde. Comd., Brigadier Eakins. On November 6th Willemstadt fell to the Div., and all Coys. concentrated at Roosendaal before moving off to their new area of operations, which was to be on the far flank of the British front, in the Venlo Sector.

A bitter drive in icy rain brought the Bn. to its new concentration area in Hamont, where C Coy. learned that it was to come under command 51 Div. for the attack towards Blerwick on the River Maas. For the initial phase the Coy. operated with its old friends 1/7 Mdx., in supporting 51 Div. advance over the Zig Canal. This successful attack completed, the Coy. returned to 56 Inf. Bde., and 49 Div. began the hard, slogging advance through mud and minefields to the Maas. Conditions during this phase put a great strain on transport, and Pls. operated mostly under command of infantry battalions. Mention may perhaps be made here of some amazing luck enjoyed by the Coy. at this stage. Repeatedly, carriers ran over mines that turned out to be anti-personnel sown among heavier mines, but did little damage. On one occasion an armoured car was blown up on a mine, immediately outside Coy. H.Q., which had been there for three days without, by some miracle, it being encountered. Again, Lieut. Jones and his "recce." party were kindly helped by an enemy 88, which opened up on them, causing their carriers to beat a hasty retreat; later, they found out that, had they gone on a few yards, they would have run on to an extensive mine-field. As it was they escaped with the loss of some minor kit.

While the attack on Blerwick was being planned, Venlo lay on the far side of the Maas, an inviting target. Attention was paid to it by a Sec. shoot from carriers touring the Bde. front. The enemy retaliated with airbursts, but did no damage. During this stage, 10 Pl. were employed in filling rather solitarily a gap between the two flanking Bns. of 56 and 146 Inf. Bdes. Meanwhile, the rain came down steadily, the mud grew deeper, and the Maas looked a formidable obstacle. However, before the attack could be launched, 49 Div. was replaced by 15 Div. and ordered to the Nijmegen–Arnhem area; on November 29th the Coy. moved to Oosterhout, west of Nijmegen, and on the following day it crossed the Waal bridge at Nijmegen and took over positions, from B Coy. 2 Cheshires, on the notorious "island" between the Waal and the Rhine.

This was, with minor changes, to be the Coy.'s scene of operations throughout the winter of 1944–45. The "island" has been fully described elsewhere, and it will suffice to say here that floods, ice, snow, mud, and slush did not help to endear it to the Coy. As against these, there were periods of rest in billets in Nijmegen, and the warm-hearted hospitality of its inhabitants. In retrospect, this period on the "island" may tend to seem inactive; in fact, all Pls. were kept busy with H.F. and D.F. tasks, often at night, and with coping with the rigours of climate and the hostility of German gunners. There were occasional shoots in support of infantry patrols, which were enjoyed as a break in the normal routine; and there were the Flying Bombs lumbering over the "island", and later, the distant roar and flash from the rocket-launching sites.

A few days after the Coy. moved to the "island" the Germans breached the dykes and all three Pls. found the flood-water rising round their positions. During the next few days the Pls. had to move repeatedly, 9 Pl. eventually settling down on a railway embankment, with guns mounted on carriers. Transport on the "island" was pruned to the minimum required for operational purposes, and a heavy strain was placed on Coy. H.Q. in servicing and supplying widely separated Pls. over water-bound roads, often under enemy shelling. On December 11th, a Sec. of 11 Pl. supported a daylight raid by our infantry on enemy platoon positions in the Elst area. The attack developed on textbook lines, the M.G. Section finding a direct fire position at right angles to the infantry line of advance, with a first-class field of fire over the approach and enemy positions. The raid was an outstanding success, thirty-six enemy being killed, wounded, or captured without a single casualty among infantry or machine-gunners. During the raid, 10 Pl. put down H.F. at the rear of the enemy positions to prevent reinforcements coming up. The platoons were delighted when later in the day the Army Commander came forward personally and congratulated the raiding party and supporting arms on the success of a cleverly-planned and boldly-executed operation, which led to the identification of enemy formations in the sector. A few days later, 9 and 10 Pls. supported another raid, by 2 Gloucesters, with a direct shoot, but on this occasion the birds had flown and the enemy positions were found to be unoccupied.

On December 17th, the Coy. was relieved by A Coy. and pulled back to the Nijmegen area, where a novel task awaited it. Lieut.-Col. D. V. G. Brock (C.O. 2 Kensingtons) had been put in comd. of a force to defend the vital Nijmegen main bridge and the subsidiary pontoon bridge, and also the town itself. It must be remembered that, at this stage, the Germans were on the banks of the Waal upstream of the bridges, and could easily float down explosives or send small parties of saboteurs through our lines, or down the river. A mixed force of infantry and one M.G. Coy. in turn was put under comd. Brock Force,[1] and C Coy. was the first of the M.G. Coys. to move into positions covering the bridges, with orders to fire on any suspicious objects floating downstream. This order was obeyed with alacrity, the Coy.'s marksmen firing joyously on pieces of wood, wreckage, hen-coops, and anything else that might harbour an explosive. Nijmegen Bridge, in full view from enemy posi-

[1] A fuller account of the composition and activities of Brock Force will be found in the chapter on Bn. H.Q.

tions near Arnhem on clear days, was frequently shelled during this stage, fortunately without serious damage to the bridge or casualties to troops. Enemy aircraft were also active.

As Christmas approached there was increasing tenseness in the area, with many rumours of an impending German paratroop attack. This was intensified when the German offensive was launched in the Ardennes and when, on Christmas Eve, Lord Haw-Haw and his female counterpart, "Mary of Arnhem", broadcast that 49 Div. (for whom the late William Joyce appeared to have a particular regard) would be annihilated during the festive season. The Div. front, thinly held, was extended still further when 51 Div. on the left were pulled out to go down to the Ardennes, and there was the uncomfortable feeling that, if the Ardennes break-through continued, the Allied forces in Holland would be cut off from their bases. Despite these threats the Coy. had an enjoyable Christmas, the Pls. coming out of action in turn to eat their Christmas dinners.

During December, the Coy. had come under comd. Brock Force and, for much of the rest of the war, operated under Bn. command. The rest of its war experiences will therefore be told in the second portion of this history. The present chapter has dealt with the period from the Normandy beach-head to Holland, when the Coy. fought mostly under Bde. comd. Limited space, and the desire to avoid repeating incidents and experiences common to all Coys., have inevitably led to the omission of much material; and many who rendered sterling services to the Coy. have not been mentioned by name. This they will understand, for an outstanding characteristic of the Coy. throughout its life was its great team spirit.

CHAPTER XXVII

D COY.

June–December 31st, 1944

D COMPANY was the only Mortar Coy. in the Battalion, and its war experiences differed in many important respects from those of the Machine-gun Coys. It was fighting with a new weapon, little tested in combat conditions; the Coy.'s organisation and tactics had therefore to be adapted, during the campaign, to meet fresh circumstances and conditions sometimes wildly unlike those envisaged in the training schools and manuals. This called for a good deal of improvisation and flexibility, and in a Battalion noted for its quick-wittedness, D Coy. was perhaps outstanding in this respect. A few words about the organisation and training of the Coy. should therefore precede the story of its operations.

The 4·2-in. mortar was developed in 1942 for the purpose of adding to the fire-power of the infantry brigade a heavier mortar than the 3-in. handled by the Mortar Platoon in the infantry battalions. The original intention was to put the 4·2-in. mortars directly under control of the Bde. Comd., who would use them over the Bde. front as a whole. In 1942 and 1943, when the Battalion was training with 49 Div. in Wales and Scotland, it was organised in three Bde. Support Groups, each consisting of one Mortar Coy., one M.G. Coy., and one Light A./A. Coy. But early in 1944 this establishment was scrapped, and the Bn. reverted to three M.G. Coys. and one Mortar Coy of four Pls. The Mortar Coy. therefore became a Divisional, rather than a Bde., fire unit, and it was clear that Pls. would frequently operate, singly or in pairs, with the Bdes. in turn. This made essential a high degree of mobility and excellent communications, and although there were few complaints on the latter score, the Lloyd carriers in which the Mortar crews moved, with their trailers, were to prove most unreliable.

"THE KENSINGTONS"

D Coy. was formed in East Anglia early in 1944, by picking the best men from the three Mortar Coys. in the former Groups. It started, therefore, with the heavy initial disadvantage of being made up, at this stage, of small groups of men, many of them sorry to leave their parent Coys., and hardly knowing men of different companies (the Bn. had been widely dispersed in Scotland in 1943). Some of the men, with many years' machine-gun training, had in the earlier stages been a little suspicious and contemptuous of the "drain-pipes", their heavy base-plates and unrifled barrels, and their inability to pinpoint a small target area. The same suspicion, it must be said, was encountered in some infantry units; in their case, a single action in Normandy, proving the weight of fire and devastating physical and moral effect of the 4·2-in. mortar on the enemy, sufficed to clear it away. As for D Coy., it fell into shape very quickly. The enthusiasm of officers and N.C.O.s was infectious, and before many weeks had passed a fine, aggressive Coy. spirit was evident. The Coy. was fortunate to have a big supply of training ammunition, and a great many field-firing exercises were carried out within the Div. For the first time, all four Pls. fired on one target, controlled by one O.P., and proved that the Div. had a new and powerful weapon at its command.

Towards the end of May it became clear that action was coming very near. Without warning, the Coy. was moved to an unknown destination, but on this occasion did not, as some expected, "get its feet wet". The destination turned out to be the Lloyd Carrier Waterproofing Camp just outside Colchester. Here there was a thorough check on all vehicles, and the main waterproofing was carried out. A few days later, on the evening of June 5th, the Coy. was ordered to its marshalling area near London, and at the grim hour of 3 a.m. on D-Day, June 6th, set out for the long drive. On this occasion all the Lloyds stood up well, and there were no vehicle casualties. Two days later, after a rousing drive through the East End to the docks, the Coy. embarked for Normandy. Its composition at that time was:

Coy. H.Q., Maj. R. Bare, Capt. G. F. Fulcher, Lieut. B. Jones, C.S.M. A. Haskell.

D COY.

12 Pl., Capt. J. Claydon, Lt. J. Asker.
13 Pl., Capt. W. King, Lt. R. Jennings.
14 Pl., Capt. W. Nicol, Lt. W. Stoltenhoff.
15 Pl., Capt. R. Archer, Lt. R. Thornhill.

Arrival and landing on the Normandy beaches were uneventful, except for one carrier of 14 Pl., which drove off the landing craft into a 6-foot-deep shell-hole, and was "drowned"; it was, however, quickly recovered, with no damage to the crew except a ducking. The Coy. moved into its concentration area near Bn. H.Q. outside the village of St. Gabriel, and waited for the first call into action. This was not to be long delayed. On June 16th the whole Coy. supported the attack on Cristot by 1/4 K.O.Y.L.I. of 146 Bde. and had the additional excitement of a B.B.C. van recording this first shoot. The recording was broadcast by the B.B.C. the next day. Two days later, in preparation for the first major Div. attack, D Coy. was split into two, with 12 and 13 Pls., under the Coy. Comd., Maj. Bare, attaching themselves to 146 Bde. and 14 and 15 Pls. under Capt. Fulcher, going to 147 Bde. The next few days were spent in reconnaissance, digging of Pl. positions, and conferences; during this period the Coy. sustained its first battle casualty, Pte. Conway, of 15 Pl., being wounded.

The Div. attacked on June 25th with two Bdes., the first objectives being Tessel Wood and Fontenay-le-Pesnel. All four Pls. were in action throughout the day, which saw the Inf. Bdes. reach their objectives. The next day the Coy. was called upon to support 8 Armoured Bde. in its advance, and excellent liaison was achieved in this first operation with tank units. The Div. consolidated the ground gained over the next few days, and the Coy. was delighted to hear that enemy prisoners were already testifying to the killing powers of the 4·2-in. mortar. One batch reported that of eighty Germans caught in a concentration of mortar bombs, only twenty remained unhurt. They had never before, according to these prisoners, experienced such a mortar concentration as this.

The next operation was the attack, against heavy opposition, by 70 Bde. on Brettevillette. This was supported by 12 and 13 Pls., who fired on targets in Le Manoire, Tessel

Bridge, Le Marie, and Queudeville. The mortar lines were repeatedly shelled, but without serious damage. During this action, a Typhoon fighter crash-landed near the mortar lines, the pilot escaping unhurt. Fierce enemy counter-attacks on 1 Tyneside Scots, in Brettevillette, developed the next day, and 12 Pl. were heavily engaged. It was clear that the enemy were building up to a major effort in this sector. It came on July 1st, with a heavy attack by German infantry and armour in the Brettevillette area. Enemy mortar positions were engaged almost continuously by D Coy., 12 and 14 Pls. being in action from 05.30 hrs. to 23.00 hrs. The Coy. was again lucky in escaping casualties during this day of bitter fighting, only one man, Pte. Heasman, being wounded. The day ended with the complete defeat of the enemy attack. By the next day it was possible to move 12 Pl. forward, and the enemy mortars, so active twenty-four hours earlier, were notably subdued. On July 3rd, after a day of heavy firing on targets in the Bordel and Brettevillette areas, all four Pls. were called upon to fire for thirty minutes in support of a 146 Bde. raid in the Juvigny area. During this the enemy retaliated with heavy concentrations of air bursts over the mortar lines. L/Sgt. Bulleid was fatally wounded, and Sgt. Hale, L/Sgt. Burwood, Cpl. Hornett, and Pte. Grisbrook were wounded. This was the Coy.'s first fatal casualty during the campaign. It was clear that the enemy here were already very sensitive to 4·2-in. mortar-fire, and was quick to retaliate on Pl. areas. When, on July 10th, 12 and 13 Pls. supported a raid by the Hallams on Vendes, counter-mortar fire fell in the Pl. areas within seconds.

Meanwhile heavy storms had delayed the landing of supplies in the beach-head, and 4·2-in. mortar ammunition became scarce. It was ordered that the mortars would fire only on known enemy mortar positions. The allotment laid down was twenty rounds per mortar per day. This restricted the Coy.'s activities, and ammunition had to be zealously hoarded for the more important shoots. On July 10th, 14 and 15 Pls. came under command 50 Div., who were preparing to attack Hottot. This attack went in the next day, the fire of both Pls. being controlled by Capt.

D COY.

Archer. Targets were engaged in Hottot, Vaast-sur-Seulles, and Pont-sur-Picavets, the enemy retaliating with mortars and air-bursts, one of which killed Pte. Smith, a driver-operator. Meanwhile, 12 and 13 Pls. supported a diversionary attack by 1/4 K.O.Y.L.I. (of 146 Bde.) on the area La Pte. Ferme.

The Coy.'s counter-mortar rôle was emphasised and improved when, on July 14th, Lieut. G. Hunt of Bn. H.Q. was appointed Counter-Mortar Officer at H.Q., R.A., and all Coys.' Tac. H.Q. wireless sets were put on the same net. On being mortared, Pls. at once sent out the code word "Poppycock", followed by an approximate bearing. The Counter-Mortar Officer had first call on the Corps and Div. artillery, 4·2-in. and 3-in. mortars, and was able to bring down quick and heavy fire on cross-bearings. This system proved efficacious, and ascendancy was established over enemy mortars which had caused heavy casualties among the Div.

On July 17th all four Pls. were under Coy. comd., preparing to support an advance by 147 and 70 Bdes. A smoke task was included, and as ranging was impossible the Coy. had the help of an Air O.P. for the first time. This proved highly satisfactory, and all tasks were completed on the next day. During this attack, Capt. Nicol was wounded when 146 Bde H.Q. was bombed, and Cpl. Dawkins, 13 Pl., was wounded by a mortar-bomb which burst near him. 12 Pl. had a hair-raising experience when a heap of about eighty mortar bombs received a direct hit. Two men in a slit-trench five yards away escaped unhurt, but all secondaries caught fire, and it was feared that the bombs would explode. All were damaged, some splitting into two or three pieces, but none exploded, and the fires were put out by Cpl. Felstead and an A/Tank Sgt.-Major.

The Coy. next enjoyed its first break, going back into Bn. H.Q. area at Cancagny for a few days. This interlude was marked by heavy rain, but arrears of sleep, maintenance, and paper work were cleared up before the Coy., with the rest of the Bn. moved over to its new sector, S.E. of Caen. The move took place on the night of July 24th, and D Coy. found itself dispersed over a wide Div. front, with orders to dig in for a long stay. Dust and massed squadrons of mosquitoes, added to enemy mortaring, shelling, and air attacks, made this seem an unpleasant prospect, only slightly alleviated by the chance of sending small parties in turn to the field cinema and mobile baths. Mortar ammunition was still scarce, the normal allotment being twenty-five rounds per mortar per day, and it was therefore all the more annoying when a light enemy bomb hit a mortar-bomb dump, destroying sixty-four rounds. On the same day Sgt. Jacobs was wounded in the back by a shell splinter. The next day, July 27th, the Coy. suffered further casualties. During shelling of 14 Pl. area, Cpl. Smith and Ptes. Pope and Edwards were wounded. As Capt. Fenwick, their Pl. Comd., was helping to load them into tpt. to take them to the Regimental Aid Post, another shell landed near by and wounded him in the leg. He was evacuated to the U.K., but rejoined the Bn. later on in the campaign. Further shelling and mortaring of Pl. areas and Coy. H.Q. followed during the next few days, destroying equipment but fortunately causing no serious casualties. A drill was laid to enable Pls. to change positions every twenty-four hours, and this helped to cut down further losses. The main task of the Coy. at this stage was still counter-mortar fire, German six-barrelled mortars being extremely active.

When the break-through at last took place and 49 Div. advanced, the Coy. had a few days of repeated moves without being able to come within range owing to the speed of the enemy withdrawal. Mortar positions had to be looked for well forward to give Pls. time to come into action, and it was while this was being done, on August 18th, that the Coy. lost Major Bare. Together with the Commanding Officer, Maj. Bare was on a reconnaissance for mortar positions. There was only scanty information about our own and enemy forward positions, and they were fired upon by a sniper covering a bridge. Major Bare was very badly wounded and had to crawl away under fire. Major Bare was later evacuated to U.K., where he underwent a number of operations, but was unable to rejoin the Bn. In him the Coy. lost a gallant and popular commander who had done sterling work in the formation and training of the Coy. as well as in these early stages of the campaign, and who richly deserved the Croix de Guerre subsequently awarded to him. He was succeeded as Coy. Comd. by Maj. G. F. Fulcher, whose cheerful and unruffled personality was soon known throughout the Div. He commanded the Coy. for the rest of the campaign and part of the occupation, winning the M.C. for his services.

August 18th was a difficult day for the Coy. In addition to the wounding of Maj. Bare, it suffered a fatal casualty, Pte. Minns, through enemy shelling. At nightfall a heavy fire-plan to assist 10 D.L.I. attack on a key hill was carried out. The hill was taken but heavily counter-attacked, and the Coy. was kept busy with D.F. and counter-mortar fire during the next day. The Inf. advance then gathered speed, and the Mortar Pls. were leap-frogged forward to keep up. There were occasions when they had not time to get into action against German rearguards, but on August 26th 14 Pl. supported the advance of 7 D.W.R. from a bridge-head over the River Risle. The infantry advanced with fixed bayonets from the mortar line, and the C.O. 7 D.W.R. later complimented the 4·2-in. mortars for their successful shoot. Two days later Pte. Laucharne bagged the first prisoners to be taken by Coy. H.Q. While parking his truck, he saw two Germans hiding in a ditch. Seizing a rifle, he leaped after them, and they surrendered before anyone had noticed that there was no bolt in the rifle. Later in the day two more prisoners were taken by less unorthodox means.

The Div. advance was now pulled up by the Seine, there being no bridge nearer than Rouen. This gave the Coy. a few days to overhaul its transport, the Lloyds carriers in particular having given some anxiety. On September 3rd the Seine was crossed at Elbeuf, and the Div. swung west for its next big task, the capture of Le Havre. Most of the Lloyds fell out at one time or another, but fine work by the M.T. personnel brought them all up in time for the set-piece, the attack on this vital port. During the earlier phases 15 Pl., supporting a probe by 146 Inf. Bde., were heavily shelled, Capt. Archer, Cpl. Clark, and Pte. Lewis being wounded.

The main attack on Le Havre provided some interesting

and successful tasks for the Coy. 12 and 14 Pls. were ranged on to their targets by Air O.P., and the mortar lines were sited so far forward that the Pls. had to withdraw during the preliminary air bombardment. 15 Pl., in support 1/4 K.O.Y.L.I., engaged opportunity targets called for by Lt. Thornhill, in addition to the prearranged fireplan. All Pls. on September 10th fired non-stop for at least $3\frac{1}{2}$ hours, the longest spell yet. Mortar barrels became overheated, and had to be cooled off, and the ammunition numbers performed a fine task in bringing up thousands of bombs. The assault went off like a perfect exercise, and by September 11th Le Havre was in British hands. The Coy. was then withdrawn into Bn. area for a few days for relaxation and an overhaul, badly needed in view of the long drive ahead before the Div. rejoined the rest of the Army Group, now beyond Antwerp. This began on September 21st, and by the time it ended on September 24th the Coy.'s Lloyds carriers were strewn over France and Belgium. One of them was lost for a fortnight, the crew eventually rejoining the Coy. minus the vehicle, which had become a write-off. This reflects no discredit on fitters and drivers; the plain fact was that the Lloyd carrier was not suitable for these long hauls.

D Coy., except for Rear Coy. H.Q., did not take part in the celebrations of liberated Vorselaar. All Pls., on September 25th, went at once into action along the Antwerp–Turnhout Canal, where the Germans were making a stand. 2 Essex (56 Bde.), with 12 Pl. in support, and 2 S.W.B., crossed the canal and occupied Rijkevorsel, and 13 Pl. moved into the bridge-head. At 02.00 hrs. on September 26th, 13 Pl., at that time commanded by Sgt. Walker, were warned by the infantry that enemy in some strength were in a house some 15 yards from the Pl. position. The infantry were unable to deal with them at that time, and the mortars were being called upon to fire. Sgt. Walker split his Pl. into two sections, closing a gap in the Inf. positions and containing the enemy, leaving enough men to fire over three hundred rounds during the day on D.F. tasks, and taking a total of fifty-eight prisoners during the day. Meanwhile, 12 Pl. moved west along the canal in support

D COY.

of 2 S.W.B., and 14 Pl. supported attacks by 11 R.S.F. of 147 Bde. 15 Pl., in support 4 Lincs., were shelled and mortared throughout the day, Pte. Patton being wounded.

For the rest of the month fighting took place along the canal and in the bridge-heads established by 56 and 147 Bdes. The advance then continued slowly, the Div. front gradually widening until there was twenty-five miles between 14 Pl. at Poppel and 12 Pl. at St. Leonards, where the Pl. Comd. had his O.P. in the steeple of a church. The first few days of October brought little change, the Div. edging its way forward, along an ever-widening front, towards the Dutch frontier. On October 4th, 14 Pl. suffered a piece of cruel ill-luck. The Pl. had just received orders to move, and kit was being loaded, when the area was shelled by enemy 88s. In a few minutes the Pl. had ten casualties, two of them fatal. Thus badly depleted, they occupied new positions and found themselves sharing slit-trenches with the forward infantry Coy. of 4 Lincs., and unable to deploy for action. The Pl. Comd. withdrew a section at a time to an area where the mortars could fire. Later in the evening some reinforcements were sent up, and a bad day ended with the Pl. in good heart.

The Div. was now preparing a main attack into Holland on the left flank and centre, while the right flank was held by Bob Force. One Pl. were put under command Bob Force, while the three remaining Pls. took part in the Div. attack. While this was being planned, a number of changes took place within the Coy. Capt. Fenwick, who had been wounded at Démouville, rejoined the Coy. on October 6th, but soon left again to take over command of H.Q. Coy. Capt. Kennedy came from B Coy. to become 2/i/C. of the Coy., and Capt. Stoltenhoff was posted to 12 Pl., with Lt. Asker as Pl. 2/i/C. Two new officers, Lt. Buttel and Lt. Krepps, joined the Coy. and were posted to 13 and 15 Pls. respectively. During this comparatively quiet spell a training cadre for new N.C.O.s was begun, and a modified baseplate tried out, with good results. There was great joy in the Coy. when ten men at a time were sent off for short leave in Antwerp.

The Div. attack north from St. Leonards began at 07.30

hrs. on October 20th, and during the next hour 12, 14, and 15 Pls. fired between them seven hundred rounds. During the night the Pls. had occupied positions 500 yards in front of the leading infantry, and were thus able to give maximum support to the attack by 56 Bde., which was a complete success. Except for one man wounded when a carrier was shelled, there were no casualties in the Coy. The next few days the Pls. were in action alternately with all three Bdes., with many calls for D.F. and H.F. tasks, until the Div. was relieved by a U.S. formation and directed on to the Dutch town of Roosendaal and the River Maas. During this operation there were no battle casualties, although in an unfortunate accident at Rear Coy. H.Q. Pte. France was fatally injured and three others hurt. The Coy. found a new rôle, during the advance to the Maas, in setting fire to buildings used by the enemy. Smoke bombs were used for this, and on October 29th Pl. positions were occupied among the smouldering ruins of buildings fired the previous day. Meanwhile, 13 Pl., with Bob Force on the right, had been put under command 4 Armoured Bde., and took part in a rapid advance north. One day, the Pl. began in positions firing north and by the evening were in a position to fire south, having gone right round a pocket of the enemy. It was not until the end of the month that this Pl. rejoined the Coy. north of Roosendaal.

By then the Div. was approaching the Maas, the enemy resistance being centred on Willemstadt. It had become very cold, and the ground at the side of the roads was becoming flooded. Farm-yards therefore became the only possible mortar positions, and they attracted unwelcome attention from enemy artillery and mortars. On November 1st, when the Coy. first fired on targets on the far side of the Maas, an enemy shell fell on 15 Pl. command post, wounding Lieut. Kreps and three others. On the other side of the account, a German section at a cross-roads was caught by 4·2-in. mortaring and wiped out. When our troops reached the cross-roads they found the enemy, all dead, lying as they had marched, in single file. In thick mud the advance went on, and became steadily more difficult to find suitable baseplate positions. On November 4th, while moving with 14

Pl. into a sugar-beet factory, Sgt. Bridges took two prisoners, and a further search revealed three more Germans. The next day 13 Pl. had to move forward under enemy observation, and Sgt. Dutch was wounded in the subsequent shelling. The next day 146 Inf. Bde. captured Willemstadt, and the Div.'s task in this sector was over. The Coy. returned to Roosendaal for a brief rest before moving with the Division to the other flank of the front, in the Venlo sector.

The long drive to Hamont, the Bn.'s concentration area, took place on November 8th and 9th in bitterly cold weather, and was one of the most trying in the Coy.'s experience, with a great many breakdowns among the Lloyds. The next day it was learned that D Coy. were to assist 53 Div. in the first stage of the attack towards Venlo, coming for this purpose under command 1 Manchesters. Positions were occupied on November 13th, and the attack went in early the following morning. Very heavy shelling followed on 13 Pl., and a direct hit on Pl. H.Q. killed two N.C.O.s, Sgt. Greenway and Cpl. Tyson, and severely wounded a third, Cpl. Walker. All these N.C.O.s were old and valued members of the Coy., and were sadly missed. Further shelling forced both 13 and 14 Pls. to move back, but by 15.00 hrs. they were in action again, and took part in a timed fire programme later in the day. Eventually, a last-minute alteration was made in the fire-plan, and radio communications having broken down had to be sent to 12 and 15 Pls. by dispatch rider. To do this, Pte. Draper had to ride over an unknown route, under enemy shelling, in pitch dark, but he succeeded in getting the message through on time. To round off a hectic day, a near miss on No. 1 mortar of 12 Pl. partially buried the crew in the mortar pit in the middle of a shoot. Pte. Kerr, the No. 1, crawled out and continued to fire his mortar until the rest of the crew were dug out.

The Coy. then reverted to 49 Div., which was preparing to pass through 51 Div. and attack Blerwick and Venlo. The first phase was again to clear up to the Maas, and the Coy. was kept together, Pls. leap-frogging on the two axis of the Div. advance. Foul weather, thick mud, and mine-fields made this a most difficult operation. Wheeled vehicles, except for jeeps, were soon useless, and the Pls. had to rely entirely on their own carriers. 13 Pl., starting with seven carriers, were soon reduced to two, these having to ferry the Pl. on each move. Wireless communications over the wide area involved were difficult, and a step-up link had to be introduced between Coy. H.Q. and the Pls. Firing during this phase, when the Coy. was able to cover the Div. front, was mainly confined to H.F. and timed programmes in support of infantry night patrols. At one stage the Div. artillery were so far forward that the 4·2-in. mortars were the only supporting arms able to provide supporting fire immediately in front of the infantry.

By November 26th the Div. advance had brought it to positions overlooking Venlo, on the far side of the Maas; but at this point it was relieved by 15 Div. and ordered to the Nijmegen–Arnhem area. No one was sorry to leave the rain, mud, and mines of the Venlo sector; and no one anticipated that Nijmegen, where the Coy. was to have such a long stay, would soon prove to be even wetter and more muddy.

The move to a concentration area west of Nijmegen took place on November 29th, and next day the Coy. took over positions from the Mortar Coy. 2 Cheshires. As transport crossing the main Nijmegen bridge had to be kept to a minimum, Pls. were limited to seven vehicles on the "island" (later reduced to six), the remainder being concentrated at Rear Coy. H.Q. 13 Pl. was the first in action on the "island", with a counter-mortar shoot on November 30th, and was also the first to be hit by floods that followed the breaking of the dykes. The other Pls. soon followed suit, and during the next few days there were frequent moves to oases of higher ground. 14 Pl. suffered an unfortunate accident on December 5th, when an explosion in the Pl. cook-house caused eight casualties.

For the rest of the month the Coy.'s activities were mainly concentrated on H.F. and D.F. tasks, usually carried out in rain or ice. On one occasion a Pl. moving to Druten, on the Div. left flank, to support 49 "Recce" Regt. had to be carried in 3-tonners, as the Lloyds could not negotiate the ice-bound roads. Two Pls. were on the "island", both in forward positions, where enemy patrols sometimes came uncomfortably close, and two in reserve at Nijmegen; but these reserve positions were by no means inactive, as, apart from garrison duties within Brock Force, reserve Pls. were often called upon for shoots on other parts of the far-flung Div. front. The Pls. on the "island", besides D.F. and H.F. tasks, supported infantry raids, and fought an endless battle against floods, rain, and ice. A great deal of use was made of alternative positions to counter enemy shelling and mortaring, and the wisdom of this was proved somewhat fortuitously when a flying-bomb made a direct hit on one of 14 Pl.'s positions, fortunately not then in occupation. The experiment, begun on the Maas, of burning down troublesome buildings in the enemy lines with smoke bombs, was carried further on the "island". One such building was a castle on which the gunners and R.A.F. made repeated attacks without much success. A section of 12 Pl. then had a go, with the aid of an Air O.P.; fifty bombs were fired, and the O.P. then reported that the castle was "burning beautifully". It burned all night, with ammunition exploding like a Crystal Palace fireworks display.

A good deal of firing at this stage was done with Air O.P.s. An incident perhaps worth recording is that when the O.P. wireless suddenly went out of action, 14 Pl. could hear the Air O.P. but the O.P. got no answers. The problem was resourcefully solved by the Pl. spelling out its messages in the snow with mortar boxes. It worked well, if a little slowly.

In these conditions D Coy. spent December—a month of activity, some hardship, and, happily, few casualties. Christmas was celebrated in turn by the Pls. in reserve in Nijmegen; concert parties, a great effort by the cooks, and the hospitality of the inhabitants combined to make it a memorable occasion. But Arnhem and part of the "island" were still in German hands, and everyone realised that some hard fighting still lay ahead.

CHAPTER XXVIII

VICTORY AND OCCUPATION

To this point there have been separate chapters on each Coy.'s part in the fighting from the Normandy beachhead to Nijmegen. These have taken this war history to the end of 1944. During December 1944, however, important changes took place, which make it easier for the Battalion's subsequent history to be dealt with as a whole.

The first of these changes was the order of the G.O.C., 49 Div., that in future the M.G. Coys. and mortars would normally be used in support of Bdes., and that they would be placed under comd. of Bdes. only for special occasions. Henceforward, the Bn. could normally expect to operate as a single fighting, as well as administrative, unit. At the time this rearrangement came into force, 49 Div. were on a very wide, thinly-held front on the "island" between Nijmegen and the approaches to Arnhem, on the Rhine. The Waal river at Nijmegen could be crossed by a road bridge or a Sapper-built pontoon bridge, and there was also a damaged railway bridge. These were vital to future operations, as well as to the present positions held by the Div.; and all were within range of enemy guns, determined raiding parties, and river-borne assault.

To defend these bridges 49 Div. created Brock Force, which was put under comd. Lt.-Col. D. V. G. Brock, comd. 2 Kensingtons. It was administered by Bn. H.Q. 2 Kensingtons, and its composition was 2 Pls. M.M.G. (provided in turn by the M.G. Coy. in reserve), 1 Bty. 25-pdrs., 1 Tp. A/Tank, 1 Tp. S/L, 1 Coy. Inf. Although the Battalion therefore provided only a portion of Brock Force, its fate was very much bound up with that heterogeneous formation, and the activities of Brock Force will find a place in this history.

An immediate result of these changes was to make possible some economies in force. A regular programme of reliefs was arranged, so that Pls. had spells of rest and overhaul in Nijmegen, and transport could be overhauled. This did not, however, mean that M.G.s and mortars carried out less firing; on the contrary, a fire-plan was made by Bn. H.Q. to cover the Div. front with H.F. and D.F. tasks, and Pls. on the "island" were kept hard at it, often at night. This, with the harsh conditions on the "island", alternating between floods and ice, made the rest-periods all the more valuable.

During most of December the enemy's activity had been confined to shelling, sneak air attacks, and infantry patrols. But as Christmas came near, and with the launching of the German offensive in the Ardennes, there were signs that he was likely to become more aggressive. There were per-

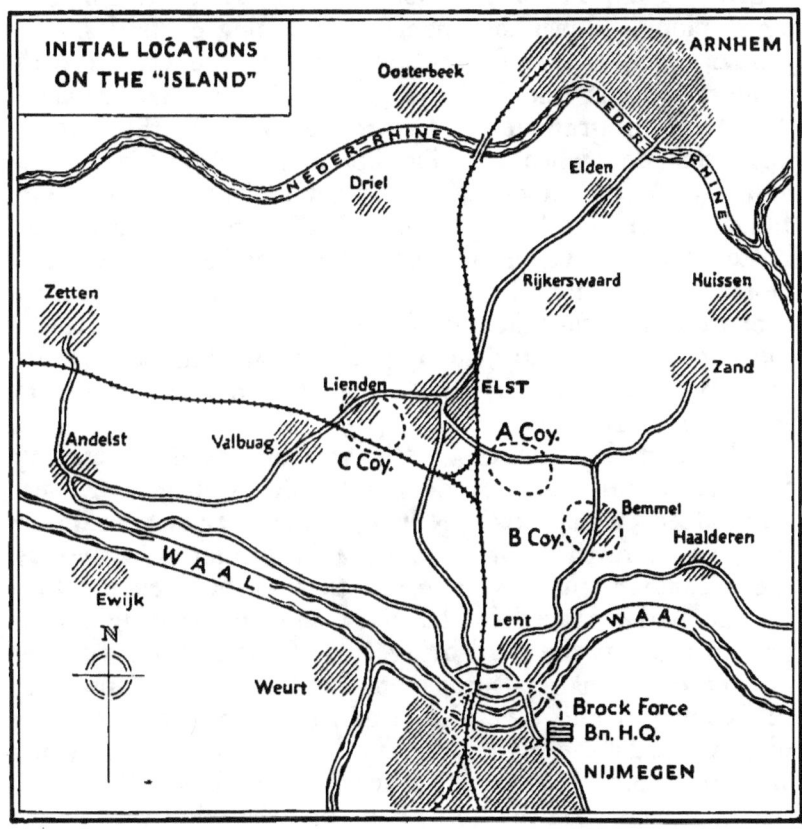

sistent reports of impending paratroop attacks on Nijmegen, shelling was intensified, and the Nijmegen bridges were obviously threatened. On Christmas Eve, Lord Haw-Haw and his female counterpart, Mary of Arnhem, broadcast that 49 Div. would be "annihilated" during the festive season; and although this spoilt nobody's Christmas dinner, precautions in Brock Force and the Bn. area in Nijmegen were intensified.

The New Year opened with aggressive, but strangely unco-ordinated, enemy activity. On January 1st three enemy aircraft over the Waal river dropped one bomb, at the cost of two of the planes seen to crash later after being engaged by Div. A./A. Two days later a party of Germans were heard at night approaching 2 S.W.B. positions on the "island" from Hemmen Castle. 5 Pl., A Coy., engaged them, pinning down the enemy and causing casualties. On January 4th, 2 S.W.B. sent a patrol to the Castle, with support from A and D Coys., while C Coy. carried out a long H.F. programme. A Coy. experienced further excitement this day when a flying bomb landed within half a mile from Tac. Coy. H.Q., without causing damage. On January 5th the Germans launched a counter-attack on Zetten, which gave the Bn. full scope for heavy M.G. and mortar fire. The Germans lost heavily without gaining ground, and during the next few days D Coy., in particular, took heavy toll among enemy positions at Hemmen Castle, which was set ablaze by smoke bombs from 4·2-in. mortars on January 12th.

The next day, January 13th, was one of great anxiety for Brock Force and of danger to the Nijmegen bridges. Soon after 3 a.m., wreckage lying in the river at the railway bridge was further shattered by an explosion. At midday the Canadian gunners reported that a small enemy submarine had surfaced in the river and was moving downstream towards the road bridge. It was then level with the advanced German positions on the Bund road, upstream of Nijmegen, and several German soldiers were seen running towards the river, waving to the submarine, which was now under fire from Canadian artillery. The submarine beached on the north bank and the pilot was seen to bale out and join the Germans. Two of them were killed by shelling and the remainder withdrew. Five minutes later a large metal object, apparently with fins, was seen floating down river in the same area. It was hit by artillery fire and blew up. At 12.15, a second submarine was seen going downstream, first at periscope level, then fully surfaced. Heavily engaged, it turned round, dived, and disappeared upstream. Almost at the same time a log was sighted below the boom covering the approach to the road bridge. It eventually ran aground and was found to have lashed to it two mines, 12 feet long and 2 feet in diameter. The mines had been hit by 40-mm. shells, but must have been actuated by a time mechanism, as they did not blow up until later, causing minor casualties but no serious damage. During the day similar logs and other floating explosives came downstream, one of them blowing a large gap in one boom; but none caused any damage to the bridge, which at the end of the day was intact, thanks largely to the alertness of Brock Force look-outs and excellent shooting by the gunners. It was later established that the submarines used in this attack were of the midget type, carrying two torpedoes. The Germans had achieved nothing, and the sub-units protecting the bridge now became known in the Div. as H.M.S. Brock Force.

The next operation in which the Bn. took part was an attack by 56 Bde. in the Zetten area. B and D Coys. supported the Bde., 8 Pl. of B Coy. enjoying a direct shoot from the first floor of a school. (The reconnaissance party for this position was accompanied by an infantry patrol which took two prisoners.) During two days' fighting, on January 20th and 21st, B Coy. Pls. fired 300,000 rounds, helping the attack to complete success. The opening burst in one shoot by 7 Pl. was seen to cause five enemy casualties.

The rest of the month passed off with routine D.F. and H.F. shoots. It was now bitterly cold, the floods had been frozen over, and large masses of ice were coming down the Waal. Brock Force was caused some anxiety by ice breaking gaps in the boom, but fortunately no further German river-borne attacks developed before they were repaired.

During January a token allotment of leave to U.K. was given the Battalion; hopes had been high that a much more generous allotment would be made, and there was some disappointment until it was learned that bigger parties would go in February and March.

The pattern was repeated in February. The Div. was still static, except for a few raids, and calls on the Bn. for M.G. and mortar fire were heavy; there was only one day in the entire month when there was no call for fire. This put a heavy strain on the Pls. on the "island", and most of the Bn. were by now longing for a change in locale. As against these drawbacks, the Bn. suffered only two casualties during this period, both wounded, and, despite the trying weather, its health record was excellent. On the lighter side it may be recorded that at the Div. individual boxing championships in Nijmegen, Pte. Panter (C Coy.) won the bantamweight, and Pte. Udall (B Coy.) was runner-up in the welterweight. Watching the boxing in the crowded Wintergarden, it was difficult to remember that the Germans still held part of the north bank of the Waal, and that the whole of Nijmegen was in range of the enemy's heavy artillery. The rest of the Allied front was slowly moving forward, and the German's last resistance was showing signs of cracking, but 49 Div. seemed rooted between Waal and Rhine.

During February Capt. I. A. Strawson relinquished the Adjutancy and joined D Coy. as 2/i/C. He was succeeded by Capt. M. Palmer, previously I.O., and Capt. Stoltenhoff joined Bn. H.Q. as I.O.

March saw little change in the Bn.'s fortunes. Relief by 53 Div. was at one stage expected, but plans were changed, and 49 Div. remained static, only extending its flanks still further. There were again heavy calls for D.F. and H.F. fire, and both 4·2-in. mortar and Mark VIII Z ammunition were in short supply. Towards the end of the month the Bn. lost its Commanding Officer, Lt.-Col. D. V. G. Brock. Having completed three years in command, he was posted away. Lt.-Col. Brock took over the Bn. on its return from Iceland in 1942, and had seen it through the trying changes and strenuous training that preceded the invasion of Normandy, and through the major part of the campaign. For his wholehearted services he was subsequently Mentioned in Dispatches. He was succeeded by Lt.-Col. D. Glover, formerly of The Manchester Regiment, who joined the Bn. in Nijmegen on March 27th, at the time when, to everyone's joy, planning had begun for the attack which was to clear the "island" and take the Div. away from an area it had come to know only too well. On March 28th and 29th, the Bn. was relieved by Princess Louise's Fusiliers of 11 Canadian Armoured Brigade, and Brock Force by the Suffolk Yeomanry.

Operation "Destroyer", to clear the eastern half of the "island", was launched on April 2nd. Bn. H.Q. had drawn up an elaborate fire-plan, and all Coys. supported 146 and 147 Inf. Bdes., who carried out the attacks. There was only scattered resistance, and by April 3rd the "island" was clear. A Coy., in support 146 Inf. Bde., now occupied positions in full view of Arnhem, but after some heavy shelling at midnight on April 3rd there was no attempt at interference by the enemy.

The next task for the Div. was one all ranks had waited for: the assault on Arnhem, where the heroic defeat of the Airborne attack in 1944 was still unavenged. Planning for this difficult operation, involving a crossing of the river in full view of enemy strong-points, began on April 5th with some difficult daylight reconnaissances watched, and occasionally fired upon, by German sentries on the other side of the Rhine. It was eventually decided to attack Arnhem from the east, the Bn.'s task in the assault stages being supporting fire, controlled from Bn. Tac. H.Q. This Fire Control Post was set up in the cellars of a heavily booby-trapped house which was shelled during the night. A Machine-gun Company of Princess Louise's Fusiliers was put under comd. of the Bn. for the initial phases.

The assault across the river, covered by a heavy barrage, was made at night on April 12th by 56 Inf. Bde., who quickly formed a bridge-head. A Coy. Tac. H.Q. followed the leading waves of infantry, with a call on the entire Bn. fire-power, and M.G. Pls. were passed over as quickly as possible for consolidation. There was great pressure on space in the Buffaloes and the inevitable changes of plan resulted in at least one D.R., Pte. Lewis of 9 Pl., C Coy., finding himself crossing the river without his Pl., together with the Assault Coys. of 2 Gloucesters. Unperturbed, he attached himself as stretcher-bearer to the Infantry Coy. H.Q.

D Coy. mortar lines had been sited well forward for the attack, and the Pls. occupied their positions at dusk on April 11th. During the night large convoys of R.A.S.C. 3-tonners brought up ammunition, and this activity must have been noted by the enemy. At dusk on April 12th, before the attack went in, 12 Pl. area was heavily and accurately shelled. Direct hits were made on stacked smoke bombs and vehicles, and fierce fires burst out. There were several casualties from burns, and for a while it seemed as if the whole platoon was in danger of being trapped. The position was saved by the great presence of mind and coolness of the Pl. Sgt., Sgt. Scott, and Cpl. Walton, who both did magnificent work in moving the Pl., and rescuing as much equipment as possible. Both these N.C.O.s were later awarded the M.M. Nevertheless, all four mortars, 1700 bombs, four carriers, and much other kit were destroyed, and the Pl. had to be taken out of action until the afternoon of April 14th. By then, heroic efforts by the Q.M. and T.O. had completely refitted the Pl., the Lloyds being replaced by new Windsor carriers.

The defences of Arnhem crumbled quickly, and the Germans retreated into Western Holland. By April 15th, the entire Bn. was in Arnhem, where Bn. H.Q. and H.Q. Coy. were established in a row of empty houses. Arnhem, after the bustle of Nijmegen, was a shock to the Bn., and an example of what German occupation during the winter had meant to the Dutch. All civilians had been evacuated after the Airborne attack, every house and shop had been looted, and what could not be carried away had been maliciously destroyed. What was left was the husk of a town, a monument to war and Nazi brutality.

On April 16th the Div. began its advance westwards in pursuit of the German Army cut off in Western Holland. The Battalion was now moving through undulating, wooded country very unlike the traditional pictures of Holland.

Enemy opposition was confined to rearguard actions, minefields, and sporadic shelling. On one occasion 6 Pl. (B Coy.) had a direct hit on a house at breakfast, but only one man was wounded. In the main, however, the Div. advance was swift, and the M.G. Coys. moved with Bdes., their main task being flank protection and provision of a firm base. By April 27th, the Div. had reached the next main German defence line, on the Grebbe, where the enemy had built strong-points and appeared to be ready to make a stand. Before an attack could be planned, news came that a truce had been arranged to enable food convoys for the starving Dutch population to pass through the German lines. There were to be no offensive patrols and no harassing fire. All positions were to remain unaltered until further orders; and an eventful month, which had seen the break-out from the "island" and the capture of Arnhem, ended with footballs being kicked about in full view of the Germans.

Those were strange days. It was clear that Hitler's Germany was collapsing into utter defeat. From the main Allied fronts, tremendous news came fast: the Americans, British, and Russians linked up, Berlin fell, and Hitler went to his squalid self-inflicted death. The end there was a matter of days; yet in Western Holland the Canadian Army, of which 49 Div. was part, still faced a compact, unbroken German Army. Would it surrender or fight with its back to the sea?

The question was answered on May 4th. Driving through the small, shattered town of Wageningen that day, an officer of the Bn. saw an unusual concentration of staff cars in the square outside a small hotel. Among them was a grey-green German car with a flag of truce. There was also a B.B.C. mobile recording van. Through the shattered windows could be seen an imposing array of red tabs. The conference ended, and a German officer, his face a grey mask of defeat, burst out of the room and hurried into his car. He was Field-Marshal Blaskowitz, Commander of the German Army in Holland, and he had just signed an unconditional surrender. He was followed out of the hotel by Gen. Bedell Smith (Chief-of-Staff to General Eisenhower), the Canadian Army Commander, and Prince Bernhard of the Netherlands, representing the Dutch Resistance forces.

The cars dispersed, the B.B.C. van went off, and the Kensington officer returned to Bn. H.Q. with the satisfied feeling that he had seen history made.

The surrender took effect at 8 a.m. on May 5th. A standstill order was in force, and civilians were not allowed to cross the lines. On that day all Coys. left their Bde. areas and concentrated near Wageningen. The next day a Bn. Thanksgiving Church Parade was held in the open near Bn. H.Q. The Commanding Officer later attended a conference at 49 Div., and returned with the news that the Div. was to take part, with I Canadian Corps, in the concentration, disarming, and guarding of all enemy in Western Holland. For this purpose the Divisional Artillery was to be formed into a separate Bde., of which 2 Kensingtons would form part. The task of the R.A. Bde. was the disarming of the notorious 34 (Landsturm Nederland) S.S. Division. This formation was composed of avowed Nazis and foreign Fascist volunteers; it had fought against 49 Div. on the "island" and was notorious in occupied Holland for its brutality.

When, next day, the Bn. moved through the Grebbe lines into Western Holland, an extraordinary situation developed. The surrender terms provided that the Germans would retain their arms until they were concentrated and under Allied guard; since they were surrounded by a hostile population with bitter memories of oppression, and contingents of Dutch Resistance fighters, this was no doubt necessary, but it meant that for some days our own troops, Germans, and Dutch Resistance were all walking around fully armed. There was great tension, but, thanks to the discipline of troops on both sides and, in particular, the amazing restraint of the Dutch, there were no armed clashes of any importance.

The Bn. was ordered to concentrate at Doorn (home after World War I of the ex-Kaiser). On the move, the following message, signed "Eisenhower", was received *via* Div. Signals:

> A representative of the German High Command signed the unconditional surrender of all German land, sea, and air forces in

VICTORY AND OCCUPATION

Europe to the Allied Expeditionary Force and simultaneously to the Soviet High Command at 070141 hours Central European time under which all forces will cease active ops. at 090001 May."

The war was over. But at that moment the Bn. was too busy for the thought to sink in. In jeeps, carriers, and trucks it was moving along the Dutch roads, while German soldiers stood silent at the doors of their billets, and orange flags waved from every window. At Doorn, a rapturous welcome by the inhabitants was awaiting them, to which the advance party could add the pleasure of evicting S.S. officers from the best houses in the town, which they had occupied with arrogant incivility for many months.

The Bn. was at once allotted the task of disarming 84 S.S. Regt. German Commanders had been ordered to sign immediately the capitulation documents and to supply information about their stores and dispositions. The Bn. 2/i/C. set off to the headquarters of an S.S. Bn. beyond Utrecht, and later wrote an account which may perhaps be quoted here:

I went off in my jeep with Pte. Hall, my driver, a Dutch Resistance interpreter, and a German S.S. officer as guide. At first, we passed through villages already reached by the Div., which were celebrating in a big way. Then we passed the "Recce" Regt. near Utrecht, and went on through a part of the district not yet occupied by Allied troops. It was a queer drive. The S.S. man, with a masklike face, didn't open his mouth except to give directions about the route. The interpreter, wildly excited, sat next to him, suggestively stroking the Sten we'd given him just before we left. The villages seemed deserted, except for armed German sentries; but as we drove through, curtains were drawn aside, windows flung open, flags put out. We could hear the hum as the streets began to fill with Dutch civilians.

The German Bn. H.Q. was a house on the far side of a canal spanned by a short bridge. We left Hall with the jeep at the bridge, and went into the house. The village streets were empty, except for German soldiers. The S.S. Colonel and his Adjutant had obviously just bathed, shaved, and put on their best uniforms. He gleamed all over; I was in rather tired battle-dress, and the interpreter wore civvies with a khaki beret at an odd angle. However, the situation was restored when I sat in the best chair and the interpreter, obviously longing for a false move, posted himself and his Sten behind me.

The German began by offering cigarettes and a drink, which were refused. He then tried the arrogant approach, saying it was impossible to answer the questions and have them at our H.Q. by midnight, as demanded. I said that if they were not there by midnight, we would send a guard to bring him in under arrest. He at once gave in, said he would see to it, and signed the capitulation document, which I took away. He came out of the house with me, and we were faced by an amazing sight. Piled high with flowers, the jeep was hemmed in on every side by men, women, and children, all perfectly quiet. But when I came out with the bit of paper in my hand, something snapped. They cheered, laughed, and cried. Led by the Pastor, they sang the Dutch National Anthem. They made speeches, the interpreter made a speech, I made a speech. It was funny, it was exciting, and it was deeply moving; for, at that moment, we realised that the war in Europe was really over.

It was not quite over for everyone. That evening, trouble was reported from Dutch S.S. Troops at Driebergen, near Doorn. 4 Pl. (A Coy.) were called out to deal with it, and in the clash two S.S. men were killed and one wounded. Nor was there much time for celebrations during the next few days. On May 10th the disarming and concentration of 84 S.S. Regt. began, and during the next forty-eight hours, 77 German officers and 1416 other ranks were disarmed, searched, and escorted to their concentration areas. It must be said that the Germans' discipline was unshaken. On May 12th planning began for Operation "Pied Piper", which was carried out by A, C, and D Coys., with a squadron of the "Recce" Regt., on May 13th and 14th. This was a sweep of the R.A. Bde. area for German deserters, Dutch Nazis in hiding in the woods, and other undesirables. A total of fifty-three arrests was made, the Dutch Resistance co-operating enthusiastically. On May 16th the Bn. went back to Wageningen, preparatory to moving into Germany, where 49 Div. was now to come under comd. of the Second British Army for occupation duties.

The move, however, was to be delayed by a gratifying experience. During its long stay in Holland, the Bn. was deeply impressed by the bearing of the people of Nijmegen, where many lasting friendships had been formed, and by the fortitude with which they, and the people in Western Holland, had faced the terrible hardships of the war and the German occupation. The Commanding Officer had conceived the idea, enthusiastically taken up by the Bn., of a collection to be presented to the Dutch Red Cross for the relief of suffering in Holland. The head of the Dutch Red Cross was Princess (now Queen) Juliana of the Netherlands, and on May 18th Lt.-Col. Glover flew to Breda and was granted an audience at which Princess Juliana agreed to accept the Bn.'s gift and to inspect the Bn. at Nijmegen on June 2nd.

This achieved, the C.O. now had to get the idea sanctioned by higher authority. The Bn. advance party was already in Germany, where the bulk of the Division was about to follow. However, the Div. Comd. agreed to the Bn. remaining in Holland until June 3rd, and on May 27th all Coys. moved back to Nijmegen. It was appropriate that the ceremony should be staged in this town, where the Bn. had been based for so long, and whose people had been so hospitable. The next few days were spent in feverish preparation for the Parade, and far-flung forays for food, blanco, paint, and polish. Capt. Palmer flew to England in a borrowed Air O.P. Auster, complete with pilot, and returned with many embellishments, such as new chevrons, R.S.M.'s stick, Regimental Flag, and ten thousand cigarettes, essential to such a function. The Regimental March, "The Silver Bugle", was orchestrated, invitations were sent to military and civic dignitaries, and the parade rehearsed. On June 2nd Princess Juliana was given a great welcome by the people of Nijmegen. She lunched with the officers of the Battalion at the Normandy Hotel, among the other guests being the G.O.C. 49 Div., and in the afternoon inspected the Battalion and accepted the cheque for £1,100 subscribed by all ranks to the Dutch Red Cross. A great day was rounded off by Coy. farewell dances, and at daybreak on June 3rd the advance party, with aching heads, left for Germany, to be followed later in the day by the rest of the Bn.

A new phase was about to begin in the life of the Battalion. The campaign and the Victory celebrations were both over, and the next task was the occupation of Germany. The area allotted to the Bn., which was now under comd. 147 Bde., was on the edge of the Ruhr. That is, it adjoined the most heavily-bombed area in Germany, where, in addition to hundreds of thousands of homeless Germans living in the cellars of shattered towns, were slave workers from all over Europe and many thousand Russian, Polish, Italian, and French prisoners-of-war. When the fighting stopped, literally millions of men, women, and children, freed from their German masters, set out for home. Home might be half the breadth of a continent away, but the roads were choked with people making their way there—by foot, pushing a handcart, by bicycle, truck, cart, lorry. It was a mass migration unparalleled in history.

By the time the Battalion arrived in their occupation area of Germany, this spontaneous homing had been to a large extent put under control. Displaced persons and prisoners-of-war had been sorted out, as far as possible, into nationalities, and put into camps to await orderly repatriation. U.N.R.R.A. teams were beginning to move in to look after health and welfare; but there were not yet enough of them, they lacked stores, transport, training, and experience, and they had to lean heavily on the Occupation Forces for help. Thus the Battalion found that their chief task in their new area was the guarding and administration of ten D.P. and P.O.W. camps, housing some 16,000–17,000 Russians, Poles, Czechs, Jugoslavs, Italians, and Ukrainians. Bn. H.Q., H.Q. Coy., and A Coy. were in Schwerte, a small, unbombed town; B and C Coy. in Emst, a village between Schwerte and Hagen (a town which had been flattened by a saturation raid). On the outskirts of Hagen were D Coy. H.Q. and Pl. areas. All billets were in requisitioned civilian houses and offices, and they were soon made comfortable.

It is difficult to give a consecutive record of the Bn.'s activities during the months that followed. On paper, there were elaborate education and training programmes, but these were at the mercy of very heavy commitments in the running of these camps and all that involved. In a typical week, Bn. H.Q. and Coy. Comds. might be called upon to deal with a looting raid by D.P.s on a German farm, a search for suspected German war criminals, the arrest of a would-be Werewolf, the departure of several hundred Italians, the non-arrival of food supplies at a camp, the death of six Poles through drinking anti-freeze stolen from a Transport store, the ever-present problem of maternity cases among women D.P.s, the visit of a Russian repatriation team, a black-market round-up, and a riot following a disputed goal at an inter-camp football match. There were tricky political obstacles to be overcome, such as a visit by King Peter of Jugoslavia to a Jugoslav camp known to contain some fervent Republicans,[1] or the passionate demand of a bunch of Ukrainians to be saved from repatriation to Soviet territory. Because of the high incidence of attacks on Germans and looting of German property, there had to be regular guards and night patrols, and the Bn. never had enough men to carry out both its occupation duties and its training programmes. The shortage of men became particularly acute when demobilisation was added to regular home leave.

Nevertheless, it would be wrong to give the impression that the life of the Bn. in Germany was all work and no play. Once the running of the camps settled down into a routine, the Coys. were able to look around, make themselves more comfortable, start up canteens and clubs, and organise recreation. Among the innovations were riding-schools and a canoeing club, while the Bn.'s football, cricket, swimming, netball, and motor-cycle cross-country teams took part in Bde. and Div. events. Progress was made, too, with educational and vocational training, Major S. R. Pinks taking charge of these activities. Gradually, as D.P.s and former prisoners-of-war were sent home, camps were closed down—usually after hectic all-night parties—and the whole of the Bn. was concentrated in Schwerte. In September the first parties for release left the Bn. They included Lt.-Col. Glover, whose crowded six months or so with the Bn. had included a visit to Britain after the end of the war to fight a northern constituency in the General Election, Major G. D. Fulcher, who had commanded the Mortar Coy. since the break-through in Normandy, and Capt. (Q.M.)

---

[1] Who were sent out of camp on a picnic for the occasion.

W. A. Blakeley, whose departure seemed like the end of an era for the Bn. he had served so well. Imperturbable, hiding a deep kindliness and sense of humour under a gruff exterior, "Bill" Blakeley had been an outstanding figure throughout the life of the Bn., and will be remembered with affection by all ranks. Towards the end of September Lt.-Col. W. Y. Kington Blair Oliphant, O.B.E., M.C., arrived to take comd. of the Bn. It was a difficult period for a new C.O. Many senior officers and N.C.O.s were on the point of release or had already gone, the future was in doubt, and it needed an exceptional personality to hold the Bn. together. Lt.-Col. Kington Blair Oliphant remained with the Bn. until it was disbanded, and impressed all who served under him with the way he steered it through these trying months.

Early in October there was a re-shuffle of senior officers. Major S. Jacobson, M.C., the 2/i/C., left for release, accompanied by Capt. Sheppard, who had done such a fine job as Bn. Transport Officer. Major R. Cannon, M.C., now became 2/i/C., Major M. Palmer took over command of D Coy., and Major Wilmot of A Coy. Capt. Kennedy became Adjutant. During the same month the Bn. said good-bye with deep regret to Brig. H. Wood, D.S.O., who was relinquishing command of 147 Inf. Bde.

With the approach of winter there were fears that food shortages might cause disturbances among German civilians in the Ruhr, and Coys. were ordered to maintain mobile reserves. However, except for minor incidents, there were no troubles, and the War Diary for December records only three exceptions to the daily "Nothing to Report" from all Coys. : On Christmas Day, it was noted, a German Light Orchestra played for the Bn.; on December 28th a Polish sentry at a D.P. Camp was attacked by an inmate, whom he fired at and killed; and on December 29th two houses near Hagen Station were blown down.

On January 15th, however, there came a piece of important, and sad, news. At a Coy. Comds.' conference, the Commanding Officer announced that the Bn. was to be prepared for disbandment by February 15th, and that C Coy. was to be disbanded in five days' time. The news was not unexpected; but its confirmation, and the nearness of the date, caused many heavy hearts that day. By January 25th C Coy. had been disbanded and the Bn. reorganised into three duty Coys., with Bn. H.Q. and H.Q. Coy. On the last day of January an advance party from 1 Cheshires arrived to arrange for the hand-over of the Bn. area; and on February 5th the Commanding Officer issued a Special Order of the Day:

The following message has been received from the Divisional Commander.

"The disbandment of your unit is, I'm afraid, now rapidly drawing to a close.

"I want, therefore, to take this opportunity of writing to tell you how much 49 Division will miss 2 KENSINGTONS from amongst its ranks.

"Throughout the campaign in N.W. Europe the Bn. maintained the highest standard of military efficiency, courage, and discipline, and the support you provided for the Infantry Bns. was such that the demand for it was incessant.

"During this period your Companies have made many friends in the Inf. Bdes., to which they have been affiliated, and it is sad that these friendships, built up by close association in battle, must now be broken up by your disbandment.

"The time since V.E. Day has not been an easy one. There have been strange and difficult tasks to be done and the disturbing influence of change and demobilisation has been a test of morale and discipline. Throughout, however, 2 KENSINGTONS have remained cheerful and enthusiastic in all they have done.

"I should like, therefore, on behalf of the whole of 49 Division to wish you, your officers, warrant officers, N.C.O.s, and men, Goodbye, God Speed, and Good Luck in whatever the future may hold in store for you. We in the Division will not forget you and I hope you all will ever have a soft spot in your hearts and pride in The Polar Bear Division.

"(Sgd.) E. T. L. GURDON,
"Major-General."

Five days later, drafts left the Bn. for 1/7 Middlesex and 1 Middlesex, and on February 12th all the remaining Kensingtons, except for a small rear party, went to 40 Reinforcement Holding Unit at Munster. The main body of 1 Cheshires arrived, and a signal was sent to Bde. H.Q. that 2 Kensingtons were now disbanded.

The Battalion's task was done. Once a close and gallant team, its members were scattered, soon to be swallowed up by the routines and responsibilities of the civilian life they had fought to preserve. This record has told only a part of its story. The rest, which cannot be put into words, remains in the hearts of the men who were proud to serve in it.

POST-WAR
(1947-1951)
By
LT.-COL. R. WASEY, M.B.E., T.D.

CHAPTER XXIX

POST-WAR (1947–1951)

By Lt.-Col. R. Wasey, M.B.E., T.D.

By 1947 both the war-time 1st and 2nd Battalions had been disbanded, and during the early part of the year Colonel Hugh Campbell, D.S.O., the Honorary Colonel, was informed that as Machine-gun Battalions were no longer to form part of the Army, the future of the Kensingtons was in doubt. Eventually the War Office decided that when the Territorial Army was reconstructed the Kensingtons should become part of Royal Signals, in order to take over the rôle of Phantom. This was a highly specialised liaison task which during the war had been performed by units staffed by all arms, but which in future was to come under Royal Signals. It would be the only unit of its kind in the Army and would be allowed to retain the privilege of wearing its own badge and carrying colours.

On May 1st the Territorial Army was officially reborn, and under the title of G.H.Q. Signal Reporting Regiment (The Kensington Regt.) the Kensingtons once more came into being. Lt.-Col. R. Wasey, M.B.E., was appointed Commanding Officer, and around him gathered a small nucleus of pre-war and war-time Kensingtons. During the year strenuous efforts were made to obtain the right kind of recruit, but the public apathy was great and progress was slow. An especial difficulty facing the Regiment was that whilst the function of the officer allowed the recruitment of a fair proportion of former Kensington officers, the task of the men in the ranks demanded in most cases that they should be Royal Signals tradesmen. For this reason many offers of war-time Kensington N.C.O.s to re-engage had to be most reluctantly refused. By November 9th the strength was forty all ranks, and on that day the Regiment and O.C.A. paraded at St. Mary Abbots Church and received back the colours, which had been laid up in 1939. Accompanied by the bands of the Life Guards and the Kensington Cadets, the parade, which included a strong detachment of the Old Comrades, marched back to H.Q. At the Kensington Town Hall the salute was taken by the Mayor of Kensington (Councillor F. R. E. Davis, C.B.E.) and by the Chief Signal Officer, London District (Lt.-Col. R. W. Morgan, O.B.E.). At H.Q. the colours were returned to the Officers' Mess, from which they had been taken eight years previously.

The year saw a slight alteration in the title of the Regiment, which now became Signal Reporting Regiment (Princess Louise's Kensington Regiment). S.S.M. Fox, who had been with the unit since its inception, was replaced by R.S.M. Bray, whose influence was to be a determining factor in the Regiment in its growth and expansion over the next four years. Few units were more fortunate in obtaining the services of one who so happily combined the traditions of the Corps and the knack of handling the volunteer soldier.

Colonel Campbell, D.S.O., finished his tour of duty as Honorary Colonel in February 1948. For nineteen years he had held this office, and the Regiment had much for which to thank him. Now it was faced with the difficult task of finding a successor, and was most fortunate in securing the services of General Sir H. Colville B. Wemyss, K.C.B., K.B.E., D.S.O., M.C., then Colonel Commandant Royal Signals. General Wemyss had held several of the highest offices in the British Army and had completed his tour as Military Secretary in 1946. Subsequent history was to prove the inestimable benefit of having one of the Royal Signals' most distinguished sons as the Honorary Colonel of Royal Signals' newest unit!

For Annual Training, which was to be for only one week, the Regiment proceeded to Canterbury in July. Here, sixty all ranks were the guests of Eastern Command Signal Regiment, and a most enjoyable but concentrated and hard-working seven days were spent.

In August the Regimental Rifle Meeting was held for the first time since the war. On the Sunday the O.C.A. arrived and a very pleasant afternoon's shooting ensued.

H.R.H. Princess Juliana (now Queen Juliana of the Netherlands) inspecting the Battalion at Nijmegen. On her Right is the Commanding Officer, Lieut.-Col. D. Glover. (See Chapter XXVIII.)
(Photo by courtesy of Imperial War Museum. Copyright reserved.)

Army Phantom Signal Regt. (Princess Louise's Kensington Regt.) March Past the Mayor of Kensington on "Adoption Day," April 15th, 1951. (*See Chapter XXIX*.)
(*Photo by courtesy of "The Kensington News."*)

POST-WAR (1947–1951)

General Wemyss presented the prizes, the Regimental Champion being Sgt. Isely and the O.C.A. Champion Major "Rocky" Knight, M.B.E., M.M.

On October 31st H.M. The King inspected the Territorial Army in Hyde Park. Much to the disappointment of the Regiment it was allowed only one representative, Cpl. E. R. Pearce, but it was given the task of running the Provost wireless communications, for which it earned many thanks from those responsible for the organisation.

On November 14th the Regiment, the O.C.A., and the Cadets paraded at Church Street Barracks and were inspected by the Hon. Colonel. They then marched to H.Q., where wreaths were laid on the Memorial and a short service was held. Later this month the regular Second-in-Command, Major E. Nanney-Wynn, left to take up another appointment and was succeeded by Major D. C. Cocks, a Territorial. Shortly after this, Capt. Maunsell, who had been Adjutant since the Regiment was re-formed, was posted away. Capt. Maunsell had been with Phantom during the war and his advice and enthusiasm had been invaluable. Capt. J. Adams, Royal Signals, took over his duties.

During the year several week-end exercises had been held and the training of the Regiment had shown great progress. Recruiting continued to be disappointing as to numbers but most satisfactory as to quality.

About this time the problem of the provision of a War Memorial for the fallen of the recent war was exercising the mind of the Commanding Officer. He approached the O.C.A., and a Committee was formed with the following members: *Chairman*: Commanding Officer; *Secretary*: E. Faircloth Stratton (1st Bn., 1939–45); *Treasurer*: H. Foren (2nd Bn., 1939–45); *Members*: Col. W. H. Godfrey, M.B.E., M.M. (President, O.C.A.), S. G. White (Hon. Sec., O.C.A.), H. Hollier (Editor, *The Kensington*).

As a result of their deliberations it was decided that the new Memorial was to be in bronze and was to be fitted beneath the existing Memorial. An appeal was launched and realised £221, of which £50 was donated by the Regiment. In addition £505 had been handed over by the

1st Battalion and kept in trust by the O.C.A. To anticipate matters it can be stated here that the total cost came to £318, and that the balance of £408 was handed to the History Committee to assist in meeting the cost of the 1939–45 *History*.

January 1949 found the Regiment 100 strong. In March a Civic Recruiting Week was held in Hammersmith, during which Field-Marshal the Viscount Montgomery of Alamein inspected a Guard of Honour in which the Regiment was well represented.

The Army Council approved the change of the title of the Regiment to Army Phantom Signal Regiment (Princess Louise's Kensington Regiment), although the change was not to be implemented until approved by H.M. The King.

The band of the Royal Corps of Signals gave a delightful concert at H.Q. on April 11th.

On May 8th the new War Memorial was unveiled by H.R.H. The Princess Royal, Colonel-in-Chief Royal Signals. It is interesting to recall that on May 8th, 1921, the existing Memorial was unveiled by her aunt The Princess Louise. Her Royal Highness was received by the Mayors of Kensington and Hammersmith and inspected a Guard of Honour commanded by Capt. A. E. B. Foxwell, son of a very famous Old Kensington. A sincere and moving service was conducted by the Rev. G. A. B. Lee, S.C.F., assisted by the band of the Irish Guards, in the presence of a large gathering of Old Comrades and serving members. The Princess dedicated the Memorial, and Bugle-Major King, of the Cadets, sounded the "Last Post" and the "Reveille". After the service H.R.H. stayed to tea and most graciously allowed the Commanding Officer to present to her over one hundred of those present, including relatives of the fallen.

In July, for the first time since the war, the Regiment had two weeks' Annual Training. This was at Crowborough, which will conjure up many memories among an earlier generation. Training proved most interesting, and the full fortnight allowed of considerable progress.

Once again the Annual Rifle Meeting of the Regiment and O.C.A. was held, this time in September, the Regimental

POST-WAR (1947–1951)

Championship being won by the Commanding Officer. Also in September the Regiment participated in the London and Middlesex Rifle Meeting and put up a very creditable performance, gaining second place against such redoubtable opponents as the Queen's Westminsters, London Scottish, R.N.V.R., etc.

During the autumn several Trade Boards were held, with most successful results. There have been several references in this narrative to the keenness of the members of the Regiment during these lean post-war years, and it is interesting to note that during this year the average number of drills performed by each man was 121 against an obligatory minimum of 30! November saw the Annual Remembrance Service at H.Q. conducted for the first time by the Regimental Chaplain, the Rev. S. Parry-Chivers. At the Regimental and O.C.A. Dance later in the same month the shooting trophies were presented by the Honorary Colonel.

The Annual Children's Party was held in early January 1950, and, thanks to the efforts of Lady Wemyss, Mrs. B. R. Wood, and Capt. Delbridge of the O.C.A., was a great success. Some sixty children of the Regt. and O.C.A. attended.

In March, at a suggestion of the Commanding Officer, the O.C.A. agreed that their journal, *The Kensington,* should include a portion allotted to the Regiment, for which it should bear the cost. It was felt that both past and present members would enjoy reading each others' activities, and that such a step would do much to weld them together. In accordance with this plan in the March issue of *The Kensington* the familiar words "The Official Journal of the Old Comrades' Association" on its cover were altered to "The Journal of the Princess Louise's Kensington Regiment Past and Present".

Week-end exercises were held in April, May, and June and were all well attended, to the great benefit of training generally.

An historic landmark was reached in June when the first contingent of National Servicemen reported to the unit. Under Government legislation all National Servicemen were now to serve four years with the Territorial Army on completion of their regular service. Obviously the efficiency of the Territorial forces would be greatly increased by this step, but eventually it must, of course, mean the death of the volunteer movement as it had for so long been constituted.

At the end of July the Regiment went to Landguard Camp, Felixstowe, for Annual Training. The strength attending was ninety-two. None of the National Servicemen so far posted were due to attend this camp. Although the first week was uncomfortable owing to overcrowding, a great deal of good work was done. For the first time since the war the O.C.A. visited the unit in Camp, many of them spending the middle week-end with the Regiment. A grand time was had by all, and the serving members were very gratified to be told by their guests that even in the pre-war years they had never been better entertained. The visit was the more appreciated by reason of the fact that it offered the first real opportunity for the Regiment to offer some token of its gratitude for the assistance and encouragement received from the Old Comrades' Association since the Regiment had been re-formed.

The usual Regimental Rifle Meeting was held in September, and was attended by over seventy of the O.C.A. The Regimental Championship was won by Dvr. Range. On September 29th the Old Comrades' Association arranged a Guest Night for those serving in the Regiment. This was a most successful function, which was much enjoyed by both parties and did much to cement an acquaintance already begun at Felixstowe in July.

Unfortunately there is little opportunity in an account such as this to mention individuals by name. It is, however, an interesting reflection on the varied rôle of the Regiment to note the names and war-time units of some of the officers serving at this time. Of the pre-war Kensingtons there were, in addition to the Commanding Officer, Majors R. Hammond, T.D., and B. R. Wood, T.D.: of the war-time Kensingtons, Major A. E. B. Foxwell, Captains A. H. Sandford, J. Downes, and F. Kendell. Others who had contributed much to the post-war progress of the unit were Major D. C. Cocks (Second-in-Command, formerly Middlesex Yeomanry and Royal Signals), Captains P. Luttman-Johnson (R.A.C. and Phantom), P. Bennett, K. E. Jones, and E. G. Jones (all of Royal Signals), W. G. Hawkins, T.D. (The Devon Regt.), and G. C. Rawlinson, T.D. (The "Recce" Regt.). In addition to the Adjutant and the R.S.M., who have already been mentioned, the Permanent Staff included Capt. T. Williamson (Q.M.), S.Q.M.S. B. Kendrick, Sgt. McGowan (Orderly Room), Sgt. Farmer (M.T.), and Sgts. Williams and S. R. Hatton (Instructors). The early days owe much also to S.S.M. Lloyd and Cpl. E. J. H. Cast, who for the first three years not only ran the Orderly Room most efficiently but also vitalised all regimental activities.

Obviously it is quite impossible to mention all the Territorial other ranks, and the author asks the forgiveness of the many staunch workers who must be omitted, but the following are some of those who had served with the Regiment for three years at this time. S.S.M.s F. B. Wright, G. O. Johnstone, and T. E. Lawson (all of R. Sigs.), S.S.M. E. Blogg ("Recce" Regt.), Sgts. A. L. Evans, H. A. North, C. E. Isely, and R. F. Dandridge (all Infantry), Sgt. B. Ireland (R. Sigs. and Phantom), Cpls. A. E. Russell, W. J. Jales, and F. W. Giles (R. Sigs.). Amongst those who had done sterling work in the earlier days but were no longer with the unit must be mentioned Cpls. E. R. Pearce and W. H. Palmer, the latter being amongst the first Kensingtons to rejoin the Regiment in 1947.

The Annual Remembrance Service was held at H.Q. in November in the presence of a goodly gathering of past and present members of the Regiment. Capt. J. Adams, Royal Signals, who had been a most enthusiastic and capable Adjutant since November 1948, was promoted and posted to a new appointment. He was succeeded by Capt. E. J. Bardell, Royal Signals.

During the year basket-ball had become a popular attraction, and in December a soccer team was formed and played its first matches, which owing to lack of a ground had to be "away". Later in the month a most successful Regimental Dance was held at H.Q., attended by over 450 serving members and Old Comrades.

The strength of the Regiment at the opening of 1951

was: officers 27, other ranks 109. This included National Servicemen.

The usual successful Children's Party was held on January 3rd.

The early part of the year brought many points of interest. It was announced that there was to be launched a scheme for the adoption of units by the Boroughs in which they were situated, and that their titles would be amended accordingly. This, of course, threatened the Regiment's title of Kensingtons, since the unit was now situated in Hammersmith. Vigorous action by the Hon. Colonel and Commanding Officer averted this blow to tradition and it was agreed by the powers-that-be that the Regiment should remain the ward of the Royal Borough by whom it had been adopted in 1905! Once again the ready assistance of the Honorary Colonel had solved a problem for the Regiment. Throughout these four years General and Lady Wemyss had participated in and enthusiastically supported every activity of the Regiment. The high reputation that the Regiment now enjoyed owed a great deal to the help and direction given it by this distinguished soldier.

The Chief Signal Officer, London District (Lt.-Col. H. R. Firth), carried out his annual inspection of the unit and the following extract from his report may interest the reader. "There may be Territorial Regiments as good as this but there can be none better than the Kensingtons, with their admirable history and high tradition."

During the early part of the year two week-end exercises were held and were notable in that they gave the Regiment its first opportunity of seeing some of its National Servicemen at work.

On April 12th the Royal Borough of Kensington, at a special meeting of the Council, formally adopted the Regiment together with other units in the Borough. On the following Sunday afternoon these units paraded in the Broad Walk for an official ceremony at which illuminated scrolls were presented to each regiment. The other units taking part were:

    499 (Mixed) H.A.A. Regt., R.A.
    64 (Mixed) Fire Command Troop, R.A.

POST-WAR (1947–1951)

11 A.A. (Mixed) Signal Regt., Royal Signals.
592 Coy. R.A.S.C.

After the ceremony units marched past the Mayor (Councillor J. G. Gapp, J.P.) and the Deputy-Lieutenant (Brigadier B. Chichester-Cooke, C.B.E.), who took the salute on the steps of the Town Hall. The Regiment was just under a hundred strong, and the colours were carried on the parade. The smartness of all ranks earned a good deal of praise from the onlookers and the local Press. In addition, there was a small motorised convoy representative of each unit. After the parade the Regiment and many Old Comrades forgathered at H.Q., and later in the evening the Mayor and Mayoress were most welcome guests. Undoubtedly the events of this day did much to strengthen the ties already linking the Regiment with the Royal Borough.

At the end of April Lt.-Col. R. Wasey handed over command to Lt.-Col. D. C. Cocks, having completed his full tour of three years plus one year's extension. The Regiment gave him a great send-off, and his successor settled down to the many tasks involved in preparing for Annual Training, which was to be at St. Martin's Plain, Shorncliffe, from May 27th to June 7th.

This camp, in a most delightful situation, was thoroughly enjoyed by all ranks, and 50 per cent. of the National Servicemen became Volunteers.

ROLL OF HONOUR

Pte. J. F. Abear
Pte. B. P. J. Alexander
Cpl. F. T. Ames
Pte. E. J. Andrews
Pte. W. H. Annett

Pte. R. Bailey
Pte. W. Baxter
Pte. J. A. Blake
Cpl. J. W. Brett
Pte. W. Bridgen
Pte. A. G. Brown
Pte. E. Brown
L/Sgt. L. G. H. Bulleid
Pte. W. H. Burt
Cpl. F. S. Bushnell

Pte. A. S. Chapman
Cpl. H. Chappell
Pte. A. Cheshire
Pte. D. J. Coombs
Pte. J. G. Coulson
Pte. H. F. Coward
Pte. G. J. Cox
Cpl. J. D. Cox
L/Cpl. R. Cross
Pte. S. Cresswell

Pte. G. Deadman
Pte. A. G. Dewey
Pte. H. R. Dillon

Sgt. J. Edmeads
Pte. F. Edwards
Pte. J. A. Evans
Pte. J. E. Eyles

Pte. R. J. Farlander
Pte. H. R. Feltham
Pte. A. R. Fetter
Pte. L. Flenley
Pte. R. M. Flint
Pte. J. Flynn
Pte. F. D. Ford
Pte. T. H. France
P.S.M. C. W. Frost

Pte. W. C. Gilbert
Pte. E. W. Graham
Pte. A. L. Gray
Pte. L. Gray
Sgt. P. N. R. Greenway
Pte. C. Greenwood
Pte. J. Gribben
Pte. S. A. Guscott

L/Cpl. H. Harvey
Pte. E. Haslam
Pte. H. H. Hassall
L/Sgt. W. W. Hebbard
Pte. R. J. Higgins
Sgt. M. R. Hilburn
Sgt. G. T. M. Holland
Sgt. S. F. Holloway
Pte. J. F. Howard
Pte. J. Hurst
Cpl. E. J. E. Husher

Pte. M. R. Jackaman
Pte. S. W. Johnson
Pte. J. A. Jones
Lieut. L. H. Jones

Pte. A. F. Kanharn
Cpl. G. A. J. Kinner

Pte. J. A. Lane
Pte. A. Laverick
Cpl. R. Lee
Sgt. L. A. Lombardi

Pte. H. McCormick
Pte. H. McNulty
Pte. A. E. Meredith
Pte. A. S. Mills
Lieut. M. G. Milner
Pte. C. T. Minns
Sgt. A. D. Monk
Cpl. T. Moran

Pte. T. Norris

Pte. T. C. O'Grady

Pte. A. E. Paley
Pte. C. A. Parish
Pte. A. G. Parrott
Pte. J. W. Patston
Pte. C. V. Payton
Pte. R. F. W. Perry
Pte. A. W. J. Piggott
Pte. A. D. Powell
Pte. H. G. Prevett
Pte. R. F. J. Pritchard

Pte. W. Ravenscroft
Pte. W. Robson

Pte. F. J. Saunders
Pte. S. A. Savage
L/Cpl. G. H. Scott
Pte. A. Seal
Pte. C. G. Sherwood
Lieut. H. S. Shillidy
Pte. C. S. Sidey
Pte. E. L. Smith
Pte. H. T. Smith
2nd-Lt. G. Smullen
Pte. G. H. Stevens
Pte. O. I. Summers
Pte. S. G. Swann

Pte. F. Tait
Pte. G. Topham
Lieut. L. J. Trott
Cpl. F. A. Tucker
Cpl. V. R. Tyson

L/Cpl. J. P. Wallace
Sgt. A. E. Williams
Sgt. G. A. Willmott
Pte. McG. J. Wilson
Pte. J. W. Wonfor
Pte. W. J. Wood
Pte. V. R. Woodard
Pte. W. Worrall
Major A. Wray

In compiling the Roll of Honour the utmost care has been taken to ensure completeness and accuracy of detail. In the event of any errors or omissions the authors tender their sincere regret.

PRINCESS LOUISE'S KENSINGTON REGIMENT
1ST BATTALION

HONOURS AND AWARDS
(1939–1945)

The authors offer their profound apologies for any errors or omissions

MILITARY CROSS

Major J. W. Doyle
Major B. V. C. Harpur
Lieut. H. S. Jupp
Lieut. J. S. McKay

Capt. R. Mitchell
Capt. B. J. G. Page
Lieut. W. H. Scott
Lieut. A. F. D. Shelley

M.B.E.

Capt. and Q.M. E. D. Knight, M.M.   R.Q.M.S. F. J. Headington

D.C.M.

Sgt. R. D. Pratt

B.E.M.

Sgt. J. F. Warner

MILITARY MEDAL

Sgt. B. B. Axten
Pte. J. L. Alsop
L/Sgt. C. E. Chidgey
L/Sgt. G. H. Claydon

Sgt. P. J. Ganley
Pte. E. C. Gordon
Sgt. A. Harvey
Sgt. A. E. Moreton

Sgt. E. Rowlands
L/Sgt. W. J. Taylor

AMERICAN BRONZE STAR

Sgt. C. E. Bland   Cpl. D. A. Box

MENTIONED IN DISPATCHES

Lt.-Col. F. G. Parker
Lt.-Col. B. L. Bryar
*Capt. R. A. Bennett
Sgt. C. E. Bland
Lieut. D. W. Blizard
Pte. G. E. Brown
Sgt. E. C. Chaston

Major C. E. Cullen
Pte. J. W. Davy
Sgt. D. D. Derrick
C.Q.M.S. C. Dixon
Pte. C. W. Donnelly
Major J. W. Doyle
*Capt. K. Duff-White

HONOURS AND AWARDS

MENTIONED IN DISPATCHES—*continued*

Major J. J. Evans
L/Sgt. H. C. Ford
Major A. E. B. Foxwell
Lieut. J. R. Gray
Major B. V. C. Harpur
Lieut. F. F. Kendell
2nd/Lt. G. Kent
Cpl. A. G. Kershaw
Sgt. L. Kibble
C.S.M. T. McGowan
Lieut. J. S. McKay
Cpl. L. W. Marks
Sgt. A. E. Moreton
Sgt. R. Muchmore
*Capt. A. R. Newstead
*Major A. Newton
Cpl. H. A. E. Outten

Sgt. R. A. Perry
Pte. S. Perowitz
*Capt. A. F. Robertson
Pte. A. C. Roxborough
Lieut. A. H. Sandford
Pte. R. B. Savoie
L/Sgt. A. Sewell
Major E. P. Shanks
Pte. J. T. Shearing
C.S.M. C. F. Skinner
Capt. R. G. Smith
Major D. B. Tregoning
R.S.M. H. A. Upchurch
L/Cpl. J. Walker
Cpl. F. Walton
Pte. R. Walton
Lieut. J. A. W. Young

*Attached to Division or higher formations.

ACTS OF GALLANTRY
Brought to notice of Army Commander and officially recorded

Pte. R. Bailey
Pte. C. Donnelly
Pte. E. Firth
Pte. F. Ford
Lieut. J. R. Gray
Pte. C. Honour
Pte. E. Hooper

Major R. May
Cpl. E. C. Stanbridge
Pte. D. Smith
R.S.M. H. A. Upchurch
Pte. J. Walker
Pte. R. Wright

ACTS OF GALLANTRY
Receiving immediate recognition from the G.O.C., by the award of 78th Division "Mark of Esteem"

Sgt. E. C. Chaston
Sgt. D. B. Coles
Pte. J. W. Davy
Cpl. H. Dennis
Cpl. A. G. Kershaw
Sgt. R. Lovejoy
C.S.M. T. J. McGowan
L/Cpl. D. J. Merrington
Pte. R. S. Milner

Pte. B. J. W. Papworth
L/Sgt. E. Ridgeway
Pte. R. B. Savoie
Cpl. E. Searle
L/Sgt. A. Sewell
Pte. R. L. Sills
Pte. W. D. Thorogood
Cpl. F. Walton
Pte. R. Wright

PRINCESS LOUISE'S KENSINGTON REGIMENT
2ND BATTALION

HONOURS AND AWARDS
(1939–1945)

The authors offer their profound apologies for any errors or omissions

MILITARY CROSS

Major R. J. Cannon
Major G. F. Fulcher
Capt. J. T. Griffiths
Major S. Jacobson

B.E.M.
Pte. A. Best

M.B.E.
Capt. (Q.M.) W. A. Blakeley

MILITARY MEDAL

Sgt. W. Calland
Sgt. L. Carter
Sgt. R. Scott
Cpl. F. Walton

CROIX DE GUERRE, GILT STAR
Major R. G. Bare

CROIX DE GUERRE, BRONZE STAR
C.S.M. R. Bund

UNITED STATES BRONZE STAR MEDAL
Major M. Palmer

MENTIONED IN DISPATCHES

Lt.-Col. D. V. G. Brock
Major R. G. Bare
Major S. R. Pinks
Major E. Dudley
Capt. R. P. Archer
Capt. Rev. C. J. Blofeld, C.F.
Capt. C. P. Douet
Capt. D. Kennedy
Lieut. R. A. Jennings
C.S.M. R. Bund
C/Sgt. G. Walker
Sgt. A. Cooper
Sgt. E. Morgan
Sgt. R. Evans
Sgt. R. Nichols
Cpl. C. Felstead
L/Cpl. D. Jacobs

INDEX

Abbeville, 28, 29
Achtel, 319
Adams, Captain J., 369, 373
Adrano, 73, 75, 82, 85
Adshead, Pte., 190, 192
Aisne, River, 34
Alatri, 145
Alexander, Pte., ~~310~~ 311
Alexandria, Battalion landed at, 161
Alife, 115
Allen, Sgt., 47
Allfrey, Lieut.-Gen. C. W., C.B., D.S.O., M.C., 105
Amberley, 47
Ambrose, Pte., 180
Ames, Cpl., 126
Amsterdam, S.S., 19
Antwerp, 306, 343
Antwerp-Turnhout Canal, 317, 330
Anzio, 113
Apennines, 106
Aquino airfield, 141
Arbuthnott, Brigadier, R. K., D.S.O., M.C., 157, 163; Major-General, C.B.E., 205; C.B., 237
Archer, Captain R., 337, 339, 341
Archer, Pte., 321
Ardennes, German offensive in, 349
Argenta, 214
Argenta Gap, 218
Argonne, Forest of, 22
Argyll and Sutherland Highlanders, 144, 145, 147, 148, 156, 175, 212
Armentières, 19, 49
Arnhem, 353, 354
Arunci Mountains, 119
Arundel, 47
Ashford, 43
Asker, Lieut. J., 337
Attrill, Lieut. K., 298, 304
Axter, Sgt., 102, 144, 180

Bagnacavallo, 210
Bagshot Moor Camp, Beaulieu, 9
Bailey, L./Cpl., 180
Bailey, Pte. R., 46, 109

Baldwin, Sgt., 307
Ball, Lieut., 182
Ballard, Captain W. A., 259, 265
Banks, Sir Donald, D.S.O., Major-General, 13
Banyard, Lieut. C. E., 298, 299, 300
Barbée Farm, 328
Bardell, Captain E. J., 373
Bare, Major R., 281, 291, 336, 340, 341
Bari, 86
Barker, L./Cpl. H., 48
Barker, Major-Gen. E. H., 279
Barrow, Pte., 114
Barter, Pte., 301
Bass, Sgt., 310
Bastia, 213
Batcombe Down, 15
Battleaxe Weekly, The, Divisional newspaper, 237
Battye, 2nd Lieut. I. H., 17; Captain, 49, 105, 108, 112
Baxter, Pte., 126
Bayeux, 299
Baylisden, near Bethersden, 49
Beaulieu, in New Forest, 254
Beaumont-Hamel, 26
Beddard, Captain D., 285
Bedford, 56
Beevor, Lieut. P., 12; Capt., 17
Bellamy, Major, 18
Belsom, Lieut. C., 225
Benevento, near Naples, 176
Beni Yusef, 162
Bennett, Captain, 234
Bennett, Captain P., 373
Bennett, Captain Rev. F. L. M., Padre, 17, 42, 50
Benson, Pte., 178
Bergensfiord, H. M. J., 263
Bernhard of the Netherlands, Prince, 355
Best, Pte., 273
Biferno, River, 91
Bird, Sgt. L. W., 96
Birmingham, Pte., 103
Bishopstone, 43
Black Watch, 24, 29

381

INDEX

Blakeley, Lieut. W. A., 253, 268;
  Captain, 285, 287, 327, 362
Blerwick, attack on, 332, 345
Blizard, Lieut. D., 177, 210
Blofeld, Rev. R. J., 285
Blogg, S.S.M. E., 373
Boccaleone, 214
Bolton, Pte. G., 96
Bone, Sgt. B., 325
Bowley, Sgt. J., 192, 196
Brake, Lieut. H., 318
Bray, R.S.M., 368
Braybrook, Captain, 287
Braybrooke, Captain E. J., 285
Breckill, C.Q.M.S., 326
Bredin, Lieut.-Col., 186
Bresle, River, 32, 33
Brett, Cpl. J., 104
Brettevillette, 325, 326, 337
Bridgeman, Pte., 152
Bridges, Sgt., 345
Bridport, 60
Brighton, 47
Broadoak, H.Q. at, 43
Brock, Lieut.-Col. D. V. G., 275, 277, 281, 285, 291, 296, 333, 348, 352
Bronte, 73
Brooke, General Sir Alan, 259
Broom, Cpl. K. R., 93
Brougham of Vaux, Lieut. the Lord, becomes Adjutant, 255
Brown, Lieut. R. W., R.A.M.C., 45;
  Capt., 50
Brown, Lieut., 145
Brown, Pte. A., 96
Brown, Pte. E., 69
Browne, Col. M., 42, 56, 259
Brussels and Antwerp liberated, 330
Bryar, Captain B. L., 13, 17, 43;
  Major, 46, 50, 54, 57, 61, 70, 95;
  Lieut.-Col. 112, 123, 159, 204, 230
Buccheri, 72
Buckland, C.S.M. H., 62
Buffs, 121
Bulford, 50
Bulleid, Sgt., 338
Bund, C.S.M., 308, 312, 321, 322
Burley, 6
Burt, Pte., 156
Burton, 2nd Lieut. A. L., 17
Burwood, Sgt., 338
Bury St. Edmunds, 51
Bushnell, Cpl. F. S., 325
Butler, C.S.M. J., 17; R.S.M., 51

Butterworth, Maj.-Gen. D. C., D.S.O., 59, 163

Caen, 315
Cairo, 161, 163
Caister-on-Sea, 309
Calabria, 85
Calland, Cpl., 312, 320, 321
Camerons, 30
Campbell, Colonel Hugh, D.S.O., O.B.E., T.D., 7, 13, 368
Campobasso, 106, 108, 109, 113
Campolieto, 115
Campomarino, 93, 95, 115
Canadian Armoured Brigade, 353
Canadian Infantry Division, 260
Canale di S. Nicolo, 215
Cancagny, 314, 327
Cannon, Lieut. R. J., 272; Captain, 277; Major, 251, 281, 298, 362
Cap d'Orlando, 82
Capracotta, 114, 115
Capua, 115
Capurso, 86
Carinthia, 220, 224
Carovilli, 108
Carroll, Pte. D., 96
Carter, Sgt., 302
Carver, Pte., 295
Casalbordino, 100
Casalnuova, 115
Casa Luca, 194
Casa Salara, 179
Cash, Pte., 155
Casoli, 112, 115
Cassibile, 72
Cassino, 115, 116, 118, 121, 141, 160, 164
Cast, Cpl. E. J. H., 373
Castel de Rio, 166, 178, 201, 203, 206
Castel di Sangro, 106
Castel-Massino, 143
Castiglione, 146, 156
Castille Umberto, 82
Catania, 85
Catenanuova, 72, 73, 74
Caulfield-Kerney, 2nd Lieut. S. F., 17
  Capt., 46
Centuripe, 74, 75
Cercipiccolo, 106, 108
Cerignola, 88
Cervaro, 126
Cesena, 204, 206

INDEX

Chamberlain, Mr., broadcast to the nation, 12
Chapman, Pte. S., 140
Chappell, Cpl. H., 156
Chappell, Sgt., 47
Cheriton, 47
Cherry Tree Camp, Colchester, 51
Cheshire Regiment, 45, 159, 206, 258
Chesterton, Lieut. P., 97
Chilton, P.S.M., 17
Chimay, Major A. A. de C., 17, 22, 39, 43, 45; Lieut.-Col., 54, 61
Churchill, Mr. Winston, 220
Civic Reception Week in Hammersmith, 370
Civita Castellano, 146
Clark, Cpl., 341
Clark, Sgt., 324
Clarke, Cpl., 341
Clarke, Sgt. J. A., 12; R.S.M., 61, 80
Claydon, Captain J., 337
Claydon, near Ipswich, 258
Clifford, Cpl., 267
Cockerill, Pte., 178
Cocks, Major D. C., 369, 372; Lieut.-Col., 375
Cohen, Capt. R. D., 62
Cohen, Pte., 301
Coliseum, 158
Colquitt, Cpl., 113
Comacchio, 218
Comaggio, 180, 182
Commings, Major-General P. C. R. C.B., C.M.G., D.S.O., 6
Consandolo, 214
Cook, C.Q.M.S., E. F., 61
Corbett, Sgt., 252
Corbridge, Lieut. J., 89, 94, 97
Corderoy, Pte., 180
Corinth, Gulf of, 232, 235
Coronation Day, May 12th, 1937, 4
Cosgrove, Lieut. A., 234
Cotignola, 208
Cotton, Pte., 153
Coward, Pte. H., 96
Cowland, Pte., 301
Cox, Cpl. J. D., 176
Cox, Pte., 304
Cramer, Captain I. D. W., 68, 81, 128
Crested Eagle, 256
Cristot taken, 300
Cross, L./Cpl., 155
Crotone, 85, 86
Crowborough, 370

Crusader, The, Eighth Army Sunday newspaper, 157
Cullen, Captain C. E., 62, 81, 130, 140, 149, 150, 163, 170, 172; Major, 229
Cupello, 99
Curtis, Major-General H. O., C.B., D.S.O., M.C., 267, 269, 278
Czechoslovakia, German forces enter, 7

D'Abo, Major R. E. N., 260, 265, 267, 270, 285
Daily Telegraph, exhibition organised by, 242
Dale, Sgt., 272
Dandridge, Sgt. R. F., 373
Daniels, Sgt., 124
Darling, C.S.M., 17
Davies, Cpl. A., 96
Davies, C.S.M. L. A., 61
Davy, Pte., 179
Dawkins, Cpl., 339
De Gaulle, General, 28
Delbridge, Captain, 371
Dennis, Cpl., 184, 188
Depinna, Lieut. C. E., 76, 117, 120; Captain, 227
Dickson, Pte., 179
Dieppe, 28, 34
Dillon, Pte., 273
Dittano, River, 73, 74
Dives, River, 328
Dix, Pte., 304
Dixon, C.Q.M.S., C., 62
Dixon, Lieut. Frank, 195, 223
Dodge, Major J. B., D.S.O., D.S.C., 15, 17, 30, 243
Doorn, 356, 357
Dorchester, 60
Douet, Lieut. C. P., 298, 300, 303
Downer, Pte., 180
Downes, Lieut. J., 155; Captain, 202, 372
Doyle, Captain J. W., M.C., 54; Major, 62, 72, 73, 81, 84, 95, 97, 105, 118, 121, 152, 157, 159, 162, 166, 167, 168, 174, 209, 228
Draper, Pte., 345
Drouet, Lt., French liaison officer, 19
Druten, 346
Dudley, Captain E., 285; Major, 295, 320
Duff, Lieut. W., 181
Duff-White, Captain K., 62, 81

INDEX

Duke of Wellington's Regiment, 268
Dunan, Cpl., 301, 302
Dungeness, 47
Durban, H.M.T., 236
Dutch, Sgt., 345
Dwyer, C.S.M. G., 62

Eakins, Brigadier, 331
Eastbourne, 260
East Surreys, 74, 91, 95, 116, 118, 153, 155, 166, 169, 212
East Yorks and East Lancs Regiments, 14
Eaton, Pte., 77
Edgcumbe, Lieut., 321
Edgecombe, R.Q.M.S. A. R., 17, 61, 80; Lt.-Q.M., 142, 202
Edmeads, Sgt., 235
Edwards, Lieut. A., 173
Edwards, Major-Gen. J. K., D.S.O., M.C., 58
Edwards, Pte. F., 326, 340
El Giza, 163
Elliott, Cpl., 320
Ellis, Captain R. H., 62, 81, 135
Empire Pride, 160
Enfidaville, 69
English, Pte., 179
Erondelle, 28
Etchells, Lieut. J., 96
Etna, Mt., 73
Evans, 2nd Lieut. J. J., 17; Captain, 54, 57; Major, 62, 63, 68, 74, 78, 81, 112, 153, 161, 202, 216; as Town Major, 222, 229, 230
Evans, Sgt. A. L., 373
Everson, Pte., 151
Eykin, Lieut.-Col., 318
Eyles, Pte., 153

Fabrica, 146
Fakenham, 56
Falcone, 82, 116
Fano, 165
Farmer, Sgt., 373
Fécamp, 35, 39
Felstead, Cpl., 339
Fenwick, Captain H., 295, 340; wounded at Démonville, 343
Ficulle, 146
Field, Cpl. R., 277; Sgt., 285
Field, Major A. H. M., 262

Fielding, Pte., 300
Fingrinhoe, 54, 56
Firenzuola, 175
Firth, Lieut.-Col. H. R., Chief Signal Officer, London District, 374
Flatvecchia, 153, 154, 155
Flenley, Pte., 304
Flint, Pte. R. M., 104
Florence, 204
Floridia, 72
Flynn, Pte. J., 48
Folkestone, 47
Fontenay-le-Pesnel, 311, 313, 325, 337
Ford, Pte., 301
Ford, Pte. F., 46
Foren, H., 369
Forêt de Bretonne, 303, 329
Forêt D'eu, 19, 28
Fort Poplar, S.S., 286, 309
Fortune, Major-General, C.B., D.S.O., 21, 34, 35, 39, 244
Fossacesia, 99, 104
Fossa Marina, 214
Foucarmont, 28, 29
Foxwell, Captain A. E. B., 62, 80, 81, 85; Major, 95, 115, 159, 168, 183, 184, 219, 220, 229, 230, 370, 372
France, Pte., 344
Frosinone, 143, 144
Frost, P.S.M., 17, 24
Fulcher, Captain G. F., 336, 337; Major, 341, 361
Fullegar, Pte., 130

Gabriel, Cpl., 103
Ganley, Sgt., 150, 151, 190, 191, 193, 194, 200
Garrad, Cpl., 179
German, Lieut. J. A., 85; Captain, 159, 205, 221, 224, 230
Gerrard, C.Q.M.S. J., 62
Gesso, 176, 191
Gessopalina, 112
Gilbert, Major, 230
Gilbert, Pte. W., 326
Giles, Col. G. M., 3
Giles, Cpl. F. W., 373
Gipping, River, 53
Gladding, Cpl., 189
Glover, Lieut.-General, 359, 361
Godfrey, Col. W. H., 369
Godfrey, Sgt., 372
Godinton Park, 51

INDEX

Gordon, P.S.M. L., 17 ; C.S.M., 62
Golden Eagle, 256
Gordons, 29, 30
Gothic Line, 165
Graham, Pte., 153
Grandpre–Varennes, 27
Grant, Major E., D.S.O., 224
Gray, 2nd Lieut. R., 68 ; Lieut., 130, 144, 184, 188
Gray, Pte. A., 140
Greatstone, 43, 47
Green, Lieut., 269, 308
Greenhill, Sgt., 26, 241
Greenland, Sgt., 326
Greenway, Sgt., 345
Greenwood, Pte., 153
Greville, Lieut. P., wins North-West Sector Boxing Championship, 267
Griffen, 222
Griffiths, Lieut. J. T., 324, 325 ; award of Military Cross, 326, 328
Griffiths, Lieut. M., 81
Grisbrooke, Pte., 338
Guelma, 67
Guglioneri, 96
Gunner, 2nd Lieut. Colin, 76
Gurdon, Major-General E. T. L., 363
Guscott, L./Cpl., 78

Hackforth, Cpl., 77
Hagondange and Talange, 22
Hale, Sgt., 338
Hall, Cpl. C., 96
Hall, Pte., 357
Hammond, 2nd Lieut. R., 17 ; Lieut., 25, 245 ; Major, T.D., 372
Hamont, 306, 345
Hancocks, Lieut.-Col. F. G., M.C., T.D., 5, 7, 13
Harfleur Hill, 316, 317
Harpur, Lieut. B. V. C., promoted Captain and Adjutant, 54, 61, 80, 81, 85, 95 ; Major, 97, 154, 162, 168, 176, 188
Hastings, 260
Harvey, L./Cpl., 109
Harvey, Sgt. A. E., 92, 93
Haughley, 53
Hawkesworth, Pte., 155
Hawkinge, 45
Hawkins, Captain W. G., T.D., 373
Hawthorn, Pte., 153, 180
Headington, C.Q.M.S. F., 62, 80, 202

Hemmen Castle, 350
Hemming, Captain, 232
Herne Bay, 43
Heydwald and Grossenwald, 23, 24
Hibberd, Sgt., 12 ; C.S.M., 17, 62, 78
Hickin, Pte., 93
Hilburn, Sgt. M. R., 329
Hill, R.S.M., 17
Hoare, Captain N. E., 5 ; Major, 13, 16
Hobden, Lieut. " Peter," 144, 156, 173
Hodges, Sgt., 74
Hog's Back, 8
Holding, Captain E. W., 16, 17, 33, 43, 46
Holdstock, Captain P., 147, 153
Holford-Strevens, Captain H. J., 62, 81, 143
Hollier, H., 369
Holloway, Sgt., 153
Honours and Awards. *See* pp. 378–380
Hooper, Pte. D., 96
Hooper, Pte. E., 96
Hopper, Captain G. E. K., 62, 81, 128
Hornett, Cpl., 338
Horrocks, General Sir Brian, 288
Howard, Pte., 97
Horton, Pte., 76
Horton Park, 43
Hothfield, 45
Hothfield Common, 49
Hothfield Place, 43, 45
Hottot, 339
Howard, Major C. N. C., 8, 13 ; Lieut.-Col., 16
Humphreys, C.Q.M.S., 17
Hunt, Lieut. G. A., 285, 289
Hunt, Sgt. M., 106
Husher, Cpl. E., 78
Hutchings, Captain R. D., 62, 151, 210 ; Major, 229
Hyderabad Barracks, 55
Hymethus, Mt., 233

Iceland, 265
Impey, Lieut. W. A., 78
Inglis, Pte., 204
Ireland, Sgt. B., 373
Irwin, Lieut.-Gen. N. M. G., C.B., D.S.O., M.C., 53
Isaakson, Sgt., 180
Iseley, Sgt. C. E., 369, 373
Isernia, 106
Isle of Man, troops embark on, 18

Ismailia, 161
Iverna Gardens, Kensington, 6
Iveson, C.Q.M.S. J., 62

Jacobs, Sgt., 340
Jacobson, Major S., M.C., 251, 280, 281, 295, 309, 362
Jales, Cpl. W. J., 373
James, Brigadier, 152
James, Pte. A. E., 73
Jarvis, Pte., 172
Jennings, Lieut. R., 337
Johnson, Lieut. V. de P. C., 324
Johnstone, S.S.M. G. O., 373
Jones, Captain E. G., 373
Jones, Captain K. E., 373
Jones, Lieut. B., 331, 336
Jones, Lieut. L., 309, 311
Jones, Pte., 173, 195
Jones, Pte. J., 321
Jones, Sgt. T., 96, 177
Juliana, Princess (now Queen), 359
Jupp, Lieut. H. S., 42, 46

Kanharn, Pte. A., 140
Kelk, C.S.M. A., 61, 90
Kemp, Pte. R., 86
Kemp, Sgt., 77
Kendell, Sgt. F., 77; commissioned, 163; Lieut., 232; Captain, 372
Kendrick, S.Q.M.S., 373
Kennedy, Lieut. D., 309, 310, 319; Captain, 343; becomes Adjutant, 362
Kensington, His Worship the Mayor, 49
Kensington, Mayor of (Councillor F. R. E. Davis, C.B.E.), 368
Kensington, Mayor of (Councillor J. G. Gapp, J.P.), 375
Kensington's National Defence Company, 10
Kensington, The, journal, 371
Kent, 2nd Lieut. G., 17, 28, 40, 41; posted to East Africa, 46
Kent, Pte., 304
Kerr, Pte., 345
Kershaw, Cpl., 179
King, Bugle-Major, 370
King, Captain W., 337
King, Cpl., 140
King, C.Q.M.S. H., 17, 47, 68

King, Pte., 328
King Edward VIII, abdication, 4
King George V, His Majesty, gravely ill, 1
King George V, His Majesty, passes peacefully away, 3
King George VI, 4; reviews ex-servicemen in Hyde Park, 5; inspects troops at Crewkerne, 16, 68, 282
King Peter of Jugoslavia, 361
King's Own Yorkshire Light Infantry, 299, 305, 339
Kinner, Cpl., 76
Kirke, General Sir Walter, Director-General of the Territorial Army, 3
Klagenfurt, 221
Kluth, C.Q.M.S. F. H., 62; C.S.M., 97, 177
Knapp, Sgt., 195
Knight, Lieut. "Rocky," 15; Captain, 17; awarded M.B.E., 54, 57, 61, 66, 86, 137, 205, 369
Knight, Pte., 202
"Knightsbridge" Camp, 226
Kotschach, 220
Kreps, Lieut., 344

Lady of Man, 40, 42
La Frascata, 213
La Morea, 168, 176, 180
Lancashire Fusiliers, 74, 91, 92, 99, 140, 148, 153, 154, 214
Lanciano, 115
Landguard Camp, Felixstowe, 373
Lane, Pte. J. A., 165
Larino, 91, 95
Last, L./Cpl., 77
La Strada, 170, 175
Laucharne, Pte., 341
Lavenham, 53
Laver, Lieut. G. A., 100; Captain, 117, 134, 177, 182
Lavington, 2nd Lieut. H. J., 17, 32; Lieut., 245
Lawrie, Lieut., 285
Lawson, S.S.M. T. E., 373
Lee, Cpl., 193
Leese, General Sir Oliver, 157
Leghorn, 210
Le Havre, 34, 35, 238, 291, 292, 316, 317, 329, 341
Leinster, S.S., 266

INDEX

Le Manoire, 337
Leonard, Lieut., 125, 144
Les Hauts Vents, 300
Lewis, Brig.-Gen., C.B., C.M.G., T.D., 13
Lewis, Lieut. J., R.A.M.C., 50
Lewis, Pte., 341
Lienz, 224
Lieser Caserne, 224
Linklater, Eric, 41; in a B.B.C. broadcast, 157
Little Spaduro House, 199
Lloyd, S.S.M., 373
Lloyd Carrier Waterproofing Camp, 336
Loenhout, attack on, 319
Lombardi, Sgt., 103
London Irish Rifles, 43, 76, 143, 148, 153, 184, 185, 187, 201
London Scottish, 43
Long, Pte., 301
Long Melford, 53
"Longstop" Barracks, Villach, 222
Longstop Hill, 101
Lorraine–Saarbruecken, 21
Lothian and Border Horse, 24, 35
Louise, H.R.H. Princess, Duchess of Argyll, C.B.E., C.I., 3, 4; passed away, 14
Lovibond, Captain T. A., 272, 273
Lower Hare Park, Commander-in-Chief's conference, 285
Loyd, Lieut.-General H. C., C.B., D.S.O., M.C., 59
Lucera, 115
Luttman-Johnson, Captain P., 373
Lydd, 47
Lympne, 5, 45

Maas, 307, 321, 331
Maas, River, 344, 345
Macchie, 148, 156
Maginot Line, 21, 22, 23, 25
Magpie, H.M.S., 234
Majendie, Major-Gen. V. H. B., 258
Maletto, 79
Manchester Regiment, 264, 266
Manston, 45
Marks, Cpl. R., 173
Marseilles, 46
Marshall, Major P. D. H., 112, 128, 158
Massafra, 86
Matthews, Lieut. L., 91; Captain, 174

Maunsell, Captain, 369
Mauthen, 220, 221
May, Captain R., 62, 63, 81, 130, 176, 224; Major, 229, 232
McCormick, Pte. H., 273
McCormick, Sgt., 252; C.S.M., 256; R.S.M., 270
McCreery, Lieut.-General Sir Richard, K.C.B., D.S.O., M.B.E., M.C., G.O.C., 225, 228
McGowan, C.Q.M.S., 193, 200
McGowan, Sgt., 373
McKay, Lieut. J. S., 96, 100, 112, 123, 152, 175, 179; Captain, 234
McLean, Lieut., 63; wounded, 69, 125, 210
McNulty, Pte. H., 327
Measures, Pte., 179
Meehan, Sgt., 95; Lieut., 210
Meikle, 2nd Lieut. A. R., 17; Lieut., 24, 245
Melfa, River, 142
Mermaid, H.M.S., 234
Messina, 82, 85
Messina, Straits, 79
Messolonghi, Byron's resting-place, 234
Mezidon, 315
Miannay, 31
Miannay–Hymmeville, 32
Middlesex Regiment, 5, 56, 57, 72
Middlewick, 54
Mignano, 123
Miles, Major-General E. G., 51, 55
Millstattersee, 227
Milnes, Sgt., 32
Milton, Lieut. "Tiny," 15, 17, 18; Captain, 46, 57
Mineo, 72
Minnis Bay, 43
Minns, Pte., 341
Minski, C.Q.M.S. T., 17, 242
Minster Abbey, 44
Mitchell, Lieut. "Bob," 116, 144, 154, 166
Mole, Lieut. C., 169, 170
Monarch of Bermuda, S.S., 163
Monastery Hill, 119
Monks, Sgt. A. D., 330
Montagano, 113, 114, 115, 116
Monte Acqua Salata, 176, 177
Monte Cairo, 118, 123
Monte Cammino, 118
Monte Castellone, 125
Montecilfone, 96, 115

Monte Croce, 220
Monte Grande, 200
Monte Merlo, 199
Monte La Pieve captured, 184
Montenero, 106, 108
Monteodorisio, 99
Monte Spaduro, 184
Monte Verro, 177, 198
Montgomery, Lieut.-General B. L., C.B., D.S.O., 48 ; General, 69, 75, 100, 101, 103 ; of Alamein, Field-Marshal the Viscount, inspects Guard of Honour, 370
Moran, Cpl. T., 103
Morgan, Lieut.-Col. R. W., O.B.E., Chief Signal Officer, London District, 368
Morgan, Major-General H. de R., 56
Morgan, Pte. J., 93
Morgan, Sgt., 304
Moro, River, 105
Morris, C.Q.M.S., 17, 62
Morris, Pte., 320
Morrow, Rev. J., 63
Motta, 115
Mount, Sgt. E., 150, 151
Mountford, Captain H. R., 17, 245
Mowbray, Lieut. F., 309, 318
Moyenneville, 32
Mozzagrogna, 103
Mullender, P.S.M., 17
Munsey, Lieut. B., 102, 168, 175
Murphy, Cpl., 301
Murphy, Pte., 151
Musselwhite, Lieut.-Col. C. C., 262, 266

N. Africa, 128
Nanney-Wynn, Major E., 369
Napier Barracks, 49
Naples, 115, 230, 231
Naples Bay, 135
Naro, 82
Nash, R.S.M., 51
Needham Market, 53
Neufchatel, 21
New Forest, 6
Newhaven, 260
Newhouse Farm, near Fisherman's Head, 56
Newman, Captain P. F., 234, 236
Newman, Pte., 176
Newstead, Captain A. R., 68, 81

Newton, Lieut., 77
Nicholson, Sgt., 153
Nicol, Captain W., 337, 339
Nijmegen, 307, 354
Nijmegen–Arnhem sector, 296, 322, 332, 333, 346, 347
Normandy, invasion of, 298 ; beaches reached, 324
North, Sgt. H. A., 373
Northamptonshire Regiment, 74, 89, 94, 95, 140, 142, 146, 214
Norton, Sgt. J., 277, 285
Nurse, Captain J. A., 62, 73, 81, 95, 134, 176

Oakes, Captain A., 85, 111, 191
Ober Drauberg, 221
Oldland, Lieut. J., 114, 116, 210
Oliphant, Lieut.-Col. W. Y. Kington Blair, O.B.E., M.C., 362
Oliver, Lieut. J. J., 61, 114 ; Captain, 223
Oosterhout, 296, 332
Orchard, Lieut., 120, 130
Orduna, H.M.T., 274
Ortanova band, 89
Orvieto, 146
Osborne, Major-General, 13
Osento, River, 99
Oude Castel, 331
Owen, Pte., 176

Padfield, Captain C. J. C., M.B.E., 16, 17 ; Major, 43, 45, 46, 49
Page, Captain B. J. G., 62, 73, 81, 86, 92, 134 ; M.C., 147, 159
Page, 2nd Lieut. H. A. C., 17 ; Captain, 53, 54 ; Major, 62, 63, 72, 78, 81 ; seriously wounded, 94, 95
Paget, General Sir Bernard, 163
Paglieto, 99
Palazzolo, 72
Palestine, Southern, 162
Palmer, Captain Mark, 262, 285, 359 ; Major, 362
Palmer, Cpl. W. H., 373
Panicale, 147, 148
Panter, Pte., 324, 352
Papenvoortbrug, 319
Parc de Boislonde, 302, 310, 313
Parker, Lieut.-Col. F. G., 16, 17, 22, 42, 43, 53, 57, 59, 61, 87, 121, 122, 137

INDEX

Parker, Pte., 153
" Parker Force," 88
Parrott, Pte., 304
Parsons, Sgt., 252
Parry, Chivers, Rev. S., Chaplain, 371
Pas de Somme, 21
Paterson, Captain G. D., 17, 22, 265, 271, 272
Patti, 82
Patton, Pte., 343
Paul, Pte., 32 ; Sgt., 152
Payton, Pte., 126
Peacock, Sgt., 180
Pearce, Cpl. E. R., 369, 373
Pearson, Major Roy, 132
Pegwell Bay, 45
Peloponnese, 232
Pencerrig, near Builth Wells, 276
Penford, Cpl., 287
Perry, Lieut. R. C. F., 181 ; Captain, 195
Perry, Pte. R. F. W., 325
Perry, Sgt., 147
Pescara, 103
Pescia, River, 151
Pescopennataro, 109
Petacciato, 97
Piano, 156
Picture Post, 8
Pignataro, 115
Pim, Major G. C., 4, 8 ; Lieut.-Col., 252, 253, 254, 261
Pinks, Captain A. W., 62, 68, 81, 112 ; Major, 137, 162, 173
Pinks, Lieut. S. R., 278 ; Major, 281, 324, 325, 361
Piper, Captain D. E. M., 62, 81, 134, 179
Piræus, 232
Plash Wood, near Haughley, 55
Po, River, 165, 209, 213, 216
Po di Volano, 216
Poland, invasion by the Germans, 11
Polderheide, 319
Pont-sur-Picavets, 339
Pope, Pte., 340
Pordenone, 220
Porter, Lieut. M., 74, 210
Porter, Pte. D., 96
Portocannone, 90, 93
Portomaggiore, 214, 215
Port Said, 163
Pratt, Sgt., 26
Price, Pte., 77

Prince, Pte., 204
Princess Louise's Fusiliers, 353
Princess Royal, the, unveils the new War Memorial, 370
Prismall, Major, 15
Pritchard, Pte., 301
Prittlewell Airfield, 57
Prize-giving and Regimental Rifle Meeting, 6
Purdom, Pte., 301
Purfleet Ranges, 309
Pyramids, 162

Quattraventi, 135
Queen Mary, H.M., opens the new Jubilee extension of the West London Hospital, 5
Queen's, 43
Queen's Westminsters, 43

Radford, Captain Rev. A. J., 50
Rae, Lieut. D., 15, 17 ; Captain, 50
Ranciano, 151, 153
Randazzo, 73, 82, 85
Range, Drv., 372
Rapido, River, 116, 117, 118, 140
Rauray, 313, 314, 325, 326
Ravenscroft, Pte., 153
Rawlinson, Captain G. C., 373
Raworth, Cpl., 300, 302
Reay, R.Q.M.S., 277
" Recce " Regiment, 99, 107, 214
Reconnaissance Regiment, 47
Reculver, 43
Redmond, 2nd Lieut., 47
Rees, Sgt., 12
Reggio, 85
Reno, River, 212, 214
Reykjavik, 264
Rhine, River, 244, 296
Ridgeway, Sgt., 192, 193
Ridley, Captain A., M.B.E., 7
Rijkevorsel, 342
Rimini, 165
Rionero, 106, 108
Ripi, 143
Ripiano, 187, 195
Ripiano Valley, 169, 170
Risborough Barracks, 49
Rivers, Pte., 97
Robbins, Pte., 114
Robertson, C.S.M., 279

INDEX

Rogers, Lieut. Basil, 195
Roll of Honour. *See* pp. 376, 377
Romney Marsh, 47
Roosendaal captured, 293, 321, 331, 344, 345
Rose-Price, Brigadier T., D.S.O., M.C., 257
Rosen, C.S.M., 322
Rouiba, 67
Royal Inniskilling Fusiliers, 95, 112, 123, 148, 186
Royal Irish Fusiliers, 75, 97, 184, 200
Royal Northumberland Fusiliers, 26, 149, 202
Royal Wanstead School, near Epping Forest, 256
Royal West Kents, 91, 96, 112, 121, 125, 144, 147, 177, 178, 212
Rueleinde, 319
Ruina, 216
Russell, Cpl. A. E., 373
Russell, Pte. A., 96
Rye, 260

S. Angelo, 117, 126
St. Donats Castle, 277, 279
St. Gabriel, 324
S. Giacomo, 95
S. Giuliano, 106
St. Leger, 325
St. Leonards, 343
S. Marco, 105
S. Maria Ridge, 99, 103
St. Marie-aux-Chenes, 27
St. Martin's Plain, Shorncliffe, 375
St. Mary Abbots Church, Kensington, Regimental colours laid up at, 12 ; parade to receive back the colours of the Regiment, 367
S. Michele, 125, 131
S. Oreste, 146
S. Patrizio, 212
St. Peter's, 158
St. Pierre, 300
S. Pietro, 109, 114, 126
St. Saens, 19
S. Severo, 105, 115
St. Valéry-en-Caux, 28, 35, 39, 163, 241
St. Valéry-sur-Somme, 29
S. Vittore, 126
Salmon, Captain A. H., 16, 17
Samaria, H.M.T., 63

San Appolinare, 166, 167, 169, 188, 191
San Clemente ford, 187, 195
Sandford, Lieut. A., 156, 169, 170 ; Captain, 372
Sanfatucchio, 148
Sangro, River, 99
San Martino, 198
San Severo, 165
Santerno, River, 211
Sarr, 43
Satchwell, C.S.M., 39, 47, 68
Saunders, Pte. F., 204
Saunders, Cpl. S., 95
Sawyer, Pte., 144
Scapelli, Mt., 73, 74
Scerni, 99
Scheldt, River, in Holland, 239, 243
Sconcola, 182
Scott, Brigadier T. P. D., D.S.O., 192, 194, 220
Scott, Lieut. W. H., 121, 144, 145, 162, 175, 178, 181 ; Captain, 234
Scott, Sgt., 354
Searle, Cpl., 195
Sharp, L./Cpl., 330
Seine, 303, 329, 341
Serracapriola, 89, 90
Shanks, 2nd Lieut. E. P., 17, 28, 41 ; appointed Adjutant, 43 ; promoted to Major, 54, 62, 68, 81, 95, 112
Shave, Captain R. G., 62, 81, 151, 163
Shaw, Lieut.-Col. D. L., M.C., 220
Shelley, Lieut. A. F. D., 74, 153
Sheppard, Captain T., 285, 288, 362
Sherman, Sgt., 67
Sherwood, Pte., 306
Shillidy, Lieut. Harvey, 188, 193
Shimield, Lieut., 232
Shoreham, 47
Shorncliffe, 47, 49
Siegfried Line, 23
Silk, Captain B. E., 81, 151
Sillaro, River, 170, 187, 195, 213
Sillian, 221
Simeto, 75
Sinello, River, 99
Shoobert, Sgt., 189
Simmance, Cpl., 190, 193
Skinner, C.S.M., 17
Skinner, Sgt. C., 74
Slade, Pte. B., 147
Small Arms School, Netheravon, 50
Smith, Captain J., 17, 45
Smith, Cpl., 340

INDEX

Smith, C.S.M., 279
Smith, C.S.M. J. W., 62
Smith, Pte., 339
Smith, Pte. E., 97
Smith, Lieut. R., 102, 144
Smith, Lieut. Smudger, 195
Smullen, 2nd Lieut. G., 77
Smythe, 2nd Lieut. P. F., 17
Sollinger, Pte., 156
Soper, C.Q.M.S. G., 62
Sousse, 69
South Petherton, 14
Spaduro captured, 184, 185, 186
Spears Military Mission, 262
" Speedy Express," 116, 117
Spencer, Pte., 113
Spinello, 186
Spittal, 223, 229
Stacey, Major E. L., 4
Stanbridge, Cpl. E. C., 91
Stanley-Clarke, Brig., 34, 39
Stanyer, Captain J. T., 324, 328
Steadman, Lieut., 88, 92
Steele, C.S.M. W. J., 62, 142
Stevens, Pte. G. H., 48
Stoltenhoff, Lieut. W., 337
Stone, Col. W. A., M.C., T.D., 4
Stopford, Maj.-Gen. M. G. M., D.S.O., M.C., 49
Stowmarket, 53
Stratton, E. F., 369
Strawberry Hill at Ilminster, 18
Strawson, Captain I. A., 285, 352
Sturmey, Pte., 287
Stuttard, Lieut. C. G., 87 ; Captain, 182
Suffolk Yeomanry, 353
" Sun Track," 85
Swain, Pte., 93
Swanage, 60
" Sweet Water Canal," 162
Sydling St. Nicholas, firing at, 60

Tamagnin, 194
Taranto, 85, 90, 160, 163
Tarvisio, 223
Tavernelle, 153, 157
Taylor, C.S.M. R., 61
Taylor, Lieut.-Col. H., M.C., 145, 155
Taylor, Pte. E., 93
Taylor, Sgt. R., 252 ; C.S.M., 261
Taylor, Sgt. W., 186
Telfer, Lieut., 308

Tessel Wood, 301, 302, 325, 337
Thomas, Cpl., 193
Thomas, Lieut. D. A., 262, 264, 265 ; Captain, 278, 298
Thomas, Pte., 301
Thomas, Pte. E., 93
Thompson, P.S.M., 17
Thornhill, Lieut. R., 337, 342
Tilly-sur-Seules, 327
Tivoli, 157
Tobin, Sgt., 77
Tondeur, Pte., 32
Topham, Pte., 149
Torrice, 143
Torricella church tower, 112
Tosland, Captain, 13
Touques, River, 291
Townland Farm, 49
Trasimeno, Lake, 147, 157
Tregoning, Captain D. B., 15, 58 ; Major, 62, 63, 81, 85, 95, 118, 121, 123, 145, 147, 152, 153, 159, 162
Termoli, 90, 92, 93, 94, 95, 115
Trew, Sgt., 287
Trigno, River, 97
Trocchio, Mount, 117, 139, 140
Trott, Lieut. H., 102, 114
Trott, R.S.M., 253, 256
Tucker, Cpl., 140
Turnock, Cpl., 310
Tuvey, Sgt. J., 170
Tyson, Cpl., 345

Udall, Pte., 352
Udine, Major J. J., 221
Underwood, Captain D., 62, 81, 95
Union Jack, Army newspaper, 150
Upchurch, C.Q.M.S. H., 61, 69, 156

Vaast-sur-Seulles, 339
Valliquerville, chateâu, 18
Vanderpump, Lieut. N., 63, 145
Vasto, 100, 115
Vatria Jokull, Iceland's greatest glacier, 272
Vaughan, Lieut. J. G., 324
Vendes, 338
Venlo, advance towards, 295, 307, 321, 345
Villach, 224
Viterbo, 146
Volturno, River, 118
Vorselaar, 317 ; liberated, 342

INDEX

Waal, 307
Waal, River, 296
Wageningen, 356
Wakeford, C.S.M., 308
Walden, Major F., 16, 17, 45
Walder, Sgt., 188
Walker, 2nd Lieut. W. E., 17, 26
Walker, Cpl., 345
Walker, Sgt., 342
Wallace, L./Cpl. J. P., 325
Walton, Cpl., 354
Warburg Barracks, 261
Ward, Pte., 192
Ware, Pte. G., 85
Wasey, Captain R., 17, 22, 46; promoted Major, 49, 54, 62, 63, 68, 70, 73, 81, 85, 95, 222; Lieut.-Col., M.B.E., T.D., 367, 375
Wasley, C.Q.M.S., 17
Wasley, Pte., 300
Wasner, Cpl., 270
Waters, Sgt., 185, 189
Watson, Captain R. M., 253, 255, 262
Watts, R.S.M. R., 285
Waymark, Sgt., 279
Welschler Wood, 26
Wemyss, General Sir H. Colville B., K.C.B., K.B.E., D.S.O., M.C., 368, 369
Wemyss, Lady, 371, 374
Wesel, 239
West, Pte., 32
Westcliff, 56
White, S. G., 369
Whitstable, 43
Wilcox, Cpl., 324
Wilding, Lieut., 120
Willard, Pte., 304
Willats, Pte., 76
Willemstadt, 306, 344, 345
Williams, Pte., 304
Williams, Sgt., 373
Williams, Sgt. "Bunny", 76
Williamson, Captain C. K., 17, 43; posted to Hong Kong, 45
Williamson, Captain T., 373

Wills, Captain S. J., 253
Willmott, Sgt., 25
Wilmot, Captain J., 309; Major, 362
Wilshire, Pte., 73
Wilson, Lieut., 182
Wilson, Pte. C., 321
Wilson, Pte. M., 273
Wimbury, Lieut. J., 114
Wimbury, Lieut. Norman, 185, 190, 223
Wimbury Pimple, 185, 187
Winchelsea, 260
Winter Line, The, 104
Winter Warfare School, 268, 271
Wolfsberg, 222
Wood, 2nd Lieut. B. R., 12, 17; Lieut., 24, 245, 247; Major, T.D., 372
Woodard, Pte., 114
Woodchurch, 49
Woodward, Pte., 301
Worrall, L./Cpl., 273
Worrall, L./Cpl. W., 140
Worsop, Pte. A., 96
Worton, Major J. B., 262; Lieut.-Col., 229, 230, 234
Wray, Captain Alastair, 254, 259, 262; Major, 265, 266, 268, 278
Wreford, Brigadier, 11
Wright, Lieut.-Col. H., 30
Wright, S.S.M. F. B., 373
Wustwezel, 293, 319
Wynne, L./Cpl., 267

Yalta, 225
Yellam, Pte., 156
Yorks and Lancs, 14
Young, C.S.M. H., 62
Young, L./Cpl., 173
Young, Lieut. John, 193
Young, R.Q.M.S., 285
Yvetot, battalion entrained for, 19

Zig Canal, 306, 331

The production of this commemorative reprint edition
would not have been possible without the use of an original copy of
the Kensingtons Second World War History from the estate of the
late Capt. J.M. Barraclough (Retd)
Princess Louise's Kensington Regiment.

For all enquiries, please contact.
The Princess Louise's Kensington Regimental Association
Honorary Secretary
Robin Watson email plkrasec@gmail.com
Website www.plkra.org.uk

"The Kensingtons"
13TH LONDON REGIMENT
The Great War 1914–18

Sgts O.F.Bailey and H.M.Hollier

A brief account of the history of the Kensingtons before the Great War is given in the opening chapter of this book. In 1908 the TF came into existence and with it the unwieldy London Regiment with its 26 battalions, among which was the 13th (County of London) Battalion (Kensington). When war broke out the battalion was already allocated to the 4th London Brigade, 2nd London Division, but in November 1914 it left the division and went to France, arriving on the 4th; it was allocated to 25th Brigade, 8th Division, a newly formed regular division, with which it fought its first major action, at Neuve Chapelle in March 1915. After a spell on the Lines of Communication the battalion joined the re-formed 1st London Division (now numbered 56th) in 168th Brigade, and it fought in that brigade on the Western Front for the rest of the war. In September 1914 a second line battalion was formed (2/13th) and assigned to179th Brigade 60th Division. An unexpected diversion occurred at the end of April 1916 when the brigade was sent to Ireland on internal security duties following the Easter rebellion. A fortnight later it returned to England and on 21 June 60th Division began its move to France. After about four months in the Vimy sector the division was transferred to Macedonia where the battalion arrived at the end of November 1916. Its spell in that theatre was comparatively short for in May 1917 the division moved again – to Palestine where it served with the EEF till the end of the war.

This history is arranged in two parts, the first deals with the first line battalion, 1/4th, and is written by Sgt Bailey; the second part is the history of the 2/4th, written by Sgt Hollier. There is a final chapter covering the post-war period up to 1935, written by one of the commanding officers. The Roll of Honour lists the dead (60 officers, 1003 men), alphabetically by ranks, without identifying battalion, nor does the list of Honours and Awards identfy the battalion. The two sergeants have a produced a very workmanlike record of the battalions even though, according to their introduction, relevant material had not been easy to come by and official records were scarce. Nevertheless, aided by the loan of diaries and the assistance of fellow members, I am sure the result was very much appreciated by the Kensingtons' Old Comrades' Association.

9781843423645

www.ingramcontent.com/pod-product-compliance
Lightning Source LLC
Chambersburg PA
CBHW052338230426
43664CB00041B/2191